The Dog Law

Second Edition

Godfrey Sandys-Winsch

B.A. (Cantab.), Solicitor

Edited by

Paul Clayden

M.A. (Oxon.), Solicitor

SWEET & MAXWELL

Published by Sweet & Maxwell, 100 Avenue Road, London NW3 3PF
part of Thomson Reuters (Professional) UK Limited
(Registered in England & Wales, Company No 1679046.
Registered Office and address for service:
Aldgate House, 33 Aldgate High Street, London EC3N 1DL)

For further information on our products and services, visit
http://www.sweetandmaxwell.co.uk

Typeset by LBJ Typesetting Ltd of Kingsclere
Printed in the UK by CPI Antony Rowe, Chippenham, Wiltshire

ISBN 978 0 414 04818 8

No natural forests were destroyed to make this product;
only farmed timber was used and replanted.

A CIP catalogue record for this book is available from the British Library

First edition published by Shaw & Sons Limited in 1993
and reprinted in 1993, 1995, 1999, 2001, 2005 and 2007

Crown copyright material is reproduced with the permission of the
Controller of HMSO and the Queen's Printer for Scotland.

All rights reserved. No part of this publication may be reproduced or
transmitted, in any form or by any means, or stored in any retrieval system
of any nature, without prior written permission, except for permitted
fair dealing under the Copyright, Designs and Patents Act 1988, or in accordance with the terms of a licence issued by the Copyright Licensing Agency
in respect of photocopying and/or reprographic reproduction. Application
for permission for other use of copyright material including permission to
reproduce extracts in other published works shall be made to the publishers.
Full acknowledgement of author, publisher and source must be given.
Application for permission for other use of copyright material controlled
by the publisher shall be made to the publishers.

Thomson Reuters and the Thomson Reuters logo are trademarks of Thomson
Reuters. Sweet and Maxwell® is a registered trademark of Thomson Reuters
(Professional) UK Limited.

© 2011 Thomson Reuters (Professional) UK Limited

The Dog Law Handbook

Second Edition

Preface

This is a new edition of a book first published in loose-leaf form in 1993. Supplements were produced at intervals, the most recent in 2007. The original author, Godfrey Sandys-Winsch, died in 2006. I prepared the 2007 supplement and was asked in 2009 by the previous publishers, Shaw and Sons Ltd, to undertake a new edition. Shaws subsequently transferred the title to Sweet & Maxwell.

The book is divided into five parts. The first sets out a summary of the law with footnotes enabling readers who wish to do so to refer to statutory sources set out in later parts. The second part supplies the Acts of Parliament relating to dogs. The third part covers other Acts dealing with animals generally. The fourth part contains the relevant statutory orders and regulations, and the fifth part reproduces Government Department circulars on the legislation. The second, third and fourth parts are fully annotated.

The book incorporates the changes in the law which have occurred since 2007.

PAUL CLAYDEN
Henley-on-Thames
January 2011

Preface to the First Edition

The passing of the Dangerous Dogs Act on 25th July 1991 and the new provisions about stray dogs in the Environmental Protection Act 1990 have prompted me to write this book in an attempt to set forth the main body of the diverse and considerable law, stretching back for more than 160 years, which now governs dogs and their activities.

The book is divided into five parts. The first sets out a summary of the law with footnotes enabling readers who wish to do so to refer to statutory sources set out in later parts. The second part supplies the Acts of Parliament relating to dogs, whilst the third covers other Acts dealing with animals generally. The fourth part contains the relevant statutory orders and regulations, and the fifth part reproduces Government Department circulars on the new legislation. The second, third and fourth parts are fully annotated.

I hope that the collection of this material in one book will provide a useful and practical guide to all those whose work involves them with canine law including, perhaps especially, dog wardens and the police.

The looseleaf format has been adopted to allow the book to be kept up to date by the insertion of supplement pages as and when new developments occur.

I would like to thank Mr. Crispin Williams of my publishers for his encouragement and great practical help, Mr. Brian Faulkner of the East Dorset District Council for his keen interest and support, and those officers of the Home Office, the Department of the Environment and the Ministry of Agriculture, Fisheries and Food who have so readily advised on matters within their respective fields.

G. SANDYS-WINSCH
Leasingham,
Lincolnshire

Abbreviations and Explanatory Notes

For those readers who are not as familiar as others with abbreviations commonly used in a book of this nature, the following are abbreviations to be found in the text and their meanings:

art: article (for the numbering of a paragraph in a Government Order).
Defra: Department for Environment, Food and Rural Affairs.
EC: European Community.
EU: the European Union.
reg: regulation (for the numbering of a paragraph in Government Regulations).
s. or ss.: section or sections of an Act.
subs. or subss.: subsection or subsections of a section of an Act.
Sch.: Schedule to an Act or to a Government Order or Regulations.

The Department for Environment, Food and Rural Affairs – created in 2001 – has taken over the functions of the former Ministry of Agriculture, Fisheries and Food, and some of the functions formerly exercised by the Department of the Environment (DoE) are now exercised by the Office of the Deputy Prime Minister, created in 2002.

In Wales, most of the functions of the former DoE and the Ministry of Agriculture are now exercised by the National Assembly for Wales.

References in this book to the Minister or to the Minister of Agriculture should now be construed as references to the Secretary of State or, in Wales, the National Assembly, unless otherwise indicated.

The "appropriate national authority" means, in England, the Secretary of State (in practice, for Environment, Food and Rural Affairs) and, in Wales, the National Assembly for Wales.

Within the text, the ellipses symbol (. . .) indicates the omission of words in Acts of Parliament, and statutory orders and regulations

Abbreviations and Explanatory Notes

which have been repealed, or which are irrelevant or unnecessary in the context of the book, or which relate to Scotland only.

The "Arrangement of sections" for each Act shows which sections of the Act have been reproduced as they have not all been reproduced in full for the reasons above.

Contents

Preface	v
Preface to the First Edition	vii
Abbreviations and Explanatory Notes	ix
Table of Cases	xvii
Table of Statutes	xix
Table of Statutory Instruments	xxiii

PART I: A SUMMARY OF THE LAW

Chapter 1 — Ownership and Theft	3
Chapter 2 — Sales of Dogs	4
Sales of Animals Generally	4
Dogs' Pedigrees	5
Pet Shops	5
Illegal Sales of Dogs	8
Chapter 3 — Owners' Responsibilities under Strict Liability and Negligence Rules	9
Chapter 4 — Dogs and Diseases	12
Chapter 5 — Dogs on the Road	14
Straying on to the Road	14
Reporting Accidents Involving Dogs	15
When a Lead is Necessary	15
Fouling Footways and Other Public Open Spaces	16
Motorway Rules	17
Dog Control Orders	18
Chapter 6 — Trespassing Dogs	20
Chapter 7 — Nuisances, Byelaws and Hygiene Regulations	25
Nuisances	25

xi

Contents

Byelaws	26
Hygiene Regulations	27
Chapter 8 — Dangerous and Ferocious Dogs	28
Dangerous Dogs	28
Dogs Act 1871	28
Dangerous Dogs Act 1991	29
Ferocious Dogs	33
Chapter 9 — Dog Collars and Stray Dogs	35
Dog Collars	35
Stray Dogs	36
Chapter 10 — The Rules about Killing and Injuring Dogs	39
The Civil Law	39
The Criminal Law	41
Chapter 11 — Boarding Kennels and Breeding Kennels	44
Boarding Kennels	44
Breeding Kennels	45
Chapter 12 — Guard Dogs	47
Chapter 13 — General Welfare of Dogs	49
Introduction	49
Prevention of Harm	49
Promotion of Welfare	53
Licensing and Registration	54
Codes of Practice	55
Animals in Distress	55
Enforcement Powers	56
Prosecutions	56
Post-Conviction Powers	57

Contents

Chapter 14 — Performing Dogs	61
Films	63
Chapter 15 — Dogs and Game	64
Prohibited Times for Taking Game	64
Poaching	65
Game Licences	65
Protection of Game from Dogs	65
Hunting with Dogs	66
Chapter 16 — Import and Export	69
Import	69
Export	72
Contact Numbers for Enquiries	72

PART II: ACTS OF PARLIAMENT RELATING TO DOGS

Night Poaching Act 1828 *ss.1, 9, 12, 13*	75
Game Act 1831 *ss.2, 3, 30*	77
Metropolitan Police Act 1839 *s.54*	80
Night Poaching Act 1844 *s.1*	81
Town Police Clauses Act 1847 *ss.2, 3, 28*	83
Dogs Act 1871 *s.2*	85
Ground Game Act 1880 *ss.1, 4, 8*	87
Dogs Act 1906 *ss.1, 3, 7*	90
Dogs (Protection of Livestock) Act 1953 *ss.1–3*	93
Animal Boarding Establishments Act 1963 *ss.1–5*	98
Breeding of Dogs Act 1973 *ss.1–5*	104
Guard Dogs Act 1975 *ss.1, 5, 7*	115
Animal Health Act 1981 *ss.13, 72–75, 86, 87*	117

Contents

Road Traffic Act 1988 ss.27, 170, 185, 189, 192	123
Dangerous Dogs Act 1989 s.1	130
Environmental Protection Act 1990 ss.149, 150	133
Breeding of Dogs Act 1991 ss.1, 2	138
Dangerous Dogs Act 1991 ss.1–7, 10	141
Protection of Badgers Act 1992 ss.1–3, 6–8, 10–14	159
Dogs (Fouling of Land) Act 1996 ss.1–8	171
Dangerous Dogs (Amendment) Act 1997 ss.1–6	179
Breeding and Sale of Dogs (Welfare) Act 1999 ss.1–11, Schedule	184
Hunting Act 2004 ss.1–11, Schedule	198
Clean Neighbourhoods and Environment Act 2005 ss.55–68	210

PART III: ACTS OF PARLIAMENT RELATING TO ANIMALS GENERALLY

Performing Animals (Regulation) Act 1925 ss.1–5, 7	225
Cinematograph Films (Animals) Act 1937 s.1	232
Pet Animals Act 1951 ss.1, 4–7	234
Veterinary Surgeons Act 1966 ss.19, 27, Schedule 3	241
Theft Act 1968 ss.1–6, 22, 23, 34	247
Animals Act 1971 ss.2, 3, 5, 6, 8, 9, 11	253
Criminal Damage Act 1971 ss.1, 5, 10	261
Public Health (Control of Disease) Act 1984 ss.55, 74	265
Animals (Scientific Procedures) Act 1986 ss.1, 2, 5, 7, 10, 16, 30, Schedule 1	267
Animal Welfare Act 2006 ss.1–45, 51–62, 68, Schedule 2	274
Fraud Act 2006 ss.1–5	337

Contents

PART IV: STATUTORY ORDERS AND REGULATIONS

Performing Animals Rules 1925	343
Rabies (Control) Order 1974	346
Motorways Traffic (England and Wales) Regulations 1982	350
Dangerous Dogs (Designated Types) Order 1991	352
Dangerous Dogs Compensation and Exemption Schemes Order 1991	353
Litter (Animal Droppings) Order 1991	360
Environmental Protection (Stray Dogs) Regulations 1992	362
Control of Dogs Order 1992	366
Control of Dogs on Roads Orders (Procedure) (England and Wales) Regulations 1995	369
Sale of Dogs (Identification Tag) Regulations 1999	376
Breeding of Dogs (Licensing Records) Regulations 1999	377
Non Commercial Movement of Pet Animals (England) Regulations 2004	379
Controls on Dogs (Non-application to Designated Land) Order 2006	390
Dog Control Orders (Procedures) Regulations 2006	393
Dog Control Orders (Prescribed Offences and Penalties, etc.) Regulations 2006	398
Controls on Dogs (Non-application to Designated Land) Order 2009	413

PART V: GOVERNMENT DEPARTMENT CIRCULARS

Home Office Circular 67/1991: Dangerous Dogs Act 1991	417
Home Office Circular 80/1992: Further Advice Concerning the Dangerous Dogs Act 1991	444
Home Office Circular 9/1994: Further Advice Concerning the Dangerous Dogs Act 1991	448

Contents

Home Office Circular 53/1999: Licensing Dog Breeding Establishments 453

Defra Guidance Circular 2006: Dog Control Orders 463

Defra Guidance Circular 2007: Guidance on Stray Dogs 474

Index 485

Table of Cases

Note: The following Tables of Cases, Statutes and Statutory Instruments cover all references to cases and legislation contained in the first section of this book – Part I: A Summary of the Law. For a full listing of the legislation and circulars reproduced in Parts II to V inclusive, please refer to the contents pages which are included at the front of the book and at the start of each Part.

Arneil v Paterson [1931] A.C. 560; 1931 S.C. (H.L.) 117; 1931 S.L.T. 399, HL	22
Campbell v Wilkinson (1909) 43 I.L.T. 237	21
Chalmers v Diwell, 74 L.G.R. 173; [1976] Crim. L.R. 134, DC	6
Clemons v Short [1969] 113 Sol. Jo. 931	25
Cummings v Grainger [1977] Q.B. 397; [1976] 3 W.L.R. 842; [1977] 1 All E.R. 104; (1958) 102 Sol. Jo. 453, CA (Civ Div)	10
Gomberg v Smith [1963] 1 Q.B. 25; [1962] 2 W.L.R. 749; [1962] 1 All E.R. 725; (1962) 106 Sol. Jo. 95, CA	11
Ives v Brewer (1951) 95 Sol. Jo. 286	21
Kite v Napp, *The Times*, June 1, 1982, CA	10
Lee v Knapp [1967] 2 Q.B. 442; [1967] 2 W.L.R. 6; [1966] 3 All E.R. 961; (1967) 131, DC	15
Parker v Walsh (1885) 1 T.L.R. 583	29
Philp (William) v Wright, 1940 J.C. 9; 1940 S.L.T. 22, 1939 S.N. 94, HCJ Appeal	29
R. v Bezzina (Anthony); R. v Codling (Sadie); R. v Elvin (Eric Everton) [1994] 1 W.L.R. 1057; [1994] 3 All E.R. 964; (1994) 99 Cr. App. R. 356; (1994) 158 J.P. 671; (1994) 158 J.P.N. 388; (1994) 91(5) L.S.G. 36; (1994) 138 S.J.L.B. 11, CA (Crim Div)	31
R. v Crown Court at Knightsbridge, Ex p. Dunne; Brock v DPP [1993] 4 All E.R. 491; (1994) 158 J.P. 213; [1993] Crim. L.R. 853; [1994] C.O.D. 3; (1993) 143 N.L.J. 1479, DC	31
Sarch v Blackburn (1830) 4 C. & P. 297	11
Smith v Sudron and Coulson (1981) Ct. of Appeal Transcripts 140	14
Harding v Price [1948] 1 K.B. 695; [1948] 1 All E.R. 283; 64 T.L.R. 111; (1948) 112 J.P. 189; 46 L.G.R. 142; [1948] L.J.R. 1624; (1948) 92 Sol. Jo. 112, DC	15
Williams v Richards (1970) 114 Sol. Jo. 864, DC	22

Table of Statutes

1828	Night Poaching Act (9 Geo. 4, c.69)			1937	Cinematograph Films (Animals) Act (1 Edw.	
	ss.1, 9	65			8 & 1 Geo.6, c.59)	63
1831	Game Act (1 & 1 Will. 4, c.32)	64, 65		1950	s.1	63
	ss.2, 3	64			Diseases of Animals Act (14 Geo. 6.	
	s.30	65			c.36)	69
1839	Metropolitan Police Act (2 & 3 Vict. c.47)	33		1951	Pet Animal Act (14 & 15 Geo., 6 c.35)	7
	s.54	34			s.1(1)	5
1847	Town Police Clauses Act (10 & 11 Vict. c.89)	33			(2)	5, 7
	s.3	33			(3)(c)	7
	s.28	33			(4), (5)	7
1848	Hares Act (11 & 12 Vict. c.30)	65			s.3	8
					s.4(1)	7
1860	Game Licences Act (23 & 24 Vict. c.90)	64, 65			s.5(1), (2)	7
1861	Offences Against the Persons Act (23 & 24 Vict. c.100)	29			(3)	8
					s.7(1)	6
					(a)	6
					(b)	7
1871	Dogs Act (34 & 35 Vict. c.56)	28			(2)(a)	6
					(3)	5, 6, 7
	s.2	28		1953	Dogs (Protection of Livestock) Act (1 & Eliz.2 c.28)	20, 22, 36
1880	Ground Game Act (42 & 43 Vict. 47)	64			s.1(1)	22
1906	Dogs Act (6 Edw. 7, c.32)	36			(2), (2A)	23
	s.1(4)	28			(3), (4)	23
	s.3(1), (1A)	36			s.2(2), (3)	24
	(2), (3)	36			s.3(1)	22, 47
	(4)–(6)	37		1961	City of London (Various Powers) Act (9 & 10 Eliz.2 c.28)	
	(8)	36				
1925	Performing Animals (Regulations) Act (15 & 16 Geo. c.38)	55, 61, 63			s.39	16
				1963	Animal Boarding Establishments Act	
	s.1(2)–(5)	61			(c.43)	55
	(6)	62			s.1(1)	44
	s.2(1)–(4)	62			(2)	44, 45
	s.3	62			(3)–(8)	45
	s.4(1), (2)	63			s.2	45
	s.5	61			s.3(2)–(4)	45
	s.7	61			s.5(1)	44

xix

Table of Statutes

1968	Theft Act (c.60)
	ss.1–6 3
1971	Animals Act (c.22) 9, 14, 21, 39
	s.2(2) 9, 10
	s.3 20
	s.5(1) 22
	(1)–(3) 9, 11
	(4) 22, 40
	s.6(3), (4) 9, 21
	(5) 11
	s.8 14
	s.9(1) 39
	(2) 40
	(3) 39
	(4), (5) 40
	s.11 .... 9, 21
	Criminal Damage Act (c.48) 41, 65
	s.1 66
	(1) 42
	s.5 66
	(2) 42
	(b) 66
	(3)................... 42
	s.10 66
	(2) 43
1972	European Communities Act (c.68) 69, 71
	Local Government Act (c.70)
	s.235(1) 16
1973	Breeding of Dogs Act (c.60) 45, 55
	s.1 46
	(1), (2) 45
	(7) 46
	s.2 46
	s.3 46
	(3) 46
	s.4A 46
1974	Rabies Act (c.17) 69
1975	Guard Dogs Act (c.50)
	s.1(1)–(3) 47
	ss.3–6 48
	s.7 47
1979	Sale of Goods Act (c.54) ... 5

1981	Animal Health Act
	(c.22) 69, 70
	s.32 13
	s.73(a) 35
1984	Police and Criminal Evidence Act (c.60) 56
1986	Animals (Scientific Procedures) Act (c.14) ... 60
1988	Road Traffic Act (c.52)
	s.27(1)–(4) 16
	(7) 16
	s.170(1), (2) 15
	(3), (4), (6) 15
1989	Dangerous Dogs Act (c.30)
	s.1(2) 29
1990	Food Safety Act (c.16) ... 27
	Environmental Protection Act (c.30)
	s.79 25
	s.82 26
	s.86(14), (15) 17
	s.149(1), (2) 38
	(5), (6), (8) 38
	s.150 37
	(2) 38
1991	Breeding of Dogs Act (c.64)
	s.1 46
	Dangerous Dogs Act (c.65)
	s.1(1) 30
	(a) 30
	(2)–(5), (7) 30
	s.2 31
	s.3(1) 31
	(2)–(4) 32
	(5) 28, 29
	(6) 29
	s.4 32
	(1)–(8) 32
	s.4A, 4B 32
	s.5(1), (2) 33
	(5) 31
	s.6 .... 30, 32
	s.7 30
	(1), (2) 30, 31
	s.10(2) 30, 31, 32
	(3) 32

xx

Table of Statutes

1992	Protection of Badgers Act (c.51) 34		Animal Welfare Act (c.45) 49
1996	Dogs (Fouling of Land) Act (c.20) 16, 19		ss.4, 5 ...... 49, 57, 58, 63
			ss.4–8 56
1997	Dangerous Dogs (Amendment) Act (c.53) 32		s.6 50
			(1), (2) 57, 58, 63
			(3) 50, 51
	ss.1–3 32		s.7 .... 51, 57, 58, 63
1999	Breeding and Sale of Dogs (Welfare) Act (c.11) 46		s.8 .... 52, 57, 58, 63
	ss.8, 9 46		(1), (2) 58
2000	Powers of Criminal Courts (Sentencing) Act (c.6) 47		s.9 .... 53, 57, 58, 63
			s.10 53
	ss.130, 131 .... 43, 48		s.11 .... 54, 58, 63
2001	Regulatory Reform Act (c.6) 65		s.12 .... 54, 57
			s.13 .... 56, 57
2003	Communications Act (c.21)		(6) 57, 58
			ss.14–17 55
	s.405 53		ss.18–21 55
2004	Hunting Act (c.37) 66		s.19(4) 59
	ss.1, 3, 4 66		s.22(4) 59
	s.5(1), (2) 67		ss.22–29 56
	ss.7–9 67		s.23(1) 59
	Sch.1 .... 66, 67		s.28(4) 59
2005	Railways Act (c.14)		s.30 56
	s.46 27		ss.31, 32 57
	Clean Neighbourhoods and Environment Act (c.16) 17		s.33 .... 57, 58
			s.34 .... 56, 57, 58
			(9) 57
	Pt 6 .... 16, 17, 18, 19		s.35 58
	s.55 .... 18, 19		s.37 58
	s.56 18		ss.38, 39 58
	s.57 18		s.40 58
	s.59 19		(2) 58
	s.68 36		ss.41–43 58
	s.108 19		ss.44, 45 59
	Sch.5		s.51 .... 53, 59
	Pt 6 36		s.52 59
2006	Fraud Act (c.35)		ss.54–57 59
	ss.2–5 3		ss.58–61 60
	s.22 3		Sch.1 55
	s.23 3		Sch.2 59

Table of Statutory Instruments

1925	Performing Animals Rules 1925 (SR & O) 1925/1219)	61	2004	Animal and Animal Products (Import and Export) Regulations
	r.9	61		(SI 2004/853) 71
1974	Rabies (Importation of Dogs, Cats and other Mammals) Order			Non-Commercial Movement of Pet Animals (England)
	(SI 1974/2211) 69,	71		Order (SI
	Rabies (Control) Order (SI 1974/2212)			2004/2363) ... 69, 70, 71 Rabies (Importation of
	art.4(1), (2)	13		Dogs, Cats and other
	art.6(1)–(4)	13		Mammals) (England)
1982	Motorways Traffic (England and Wales) Regulations (SI 1982/			(Amendment) Order (SI 2004/2364) ... 71, 72 General Food Regulations
	1163)			(SI 2004/3279) 27
	reg.14	17	2006	Controls on Dogs (Non-
	reg.16(1)(a)	17		application to
1991	Litter (Animal Droppings) Order 1991 (SI			Designated Land) Order (SI 2006/779) ... 18
	1991/961)	17		Clean Neighbourhoods
	Dangerous Dogs Act 1991 (Commencement and Appointed Day) Order (SI 1991/1742)			and Environment Act 2005 (Commencement No.1, Transitional and Savings Provisions) (England) Order (SI
	art.3	30		2006/795) 19
	Dangerous Dogs Compensation and Exemption Schemes Order (SI 1991/ 1744)			Dog Control Orders (Procedures) Regulations (SI 2006/798) .... 18 Dog Control Orders
	Pt III	30		(Prescribed Offences
1992	Environmental Protection (Stray Dogs) Regulations			and Penalties etc.) Order (SI 2006/
	(SI 1992/288)	37		1059) 18
	reg.2	38		Clean Neighbourhoods
	reg.3	38		and Environment Act
	Control of Dogs Order			2005 (Commencement
	(SI 1992/901)	35		No.2, Transitional
	art.2(1), (2)	35		Provisions and Savings)
	art.3	35		(Wales) Order (SI
	art.4	35		2006/2797) 19

xxiii

Table of Statutory Instruments

2007 Environmental Offences (Fixed Penalties) (Miscellaneous Provisions) Regulations (SI 2007/175) 19
Controls on Dogs (Non-application to Designated Land) (Wales) Orders (SI 2007/701) 18
Dog Control Orders (Miscellaneous Provisions) (Wales) Regulations (SI 2007/702) 18
Docking of Working Dogs' Tails (Wales) Regulations (SI 2007/1028) 51
Mutilations (Permitted Procedures) (Wales) Regulations (SI 2007/1029) 50

Mutilations (Permitted Procedures) (England) Regulations (SI 2007/1100) 50
Docking of Working Dogs' Tails (England) Regulations (SI 2007/1120) 51
Regulatory Reform (Game) Order (SI 2007/2007) 65

2008 Environmental Offences (Fixed Penalties) (Miscellaneous Provisions) (Wales) Regulations (SI 2008/663) 19
Clean Neighbourhoods and Environment Act 2005 (Commencement No.5) Order (SI 2008/956) 36

2010 Welfare of Racing Greyhounds Regulations (SI 2010/543) 55

Part I

A Summary of the Law

Chapter 1	OWNERSHIP AND THEFT	3
Chapter 2	SALES OF DOGS	4
	Sales of Animals Generally	4
	Dogs' Pedigrees	5
	Pet Shops	5
	Illegal Sales of Dogs	8
Chapter 3	OWNERS' RESPONSIBILITIES UNDER STRICT LIABILITY AND NEGLIGENCE RULES	9
Chapter 4	DOGS AND DISEASES	12
Chapter 5	DOGS ON THE ROAD	14
	Straying on to the Road	14
	Reporting Accidents Involving Dogs	15
	When a Lead is Necessary	15
	Fouling Footways and Other Public Open Spaces	16
	Motorway Rules	17
	Dog Control Orders	18
Chapter 6	TRESPASSING DOGS	20
Chapter 7	NUISANCES, BYELAWS AND HYGIENE REGULATIONS	25
	Nuisances	25
	Byelaws	26
	Hygiene Regulations	27
Chapter 8	DANGEROUS AND FEROCIOUS DOGS	28
	Dangerous Dogs	28
	Dogs Act 1871	28
	Dangerous Dogs Act 1991	29
	Ferocious Dogs	33
Chapter 9	DOG COLLARS AND STRAY DOGS	35
	Dog Collars	35
	Stray Dogs	36
Chapter 10	THE RULES ABOUT KILLING AND INJURING DOGS	39
	The Civil Law	39
	The Criminal Law	41

Chapter 11	BOARDING KENNELS AND BREEDING KENNELS	44
	Boarding Kennels	44
	Breeding Kennels	45
Chapter 12	GUARD DOGS	47
Chapter 13	GENERAL WELFARE OF DOGS	49
	Introduction	49
	Prevention of Harm	49
	Promotion of Welfare	53
	Licensing and Registration	54
	Codes of Practice	55
	Animals in Distress	55
	Enforcement Powers	56
	Prosecutions	56
	Post-Conviction Powers	57
Chapter 14	PERFORMING DOGS	61
	Films	63
Chapter 15	DOGS AND GAME	64
	Prohibited Times for Taking Game	64
	Poaching	65
	Game Licences	65
	Protection of Game from Dogs	65
	Hunting with Dogs	66
Chapter 16	IMPORT AND EXPORT	69
	Import	69
	Export	72
	Contact Number for Inquiries	72

Chapter 1

OWNERSHIP AND THEFT

Dogs, being domestic animals, are owned in the same way as inanimate objects such as cars and furniture. Ownership is retained when a dog is lost and, subject to the statutory rules in Chapter 9, when it strays. An owner whose dog is detained without the owner's permission by another person may sue that person in court for its return. He may also lawfully retake the dog from that person; although the law says that he is justified in the use of reasonable force if that person resists him, force should be used with caution because of possible ensuing complications.

The keeping and feeding of another person's dog does not by itself permit retention of the dog until its keep is paid.

Puppies are owned by the owner of their mother, unless there is a special agreement to the contrary.

It naturally follows from what has been said about ownership that a dog may be the subject of theft – though, strangely, this was not the case until 1968. Basically, a dog will be stolen when it is taken from its owner, or anyone else who has possession or control of it, with the intention of permanently depriving that person of it.[1] A dog may also be the subject of offences associated with theft, such as obtaining property by deception[2] and receiving stolen goods.[3]

It is an offence to advertise publicly a reward for the return of a dog stolen or lost using any words to the effect that no questions will be asked, or that the person producing the dog will be safe from apprehension or inquiry, or that any money paid for its purchase or advanced by way of loan on it will be repaid. The offence will be committed by the printer and publisher of the advertisement as well as by the advertiser himself.[4]

---

1 Theft Act 1968 ss.1–6, pp.247–250.
2 Fraud Act 2006 ss.2–5, pp.338–339.
3 Theft Act 1968 s.22, p.251.
4 Theft Act 1968 s.23, p.251.

Chapter 2

SALES OF DOGS

Sales of Animals Generally

The first rule applying to the sale of domestic animals, as it applies to goods, is "caveat emptor", or let the buyer beware. In other words, the buyer must accept the animal as he finds it then and later and have no redress for any defects. But the common law and Acts of Parliament have superimposed on this basic rule a number of measures to give buyers some protection.

There can be included as part of the transaction of selling a condition or warranty about a particular quality of the animal, which it is for the buyer to obtain from the seller for the buyer's protection. As will be described later, certain matters will be covered by statute. In so far as they are not, a buyer should cover himself by condition or warranty for particular qualities or virtues which he wants in the animal. A buyer who is concerned that the animal should be fit for a particular purpose which he wants will have protection by statute if his seller is acting in the course of a business (see item (b) on p.5); if not, he should obtain a condition or warranty to that effect. The health and breeding of the animal may be further aspects to be covered.

Such matters are normally secured by a warranty. The difference in legal consequences between a warranty and a condition is that on a breach of warranty the sale is not invalidated and the buyer is entitled only to sue the seller for the loss thereby suffered; but a breach of condition enables the buyer to repudiate the contract of purchase, which means that he may return the animal and be entitled to have his money back.

A buyer should consider which form of protection he needs. Both conditions and warranties are effective if given verbally, but then dispute may follow about which it was and about the terms used. It is therefore safer to have it in writing and signed by the seller.

If a diseased dog is sold without warranty or condition, then, unless the seller was guilty of fraud, the buyer suffers the loss under the caveat emptor principle.

The statutory provisions protecting buyers have in modern times grown to substantial proportions and are sometimes complicated. A consideration of these provisions is outside the scope of this book, except to mention that under the Sale of Goods Act 1979:

(a) there will be an implied condition that the seller has the right to sell the animal;

(b) if the seller is acting in the course of a business, there will be an implied condition that the animal is reasonably fit for any particular purpose which the buyer makes known to the seller showing that the buyer is relying on the seller's skill or judgment;

(c) there will be an implied warranty that the animal is not subject to any charge or incumbrance not disclosed or known to the buyer before the contract of sale.

The remedies for breach of these implied conditions and this warranty are as described above for express conditions and warranties.

Dogs' Pedigrees

It will be a condition of sale, when a dog is sold with a given pedigree, that the pedigree is truly stated. If it is shown to be false, there will be a breach of condition entitling the buyer to repudiate the contract of purchase and claim his money back.

To sell with a false pedigree at a price reflecting the pedigree if true constitutes the criminal offence of obtaining money by false pretences. In cases of disputes, the trading standards officers of the local council will sometimes be able to help, and the Kennel Club will exceptionally arbitrate if the dog is registered with them.

Pet Shops

The Pet Animals Act 1951 requires that a person keeping a pet shop must be licensed by the district council (in London, by the City Corporation or the borough council, according to the shop's location).[1] The effect of the definition in the Act of "keeping a pet shop" is that

---

1 Pet Animals Act 1951 ss.1(1), (2), 7(3), pp.234, 238.

Sales of Dogs

persons selling dogs (or other pets) otherwise than in a shop may need to be licensed.[2]

Such a keeping is defined (but with the two qualifications mentioned below) as the carrying on at premises of any nature (including a private dwelling) of a business of selling animals as pets, and includes the keeping of animals in any such premises with a view to their being sold in the course of such a business, whether by their keeper or any other person.[3] Several ingredients of this definition need to be examined.

"Premises" in general legal terminology includes open land as well as buildings, and it is thought that sales in the open air will be equally subject to the Act. See also p.7.

The meaning of "business" is discussed on p.44, and it is suggested that the principles mentioned there should be applied.

The phrase "selling animals as pets" includes, so far as dogs are concerned, their selling wholly or mainly for domestic purposes.[3] The word "animal" is itself defined in the Act as including any description of vertebrate.[4]

The second part of the definition makes it clear that the keeping of animals in one place with the object of their being sold by someone other than their keeper at any place or by their keeper at another place will not escape the Act's provisions; that keeping must be licensed. Following this clarification, a case in 1975 decided that a person keeping animals on premises for short periods (48 hours in that case) for the purpose of exporting them nevertheless was keeping a pet shop within the definition, even though the public did not go to the premises to buy animals.[5]

The foregoing definition of "keeping a pet shop" is qualified in two ways. First, a person is not to be treated as keeping a pet shop **only** because he keeps or sells pedigree animals bred by him or the offspring of an animal kept by him as a pet.[6] A pedigree animal is defined

---

2   Pet Animals Act 1951 s.7(1), p.238.
3   Pet Animals Act 1951 s.7(2)(a), p.239.
4   Pet Animals Act 1951 s.7(3), p.239.
5   *Chalmers v Diwell*, p.240.
6   Pet Animals Act 1951 s.7(1)(a), p.238.

to mean an animal of any description which is by its breeding eligible for registration with a recognised club or society keeping a register of animals of that description.[7]

The second qualification arises as follows. If:

(a) a person carries on a business of selling animals as pets; **and**

(b) that business is carried on in conjunction with a business of breeding pedigree animals (as defined above); **and**

(c) the district council are satisfied that the animals sold in the business were acquired by the person with a view to being used, if suitable, for breeding or show purposes; **and**

(d) those animals are not pedigree animals bred by that person; **and**

(e) after their acquisition those animals were found by that person not to be suitable or required for either of the uses described at (c) above;

the district council may direct that the person shall not be treated as keeping a pet shop **by reason only** of his business of selling animals as pets.[8] A pet seller who believes that he should be exempt from licensing on this account should apply to the council for a direction in these terms.

The rules about the licensing of pet shops are similar to those for boarding kennels, for which see pp.44–45. The licensing fee, the right of appeal, the duration of the licence and the powers to inspect premises are the same,[9] and corresponding offences are created.[10] The Pet Animals Act 1951 enables the council to attach a condition to the licence providing that mammals will not be sold at too early an age,[11] but the Act does not require the pet shop proprietor to keep a register. Similarly, too, a person convicted of offences under the Act, or under the Protection of Animals Acts (for which, generally, see Chapter 13),

---

7 Pet Animals Act 1951 s.7(3), p.239.
8 Pet Animals Act 1951 s.7(1)(b), p.238.
9 Pet Animals Act 1951 ss.1(2), (4), (5), 4(1), pp.234–236.
10 Pet Animals Act 1951 s.5(1), (2), p.237.
11 Pet Animals Act 1951 s.1(3)(c), p.234.

Sales of Dogs

may be disqualified by the court from having a pet shop licence and may have any licence held by him cancelled.[12]

Illegal Sales of Dogs

It is an offence, whether or not the vendor is operating such a business, to sell an animal as a pet to a person whom the seller has reasonable cause to believe to be under the age of 12. The definitions of "animals" and "selling animals as pets" given on p.6 apply.

---

12 Pet Animals Act 1951 s.5(3), p.237.

Chapter 3

OWNERS' RESPONSIBILITIES UNDER STRICT LIABILITY AND NEGLIGENCE RULES

As will be seen from later chapters, there are many legal rules made, some by Acts of Parliament and some by case law, which govern people's responsibilities for various acts of dogs. These rules relate specifically to dogs. There are also rules framed in wider terms which apply to animals generally, and hence their application to dogs needs to be mentioned here. The rules are found under two headings: strict liability and negligence.

The position under strict liability is regulated by the Animals Act 1971 and is, unfortunately, complicated. In outline, the Act says that a **keeper** of a dog will be **strictly liable** for **damage** caused by the dog **in certain circumstances**[1] but **will be excused liability** in particular cases.[2] We have to look at each of the emphasised parts of this summary in turn.

A **keeper** of a dog has a special definition[3] which is given in full and discussed on pp.20–21.

"**Strictly liable**" means simply that a dog's keeper will be liable if the dog causes damage, whatever the circumstances; negligence on his part does not have to be proved.

The meaning of "**damage**" is defined to **include** the death of, or injury to, any person, and that in turn includes any disease or any impairment of physical or mental condition.[4] The result of using this definition is not entirely clear, but appears to be that damage to inanimate objects will be within its scope but injury to other animals will not.

The **circumstances** in which there will be liability, unless one of the excuses mentioned below applies, are as follows:

---

1 Animals Act 1971, s.2(2), p.253.
2 Animals Act 1971 s.5(1)–(3), p.255.
3 Animals Act 1971 s.6(3), (4), p.257.
4 Animals Act 1971 s.11, p.260.

Owners' Responsibilities Under Strict Liability and Negligence Rules

(a) the damage is of a kind which the dog, unless restrained, was likely to cause or which, if caused by the dog, was likely to be severe; **and**

(b) the likelihood of the damage or of its being severe was due to characteristics of the dog not normally found in dogs or not normally so found except at particular times or in particular circumstances; **and**

(c) those characteristics were known to the dog's keeper or were at any time known to a person who at that time had charge of the dog as the keeper's servant or, where the keeper is the head of a household, were known to another keeper of the dog who is a member of that household and under the age of 16.[5]

This is the complicated part of this piece of law. A High Court judge, no less, once confessed that he had struggled for a considerable time to ascertain its meaning through its remarkably opaque language![6] Much will depend in each case on the view which the court takes about the characteristics of dogs. In one case it was decided that a propensity to attack people carrying bags is not a normal characteristic of dogs.[7]

The circumstances in which the keeper of a dog **will be excused liability** for damage which it causes are:

(a) Where the damage was due wholly to the fault of the person suffering it; **or**

(b) if the person injured voluntarily accepted the risk of injury, but the employee of a dog's keeper who incurs a risk incidental to his employment is not to be treated as accepting the risk voluntarily; **or**

(c) if the damage was caused by a dog kept at any place to a trespasser there if it is proved:

   (i) **either** that the dog was not kept there for the protection of persons or property;

---

5 Animals Act 1971 s.2(2), p.253.
6 Ormrod L.J., in *Cummings v Grainger* [1977] 1 All E.R. 104 at 110.
7 *Kite v Knapp*, p.254.

(ii) **or**, if the dog was kept there for that purpose, that the keeping for the purpose was not unreasonable.[8]

What is reasonable in case (ii) will depend upon the circumstances; in an old court case it was decided (not surprisingly!) that the keeping of a fierce dog in the access to a house which injured innocent visitors on lawful business was not excusable.[9] See also p.29.

The negligence rules, too, are imprecise. They are based on common law, that is, the decisions of the courts through the years. Liability depends on the person seeking redress being able to satisfy the court that the person whose dog caused the injury or damage owed him a duty to take care, that he failed in that, and that the injury or damage was the result.

The difficulty in this area is being able to establish that duty. Case law is not very helpful, though it does indicate that there is a duty to keep a dog under reasonable control on a public road[10]; this is reinforced by statute – see p.14. It may well be that a failure of control in other situations could lead to liability. Clearly, reasonable control of a dog at all times is advisable to prevent accidents and ensuing claims.

Under the negligence rules the person liable will generally be the person having control of the dog at the time of injury or damage; but an owner, even when not such a person, may also be liable in some circumstances.

Claims under the two heads of strict liability and negligence are not mutually exclusive, and may be made in the alternative.

---

8 Animals Act 1971 ss.5(1)–(3), 6(5), pp.255–257.
9 *Sarch v Blackburn* (1830) 4 C. & P. 297 at 300.
10 *Gomberg v Smith* [1963] 1 Q.B. 25; [1962] 1 All E.R. 725, CA.

Chapter 4
DOGS AND DISEASES

If a dog has an infectious or contagious disease, its keeper will be responsible for any damage or injury caused by the disease in the following cases:

(a) If, when he knows it to be diseased, he allows it to mingle with other persons' animals.

(b) If, when he knows it to be diseased and infectious to persons handling it, he employs a person to handle its carcass who is ignorant of the state of the dog, and that person becomes infected.

(c) If, when he knows it to be diseased, he leaves the dog with another person for an agreed purpose, knowing that he probably will or may place it with healthy animals, and does not warn that person of the dog's disease.

(d) If he sells the dog with a warranty that it is free from disease, whether he knows of the disease or not.

(e) If he is guilty of fraud or concealment about its disease when selling it.

(f) If, knowing the dog to be diseased and that it may be put in with healthy animals, he sells it at public market, fair or auction or, possibly, in a private sale.

A further provision about the sale of diseased dogs may be found on p.4.

It is perhaps worth mentioning here the very strict provisions which would apply if, unfortunately, there were to be an outbreak of rabies in this country.

If a dog's keeper knows or suspects that his dog is affected with rabies, or was so affected at its death –

(a) he must with all practicable speed give written notice of the fact to a diseases of animals inspector of the Department of the

Dogs and Diseases

Environment, Food and Rural Affairs (in England) or (in Wales), or local authority or to the police, unless he reasonably believe that someone else has done so; and

(b) he must, as far as practicable, keep the dog or its carcase separated from other animals.[1]

Government veterinary inspectors are given very wide powers of action if rabies is suspected. They may enter any premises to make enquiries, to examine animals and their carcases, to take samples for diagnosis, and to remove (for veterinary observation or diagnostic tests) animals which are affected with rabies or suspected of infection or which have been in contact with affected or suspected animals.[2] Such animals may be slaughtered by Departmental officials; compensation is payable.[3]

Those involved with animals in these circumstances, e.g. the occupier of the premises where the animals are and those having charge of them, must give information and reasonable assistance to the veterinary inspectors.[4]

The controls on the import of dogs aimed at preventing the introduction of rabies into this country are described in Chapter 16.

---

1 Rabies (Control) Order 1974 art.4(1)(2), p.347.
2 Rabies (Control) Order 1974 art.6(1)(2), p.347.
3 Animal Health Act 1981 s.32.
4 Rabies (Control) Order 1974 art.6(2)–(4), pp.347–348.

Chapter 5
DOGS ON THE ROAD

Straying on to the Road

The Animals Act of 1971 provides that owners of animals and those having control of them have a duty to take reasonable care to see that injury or damage is not caused by their animals straying on to the road.[1] The term "reasonable care" is commonly used in legal parlance to indicate a standard which is flexible enough to take account of varying circumstances. It is not an absolute or strict standard, as with the strict liability provisions mentioned on p.9, but nevertheless demands a fairly high degree of care. The point arose in a case decided in 1981 when the court gave its opinion that if a fence, though not 100% secure, is reasonably adequate to prevent escape, the duty to take reasonable care is fulfilled.[2]

This duty does not automatically demand fencing or other means of containment against the road, but this is generally advisable when a dog is customarily let loose, and is strongly advised if the road is heavily trafficked. On the other hand, if a dog can be trained well enough to keep itself within bounds, no fencing is needed. Responsibility in each case will be determined by the total circumstances of that case.

The duty is only operative in cases of highways (for the meaning of which see p.35), and therefore does not apply to private roads and other private ways.

Clearly, the most serious consequences which could ensue when this duty is breached and a dog causes damage or injury is a motor vehicle accident with ensuing death or injury or a heavy claim for repairs, or all of these. But there will be responsibility also for such lesser incidents as cycle accidents and the knocking over of pedestrians.

---

1 Animals Act 1971 s.8, p.257.
2 *Smith v Sudron and Coulson*, p.258.

Reporting Accidents Involving Dogs

The Road Traffic Act 1988 has laid down rules for conduct when a dog (and certain other animals) is injured in an accident with a motor vehicle on a public road or other road to which the public has access. The rules do not apply when: the dog is in a vehicle or trailer drawn by it; or the vehicle is not intended or adapted for use on roads or is one which can only be used for cutting grass and is controlled by a pedestrian.

The driver of the vehicle must stop. A person having "reasonable grounds" for doing so may ask the driver to supply the name and address of the driver and, if he is not the owner, of the owner of the vehicle, and the vehicle's registration number; the driver must give this information.[3] The "reasonable grounds" are not specified. Clearly, the dog's owner has such grounds and, it is suggested, any person controlling the dog at the time and any member of the owner's family.

The driver should stop for such length of time as in the circumstances will enable any person entitled to do so to require the information from the driver personally.[4] If no one does that, or if for any other reason the driver does not give his name and address, the driver must report the accident to the police as soon as reasonably practicable, and in any case within 24 hours of the accident.[5]

Failure to do any of the things required of him renders the driver liable to prosecution.[6] But (assuming the magistrates believe him) no offence is committed if the driver is unaware of the accident and does not stop.[7]

When a Lead is Necessary

A local authority may by order designate particular roads the effect of which is that it becomes an offence for a person to cause or permit a dog to be on a designated road without it being held on a lead. This is not to apply to dogs proved to be kept for driving or tending sheep

---

3 Road Traffic Act 1988 s.170(1), (2), pp.125–126.
4 *Lee v Knapp*, p.127.
5 Road Traffic Act 1988 s.170(3), (6), p.126.
6 Road Traffic Act 1988 s.170(4), p.126.
7 *Harding v Price*, p.127.

Dogs on the Road

or cattle in the course of a trade or business, or proved to be at the time in use under proper control for sporting purposes.

The local authorities which have these powers are, in London, the City Corporation and the London borough councils, elsewhere in England county councils and metropolitan district councils and in Wales county and county borough councils.[8] If they are proposing to make an order, it must be advertised in the local press so that the public may have an opportunity to comment and object, and a public inquiry may be held.

When an order is made, signs giving information about its effect are to be erected in the roads concerned.

Fouling Footways and Other Public Open Spaces

Prior to the coming into force of Part 6 of the Clean Neighbourhoods and Environment Act 2005 (see under "Dog Control Orders" below), district councils (in London, the City Corporation or a borough council) were enabled to make byelaws about this.[9] There was no set form of byelaw and its wording may have varied from place to place, but the following format was commonly found.

The byelaw made it an offence for a person in charge of a dog to allow it to foul the footway of any street or public place by deposit of its excrement. It usually provided that it would be a defence if that person satisfied the court that the fouling was not due to culpable neglect or default on his part; and the byelaw might go on to say that the owner of the dog should be deemed to be in charge of it unless the court was satisfied that at the time of fouling the dog was in the charge of another person. Offences were prosecuted before the magistrates.

Notices warning of the byelaw had to be displayed in the places where the byelaw operated.

Under the Dogs (Fouling of Land) Act 1996, local authorities could designate land on which it would be an offence, with certain exceptions, for a dog owner to allow his dog to defecate. The 1996 Act has been superseded by Part 6 of the Clean Neighbourhoods and

---

8 Road Traffic Act 1988 s.27(1)–(4), (7), p.124.
9 Local Government Act 1972 s.235(1); City of London (Various Powers) Act 1961 s.39.

Motorway Rules

Environment Act 2005 (see below), but any designations made before Part 6 of the 2005 Act came into force (on April 6, 2006) remain effective until superseded by a dog control order made under Part 6 of the 2005 Act or by a revocation of the designation order.

Under environmental protection legislation designated authorities and others have a duty to keep land under their control clear of litter and refuse. Dog faeces have been declared to be refuse for this purpose.[10] These provisions do not apply directly to dog owners; their liability will depend upon the terms of any byelaws operating on the land and upon whether the land is designated as described above.

Motorway Rules

The Motorways Traffic (England and Wales) Regulations 1982 (as amended) contain rules about the handling of all kinds of animals which are carried in a vehicle using a motorway ("vehicle" will include a trailer). To disobey the rules is a criminal offence. The Regulations say that the person in charge of the animal shall so far as practicable secure that:

(a) the animal is not removed from or permitted to leave the vehicle while the vehicle is on the motorway; and

(b) if it escapes from, or it is necessary for it to be removed from or permitted to leave, the vehicle:

    (i) it shall not go or remain on any part of the motorway except the verge, which is defined to mean any part of the road other than a carriageway or central reservation, and

    (ii) while it is not on or in the vehicle, it must be held on a lead or otherwise kept under proper control.[11]

But the person in charge of the animal need not comply with these requirements if so directed by the police or if such is indicated by a traffic sign.[12]

---

10 Environmental Protection Act 1990 ss.86(14)(15), 89; Litter (Animal Droppings) Order 1991, p.360.
11 Motorways Traffic (England and Wales) Regulations 1982 reg.14, p.351.
12 Motorways Traffic (England and Wales) Regulations 1982 reg.16(1)(a).

Dogs on the Road

Dog Control Orders

Dog control orders were introduced by Part 6 of the Clean Neighbourhoods and Environment Act 2005. Section 55 empowers a primary authority and a secondary authority to make an order providing for an offence or offences in relation to the control of dogs in its area. A primary authority is a district council in England, a county council in England for an area for which there are no district councils, a London borough council, the Common Council of the City of London, the Council of the Isles of Scilly and a Welsh county or county borough council. A secondary authority is a parish council in England and a community council in Wales.

A dog control order may relate to one or more of the following:

(a) fouling of land by dogs and the removal of dog faeces;

(b) keeping of dogs on leads;

(c) exclusion of dogs from land;

(d) the number of dogs which a person may take on to any land.

Section 56 requires the Secretary of State to make regulations prescribing the penalties for breach of a dog control order (which cannot exceed level 3 on the standard scale) and prescribing the form and content of a dog control order. The relevant regulations for England are the Dog Control Orders (Prescribed Offences and Penalties, etc.) Order 2006 (SI 2006/1059) and the Dog Control Orders (Procedures) Regulations 2006 (SI 2006/798); and for Wales, the Dog Control Orders (Miscellaneous Provisions) (Wales) Regulations 2007 (SI 2007/702).

Section 57 provides that dog control orders may only apply to land in the open air to which the public are entitled or permitted to have access with or without payment. Covered land is in the open air if it is open to the air on at least one side. The Secretary of State may designate land which is not to be subject to dog control orders. The Controls on Dogs (Non-application to Designated Land) Order 2006 (SI 2006/779) and the Controls on Dogs (Non-application to Designated Land) (Wales) Order 2007 (SI 2007/701) designate Forestry Commission land and land over which a road passes. Where land is regulated under a private Act otherwise than by a primary or a secondary authority, the person

Dog Control Orders

who has the powers of regulation may by notice in writing to those authorities in whose area the land is situated exclude the land from the ambit of Part 6.

Section 59 empowers an authorised officer of a primary or secondary authority to issue a fixed penalty notice where he has reason to believe an offence has been committed under a dog control order made by the authority. In addition, such an officer of a secondary authority may issue a fixed penalty notice where he has reason to believe an offence has been committed under a dog control order made by a primary authority. The amount of the fixed penalty is the amount specified by the authority (which may differ for different offences) or, if none, £75. The Secretary of State has power to prescribe maximum and minimum penalty amounts. In England, the Environmental Offences (Fixed Penalties) (Miscellaneous Provisions) Regulations 2007 (SI 2007/175) prescribe £80 and £50 as the maximum and minimum amounts. In Wales, the Environmental Offences (Fixed Penalties) (Miscellaneous Provisions) (Wales) Regulations (SI 2008/663) prescribe £75 and £150 as the maximum and minimum amounts.

Where a primary or a secondary authority has byelaws which make similar provision to a dog control order under s.55 of Pt 6 of the Clean Neighbourhoods and Environment Act 2005, the byelaws cease to have effect in relation to any land once it becomes subject to a dog control order.

Part 6 supersedes the Dogs (Fouling of Land) Act 1996, which is repealed. Nevertheless, the 1996 Act will continue to apply to land designated under that Act until a dog control order is made over it or the land ceases to be designated.[13]

Defra has issued guidance on dog control in its guidance circular "Dog Control Orders" (see p.463). It has also issued particular guidance to parish councils in its publication "Getting to grips with the Clean Neighbourhoods and Environment Act 2005 – a parish council guide to environmental enforcement".

---

13 Clean Neighbourhoods and Environment Act 2005 s.108 and Clean Neighbourhoods and Environment Act 2005 (Commencement No. 1, Transitional and Savings Provisions) (England) Order 2006 (SI 2006/795). The equivalent Welsh Order is the Clean Neighbourhoods and Environment Act 2005 (Commencement No. 2, Transitional Provisions and Savings) (Wales) Order 2006 (SI 2006/2797).

Chapter 6

TRESPASSING DOGS

A dog may be said to be trespassing when it is on property where it has no right to be or, more correctly, where its owner has no right or permission to allow it to be. The law is fairly precise about liability for certain kinds of trespass by a dog, but is not so clear in other instances.

If a dog of its own accord enters land without permission but does no more, its owner is not liable under civil law for the trespass; nor is it any criminal offence.

Nineteenth century cases have decided that a dog's owner is liable under civil law if he deliberately sends his dog on to somebody else's land in pursuit of game (no entry on the land by the owner being necessary), or if he allows the dog to roam at large knowing it to be addicted to destroying game. It is not clear what the consequences are if the dog is so sent for another purpose; possibly the owner would be liable for damage thereby caused.

Special rules operate when a trespassing dog kills or injures livestock, and these will be considered in a moment. There then remains the situation in which the dog of its own accord trespasses and causes damage otherwise than to livestock. Again, the law is not clear, but probably the position is that the dog's owner will be liable for any damage which it is in the nature of a dog to commit.

Cases of dogs worrying livestock are governed by two statutes: the Animals Act 1971 deals with civil liability; and the Dogs (Protection of Livestock) Act 1953 regulates criminal responsibility. Liability under one head does not of course exclude liability under the other.

Except as noted below, the keeper of a dog is liable for the damage it causes by killing or injuring livestock.[1] Three parts of this statement need individual examination.

The 1971 Act gives a special meaning to the word "keeper". A person is a keeper of a dog if he either owns it, or has it in his possession, or is

---

1 Animals Act 1971 s.3, p.255.

Trespassing Dogs

the head of a household of which a member under 16 years old owns the dog or possesses it. Such a person remains the keeper of the dog until someone else fulfilling these qualifications succeeds him as keeper. But a person who takes possession of a dog to prevent it causing damage or to restore it to its owner does not, just because of that possession, become its keeper.[2]

Despite all this detail, some imprecision remains about the identity of the head of a household. Probably, and despite modern trends, in the common case of a household with husband, wife and children the husband is assumed to be its head. But proof of the fact could be difficult, and establishing the identity of the head in many households of different composition more so.

Cases decided prior to the Act indicate that injury in this context may include indirect injury. For example, foals injuring themselves as the result of a dog barking at them[3] and poultry ceasing to lay as a result of shock following a dog's presence.[4]

The 1971 Act has a long definition of "livestock". It means all of the following:

(a) Cattle, horses, asses, mules, hinnies (which are the off-spring of she-asses by stallions), sheep, pigs, goats, and deer not in a wild state.

(b) The domestic varieties of fowls, turkeys, ducks, geese, guinea-fowls, pigeons, peacocks and quail.

(c) While in captivity only, pheasants, partridges and grouse.[5]

Liability is avoided in the cases listed below. But otherwise it matters not what active or passive role is played by the dog's keeper (as defined). It is enough that he is its keeper and the dog does the damage. There is no liability:

---

2 Animals Act 1971 s.6(3), (4), p.257.
3 *Campbell v Wilkinson*, p.255.
4 *Ives v Brewer*, p.255.
5 Animals Act 1971 s.11, p.260.

(1) if the damage to the livestock is due wholly to the fault of the person whose livestock it is; **or**

(2) if the livestock was killed or injured on land on to which it had strayed **and**:

    (i) **either** the dog belonged to the occupier of that land, **or**
    (ii) its presence on that land was authorised by him.[6]

Where damage is caused by two or more dogs acting together, the law regards each dog as causing the whole of the damage, and consequently the keeper of each can be held responsible for the whole damage.[7]

Under the Dogs (Protection of Livestock) Act 1953, if a dog worries livestock on agricultural land, its owner and, if it is in the charge of anyone else, that person also, is guilty of an offence and can be prosecuted and fined,[8] unless one of the defences later mentioned can be established. Here, again, there are definitions of a number of the terms used.

"Livestock" are: bulls, cows, oxen, heifers, calves, sheep, goats, swine, horses, asses, mules, and domestic fowls, turkeys, geese and ducks.

"Agricultural land" means land used as arable, meadow or grazing land, or for the purposes of poultry or pig farming, market gardens, allotments, nursery grounds or orchards[9]; and, it has been decided, a cricket field on which sheep are grazing will come within this definition.[10]

There is a long definition of what worrying livestock (as that word is already defined) means. It is:

(a) attacking livestock; **or**

(b) chasing them (which will include running among them so as to alarm them) in such a way as may be reasonably expected to cause them injury (which here has the same meaning as

---

6 Animals Act 1971 s.5(1), (4), pp.255–256.
7 *Arneil v Paterson*, p.255.
8 Dogs (Protection of Livestock) Act 1953 s.1(1), p.93.
9 Dogs (Protection of Livestock) Act 1953 s.3(1), p.96.
10 *Williams v Richards*, p.97.

Trespassing Dogs

described on p.21) or suffering or, in the case of females, abortion or loss or diminution in their produce; **or**

(c) being at large (i.e., not on a lead or otherwise under close control) in a field or enclosure in which there are sheep.[11]

But case (c) does **not** apply to the following dogs:

(i) a dog owned by, or in the charge of, the occupier of the field or enclosure, the owner of the sheep or a person authorised by that occupier or owner. (This authorisation appears to mean authority or permission given to the person to have his dog in the field or enclosure. The authority is not required to be in writing, but ideally it should be to safeguard the authorised person's position if he were to be prosecuted);

(ii) police dogs, guide dogs, trained sheep dogs, working gun dogs, and packs of hounds.[12]

The offence of worrying livestock will not be committed (and the defendant therefore is entitled to be acquitted) in either of the following cases:

(a) if, being the owner of the dog, he satisfies the court that at the time in question the dog was in the charge of some other person whom he reasonably believed to be a fit and proper person to be in charge of it[13];

(b) if, being the owner of the dog or in charge of it, he satisfies the court that at the material time the livestock were trespassing on the land in question and the dog was owned by, or in the charge of, the occupier of that land or a person authorised by that owner or occupier. (As to "authorise", see paragraph (i) above). But this will not be a defence if the authorised person causes the dog to attack the livestock.[14]

---

11 Dogs (Protection of Livestock) Act 1953 s.1(2), p.93.
12 Dogs (Protection of Livestock) Act 1953 s.1(2A), p.93.
13 Dogs (Protection of Livestock) Act 1953 s.1(4), p.94.
14 Dogs (Protection of Livestock) Act 1953 s.1(3), p.93.

Trespassing Dogs

The police may intervene in some cases of dogs worrying livestock. If a police officer reasonably believes that a dog found on what appears to him to be agricultural land has been worrying livestock there, and no person is present who admits to being its owner or in charge of it, the officer may, in order to find out the owner, seize and keep the dog until the owner has claimed it and paid the expenses of detention.[15] (The same definitions for "livestock" and "agricultural land" as are given on p.22 apply in this situation). The procedure to be operated by the police after seizure is that used when a stray dog is detained[16] for which see p.36.

For the occasions when the killing or injuring of a dog which is attacking animals or human beings is justified, see Chapter 10.

---

15 Dogs (Protection of Livestock) Act 1953 s.2(2), p.95.
16 Dogs (Protection of Livestock) Act 1953 s.2(3), p.95.

Chapter 7

NUISANCES, BYELAWS AND HYGIENE REGULATIONS

Nuisances

The keeping of any animals in such a position or in such circumstances as to cause a substantial discomfort or annoyance to the public in general or to a particular person constitutes in law the civil wrong of nuisance. The remedy is by action in the courts claiming, as appropriate, an award of damages and/or an injunction; the latter is an order of the court forbidding the continuance of the nuisance on penalty of a fine or imprisonment.

Dogs may cause discomfort or annoyance, for example, by excessive barking, especially if late at night, or by a number of them running loose. But the effect must be substantial, and it is always a question of degree whether a particular activity in given circumstances constitutes a nuisance; some inconveniences have to be tolerated.

In addition to nuisances at common law which have just been described, Acts of Parliament have created what are known as statutory nuisances. Amongst other things, it is a statutory nuisance to keep any animal in such a place or manner as to be prejudicial to health or a nuisance, or to emit noise from premises so as to be similarly prejudicial or a nuisance.[1] It appears that what is meant by being a nuisance in this context is carrying on an activity affecting public health, though not necessarily causing injury to health or annoyance to any particular person, or injury to any particular property. Judicial opinion indicates that the keeping of noisy dogs may be a statutory nuisance.[2]

There is a statutory procedure which is operated by district councils for dealing with these nuisances. It involves: the service of an abatement notice and, if that is not heeded, a summons to, and an order by, the magistrates' court; fines for non-compliance; abatement by the council; and recovery of the council's costs of abatement and legal costs.

---

1 Environmental Protection Act 1990 s.79.
2 *Clemons v Short* [1969] 113 Sol. Jo. 931.

Proceedings in the magistrates' court to remedy a statutory nuisance may also be taken by a private individual who is aggrieved by the nuisance.[3]

Basically, common law and statutory nuisances are concerned with the same thing; the causing of substantial discomfort or annoyance to people. The latter type of nuisance is generally more concerned with public health considerations, whilst the common law is more likely to be called in aid to settle private disputes.

Byelaws

Byelaws are a kind of subordinate legislation which may be made by a variety of organisations and for many different purposes and situations. Some byelaws affect dogs and the following are the most common instances of these.

Many organisations controlling public open spaces have byelaws; the details are sometimes accessible on site, but in other cases enquiries must be made. Byelaws may be made for national parks, areas of outstanding natural beauty, National Trust property, nature reserves, common land, large forest areas, and land and waterways to which the public have access by agreement or order.

The Forestry Commission Byelaws of 1982 operate on Forestry Commission land to which the public have access. So far as dogs may be concerned, these provide that a person shall not, except with the Commissioners' written authority:

(a) permit any animal in the person's charge to be out of control;

(b) permit a dog for which the person is responsible to disturb, worry or chase any bird or animal or, on being requested by an officer of the Commissioners to do so, fail to keep the dog on a leash;

(c) intentionally disturb, injure, catch, destroy or take any bird, fish, reptile or animal, or attempt to do so;

(d) intentionally disturb, damage or destroy the burrow, den, set or lair of any wild animal.

---

3 Environmental Protection Act 1990 s.82.

Hygiene Regulations

Water authorities and internal drainage boards may make byelaws applying to reservoirs, waterways, other inland waters and land under their control. These may deal with such matters as:

(a) prohibiting the washing of animals in the water. (The British Waterways Board have a similar byelaw relating to their canals – except the Gloucester and Sharpness Canal);

(b) prohibiting the destruction, injury or disturbance of wild animals;

(c) ordering dog owners and others in charge of them to keep them under proper control and to restrain them from causing annoyance to other people, from worrying other animals or water fowl and from entering the water.

The Railways Act 2005 s.46 empowers railway operators to make byelaws relating, among other matters, to the maintenance of order and the prevention of nuisance on stations and platforms. The section also saves any byelaws made under earlier legislation until they are amended or revoked under the 2005 Act. The British Railways Board's byelaws of 1971 have several provisions affecting animals generally. These include: the power to exclude animals causing or likely to cause annoyance or damage; the exclusion of animals from moving platforms; and directions about where animals may be left or placed.

Local authorities' byelaws about the fouling of footways by dogs have already been considered on p.16.

Hygiene Regulations

Under the General Food Regulations 2004 (SI 2004/3279) (as amended), made under the Food Safety Act 1990, a business or undertaking, whether run for profit or not, in which food is sold or supplied for human consumption is required to observe a number of hygiene regulations. These include rules designed to prevent dogs and other live animals from coming into contact with food.

Shops serving food and their customers are exhorted by the public health authorities to exclude dogs from the shops, but guide dogs for the blind are permitted entry.

Chapter 8

DANGEROUS AND FEROCIOUS DOGS

Dangerous Dogs

Until 1991 the only Act of Parliament which provided court procedures for dealing with dangerous dogs as such was the Dogs Act of 1871. Following a series of attacks on people by the more vicious kinds of dogs, a Dangerous Dogs Act was passed in the summer of 1991; this provided better means for dealing with such dogs. First, however, we look at the provisions of the 1871 Act.

Dogs Act 1871

Under this Act a complaint may be made to a magistrates' court that a dog is dangerous and not kept under proper control. If the magistrates find that the dog is dangerous, they may either order the dog's owner to keep it under proper control or order it to be destroyed. A fine can be imposed for breach of either kind of order.[1]

The main defects of this procedure were remedied by the Dangerous Dogs Act 1991. Previously, there was doubt about when a dog could be said to be dangerous. If a dog was proved to have injured cattle or poultry, or to have chased sheep, an order under the 1871 Act could be made.[2] Whilst attacks on people would generally justify an order, the position was uncertain in the case of incidents involving other kinds of animals.

Following the enactment of the 1991 Act, magistrates may make an order without proof that any person had been injured.[3] Injuring cattle or poultry still provides justification for an order. It appears that the resultant position is that magistrates now have a wide discretion and may make an order in any circumstances where they find a dog to be dangerous.

Before 1991, magistrates could not elaborate on the means of control when making a proper control order. Since the 1991 Act came into

---

1 Dogs Act 1871 s.2, p.85.
2 Dogs Act 1906 s.1(4), p.90.
3 Dangerous Dogs Act 1991 s.3(5), p.146.

28

Dangerous Dogs Act 1991

force, their order may specify those means; muzzling, keeping on a lead, exclusion from named places and any other measures of control are permitted.[4] Also, if magistrates believe that neutering of a male dog would make it less dangerous, they may order that to be done.[5]

The need for proper control is not limited to public places, but extends, it has been decided, to places where the dog is on the owner's private property to which other people have a right of access.[6]

A control order or a destruction order may be made even though the owner did not know that his dog was dangerous.[7] Although normally a control order will first be made, magistrates would not be acting improperly solely because they made a destruction order in the first instance.

The police are the proper people in the majority of cases to start proceedings in the magistrates' court, but others may do so. An appeal may be made to the Crown Court against a destruction order or a control order.[8]

A person who sets his dog on another person who is wounded by the dog will be guilty of the offence of malicious wounding under the Offences Against the Persons Act 1861.

Dangerous Dogs Act 1991

This Act tackles the problem of dangerous dogs in four ways:

(1) By prohibiting possession of named breeds except under strictly controlled conditions.

(2) By authorising the imposition of restrictions on other dogs believed to be a serious danger to the public.

(3) By imposing sanctions on the owners of dogs and those in charge of them which are dangerously out of control in a public place.

---

4 The 1991 Act s.3(5), p.146.
5 The 1991 Act s.3(6), p.146.
6 *Philip v Wright* (1940) S.C. (J) 9; 1939 S.N. 94; 1940 S.L.T. 22.
7 *Parker v Walsh* (1885) 1 T.L.R. 583.
8 Dangerous Dogs Act 1989 s.1(2), p.130.

Dangerous and Ferocious Dogs

(4) By imposing sanctions on the owners of dogs and those in charge of them who allow them to injure persons on private property.

(1) Four types of dog are named by, or under powers in, the 1991 Act. These are: the pit bull terrier; the Japanese Tosa; the Dogo Argentino and the Fila Braziliero.

The Secretary of State may add other dogs of a type appearing to be bred for fighting or to have the characteristics of such a type to this list.[9]

Under the 1991 Act it is an offence: to breed or breed from any such dog; to sell, exchange, or to offer, advertise[10] or expose it for sale or exchange; to make, or offer to make, a gift of it, or advertise or expose it as a gift; to allow it to be in a public place[11] without being muzzled or kept on a lead[12]; or to abandon it or allow it to stray.[13] It is also an offence for a person to have possession or custody of any of the listed dogs unless the following requirements are met. These are, briefly, that particulars of the dog be reported to the police, that the dog be neutered and carry identification of neutering, that third party insurance cover be provided, and that a certificate of exemption shall be in force and its requirements complied with.[14] The Index of Exempted Dogs has been appointed as agent by Defra to manage these exemption arrangements.[15]

In practice, these measures are aimed at the pit bull terrier, the other named breeds being very rare in this country. On the face of it, the measures would appear to be sufficiently drastic to deal with the situation. The problem arises in determining whether or not a dog is a pit bull terrier. The Act's definition is "any dog of the type known as the pit bull terrier",[16] and it provides that in any prosecution it is

---

9 Dangerous Dogs Act 1991 s.1(1), p.141; SI 1991/1743, p.352.
10 For the definition of "advertise", see the 1991 Act s.10(2), p.157.
11 For the definition of "public place" and an interpretation in a decided case, see the 1991 Act s.10(2), p.157 and the Commentary thereon.
12 For the meanings of "muzzled" and "kept on a lead", see the 1991 Act s.7(1)(2), p.156.
13 Dangerous Dogs Act 1991 ss.1(2), (4), (7), 6, 7, 10(2), pp.141–157.
14 The 1991 Act s.1(3), (5), (7), p.142; SI 1991/1744, Part III, p.354.
15 The address of the Index of Exempted Dogs is PO Box 1544, London W7 2ZB; telephone 0844 8563303; email: office@endangereddogs.com; website: *http://www.endangereddogs.com*.
16 The 1991 Act s.1(1)(a), p.141.

to be presumed that the dog is a pit bull terrier unless the accused brings sufficient evidence to the contrary.[17] Several early prosecutions under the Act have failed because the defendant has been able to convince the court, through the evidence of an expert witness, that his dog was not a pit bull terrier but a dog of a similar appearance, such as a Staffordshire bull terrier, a Labrador cross or other cross-breed which cannot rightly be called a pit bull terrier.

The true pit bull terrier is itself a cross-breed; but canine purists and Defra (who are responsible for the legislation) disagree about the breeds from which it is bred. However, a case in 1993 provided some clarification.[18] It decided that the provisions described above do not apply only to the breed of dogs known as pit bull terriers, since the word "type" is not synonymous with the word "breed", but apply to a dog having a substantial number or most of the physical characteristics of a pit bull terrier, which is a matter of fact for the adjudicating court to decide.

(2) Distinct arrangements are made under the 1991 Act for types of dog which, though not partly banned as described, are seen by the Government to present a serious danger to the public. These arrangements, which are yet to be brought into force by Government order, will nominate types of dogs of this description and impose restrictions on them. The restrictions, breach of which may lead to prosecution, fines and imprisonment, can only include banning the dogs from public places[19] without being muzzled or kept on a lead,[20] and prohibiting their abandonment or straying.[21]

(3) An offence is committed by the owner of a dog, **and** by any other person in charge of it at the time, if the dog is dangerously out of control in a public place. The offence is one of strict liability. A more serious offence will be committed if the dog, while so out of control, injures a person.[22]

The owner of a dog, who was not in charge of it at the time, will have a defence if he proves that the dog was then in the charge of

---

17 The 1991 Act s.5(5), p.154.
18 *R. v Crown Court at Knightsbridge, Ex p. Dunne* (1993) 4 All E.R. 491.
19 For the definition of "public place" and an interpretation in a decided case, see the 1991 Act s.10(2), p.157 and the Commentary thereon; *R. v Bezzina* (1994) 3 All E.R. 964, CA.
20 For the meanings of "muzzled" and "kept on a lead", see the 1991 Act s.7(1), (2), p.156.
21 The 1991 Act s.2, p.144–145.
22 The 1991 Act s.3(1), p.146.

somebody whom he reasonably believed to be a fit and proper person to be in charge of it.[23]

Where the dog is owned by a person less than 16 years old, the owner, for the purpose of this offence, will include the head of the household, if any, of which that person is a member.[24]

(4) An offence is committed by the owner of a dog who allows it to enter a place which is not a public place[25] and, while it is there, it injures any person or there are grounds for reasonable apprehension[26] that it will do so. If a person other than the owner of the dog is in charge of it at the time, that person, and not the owner, will be liable.[27] The maximum penalties on conviction are more serious if injury occurs.[28]

It will be seen that this offence governs control of dogs on private property, whilst that relating to public places is as described at (3) above.

In addition to imposing fines and imprisonment, a court convicting a person for any of the offences described at (1), (2), (3) and (4) above may order the destruction of the dog involved. Formerly, a court was required to order destruction if the offence concerned one of the partly banned breeds or if the offence under (3) or (4) involved actual injury. A number of cases of hardship led to the passing of the Dangerous Dogs (Amendment) Act 1997 which came into force on June 8, 1997. This Act relaxes the mandatory requirement for destruction and, within limitations, gives magistrates a discretion.[29]

The court **may** also disqualify the offender in cases (1), (3) or (4) above, for as long as it thinks necessary, for having custody of a dog.[30]

---

23 The 1991 Act s.3(2), p.146.
24 The 1991 Act s.6, p.156. For comment on "head of the household", see p.21.
25 For the definition of "public place" and an interpretation in a decided case, see the 1991 Act s.10(2), p.157 and the Commentary thereon.
26 For "injury" and "reasonable apprehension" of it when the dog is being used for lawful purposes, see the 1991 Act s.10(3), p.157.
27 The 1991 Act s.3(3), p.146.
28 The 1991 Act s.3(3), (4), p.146.
29 The 1991 Act ss.4, 4A, 4B, pp.148–153; Dangerous Dogs (Amendment) Act 1997 ss.1–3, pp.179–182.
30 The 1991 Act s.4(1), p.148. For other matters concerned with the destruction of dogs, for appeals against orders, and the removal of, and consequences of disregarding, a disqualification order, see the 1991 Act s.4(2)–(8), pp.148–149.

Police officers and authorised officers of a local authority are given wide powers to enter and search premises and to seize dogs involved in offences or suspected offences; in some cases a magistrate's warrant is needed.[31]

Ferocious Dogs

Except in the Greater London area, it is an offence, which originates in the Town Police Clauses Act 1847, for any person in any street: to let an unmuzzled ferocious dog be at large so that it obstructs or annoys the residents or passengers in the street or puts them in danger; or to set on or urge any dog to attack, worry or put in fear any person or animal.[32] The word "street" here is given an extended meaning to include any road, square, court, alley, thoroughfare or public passage.[33]

The courts have not pronounced on the meaning to be given to "ferocious", but a dog may be regarded as ferocious if it appears to be untamed and certainly if it is shown to have unusually vicious tendencies. In adjudicating in any prosecution the magistrates will form a view based on the behaviour of the dog at the time and on any evidence given about its previous conduct. Less extreme behaviour may make the dog liable to be dealt with as a dangerous dog, for which see the preceding pages.

Clearly, a dog will not be at large when it is held on a lead. It may be argued, since "at large" means at liberty or free, that an unleashed dog answering obediently to the commands of the person in charge of it is also not at large; though in that situation the dog should not be annoying or endangering people or other animals, but may be obstructing people. If a dog may exhibit tendencies in a street which might be described as ferocious, it is sensible (if it has to be there) for it to be muzzled when, whatever its behaviour, the offence of letting it be at large cannot be committed.

In the Metropolitan Police District a similar offence has been created by the Metropolitan Police Act 1839. This differs only from the first part of the 1847 Act offence in that it is sufficient that an unmuzzled dog be at large (no obstruction, annoyance or danger need be shown),

---

31 The 1991 Act s.5(1), (2), p.154.
32 Town Police Clauses Act 1847 s.28, p.83.
33 Town Police Clauses Act 1847 s.3, p.83.

Dangerous and Ferocious Dogs

and that the place of the offence is described as any thoroughfare or public place.[34]

Under the Protection of Badgers Act 1992, dogs involved in offences against badgers may be destroyed by court order and their owners disqualified from keeping dogs.[35]

---

34 Metropolitan Police Act 1839 s.54, p.80.
35 Protection of Badgers Act 1992 s.13, p.167.

Chapter 9

DOG COLLARS AND STRAY DOGS

Dog Collars

Under the Control of Dogs Order of 1992 every dog other than one excepted by the Order, while in a highway or place of public resort, must wear a collar with the name and address of its owner inscribed on it or on a plate or badge attached to it.[1]

A highway is a road or other way over which the public have the right to pass to and fro; it need not necessarily be maintained by a highway authority. A place of public resort has been said to mean a place to which the public goes as a matter of fact, as distinct from a matter of right, and notwithstanding that a charge is made for admission.

A dog collar is not needed for:

(a) a pack of hounds; or

(b) any dog while being used for sporting purposes, for the capture or destruction of vermin, or for the driving or tending of cattle or sheep; or

(c) any dog while being used on official duties by the Armed Forces, Customs and Excise officers or the police; or

(d) any dog while being used in emergency rescue work; or

(e) any dog registered with the Guide Dogs for the Blind Association.[2]

If a collar is not worn when required, the dog may be seized by the police and treated by them as a stray,[3] for which see the heading "Stray Dogs" below. Also, its owner and any person in charge of it causing or permitting the dog to be in a highway or place of public resort are each guilty of an offence and may be prosecuted and fined, unless they had lawful authority or excuse.[4]

---

1 Control of Dogs Order 1992 arts 2(1), 3, pp.366–367.
2 Control of Dogs Order 1992 art.2(2), p.366.
3 Control of Dogs Order 1992 art.4, p.367.
4 Control of Dogs Order 1992 art.3, p.367; Animal Health Act 1981 s.73(a), p.119.

It is unlikely that an ordinary defendant could plead lawful authority as a defence; that would however bar the conviction of a policeman during the course of seizing the dog. The other defence – having a lawful excuse – could be available, for example, to an owner who was prosecuted and who was able to satisfy the magistrates that he was neither in charge of the dog at the time nor had any part in allowing it to be in a highway or place of public resort; and, further, that he honestly but mistakenly believed on reasonable grounds that the dog was to be used by another person for one of the purposes described in item (b) above.

Stray Dogs

(1) Seizure by the police

Since the coming into force of s.68 of and Pt 6 of Sch.5 to the Clean Neighbourhoods and Environment Act 2005,[5] the responsibility for stray dogs rests solely with local authorities. However, the previous powers under the Dogs Act 1906 for police to seize and detain stray dogs still apply in relation to dogs worrying or chasing livestock, etc. in breach of the Dogs (Protection of Livestock) Act 1953.

In this respect, the Dogs Act 1906 enables a police officer to seize any dog found in a highway or place of public resort (for the meanings of these terms, see p.35) which he has reason to believe is a stray. A dog found on any other land or premises may be similarly seized if the owner or occupier consents. The officer seizing the dog may then detain it until the owner has claimed it and paid all expenses incurred in its detention.[6]

If the dog is wearing a collar showing an address, or the owner is otherwise known, the officer must serve on the person whose address is given or the known owner (as the case may be) written notice that the dog has been seized and is liable to be sold or destroyed if not claimed within seven clear days after service of the notice.[7] The dog must be properly fed and maintained during detention by the person having charge of it.[8]

---

5 On April 6, 2008, by virtue of the Clean Neighbourhoods and Environment Act 2005 (Commencement No. 5) Order 2008 (SI 2008/956).
6 Dogs Act 1906 s.3(1), (1A), p.90.
7 Dogs Act 1906 s.3(2), (3), p.91.
8 Dogs Act 1906 s.3(8), p.91.

Stray Dogs

After seven days from service of the notice, or from original detention of the dog if the police have not been able to serve a notice, if the owner has not claimed it and paid the expenses of its detention, the detaining officer may sell the dog or have it destroyed. But it must not be given or sold for purposes of vivisection and, if destroyed, that must be done so as to cause as little pain as possible.[9]

The police must keep a register of all dogs seized by them and record their particulars. It is open for public inspection at all reasonable times for a fee of 5p.[10]

(2) Finding by a private person

The finder of a stray dog must at once either return it to its owner or to the dog warden of the local authority for the area, advising them where it was found.

If the finder takes the dog to the local authority's dog warden, the ensuing procedure is more involved. The finder may again choose to keep the dog or not. If he decides to keep it, the following steps are taken[11]:

(a) the finder supplies his particulars to the dog warden;

(b) the dog warden also records a description of the dog, any information on the dog's collar, and particulars about its finding;

(c) where the dog's owner can be identified and readily contacted, the dog warden will try to contact him and give him an opportunity to collect the dog;

(d) failing collection by the owner, the finder will be allowed to keep the dog if the dog warden's enquiries about his suitability as a dog owner are satisfactory;

(e) the dog warden warns the finder of his obligation to keep the dog for at least one month (if unclaimed by the owner) on pain of prosecution.

---

9 Dogs Act 1906 s.3(4), (5), p.91.
10 Dogs Act 1906 s.3(6), p.91.
11 Environmental Protection Act 1990 s.150, p.136; SI 1992/288, p.362.

Dog Collars and Stray Dogs

If the finder of a stray, having taken it to the dog warden, tells him that he does not want to keep it, the dog warden will retain the dog and, unless he believes that it is not a stray, will treat it as a dog seized by him,[12] for which see "Seizure by dog wardens" below.

(3) Seizure by dog wardens

Every local authority must appoint an officer to deal with stray dogs. The title of the officer is for the authority to determine. For the sake of simplicity, he is referred to here as a dog warden. It is his duty to seize (if practicable) any dog which he believes to be a stray and to detain it. Where it is found on private property, he must have the prior consent of the owner or occupier.[13]

The dog warden must then serve notice on the dog's owner if he can be identified. If the owner claims the dog, he is not entitled to its return unless he pays the expenses of detention and the prescribed sum of £25.[14]

If not claimed within seven days of seizure or, if a notice has been served, within seven days of its service, the dog warden may sell or give the dog to a suitable person or to a dogs' home (who in either case will become its owner), or may have it destroyed. It is not to be disposed of for vivisection.[15]

The dog warden is obliged to keep a register of dogs seized. This will include a description of each dog, any information on its collar, particulars of its finding and of any seven-day notice served, and details of the dog's disposal or of its return to its owner. The register will be available for free inspection by the public.[16]

---

12 Environmental Protection Act 1990 s.150(2), p.136.
13 Environmental Protection Act 1990 s.149(1), (2), p.133.
14 Environmental Protection Act 1990 s.149(5), p.134; Environmental Protection (Stray Dogs) Regulations 1992 reg.2, p.362.
15 Environmental Protection Act 1990 s.149(6), p.134.
16 Environmental Protection Act 1990 s.149(8), p.134; Stray Dogs Regulations 1992 reg.3, p.362.

Chapter 10

THE RULES ABOUT KILLING AND INJURING DOGS

The Civil Law

If his dog is wrongfully killed or injured by another person, the dog's owner will be able to sue that person and recover damages for his loss. The law says that there are three situations in which a killing or injury is not wrongful, and it is only in those situations that the owner will have no claim.

The first of these situations, which is regulated by the Animals Act 1971 and is rather complicated, is when a person (called below "the killer") kills or injures another dog to protect livestock. The meaning of "livestock" is as given on p.22. The killer will be excused liability if he fulfils all of the following conditions:

(1) he was acting for the protection of livestock;

(2) he was entitled to act for the protection of livestock; and

(3) within 48 hours of the killing or injury he gave notice of it to the officer in charge of a police station.[1]

The 1971 Act goes on to lay down more precisely when a killer shall be treated as acting for the protection of livestock and when he shall be treated as entitled so to act. So, to fulfil condition (1):

(a) **either** the dog must have been worrying or about to worry livestock and there were no other reasonable means of ending or preventing the worrying;

(b) **or** the dog had been worrying livestock, had not left the vicinity and was not under the control of any person, and there were no practicable means of ascertaining to whom it belonged.[2]

---

1 Animals Act 1971 s.9(1), p.258.
2 Animals Act 1971 s.9(3), p.259.

The Rules About Killing and Injuring Dogs

And, to fulfil condition (2):

(i) the livestock, or the land on which it was at the time of killing, must belong to the killer or to some other person under whose express or implied authority the killer was acting; **but**

(ii) the situation must **not** be one in which the livestock was killed or injured on land on to which it had strayed **and** the dog belonged to the occupier of that land or its presence there was authorised by the occupier.[3] (In these circumstances the 1971 Act provides that the dog's keeper shall not be liable for damage to the livestock; see item (2) on p.22).

The following points of detail arise on the foregoing.

Written notice to the police is not mandatory but is advisable for the killer's protection in the case of later proceedings against him. He should have a copy of the notice receipted by the police officer and endorsed by the officer with the time and date of receipt.

The 1971 Act does not have a definition of "worrying". It is suggested that the definition given on pp.22–23 be used as a guide, but omitting part (c) of it as being as too artificial in the present context.

In the case of items (a) and (b) above, the Act states that a belief on reasonable grounds that the conditions described were so will be sufficient.[4] In other words, a killer pleading those conditions will be successful if he can satisfy the court that he believed they were so and had reasonable grounds for that belief, even though others might have taken a different view at the time.

For the purpose if items (i) and (ii) above, an animal belongs to any person if he owns it or has it in his possession, and land belongs to any person if he is the occupier of it.[5]

The second situation in which the killing or injuring of a dog is justified is when it is done by a human being in self-defence. Presumably there would be justification for a killer so acting in defence of another

---

[3] Animals Act 1971 ss.5(4), 9(2), pp.256, 258.
[4] Animals Act 1971 s.9(4), p.259.
[5] Animals Act 1971 s.9(5), p.259.

The Criminal Law

person being attacked. It is also uncertain whether a killing or injury is justified when the dog is running away after such an attack.

It seems clear that there would have to be some correlation between the severity of the attack and the severity of the counter-measures used. At one extreme, to kill a dog following a nip in the leg would not be justified; and, at the other, a person is not required to fear for his life before hurting the dog.

The third situation arises when a dog attacks domestic animals which are not livestock (as that word is defined on p.22). In this case the killing or injuring of a dog is justified if:

(a) at the material time the dog was actually attacking the animals **or**, if left at large, would renew the attack so that the animals would be left in real and imminent danger unless renewal was prevented; **and**

(b) **either** there was in fact no practicable means other than shooting of stopping the present attack or a renewal of attack, **or** that, having regard to all the circumstances in which he found himself, the killer acted reasonably in regarding the shooting as necessary.

The rules in this third situation derive from case law (as, too, do those in the second situation). There is therefore no such specific protection for a defendant on the grounds of reasonable belief as applies to items (a) and (b) in the first situation – see above. A court would assess all the circumstances and evidence, including the reasonableness of the killer's behaviour.

It is doubtful whether there is a defence to a civil claim for killing or injuring another's dog because it is attacking wild animals on one's land; though protective measures for game may be taken – see p.65.

It is not permissible to tempt other people's dogs to destruction by devices on one's own land; the dogs' owners would be entitled to sue for damages. This rule derives from an old law case concerned with traps baited with strong smelling meat.

The Criminal Law

The criminal law is found in the Criminal Damage Act 1971 which is concerned with the destruction or damage by one person of another

The Rules About Killing and Injuring Dogs

person's property. Since domestic animals are capable of ownership (see p.3), the 1971 Act applies to the killing or injuring of dogs and other domestic animals.

An offence is committed if a person without lawful excuse kills or injures a dog belonging to another person intending to do so or being reckless as to whether the dog would be killed or injured.[6] Certain ingredients of this statement need examination.

The 1971 Act sets out the circumstances in which a person shall be treated as having a lawful excuse and in which therefore no offence is committed. This is so, firstly, if at the time of the alleged offence he believed that the person or persons whom he believed to be entitled to consent to the injury or killing had so consented or would have so consented if he or they had known of the injury or killing and its circumstances.

There is also a lawful excuse if the person killed or injured the dog in order to protect property belonging to himself or to another person, or to protect a right or interest in property which was or which he believed to be vested in himself or another person; **and** at the time of the alleged offence he believed that:

(a) the property, right or interest was in immediate need of protection; **and**

(b) the means of protection adopted or proposed were or would have been reasonable having regard to all the circumstances.[7]

In the cases where in the last two paragraphs there are references to the person's beliefs, the Act provides that it is immaterial whether those beliefs were justified, provided they were honestly held.[8]

The Act says that, for the purpose of interpreting the foregoing paragraphs, a dog or other property is to be treated as belonging to any person who has:

---

6 Criminal Damage Act 1971 s.1(1), p.261.
7 Criminal Damage Act 1971 s.5(2), p.262.
8 Criminal Damage Act 1971 s.5(3), p.263.

The Criminal Law

(a) the custody or control of it; **or**

(b) any proprietary right or interest in it, but not an interest arising only from an agreement to transfer or grant an interest; **or**

(c) a mortgage of it.[9]

It appears that the word "proprietary" is here used to mean more than simple ownership and might extend to a leasing or hiring of, or a licence to use, property.

As a final comment on the original statement of the offence, it is emphasised that an accidental killing or injuring of a dog, without intention or recklessness in the act, will not be an offence.

The killing or injuring of one's own dog is not by itself an offence, but it would be so if cruelty were used, for which see Chapter 13.

A person convicted of an offence of killing or injuring another's dog may be ordered by a magistrates' court to pay compensation of up to £5,000 for any loss or damage resulting from the offence.[10] In many cases therefore it will be unnecessary for an aggrieved dog owner to use the civil law with its attendant expense. It is possible to prosecute the criminal offence privately if the law enforcement authorities do not do so.

---

9 Criminal Damage Act 1971 s.10(2), p.263.
10 Powers of Criminal Courts (Sentencing) Act 2000 ss.130–131.

Chapter 11

BOARDING KENNELS AND BREEDING KENNELS

Boarding Kennels

The Animal Boarding Establishment Act 1963 requires boarding kennels for dogs and cats to be licensed by district councils in England, county and county borough councils in Wales and, in London, by the City Corporation or the borough council according to the kennels' location.[1]

The activity requiring a licence is the keeping of such kennels, and this is defined as the carrying on at any premises (including a private dwelling) of a business of providing accommodation for other people's dogs and cats. But the Act states that a licence is not needed if :

(a) the accommodation is provided only in connection with a business of which the provision of boarding accommodation is not the main activity, e.g. a vet temporarily boarding animals before, during or after treatment; **or**

(b) if dogs or cats are kept on premises pursuant to a requirement under the diseases of animals legislation.[2]

Since this definition incorporates a business element, if the boarding of the animals is not a business, a licence is unnecessary. Whilst the word "business" commonly means an activity carried on for profit, it is not safe to assume, in the light of past court cases considering the meaning in other contexts, that profit is a necessary ingredient. It is suggested that: if boarding is a regular practice, it needs a licence, whether done for profit or not; but if done for friends when on holiday, or in similar helping circumstances, on payment only of the cost of the animals' keep, it does not.

The granting of a licence is at the council's discretion. The 1963 Act requires them to pay particular attention to ensuring that the animals will be suitably accommodated, fed, exercised and protected

---

1 Animal Boarding Establishments Act 1963 s.1(1), (2), p.98.
2 Animal Boarding Establishments Act 1963 s.5(1), p.103.

44

from disease and fire, and that a proper register is kept showing their dates of arrival and departure and their owners' names and addresses. A licence should contain conditions to these ends, and the council may add other conditions.

A fee for the licence will be charged; there is no maximum.[3] The licence will run, at the applicant's choice, from the day it is granted to the end of the year, or from the beginning of next year to the end of that year.[4] An applicant aggrieved by the refusal of a licence or by any of the conditions included in a licence granted to him may appeal to a magistrates' court.[5]

Councils may authorise their officers, and vets, to inspect licensed kennels. It is an offence intentionally to obstruct or delay their entry or inspection.[6] It is also an offence to keep kennels without a licence when one is needed, or to fail to comply with a condition of a licence.[7]

As well as imposing any other punishment, a court convicting for these offences (or for a number of other offences under Acts concerned with animals) may cancel the defendant's licence and disqualify him from keeping kennels for as long as it thinks fit. The defendant may appeal against these decisions to the Crown Court.[8]

When the licence holder dies, the licence is treated as having been granted to his personal representatives for three months after the death. The council may extend and re-extend the three months if satisfied that that is necessary for winding up the deceased's estate and that no other circumstances make it undesirable.[9]

Breeding Kennels

The Breeding of Dogs Act 1973 requires dog breeding kennels to be licensed by district councils in England, county and county borough councils in Wales and, in London, by the City Corporation or the borough council according to the kennels' location.[10]

---

3 Animal Boarding Establishments Act 1963 s.1(2), (3), p.98.
4 Animal Boarding Establishments Act 1963 s.1(5), (6), p.99.
5 Animal Boarding Establishments Act 1963 s.1(4), p. 99.
6 Animal Boarding Establishments Act 1963 s.2, p.101.
7 Animal Boarding Establishments Act 1963 ss.1(8), 3(2), p.100, p.102.
8 Animal Boarding Establishments Act 1963 s.3(3), (4), p.102.
9 Animal Boarding Establishments Act 1963 s.1(7), p.99.
10 Breeding of Dogs Act 1973 s.1(1), (2), p.104.

Boarding Kennels and Breeding Kennels

The activity requiring licensing is basically the breeding of dogs for sale; however, the definition of the activity takes account of the number of bitches involved, the sale of puppies and the breeder's arrangements with relatives and others.[11]

When an application for a licence is received, the kennels will be inspected by a vet and/or a local authority officer, and conditions to secure the safety and well-being of the dogs will be imposed if a licence is granted.[12] Licences last for one year, but may be cancelled by a court for offences by the licensee.[13]

A power of entry to kennels may be granted by a magistrate's warrant when offences against the 1973 Act are suspected.[14]

Offences about the sale of dogs are enacted in the Breeding and Sale of Dogs (Welfare) Act 1999[15] and penalties for offences can include disqualification from keeping kennels and from having custody of particular dogs.[16]

---

11 Breeding of Dogs Act 1973 s.4A, p.112.
12 Breeding of Dogs Act 1973 ss.1, 2, pp.104–108.
13 Breeding of Dogs Act 1973 ss.1(7), 3(3), pp.106, 109.
14 Breeding of Dogs Act 1991 s.1 p.138.
15 Breeding and Sale of Dogs (Welfare) Act 1999 s.8, p.192.
16 Breeding of Dogs Act 1973 s.3, p.109; Breeding and Sale of Dogs (Welfare) Act 1999 s.9, p.194.

Chapter 12

GUARD DOGS

The controlling legislation relating to guard dogs is the Guard Dogs Act 1975. For the purposes of the Act a guard dog is defined as a dog which is being used to protect premises, or property kept on the premises, or a person guarding the premises or such property. The word "premises" is defined, and two parts of that definition also need explanation.

"Premises" means land (other than agricultural land and land within the curtilage of a dwelling house) and buildings, including parts of buildings other than dwelling houses. "Agricultural land" means land used as arable, meadow or grazing land, or for the purpose of poultry farming, pig farming, market gardens, allotments, nursery grounds or orchards.[1] A curtilage of a dwelling house is its garden and more immediate surrounds. In summary, therefore, the rules about guard dogs which follow apply to all land and buildings except houses, their surrounds and farmland in a wide sense of that word.

The 1975 Act makes it an offence to use, or permit the use of, a guard dog at any premises (as defined above) unless a person (in the Act and here called "the handler") who is capable of controlling the dog is present on the premises, and the dog is under the control of the handler at all times while it is being used as a guard dog, except while it is secured so that it is not at liberty to roam the premises. The handler's duty to control the dog may only be relaxed if another handler capable of controlling it has control of it so that it cannot roam.[2] A guard dog is not to be used at all unless a notice warning of its presence is clearly shown at each entrance to the premises.[3]

The foregoing provisions are matters of criminal law and do not themselves provide for compensation for a person attacked by a guard dog. However, the Powers of Criminal Courts (Sentencing) Act 2000 empowers a court in any case where a defendant is convicted of an

---

1 Guard Dogs Act 1975 s.7, p.116; Dogs (Protection of Livestock) Act 1953 s.3(1), p.96.
2 Guard Dogs Act 1975 s.1(1), (2), p.115.
3 Guard Dogs Act 1975 s.1(3), p.115.

Guard Dogs

offence to award compensation of up to £5,000 to any person for personal injury, loss or damage resulting from that offence.[4] If there is no prosecution (a private prosecution may be undertaken), or if that is unsuccessful, the person attacked must rely on such rights as he has under the civil laws of strict liability and negligence, for which see Chapter 3.

Sections 3–6 of the 1975 Act are not yet in force. They relate to the licensing by district councils in England, county and county borough councils in Wales and the City Corporation in London of kennels at which guard dogs are kept.

---

4   Powers of Criminal Courts (Sentencing) Act 2000 ss.130–131.

Chapter 13

GENERAL WELFARE OF DOGS

Introduction

The legislation which primarily relates to the general welfare of animals is the Animal Welfare Act 2006. The 2006 Act generally applies to all animals, i.e. vertebrates other than man. However, there is power to extend the Act to invertebrates. Some provisions, noted below, apply only to "protected animals", i.e. animals of a kind commonly domesticated in the British Islands which are under the control of man and are not living in a wild state. Most dogs will thus be protected animals for the purposes of the 2006 Act.

There are many other protective laws which serve to eliminate or reduce the suffering of animals. So far as they affect dogs, such laws are dealt with in Chapter 2 (pet shops), Chapter 4 (diseased dogs), Chapter 10 (killing and injuring dogs), Chapter 11 (boarding and breeding kennels) and Chapter 14 (performing dogs).

Prevention of Harm

Unnecessary suffering

Section 4 of the 2006 Act creates two offences:

(a) acting, or failing to act, in such a way that unnecessary suffering is caused to a protected animal;

(b) being responsible for an animal, permitting or culpably failing to prevent another person causing unnecessary suffering to that animal.

The section also sets out relevant considerations which apply when determining whether suffering is unnecessary: see p.278. It should be noted that these considerations are not conclusive; the courts are entitled to have regard to any other relevant considerations.

Mutilation

Section 5 of the 2006 Act creates three offences:

General Welfare of Dogs

(a) carrying out a "prohibited procedure" (defined below) on a protected animal;

(b) causing such a procedure to be carried out on a protected animal;

(c) being responsible for an animal, permitting or culpably failing to prevent another person carrying out a prohibited procedure on an animal.

A prohibited procedure is one which involves interference with the sensitive tissues or bone structure of the animal otherwise than for medical treatment. However, the docking of a dog's tail is not covered by the foregoing offences; this is treated separately in s.6 (see below).

The appropriate national authority (for definition, see Abbreviations and Explanatory Notes) may by regulations specify circumstances in which the foregoing actions are not classed as offences. The following regulations have been made: the Mutilations (Permitted Procedures) (England) Regulations 2007 (SI 2007/1100) (as amended) and the Mutilations (Permitted Procedures) (Wales) Regulations 2007 (SI 2007/1029) (as amended).

Docking of dogs' tails

Section 6 of the 2006 Act creates five offences, to which statutory defences apply:

(a) removing, or causing to be removed by another person, the whole or part of a dog's tail, except for medical treatment;

(b) being responsible for a dog, permitting or culpably failing to prevent another person from removing the whole or part of the dog's tail, except for medical treatment;

(c) being the owner of a "subsection (3) dog)" (a term defined in (i) below), failing to take reasonable steps before the dog is three months old to ensure that the dog is a subs.(3) dog in accordance with regulations made by the appropriate national authority;

(d) after the commencement of s.6, showing a dog from which the tail has been wholly or partly removed at an event to which members of the public are admitted on payment of a fee;

Prevention of Harm

(e) knowingly giving false information to a veterinary surgeon in relation to the certification of a dog as a subs.(3) dog.

The statutory defences are as follows:

(i) no offence under (a) or (b) above is committed where the dog is a certified working dog (i.e. a subs.(3) dog) that is not more than five days old. A dog is certified if a veterinary surgeon certifies that, in accordance with regulations made by the appropriate national authority, the following conditions are met:

— evidence is produced to the vet that the dog is likely to be used in connection with law enforcement, the armed forces, emergency rescue, lawful pest control or the lawful shooting of animals;

— the dog is of a type specified for the purposes of legislation by regulations made by the appropriate national authority;

(ii) a reasonable belief by a person accused of an offence under (a) or (b) above that the dog was a subs.(3) dog;

(iii) showing a dog in public contrary to (d) above is not an offence if the dog is shown solely to demonstrate its working abilities;

(iv) in relation to an offence under (d) above, a reasonable belief that the event was not one to which the public paid for admittance, the event took place before the legislation commenced or the dog was a subs.(3) dog.

The section gives the appropriate national authority power to make regulations for the purposes of the section. The Secretary of State has made the Docking of Working Dogs' Tails (England) Regulations 2007 (SI 2007/1120) and the National Assembly has made the Docking of Working Dogs' Tails (Wales) Regulations 2007 (SI 2007/1028).

Poisons and drugs

Section 7 of the 2006 Act creates three offences:

(a) without lawful authority or excuse, administering poison or injurious drug to a protected animal (see above for definition), knowing the substance to be poisonous or injurious;

General Welfare of Dogs

(b) causing a protected animal to take poison or an injurious drug, knowing the substance to be poisonous or injurious;

(c) being responsible for an animal, without lawful authority or reasonable excuse, permitting or culpably failing to prevent another person from administering a poisonous or injurious drug to that animal.

Fighting, wrestling and baiting

Section 8 of the 2006 Act creates a number of offences related to fighting, wrestling or baiting involving animals and animals and humans:

(a) causing or attempting to cause an animal fight to take place;

(b) knowingly receiving money for admission to an animal fight;

(c) knowingly publicising an animal fight;

(d) providing information about an animal fight to another person with the intention of enabling or encouraging attendance at such a fight;

(e) making or accepting bets on the outcome of an animal fight, or of anything occurring during an animal fight;

(f) taking part in an animal fight;

(g) having possession of anything designed to be used in connection with an animal fight with the intention that it is used in a fight;

(h) keeping or training an animal for use in an animal fight;

(i) keeping premises for use in an animal fight;

(j) knowingly supplying a video recording of an animal fight;

(k) knowingly publishing such a recording;

(l) knowingly showing such a recording to another person;

(m) possessing such a recording, knowing it to be a recording of an animal fight and with the intention of supplying it.

However, no offence is committed in relation to (j) to (m) above if the event took place outside Great Britain or before s.8 came into force. There are also exceptions to liability in relation to (j), (k) and (l) above in relation to video recordings included in a programme service (as defined in s.405 of the Communications Act 2003).

There is provision to extend the offences in (j) to (m) above to other member states of the European Union.

Promotion of Welfare

Duty of person responsible for animal to ensure welfare

Section 9 of the 2006 Act makes it an offence for a person not to take, in all the circumstances specified in the section, reasonable steps to ensure that the needs of an animal for which he is responsible are met to the extent required by good practice. The specified circumstances are any lawful purpose for which the animal is kept and any lawful activity undertaken in relation to the animal. The needs of an animal are taken to include:

(a) a suitable environment;

(b) a suitable diet;

(c) being able to exhibit normal behaviour patterns;

(d) being housed with, or apart from, other animals; and

(e) being protected from pain, suffering, injury and disease.

Nothing in s.9 applies to the destruction of an animal in an appropriate and humane manner.

Improvement notices

Section 10 of the 2006 Act empowers an inspector to serve an improvement notice on a person who is failing to comply with the requirement in s.9 to ensure that the needs of an animal are being met in accordance with good practice. An inspector is defined in s.51 as a person appointed for that purpose by the appropriate national authority or by a local authority (a county council, district council, London borough council, the Common Council of the City of London and the Council of the Isles of Scilly in England and county or county borough council in Wales).

General Welfare of Dogs

Transfer of animals by sale or prize to persons under 16

It is an offence under s.11 of the 2006 Act:

(a) to sell an animal to a person whom the seller reasonably believes to be under 16; and

(b) to enter into an arrangement with such a person under which that person has an opportunity to win the animal as a prize.

No offence is committed where the arrangement is made in the presence of a person under 16 and that person is accompanied by a person over that age, nor where the person under 16 is not present but the transferor has reason to believe that the consent of the person who has care or control over the person under 16 (e.g. a parent or legal guardian) has been given.

No offence is committed under the section where the arrangement takes place in a family context (e.g. transfer from parent to child).

Regulations to promote welfare

Section 12 of the 2006 Act empowers the appropriate national authority to make regulations for the promotion of the welfare of animals (and their progeny) for which a person is responsible (thus excluding animals in a wild state).

The regulations may cover, for example:

(a) specific requirements for meeting the needs of animals;

(b) facilitating or improving co-ordination between those with responsibilities relating to the welfare of animals;

(c) establishing a body or bodies to give advice about the welfare of animals.

Licensing and Registration

Licensing or registration of activities involving animals

Section 13 of the 2006 Act empowers the appropriate national authority to make regulations covering the licensing and registration

Animals in Distress

of activities involving animals. The authority is given power to repeal or amend the licensing or registration provisions in the Performing Animals (Regulation) Act 1925 (see pp.61 and 225), the Animal Boarding Establishments Act 1963 (see pp.44 and 98) and the Breeding of Dogs Act 1973 (see pp.45 and 104). The Secretary of State has made the Welfare of Racing Greyhounds Regulations 2010 (SI 2010/543). These apply only in England.

Schedule 1 to the 2006 Act makes detailed provision about the making of regulations.

Codes of Practice

Sections 14 to 17 of the 2006 Act empower the appropriate national authority to issue, approve and revoke codes of practice giving practical guidance on the Act.

Animals in Distress

Sections 18 to 21 of the 2006 Act:

(a) empower an inspector or a constable who reasonably believes that a protected animal is suffering to take immediate steps (other than destruction) to alleviate the animal's suffering;

(b) empower an inspector or a constable to destroy a protected animal when a veterinary surgeon certifies that the animal should in its own interests be destroyed;

(c) empower an inspector or a constable to destroy a protected animal where there appears to be no reasonable alternative because of the animal's condition and it is not reasonably practicable to wait for a vet;

(d) empower an inspector or a constable to take a protected animal into possession if a vet certifies that the animal is suffering;

(e) empower an inspector or a constable to take a protected animal into possession where it is suffering and it is not reasonably practicable to wait for a vet;

(f) empower an inspector or a constable acting under (d) above to arrange for the animal to be cared for at a place of safety;

General Welfare of Dogs

(g) make it an offence to deliberately obstruct a person exercising the foregoing powers;

(h) entitle those exercising the foregoing powers to apply to a magistrates' court for an order to reimburse their expenses and for a person so ordered to appeal to the Crown Court;

(i) give powers of entry for the foregoing purposes;

(j) empower a magistrates' court to authorise the provision of treatment to, the sale or other disposal of, or the destruction of an animal taken into possession in accordance with (e) above;

(k) provide for appeals against orders made under (j) above to the Crown Court.

Enforcement Powers

Sections 22 to 29 of the 2006 Act make provision for the enforcement of the Act. The main provisions are:

(a) sections 22 to 24 empower a constable to seize animals involved in fighting offences, to obtain a justice's warrant to enter and search premises to obtain evidence of an offence under ss.4–8, 13 and 34 of the Act and to enter premises for the purpose of making an arrest in accordance with the Police and Criminal Evidence Act 1984;

(b) sections 25 to 29 relate to the inspection of licences, licensed premises, registration, farm premises and in respect of Community obligations.

Prosecutions

Power of local authorities to prosecute offences

Section 30 of the 2006 Act empowers local authorities to prosecute offenders. Those authorities are: in England, a county council, a district council, a London borough council, the Common Council of the City of London and the Council of the Isles of Scilly; in Wales, a county or county borough council.

Time limits for prosecutions

Section 31 of the 2006 Act sets out time limits for prosecutions. The limit is three years from the date of the commission of the offence and six months from the date when the prosecutor thinks there is sufficient evidence to justify proceedings.

Post-Conviction Powers

Imprisonment or fine

Section 32 of the 2006 Act provides the following penalties on summary conviction:

(a) for offences under ss.4, 5, 6(1) and (2), 7 and 8: imprisonment for up to 51 weeks or a fine not exceeding £20,000, or both;

(b) for offences under ss.9, 13(6) and 34(9): imprisonment for up to 51 weeks or a fine not exceeding level 5 on the standard scale (currently £5,000), or both;

(c) for offences under regulations made under ss.12 and 13: as provided in the regulations;

(d) for any other offence under the Act: imprisonment not exceeding 51 weeks or a fine not exceeding level 4 on the standard scale (currently £2,500), or both.

Deprivation

Section 33 of the 2006 Act enables the owner of an animal who is convicted of an offence under ss.4, 5, 6(1) and (2), 7, 8 or 9 to be deprived of ownership of the animal instead of, or in addition to, being imprisoned or fined. A similar provision relates to a person who is convicted of an offence under s.34 (see below).

Disqualification and seizure

Section 34 of the 2006 Act enables a person convicted of an offence under ss.4, 5, 6(1) and (2), 7, 8, 9, 13(6) or 34(9) (breach of a disqualification order) to be disqualified from owning, keeping or participating in the keeping of animals, or being party to an arrangement whereby he is able to control or influence the way in which animals are kept.

The disqualification extends to transporting animals or arranging for their transport. Breach of a disqualification order is an offence.

Section 35 empowers the court which makes a disqualification order under s.34 to order the seizure of an animal which is owned or kept in breach of the disqualification order.

Destruction of animals

Where a person is convicted of an offence under s.4, 5, 6(1) and (2), 7, 8(1) and (2) or 9 of the 2006 Act, s.37 empowers the court, on the evidence of a vet, to order the destruction of an animal in relation to which the offence was committed. Section 38 makes similar provision in relation to animals involved in fighting offences.

Section 39 empowers the court to order a person convicted of an offence under s.8(1) or (2), or another person, to reimburse the expenses of the police in looking after the animal.

Forfeiture of equipment used in offences

Under s.40 of the 2006 Act, a person convicted of an offence under s.4, 5, 6(1) and (2), 7 or 8 may be required by the court to forfeit a "qualifying item", which may be destroyed or otherwise dealt with as specified in the order. Qualifying items are defined in s.40(2) and comprise equipment used in the commission of offences under the specified sections of the Act.

Pending appeals

Section 41 of the 2006 Act provides that nothing may be done under ss.33, 35, 37, 38 or 40 until the time for making an appeal has expired or an appeal has been determined or withdrawn.

Orders with respect to licences

Under s.42 of the 2006 Act, a person convicted of an offence under ss.4, 5, 6(1) and (2), 7–9, 11 or 13(6) may have his licence cancelled and he may be disqualified from holding a licence for a period specified by the court.

Termination of disqualification

Section 43 of the 2006 Act enables a person disqualified under s.34 or 43 to apply to the court for the disqualification to be lifted. At least

Post-Conviction Powers

one year must pass after the disqualification was imposed before an application can be made.

Reimbursement of expenses

Section 44 of the 2006 Act provides that, where a person is required on conviction to reimburse the expenses of looking after an animal, those expenses are recoverable as a civil debt.

Section 45 provides that a non-offender may appeal against the imposition of an order to reimburse expenses.

General

The remainder of the 2006 Act includes provisions covering the following:

(a) section 51 of the 2006 Act defines an inspector as a person so appointed by the appropriate national authority or the local authority. The appropriate national authority may issue guidance, to which a local authority must have regard. An inspector is not liable in civil or criminal proceedings for anything done in purported performance of his functions under the Act if he acted in good faith and had reasonable grounds for so acting;

(b) section 52 lays down conditions for granting warrants under ss.19(4), 22(4), 23(1) and 28(4);

(c) section 52 brings into effect Sch.2 which makes supplementary provision relating to the powers of entry, inspection and search;

(d) section 54 gives power for a constable in uniform, or an inspector accompanied by such a person, to stop and detain vehicles in pursuance of specified provisions of the Act;

(e) section 55 gives a similar power in relation to the detention of vessels, aircraft and hovercraft;

(f) section 56 gives power to obtain documents;

(g) section 57 provides for the commission of offences by bodies corporate;

(h) section 58 generally exempts from action under the 2006 Act anything done lawfully under the Animals (Scientific Procedures) Act 1986 (see p.267);

(i) section 59 states that nothing in the 2006 Act applies to normal fishing;

(j) section 60 deals with the application of the 2006 Act to the Crown;

(k) section 61 confers powers on the appropriate national authority to make orders and regulations.

Chapter 14

PERFORMING DOGS

The exhibition of performing animals at any entertainment to which the public is admitted, whether on payment or not, and the training of performing animals for such exhibitions, are controlled by the Performing Animals (Regulation) Act 1925 and the Performing Animals Rules 1925. No definitions of "performing" or "performing animal" are attempted, but all animals are included except invertebrates.[1]

The basis of this control is registration with the county or metropolitan district council backed up by powers to inspect the animals and the places where they are kept and sanctions by the court. (In London, registration is with the City Corporation or the borough council.) The person exhibiting or training animals should register with that one of these authorities within whose area he lives.[2]

The training of animals for bona fide military, police, agricultural or sporting purposes, and the public exhibition of animals so trained, are exempted from registration.[3] No definition of any of these terms in this context is available and, apart from gun dogs and sheep dogs, the scope of agricultural and sporting purposes seems to be limited.

Applications for registration must contain particulars of the animals and of the general nature of the performances for which they are to be exhibited or trained.[4] A fee, as fixed by the registration authority, must accompany the application.[5]

The authority appears to have no discretion to refuse registration provided the application is correctly made out and the fee paid, unless the applicant is disqualified from registration, for which see p.63. A certificate of registration is issued. It will contain the particulars on the application form, and they will also be entered on the authority's register, which is open to inspection.[6] An applicant may later apply

---

1 Performing Animals (Regulation) Act 1925 s.5, p.230.
2 Performing Animals (Regulation) Act 1925 s.1(2), p.225.
3 Performing Animals (Regulation) Act 1925 s.7, p.231.
4 Performing Animals (Regulation) Act 1925 s.1(3), p.225.
5 Performing Animals Rules 1925 r.9, p.344.
6 Performing Animals (Regulation) Act 1925 s.1(4), (5), pp.225–226.

Performing Dogs

to have these particulars varied, when the authority will cancel the existing certificate and issue a new one without charging a further fee.[7]

If a magistrates' court is satisfied on a complaint made by the police or an officer of the registering authority that the training or public exhibition of any performing animal has been accompanied by cruelty and should be prohibited or allowed only subject to conditions, the court may make an order accordingly.[8] There is a right of appeal to the Crown Court.[9] The order comes into force seven days after it is made or, if an appeal is lodged within that time, when the appeal is determined but subject, of course, to the outcome of the appeal.[10] Particulars of the order will be endorsed on the issued certificate and entered in the authority's register.[11]

Police officers and authorised officers of the registering authority have power to enter premises, and to inspect them and performing animals there, but may not go on or behind the stage during a public performance.[12]

Offences punishable by fine have been created if a person does any of the following things:

(a) exhibits or trains (in the terms described at the beginning of this chapter) a performing animal without being registered unless he is exempted, or does so outside the terms of registration;

(b) fails to comply with an order of the magistrates' court;

(c) obstructs or deliberately delays an officer when exercising his powers of entry and inspection;

(d) conceals any animal to avoid its inspection;

(e) fails to produce his certificate to the court for endorsement;

---

7 Performing Animals (Regulation) Act 1925 s.1(6), p.226.
8 Performing Animals (Regulation) Act 1925 s.2(1), p.227.
9 Performing Animals (Regulation) Act 1925 s.2(2), p.227.
10 Performing Animals (Regulation) Act 1925 s.2(3), p.227.
11 Performing Animals (Regulation) Act 1925 s.2(4), p.227.
12 Performing Animals (Regulation) Act 1925 s.3, p.228.

(f) applies to be registered when disqualified by a court for registration.[13]

When a person is convicted of any of these offences, or of offences under ss.4, 5, 6(1) and (2), 7–9 and 11 of the Animal Welfare Act 2006 (for which, see Chapter 13), the convicting court may, as well as or instead of fining the offender:

(a) if he is registered under the Performing Animals (Regulation) Act 1925, order that his name be removed from the register; and

(b) order him to be disqualified from being registered, either permanently or for such time as the order may stipulate.

The same provisions about appeal, the effective date of the order and the recording of the order as apply to an order made after a complaint of cruelty (for which see p.62) will apply to the orders described above.[14]

Films

The Cinematograph Films (Animals) Act 1937 is concerned with the depiction of scenes involving cruelty to dogs and many other kinds of domestic and captive animals. Briefly, it is an offence, punishable with fine or imprisonment or both, to exhibit to the public any film if in connection with its production any scene represented in the film was organised or directed in such a way as to involve the cruel infliction of pain or terror on an animal or the cruel goading of an animal to fury.[15]

---

13 Performing Animals (Regulation) Act 1925 s.4(1), p.228.
14 Performing Animals (Regulation) Act 1925 s.4(2), p.229.
15 Cinematograph Films (Animals) Act 1937 s.1, p.232.

Chapter 15

DOGS AND GAME

It is not perhaps widely known that the pursuit of game by a dog and associated activities are as much subject to the game laws as the shooting of game with guns. There are four branches of the game laws to be looked at: prohibited times for taking game, poaching, game licences and the protection of game from dogs. The statutes involved are principally the Game Act 1831, the Game Licences Act 1860 and the Ground Game Act 1880.

The laws about deer are not considered here.

Prohibited Times for Taking Game

Certain game birds are protected by close seasons. These are as follows, all dates being inclusive:

Black game	December 11 to August 19, except in Somerset, Devon and that part of the New Forest which lies in Hampshire where it is December 11 to August 31.
Bustard or wild turkey	March 2 to August 31.
Grouse or red game	December 11 to August 11.
Partridge	February 2 to August 31.
Pheasant	February 2 to September 30.

It is an offence to kill or take these birds during the above times.[1] This means that they must not be killed or captured by any means, and tame game and carcases of game are included. The killing by a dog or the use of a dog for the purpose of killing or taking some kinds of game on a Sunday or on Christmas Day is also prohibited. The kinds concerned are hares, pheasants, partridges, grouse, heath or moor game, and black game.[2] As well as an actual killing by a dog, the use of a dog to put up game, to retrieve it or to point at it is consequently an offence on those days.

---

1 Game Act 1831 s.3, p.77.
2 Game Act 1831 s.2, p.77.

Poaching

Nineteenth century statutes have created several offences to deal with poaching, both by day and night. Each varies in some manner from the other. The birds and animals which are the subject of the offences collectively are: hares, pheasants, partridges, grouse, heath or moor game, black game, woodcock, snipe, rabbits and bustards.[3]

These matters are mentioned here because dog owners may often not appreciate the wide scope of these laws. Basically, a poacher is a person pursuing game when he has no right to it, and that right can only be obtained through occupation or ownership of land or by a document granting the right. The nature of the land is immaterial, and a member of the public has no more right to game on, say, roadside verges than he has to it on "private land". A person may poach with a dog as much as with a gun or snare. And lastly, though some offences require the taking or killing of game, others are committed simply by being on land in search or pursuit of game.

Game Licences

Until July 31, 2007, a game licence was required (with certain exceptions) to use a dog to search for, kill or pursue game or to assist in so doing (Game Act 1831, Hares Act 1848 and Game Licences Act 1860). The Regulatory Reform (Game) Order 2007 (SI 2007/2007) (made under the Regulatory Reform Act 2001), which applies in both England and Wales, repealed the relevant sections of the 1831 Act relating to game licences and the whole of the Hares Act 1848 and the Game Licences Act 1860 with effect from August 1, 2007.

Protection of Game from Dogs

Although under the criminal law the Criminal Damage Act 1971 allows, subject to reservations, a person to kill or injure a dog to protect his property, the definition of "property" in the Act excludes game in a wild state.

The Act has the effect of allowing such action against a dog only if the game has been tamed, or is ordinarily kept in captivity, or is

---

3   Game Act 1831 s.30, p.78; Night Poaching Act 1828 ss.1, 9, pp.75–76.

Dogs and Game

otherwise in the possession of a person,[4] e.g. hand-reared and penned game birds. Further, the person taking such action is only justified in doing so if he believed that the game was in immediate need of protection and that the action taken was reasonable in the circumstances.[5] Even if there is justification as described, there is apparently no protection from civil proceedings, and a protector of game could face a claim from the dog's owner.

There is some rather ancient legal authority (two cases concerned with dog spears!) for saying that an occupier of land may take steps to protect his game in his absence. In modern times an occupier may be expected to be more circumspect. Spring traps may not be used against dogs, and devices such as spring guns and man traps which may kill or cause grievous bodily harm to a human trespasser are forbidden; but electrified wires are not, provided no injury is caused.

Hunting with Dogs

After a long political campaign, the banning of hunting wild animals with dogs was enacted in the Hunting Act 2004, which came into force on February 18, 2005. The Act creates the following offences relating to hunting:

(a) hunting a wild mammal with a dog unless the hunting is exempt by coming within the scope of Sch.1 to the Act.[6] It is a defence for a person charged with an offence under s.1 to show that he reasonably believed that the hunting was exempt[7];

(b) as the owner of land, knowingly to permit hunting with dogs on the land and, as the owner of a dog, knowingly to permit the dog to take part in unlawful hunting.[8]

The Act also bans hare coursing and creates the following offences:

(a) participating in a hare coursing event;

(b) attending a hare coursing event;

---

4 Criminal Damage Act 1971 ss.1, 5 and 10, pp.261–263.
5 Criminal Damage Act 1971 s.5(2)(b), p.262.
6 Hunting Act 2004 s.1, p.199.
7 Hunting Act 2004 s.4, p.200.
8 Hunting Act 2004 s.3, p.199.

Hunting with Dogs

(c) knowingly facilitating a hare coursing event;

(d) as owner, permitting land to be used for a hare coursing event[9];

(e) entering a dog for the event;

(f) permitting a dog to be entered; and

(g) controlling or handling a dog in the course of or for the purpose of the event.[10]

The penalty on conviction for any of the foregoing offences is a fine not exceeding level 5 on the standard scale (currently £5,000).

A constable without a warrant may arrest a person who commits one of the above offences.[11] He may stop and search a person he reasonably suspects of committing any of these offences; he may also stop and search any animal, vehicle or other thing in the possession or control of that person where he suspects that evidence is likely to be found there. He may seize and detain any animal etc. if required as evidence in criminal proceedings or subject to forfeiture proceedings. He may enter land, premises or vehicles without a warrant in order to exercise his power to seize and detain.[12]

A court may order forfeiture of any dog or hunting article used in the commission of any of the above offences.[13]

Exempt hunting is defined in Sch.1 and comprises:

(a) stalking and flushing out;

(b) use of dogs below ground to protect birds for shooting;

(c) hunting of rats;

(d) hunting of rabbits;

(e) retrieval of hares;

---

9 Hunting Act 2004 s.5(1), p.200.
10 Hunting Act 2004 s.5(2), p.200.
11 Hunting Act 2004 s.7, p.201.
12 Hunting Act 2004 s.8, p.201.
13 Hunting Act 2004 s.9, p.202.

Dogs and Game

(f) falconry;

(g) recapture of a wild mammal;

(h) rescue of wild a mammal, research and observation.

In each case, the Schedule sets out conditions which must be observed for the exemption to apply.

Chapter 16

IMPORT AND EXPORT

Import

Different rules are applicable to the import of dogs according to whether they are classified as commercially traded dogs or pet dogs. Those concerned with the former category should consult Defra at the address given at the end of this chapter. The remainder of this section of the chapter relates only to the import of pet dogs on a non-commercial basis.

The principal legislation covering the import of pet dogs is the Non-Commercial Movement of Pet Animals (England) Order 2004 (SI 2004/2363), made under the European Communities Act 1972 to implement EC Regulation No. 998/2003.

The importation of pet dogs otherwise than in accordance with the 2004 Order is covered by the Rabies (Importation of Dogs, Cats and other Mammals) Order 1974 (as frequently amended), made under the Diseases of Animals Act 1950 and the Rabies Act 1974 (both now repealed) and continued in force under the Animal Health Act 1981.

The amended 1974 Order establishes the general rule that a dog may not be imported into Great Britain unless an import licence has been granted by the Secretary of State. There are two exceptions, namely:

(a) the dog has been in quarantine for six months or more or has been resident all its life in Northern Ireland, the Republic of Ireland, the Channel Islands or the Isle of Man;

(b) when the dog is landed with the intention or re-exporting it within 48 hours from the same port or airport. Satisfactory arrangements must previously be made for its re-export, otherwise the landing will be regarded as illegal.

The 2004 Order was made under the European Communities Act 1972 to enforce EC Regulation 998/2003 (the EC pets regulation), which establishes health conditions for pet dogs, cats, ferrets and some other species, including rabbits and rodents. The Regulation

Import and Export

covers movement within the EU and imports from third countries. As the EC pets regulation is directly applicable, its provisions are not spelt out in domestic legislation.

The EC pets regulation allows the UK broadly to continue with its domestic Pet Travel Scheme for dogs and cats until at least the end of 2011, and specifies the conditions under which these animals can enter the UK. Under the Regulation, dogs, cats and ferrets can move within the EU and from certain third countries provided they meet specified conditions. The UK can also retain its national requirements in some respects. These national requirements are laid down in the 2004 Order.

There is a limit of five dogs, cats and ferrets that can be imported into and around EU countries. The limit came into force on May 26, 2010. Dogs, cats and ferrets must enter the UK on approved routes. The responsibilities of transport companies operating these routes, including the checks they must carry out to ensure that these animals comply with the relevant requirements, are laid down in agreements with Defra. Approval of such routes is subject to any conditions considered necessary by the Secretary of State. This gives assurances that all such animals are checked for compliance with the UK's requirements. The Regulation requires carriers to comply with the conditions of their approval and also sets out the general duties of transport companies in this respect. It also requires vets given approval to issue passports to comply with the terms and conditions of their approval. The 2004 Order also provides for inspectors to carry out spot checks on animals which have entered the UK in this way. Inspectors appointed under the Animal Health Act 1981 are inspectors for the purpose of the Regulation. It also provides for powers to carry out checks required to verify compliance with the rules.

Under the Regulation, dogs, cats and ferrets may move within the EU with a passport, and enter from third countries with a third country certificate. The format of both of these documents has been established in Brussels, and is designed to provide details of the requirements of the EC pets regulation (including the requirements for entry to the UK). To facilitate a smooth transition, as a temporary measure, these animals may also move within, and enter, the EU under previously agreed certification, provided this was issued before October 1, 2004 and is still valid. This means that, as an alternative to the passport/third country

Import

certificate, dogs and cats can enter the UK with Pet Travel Scheme (PETS) certification (designed for entry under PETS before the EC pets regulation came into effect), which meets these conditions. The 2004 Order requires carriers to check these documents appropriately.

The Regulation makes it an offence for a transport company to fail to comply with the conditions of its approval or its duties as laid down in legislation, and also for an individual to provide false information or to obstruct any person executing the Regulation. Other offences relate to other failures to comply with approvals and falsification of documents. It is also an offence under the Regulation for pet owners to fail to produce appropriate documentation at the port of arrival in the UK upon demand by an inspector. Penalties are laid down in the Regulation which are in line with those previously applied under the UK's pet passport scheme and comply with the limits set by the European Communities Act. The Regulation is enforced by the local authority but may, in particular cases, be enforced by officials acting on behalf of the Secretary of State.

Consequential amendments have been made to two other pieces of domestic legislation as a result of the EC pets regulation. Exemptions from the UK's quarantine requirements are set out in the Rabies (Importation of Dogs, Cats and Other Mammals) Order 1974, and amendments to this Order have been made by the Rabies (Importation of Dogs, Cats and Other Mammals) (England) (Amendment) Order 2004 (SI 2004/2364). The EC pets regulation also amends Council Directive 92/65/EEC, which deals with commercially traded animals, and subjects some large groups of pets to its requirements. This Directive is implemented in the UK by the Animal and Animal Products (Import and Export) Regulations 2004 (SI 2004/853).

Under the Regulation, dogs and cats can be imported into the UK from Member States and listed third countries provided that they have been microchipped, then vaccinated, and blood tested. These animals must wait at least six months after the blood sample was drawn before they are able to enter the UK without quarantine, and must be treated against ticks and tapeworms 24–48 hours before being imported. Dogs and cats which come from other third countries, or do not meet the Regulation's requirements, must continue to undergo quarantine. Where a dog or cat has been microchipped etc. an EU pet passport must be obtained from an appropriately licensed veterinary

Import and Export

surgeon if the animal is to travel within the European Union. For travel outside the EU, some countries accept the EU pet passport, others have their own requirements. The Defra website gives detailed advice on the pet travel scheme.

Export

For the export of a dog, the requirements of the importing country's regulations must be met. For EU and other countries covered by the 2004 Order described above, those requirements are likely to be identical or very similar to those in the 2004 Order. For other countries, enquiries should be made to Defra at the address below.

Contact Numbers for Enquiries

PETS: 0870 241 1710.

Quarantine: 01245 454860.

Export/Trade: 01228 403600.

The Defra website *http://www.defra.gov.uk* carries a great deal of information about animals in general and dogs in particular.

Part II

Acts of Parliament Relating to Dogs

Night Poaching Act 1828 ss.1, 9, 12, 13 75
Game Act 1831 ss.2, 3, 30 77
Metropolitan Police Act 1839 s.54 80
Night Poaching Act 1844 s.1 81
Town Police Clauses Act 1847 ss.2, 3, 28 83
Dogs Act 1871 s.2 85
Ground Game Act 1880 ss.1, 4, 8 87
Dogs Act 1906 ss.1, 3, 7 90
Dogs (Protection of Livestock) Act 1953 ss.1–3 93
Animal Boarding Establishments Act 1963 ss.1–5 98
Breeding of Dogs Act 1973 ss.1–5 104
Guard Dogs Act 1975 ss.1, 5, 7 115
Animal Health Act 1981 ss.13, 72–75, 86, 87 117
Road Traffic Act 1988 ss.27, 170, 185, 189, 192 123
Dangerous Dogs Act 1989 s.1 130
Environmental Protection Act 1990 ss.149, 150 133
Breeding of Dogs Act 1991 ss.1, 2 138
Dangerous Dogs Act 1991 ss.1–7, 10 141
Protection of Badgers Act 1992 ss.1–3, 6–8, 10–14 159
Dogs (Fouling of Land) Act 1996 ss.1–8 171
Dangerous Dogs (Amendment) Act 1997 ss.1–6 179
Breeding and Sale of Dogs (Welfare) Act 1999 ss.1–11, Schedule 184

Hunting Act 2004 ss.1–11, Schedule 198
Clean Neighbourhoods and Environment Act 2005 ss.55–68 210

NIGHT POACHING ACT 1828
c. 69

Arrangement of sections

1. Trespassing in pursuit of game by night
9. Armed trespass in pursuit of game by night by three or more persons
12. What time shall be considered night
13. What shall be deemed game

1. Trespassing in pursuit of game by night
If any person shall, by night, unlawfully take or destroy any game or rabbits in any land, whether open or enclosed, or shall by night unlawfully enter or be in any land, whether open or enclosed, with any gun, net, engine, or other instrument, for the purpose of taking or destroying game, he shall be liable on summary conviction to a fine not exceeding level 3 on the standard scale.
. . .

Definitions and Meanings
"*game*": s.13.
"*level 3 on the standard scale*": currently £1,000.
"*night*": s.12.

Commentary
This section is concerned with trespassing in pursuit of game and rabbits by night. The unauthorised hunting of rabbits with a dog at night is clearly an example of an offence under this section.

Further References
For an extension to the scope of this section, see the Night Poaching Act 1844, s.1, at p.81 below.

Night Poaching Act 1828

For a similar offence committed by day, see the Game Act 1831, s.30, at p.78 below.

9. Armed trespass in pursuit of game by night by three or more persons

If any persons, to the number of three or more together, shall by night unlawfully enter or be in any land, whether open or inclosed, for the purpose of taking or destroying game or rabbits, any of such persons being armed with any gun, crossbow, fire arms, bludgeon, or any other offensive weapon, each and every of such persons shall be guilty of a misdemeanour, and being convicted thereof shall be liable on summary conviction to imprisonment for a term not exceeding six months or to a fine not exceeding level 4 on the standard scale, or to both.

Definitions and Meanings
"game": s.13.
"level 4 on the standard scale": currently £2,500.
"night": s.12.

Commentary
This section, which is otherwise similar to that created by the second part of s.1, creates a more serious offence when three or more armed trespassers are acting together at night.

Further References
For an extension of the scope of this section, see the Night Poaching Act 1844, s.1, at p.81 below.

12. What time shall be considered night

Provided always that for the purposes of this Act the night shall be considered and is hereby declared to commence at the expiration of the first hour after sunset, and to conclude at the beginning of the last hour before sunrise.

13. What shall be deemed game

For the purposes of this Act the word "game" shall be deemed to include hares, pheasants, partridges, grouse, heath or moor game, black game, and bustards.

Commentary
Sections 12 and 13 provide definitions of "night" and "game" when used in the earlier parts of this Act.

GAME ACT 1831

c. 32

Arrangement of sections

2. Definition of "game" under this Act

3. Penalty for killing or taking game on certain days and during certain seasons

30. Penalty on persons trespassing in the daytime upon lands in search of game or woodcocks, etc.

2. Definition of "game" under this Act

The word "game" shall for all the purposes of this Act be deemed to include hares, pheasants, partridges, grouse, heath or moor game, black game. . . .

3. Penalty for killing or taking game on certain days and during certain seasons

If any person whatsoever shall kill or take any game, or use any dog, gun, net, or other engine or instrument for the purpose of killing or taking any game, on a Sunday or Christmas Day, such persons shall, on conviction thereof before two justices of the peace, forfeit and pay for every such offence such sum of money, not exceeding level 1 on the standard scale, as to the said justices shall seem meet; and if any person whatsoever shall kill or take any partridge between the first day of February and the first day of September in any year, or any pheasant between the first day of February and the first day of October in any year, or any black game (except in the county of Somerset or Devon, or in the New Forest in the county of Southampton) between the tenth day of December in any year and the twentieth day of August in the succeeding year, or in the county of Somerset or Devon, or in the New Forest aforesaid, between the tenth day of December in any year and the first day of September in the succeeding year, or any grouse commonly called red game between the tenth day of December in any year and the twelfth day of August in the succeeding year, or any bustard between the first day of March

Game Act 1831

and the first day of September in any year, every such person shall, on conviction of any such offence before two justices of the peace, forfeit and pay, for every head of game so killed or taken, such sum of money, not exceeding level 1 on the standard scale, as to the said justices shall seem meet; ...

Definitions and Meanings
"game": s.2.
"level 1 on the standard scale": currently £200.

Commentary
This section falls into two parts:
 (1) The first part makes it an offence (amongst other things) to use a dog to kill or take game on a Sunday or on Christmas Day. Such use will include, as well as actual killing, the use of a dog to put up game, to retrieve it or to point at it.
 (2) The offence in the second part is, more simply, the killing or taking of game outside the named seasons. Retrieving and actual killing by a dog will fall within this offence.

30. Penalty on persons trespassing in the daytime upon lands in search of game, or woodcocks, etc.

... If any person whatsoever shall commit any trespass by entering or being in the daytime upon any land in search or pursuit of game, or woodcocks, snipes, or conies, such person shall, on conviction thereof before a justice of the peace, forfeit and pay such sum of money, not exceeding level 3 on the standard scale, as to the justice shall seem meet; and that if any persons to the number of five or more together shall commit any trespass, by entering or being in the daytime upon any land in search or pursuit of game, or woodcocks, snipes, or conies, each of such persons shall, on conviction thereof before a justice of the peace, forfeit and pay such sum of money, not exceeding level 4 on the standard scale, as to the said justice shall seem meet, together with the costs of the conviction: Provided always, that any person charged with any such trespass shall be at liberty to prove, by way of defence, any matter which would have been a defence to an action at law for such trespass; save and except that the leave and licence of the occupier of the land so trespassed upon shall not be a sufficient defence in any case where the landlord, lessor, or other person shall have the

Game Act 1831

right of killing the game upon such land, by virtue of any reservation or otherwise, as herein-before mentioned . . .

Definitions and Meanings
"coney": rabbit.
"game": s.2.
"levels 3 and 4 on the standard scale": currently £1,000 and £2,500.

Commentary
This section, which deals with trespassing by day in pursuit of game, falls into two parts.

The first part deals with trespass by up to four people. The second relates to the same offence by five or more people acting together and is punishable by a heavier fine.

The hunting of rabbits with a dog without permission is clearly an example of an offence under this section.

Further References
For trespassing in pursuit of game by night, see the Night Poaching Acts 1828 and 1844 on pp.75 and 81.

METROPOLITAN POLICE ACT 1839
c. 47

Arrangement of sections

54. Prohibition of nuisances by persons in the thoroughfares

54. Prohibition of nuisances by persons in the thoroughfares
Every person shall be liable to a penalty not more than level 2 on the standard scale who, within the limits of the metropolitan police district, shall, in any thoroughfare or public place, commit any of the following offences; (that is to say,) . . .
2. Every person who shall . . . suffer to be at large any unmuzzled ferocious dog, or set on or urge any dog or other animal to attack, worry, or put in fear any person, horse, or other animal.

Meanings
"level 2 on the standard scale": currently £500.
"metropolitan police district": Greater London (except the City and the Inner and Middle Temples) (London Government Act 1963 s.76).

Commentary
The offence created by this section is almost identical in terms to that created by the Town Police Clauses Act 1847 s.28, at p.83, which operates outside the Metropolitan Police District. For commentary on terms used, see under that section.

Further References
For legislation regarding the muzzling of dogs, see the Dangerous Dogs Act 1991 ss.1(2)(d), 2, 3(5) and 7(1)(a) at pp.141, 144, 146 and 156.

NIGHT POACHING ACT 1844
c. 29

Arrangement of sections

1. Provisions supplementary to the Night Poaching Act 1828

1. Provisions supplementary to the Night Poaching Act 1828

All the pains, punishments, and forfeitures imposed by the said Act upon persons by night unlawfully taking or destroying any game or rabbits in any land, open or inclosed, as therein set forth, shall be applicable to and imposed upon any person by night unlawfully taking or destroying any game or rabbits on any public road, highway, or path, or the sides thereof, or at the openings, outlets, or gates from any such land into any such public road, highway, or path, in the like manner as upon any such land, open or inclosed; and it shall be lawful for the owner or occupier of any land adjoining either side of that part of such road, highway, or path where the offender shall be, and the gamekeeper or servant of such owner or occupier, and any person assisting such gamekeeper or servant, and for all the persons authorized by the said Act to apprehend any offender against the provisions thereof, to seize and apprehend any person offending against the said Act or this Act; and the said Act, and all the powers, provisions, authorities, and jurisdictions therein or thereby contained or given, shall be as applicable for carrying this Act into execution as if the same had been herein specially set forth.

. . .

Definitions
"night" and *"game":* see, by virtue of this section, the Night Poaching Act 1828 ss.12, 13, at p.76.
"the said Act": the Night Poaching Act 1828.

81

Night Poaching Act 1844

Commentary
Sections 1 and 9 of the Night Poaching Act 1828 relate to "any land, whether open or enclosed". In the ensuing years it was found that poachers were able to evade conviction when poaching on roadsides. The purpose of the 1844 Act was to close that loophole by extending the scope of the offence to "any public road, highway, or path, or the sides thereof, or at the openings, outlets, or gates from any such land into any such public road, highway, or path".

TOWN POLICE CLAUSES ACT 1847
c. 89

Arrangement of sections

2. "The special Act"
3. Interpretations in this and the special Act
28. Penalty on persons committing any of the offences herein named

2. "The special Act"
The expression "the special Act" used in this Act shall be construed to mean any Act which shall be hereafter passed for the improvement or regulation of any town or district defined or comprised therein, and with which this Act shall be incorporated; . . .

3. Interpretations in this and the special Act
The following words and expressions in both this and the special Act, and any Act incorporated therewith, shall have the meanings hereby assigned to them, unless there be something in the subject or context repugnant to such construction; (that is to say,) . . .

The word "person" shall include a corporation, whether aggregate or sole:

. . .

The word "street" shall extend to and include any road, square, court, alley, and thoroughfare, or public passage, within the limits of the special Act . . .

Commentary
Sections 2 and 3 define a number of terms which are used in ss.28 and 36 which follow.

28. Penalty on persons committing any of the offences herein named
Every person who in any street, to the obstruction, annoyance, or danger of the residents or passengers, commits any of the following offences, shall be liable to a penalty not exceeding level 3 on the standard scale for

Town Police Clauses Act 1847

each offence, or, in the discretion of the justice before whom he is convicted, may be committed to prison, there to remain for a period not exceeding fourteen days; ... (that is to say,) ...
Every person who suffers to be at large any unmuzzled ferocious dog, or sets on or urges any dog or other animal to attack, worry, or put in fear any person or animal. ...

Definitions and Meanings
"level 3 on the standard scale": currently £1,000.
"person": s.3.
"street": s.3.

Commentary
The courts have not given any meaning to the word "ferocious" in this context. It is suggested that a dog may be regarded as ferocious if it appears to be untamed, and certainly if it is shown to have unusually vicious tendencies.

A dog on a lead is not at large, and this section will not apply when a person could exercise control by means of a lead but did not do so (*Ross v Evans* (1959) 2 Q.B. 79; [1959] 2 All E.R. 222).

A person who sets his dog on another person who is wounded by the dog will be guilty of the offence of malicious wounding under the Offences Against the Person Act 1861.

This section does not apply in the Greater London Area. For a similar offence which can be committed in the Metropolitan Police District, see the Metropolitan Police Act 1839 s.54, at p.80.

Further References
For modern legislation on the muzzling of dogs, see the Dangerous Dogs Act 1991 ss.1(2)(d), 2, 3(5) and 7(1)(a) at pp.141, 144, 146 and 156.

For further commentary on the provisions of this section, see p.33.

DOGS ACT 1871
c. 56

Arrangement of sections

2. Dangerous dogs may be destroyed

2. Dangerous dogs may be destroyed
Any court of summary jurisdiction may take cognizance of a complaint that a dog is dangerous, and not kept under proper control, and if it appears to the court having cognizance of such complaint that such dog is dangerous, the court may make an order in a summary way directing the dog to be kept by the owner under proper control or destroyed. . . .

Meanings
"Court of summary jurisdiction": i.e. a magistrates' court.

Commentary
The effectiveness of this section has been strengthened by the Dangerous Dogs Act 1991 s.3(5), (6) – see p.146. A s.2 order may now be made whether or not the dog injured any person (1991 Act s.3(5)). A dog which is proved to have injured cattle or poultry, or to have chased sheep, may be dealt with as a dangerous dog (Dogs Act 1906 s.1(4), at p.90).

Whether or not it can be said that a dog is kept under proper control appears to be a question of fact for the court to decide. The case of *Ex parte Hay* (1886) 3 T.L.R. 24 decided that, unless otherwise shown, the fact that a dog was neither muzzled nor led was sufficient proof that it was not under proper control.

The powers of a magistrates' court on hearing a complaint under this section have also been extended by the Dangerous Dogs Act 1989, s.1 – see p.130.

A s.2 order may be made though the owner did not know that the dog was dangerous (*Parker v Walsh* (1885) 1 T.L.R. 583). An order to destroy a dog may be made without giving the owner the option of keeping it under proper control

Dogs Act 1871

(*Pickering v Marsh* (1874) 38 J.P. 678; 43 L.J.M.C. 143; 22 W.R. 798), though normally a control order would first be made.

An appeal against a control order or a destruction order may be made to the Crown Court (Dangerous Dogs Act 1989 s.1(2), at p.130).

Further References
For failure to comply with a s.2 order, see the Dangerous Dogs Act 1989 s.1(3), at p.130.

For other legislation dealing with dangerous dogs, see the Dangerous Dogs Act 1991 at pp.141–158.

For the relevance of s.2, as strengthened by the 1989 and 1991 Acts, to particular circumstances, see Home Office Circular 67/91, paras 48–50, at p.427.

GROUND GAME ACT 1880

c. 47

Arrangement of sections

1. Occupier to have right to kill ground game
4. Exemption from game licences
8. Interpretation clause

1. Occupier to have right to kill ground game
Every occupier of land shall have, as incident to and inseparable from his occupation of the land, the right to kill and take ground game thereon, concurrently with any other person who may be entitled to kill and take ground game on the same land: Provided that the right conferred on the occupier by this section shall be subject to the following limitations:
   (1) The occupier shall kill and take ground game only by himself or by persons duly authorised by him in writing:
   (a) The occupier himself and one other person authorised in writing by such occupier shall be the only persons entitled under this Act to kill ground game with fire-arms;
   (b) No person shall be authorised by the occupier to kill or take ground game, except members of his household resident on the land in his occupation, persons in his ordinary service on such land, and any one other person bona fide employed by him for reward in the taking and destruction of ground game;
   (c) Every person so authorised by the occupier, on demand by any person having a concurrent right to take and kill the ground game on the land or any person authorised by him in writing to make such demand, shall produce to the person so demanding the document by which he is authorised, and in default he shall not be deemed to be an authorised person.
   (2) A person shall not be deemed to be an occupier of land for the purposes of this Act by reason of his having a right of common over such lands; or by reason of an occupation for the purpose of grazing or pasturage of sheep, cattle, or horses for not more than nine months.

Ground Game Act 1880

(3) In the case of moorlands, and uninclosed lands (not being arable lands), the occupier and the persons authorised by him shall exercise the rights conferred by this section only from the eleventh day of December in one year until the thirty-first day of March in the next year, both inclusive; but this provision shall not apply to detached portions of moorlands or uninclosed lands adjoining arable lands, where such detached portions of moorlands or uninclosed lands are less than twenty-five acres in extent.

Definitions
"ground game": s.8.

Commentary
This section authorises occupiers of land, and others authorised by them as described in the section, to kill hares and rabbits on the land concurrently with the exercise of gaming rights held by others.
This section is relevant to the consideration of s.4 below.

4. Exemption from game licences
The occupier and the persons duly authorised by him as aforesaid shall not be required to obtain a licence to kill game for the purpose of killing and taking ground game on land in the occupation of such occupier, and the occupier shall have the same power of selling any ground game so killed by him, or the persons authorised by him, as if he had a licence to kill game. . . .

Definition
"ground game": s.8.

Commentary
This section allows an occupier of land, and others properly authorised by him under s.1, to kill hares and rabbits on the land without a game licence.

8. Interpretation clause

For the purposes of this Act—
   The words "ground game" mean hares and rabbits.

Commentary

This section provides the meaning to be given to "ground game" in ss.1 and 4 of the Act.

DOGS ACT 1906
c. 32

Arrangement of sections

1. Liability of owner of dog for injury to cattle
3. Seizure of stray dogs
7. Definition of cattle

1. Liability of owner of dog for injury to cattle

. . .

(4) Where a dog is proved to have injured cattle or chased sheep, it may be dealt with under section two of the Dogs Act, 1871, as a dangerous dog.

Definitions
"cattle": includes horses, mules, asses, sheep, goats and swine (s.7).
"poultry": means domestic fowls, turkeys, geese, ducks, guinea fowls and pigeons (Dogs (Amendment) Act 1928, s.1(2), now repealed). The term may also include pheasants and partridges.

Commentary
Section 1(4) provides the only specific instance in which a dog can be said to be dangerous for the purposes of the Dogs Act 1871 s.2, at p.85.

3. Seizure of stray dogs

(1) Where a police officer has reason to believe that any dog found in a highway or place of public resort or on any other land or premises is a stray dog, he may seize the dog and may detain it until the owner has claimed it and paid all expenses incurred by reason of its detention.

(1A) The powers under subsection (1) of this section shall not be exercised in relation to a dog found on any land or premises other than a highway or place of public resort unless the owner or occupier of the land or premises has consented to such exercise.

Dogs Act 1906

(2) Where any dog so seized wears a collar having inscribed thereon or attached thereto the address of any person, or the owner of the dog is known, the chief officer of police, or any person authorised by him in that behalf, shall serve on the person whose address is given on the collar, or on the owner, a notice in writing stating that the dog has been so seized, and will be liable to be sold or destroyed if not claimed within seven clear days after the service of the notice.

(3) A notice under this section may be served either—
 (a) by delivering it to the person on whom it is to be served; or
 (b) by leaving it at that person's usual or last known place of abode, or at the address given on the collar; or
 (c) by forwarding it by post in a prepaid letter addressed to that person at his usual or last known place of abode, or at the address given on the collar.

(4) Where any dog so seized has been detained for seven clear days after the seizure, or, in the case of such a notice as aforesaid having been served with respect to the dog, then for seven clear days after the service of the notice, and the owner has not claimed the dog and paid all expenses incurred by reason of its detention, the chief officer of police, or any person authorised by him in that behalf, may cause the dog to be sold or destroyed in a manner to cause as little pain as possible.

(5) No dog so seized shall be given or sold for the purposes of vivisection.

(6) The chief officer of police of a police area shall keep, or cause to be kept, one or more registers of all dogs seized under this section in that area which are not transferred to an establishment for the reception of stray dogs. The register shall contain a brief description of the dog, the date of seizure, and particulars as to the manner in which the dog is disposed of, and every such register shall be open to inspection at all reasonable times by any member of the public on payment of a fee of one shilling.

(7) The police shall not dispose of any dog seized under this section by transferring it to an establishment for the reception of stray dogs unless a register is kept for that establishment containing such particulars as to dogs received in the establishment as are above mentioned, and such register is open to inspection by the public on payment of a fee not exceeding one shilling.

(8) The police officer or other person having charge of any dog detained under this section shall cause the dog to be properly fed and maintained.

Dogs Act 1906

(9) All expenses incurred by the police under this section shall be defrayed out of the police fund, and any money received by the police under this section shall be paid to the account of the police fund.

. . .

Commentary
As a result of repeals in the Clean Neighbourhoods and Environment Act 2005, this section now only applies in cases where the police seize a dog which is worrying livestock in breach of s.1 of the Dogs (Protection of Livestock) Act 1953 – see p.93.

Notice of seizure is to be served on the person whose name is given on the dog's collar or on the dog's owner if known (subss.(2), (3)). That person is given seven days in which to reclaim the dog. Failure to do so and to pay the expenses of its detention by the police enable the police to sell the dog or have it destroyed (subss.(4), (5)).

A register containing particulars of dogs seized is to be kept by the police and be available for public inspection (subs.(6)). The dog is not to be transferred to any home for stray dogs unless it keeps such a register available for public inspection (subs.(7)). The dog must be properly fed and maintained by the police while in their custody (subs.(8)).

Further References
For the seizure of stray dogs by local authority dog wardens, see the Environmental Protection Act 1990 s.149, at p.133.

For the procedure to be followed when a private person takes possession of a stray, see s.150 of the 1990 Act at p.136.

For a view on the meaning of "stray dog", see pp.135–136.

7. Definition of cattle
In this Act the expression "cattle" includes horses, mules, asses, sheep, goats and swine.

DOGS (PROTECTION OF LIVESTOCK) ACT 1953

c. 28

Arrangement of sections

1. Penalty where dog worries livestock on agricultural land
2. Enforcement
2A. Power of justice of the peace to authorise entry and search
3. Interpretation and supplementary provisions

---

1. Penalty where dog worries livestock on agricultural land

(1) Subject to the provisions of this section, if a dog worries livestock on any agricultural land, the owner of the dog, and, if it is in the charge of a person other than its owner, that person also, shall be guilty of an offence under this Act.

(2) For the purposes of this Act worrying livestock means—
 (a) attacking livestock, or
 (b) chasing livestock in such a way as may reasonably be expected to cause injury or suffering to the livestock or, in the case of females, abortion, or loss of or diminution in their produce.
 (c) being at large (that is to say not on a lead or otherwise under close control) in a field or enclosure in which there are sheep.

(2A) Subsection (2)(c) of this section shall not apply in relation to—
 (a) a dog owned by, or in the charge of, the occupier of the field or enclosure or the owner of the sheep or a person authorised by either of those persons; or
 (b) a police dog, a guide dog, a trained sheep dog, a working gun dog or a pack of hounds.

(3) A person shall not be guilty of an offence under this Act by reason of anything done by a dog, if at the material time the livestock are trespassing on the land in question and the dog is owned by, or in the charge of, the occupier of that land or a person authorised by him, except in a case where the said person causes the dog to attack the livestock.

Dogs (Protection of Livestock) Act 1953

(4) The owner of a dog shall not be convicted of an offence under this Act in respect of the worrying of livestock by the dog if he proves that at the time when the dog worried the livestock it was in the charge of some other person, whom he reasonably believed to be a fit and proper person to be in charge of the dog.

(5) Where the Minister is satisfied that it is inexpedient that subsection (1) of this section should apply to land in any particular area, being an area appearing to him to consist wholly or mainly of mountain, hill, moor, heath or down land, he may by order direct that that subsection shall not apply to land in that area.

(6) A person guilty of an offence under this Act shall be liable on summary conviction to a fine not exceeding level 3 on the standard scale.

Orders
No order has yet been made under subs.(5).

Definitions and Meanings
"agricultural land": s.3(1).
"level 3 on the standard scale": currently £1,000.
"livestock": s.3(1).
"the Minister": s.3(2).
"worrying livestock": subss.(2)–(4).

Commentary
Under subs.(1) both the owner of a dog and the person in charge of it at the time are made guilty of an offence if the dog worries livestock. The maximum fine is given in subs.(6).

The definition of "worrying livestock" is supplied by subs.(2). This is qualified by the provisions in subss.(2A), (3) and (4). It appears that indirect injury is within the definition (*Campbell v Wilkinson* (1909) 43 I.L.T. 237: a case in which foals injured themselves following a dog barking at them). Poultry ceasing to lay after shock caused by dogs is clearly within the definition and was the subject of a case decided before the Act ((1951) 95 S.J. 286). Actual pursuit need not be proved; it is enough for the dog to run among the livestock so as to alarm them (*Stephen v Milne* (1960) S.L.T. 276; 1960 S.C. (J.) 119).

Dogs (Protection of Livestock) Act 1953

Further References
This section relates to the criminal law only. For civil liability for the worrying of livestock by dogs, see the Animals Act 1971 ss.3, 5(1), (4) at pp.255–256.

As to when a person is justified in killing a dog which is worrying livestock, see s.9 of the 1971 Act at p.258.

2. Enforcement

(1) As respects an offence under this Act alleged to have been committed in respect of a dog on any agricultural land in England or Wales, no proceedings shall be brought except—
- (a) by or with the consent of the chief officer of police for the police area in which the land is situated, or
- (b) by the occupier of the land, or
- (c) by the owner of any of the livestock in question.

(2) Where in the case of a dog found on any land—
- (a) a police officer has reasonable cause to believe that the dog has been worrying livestock on that land, and the land appears to him to be agricultural land, and
- (b) no person is present who admits to being the owner of the dog or in charge of it,

then for the purpose of ascertaining who is the owner of the dog the police officer may seize it and may detain it until the owner has claimed it and paid all expenses incurred by reason of its detention.

(3) Subsections (4) to (10) of section three of the Dogs Act, 1906 (which provide for the disposal of dogs seized under subsection (1) of that section if unclaimed after seven days) shall apply in relation to dogs seized under the last preceding subsection as they apply in relation to dogs seized under subsection (1) of that section (which provides for the seizure and detention of dogs found in highways and places of public resort and believed to be stray dogs).

Definitions
"agricultural land": s.3(1).
"livestock": s.3(1).
"worrying livestock": s.1(2)–(4).

Commentary
Subsection (1) describes the persons who may bring proceedings under the Act; alternatively, the chief constable may authorise a prosecution.

Dogs (Protection of Livestock) Act 1953

Subsection (2) gives police officers powers to seize and detain dogs suspected of worrying livestock. These are supplemented by the powers of entry given by s.2A below.

Dogs seized under subs.(2) will be dealt with as strays under the procedures in the Dogs Act 1906, s.3(4)–(9), which are reproduced at pp.91–92.

2A. Power of justice of the peace to authorise entry and search

If on an application made by a constable a justice of the peace is satisfied that there are reasonable grounds for believing—
  (a) that an offence under this Act has been committed; and
  (b) that the dog in respect of which the offence has been committed is on premises specified in the application,
he may issue a warrant authorising a constable to enter and search the premises in order to identify the dog.

Commentary
This section gives further powers to the police in aid of prosecutions under the Act. These are limited to entry and search of premises to identify a dog. Some powers of seizure are given by s.2 above.

3. Interpretation and supplementary provisions

  (1) In this Act—
"agricultural land" means land used as arable, meadow or grazing land, or for the purpose of poultry farming, pig farming, market gardens, allotments, nursery grounds or orchards; and
  "livestock" means cattle, sheep, goats, swine, horses, or poultry, and for the purposes of this definition "cattle" means bulls, cows, oxen, heifers or calves, "horses" includes asses and mules, and "poultry" means domestic fowls, turkeys, geese or ducks.
  (2) In this Act the expression "the Minister" as respects England and Wales means the Minister of Agriculture Fisheries and Food . . .
  (3) The power of the Minister to make orders under subsection (5) of section one of this Act shall be exercisable by statutory instrument and shall include power, exercisable in the like manner, to vary or revoke any such order.

Commentary
This section supplies definitions for a number of terms used earlier in the Act.

A cricket field on which sheep are grazing will fall within the definition of agricultural land *(Williams v Richards* (1970) 114 S.J. 864;, November 5, 1970, D.C.).

ANIMAL BOARDING ESTABLISHMENTS ACT 1963

c. 43

Arrangement of sections

1. Licensing of boarding establishments for animals
2. Inspection of boarding establishments for animals
3. Offences and disqualifications
4. Power of local authorities to prosecute
5. Interpretation

1. Licensing of boarding establishments for animals

(1) No person shall keep a boarding establishment for animals except under the authority of a licence granted in accordance with the provisions of this Act.

(2) Every local authority may, on application being made to them for that purpose by a person who is not for the time being disqualified—
 (a) under this Act, from keeping a boarding establishment for animals; or
 (b) under the Pet Animals Act, 1951, from keeping a pet shop; or
 . . .
 (e) under the Protection of Animals (Amendment) Act, 1954, from having the custody of animals; or
 (f) under section 34(2), (3) or (4) of the Animal Welfare Act 2006,
and on payment of such fee as may be determined by the local authority, grant a licence to that person to keep a boarding establishment for animals at such premises in their area as may be specified in the application and subject to compliance with such conditions as may be specified in the licence.

(3) In determining whether to grant a licence for the keeping of a boarding establishment for animals by any person at any premises, a local authority shall in particular (but without prejudice to their discretion to withhold a licence on other grounds) have regard to the need for securing—

Animal Boarding Establishments Act 1963

(a) that animals will at all times be kept in accommodation suitable as respects construction, size of quarters, number of occupants, exercising facilities, temperature, lighting, ventilation and cleanliness;

(b) that animals will be adequately supplied with suitable food, drink and bedding material, adequately exercised, and (so far as necessary) visited at suitable intervals;

(c) that all reasonable precautions will be taken to prevent and control the spread among animals of infectious or contagious diseases, including the provision of adequate isolation facilities;

(d) that appropriate steps will be taken for the protection of the animals in case of fire or other emergency;

(e) that a register be kept containing a description of any animals received into the establishment, date of arrival and departure, and the name and address of the owner, such register to be available for inspection at all times by an officer of the local authority, veterinary surgeon or veterinary practitioner authorised under section 2(1) of this Act;

and shall specify such conditions in the licence, if granted by them, as appear to the local authority necessary or expedient in the particular case for securing all the objects specified in paragraphs (a) to (e) of this subsection.

(4) Any person aggrieved by the refusal of a local authority to grant such a licence, or by any condition subject to which such a licence is proposed to be granted, may appeal to a magistrates' court; and the court may on such an appeal give such directions with respect to the issue of a licence or, as the case may be, with respect to the conditions subject to which a licence is to be granted as it thinks proper.

(5) Any such licence shall (according to the applicant's requirements) relate to the year in which it is granted or to the next following year. In the former case, the licence shall come into force at the beginning of the day on which it is granted, and in the latter case it shall come into force at the beginning of the next following year.

(6) Subject to the provisions hereinafter contained with respect to cancellation, any such licence shall remain in force until the end of the year to which it relates and shall then expire.

(7) In the event of the death of a person who is keeping a boarding establishment for animals at any premises under the authority of a licence granted under this Act, that licence shall be deemed to have been granted to his personal representatives in respect of those premises and shall, notwithstanding subsection (6) of this section (but subject to the

Animal Boarding Establishments Act 1963

provisions hereinafter contained with respect to cancellation), remain in force until the end of the period of three months beginning with the death and shall then expire:
Provided that the local authority by whom the licence was granted may from time to time, on the application of those representatives, extend or further extend the said period of three months if the authority are satisfied that the extension is necessary for the purpose of winding up the deceased's estate and that no other circumstances make it undesirable.

(8) Any person who contravenes the provisions of subsection (1) of this section shall be guilty of an offence; and if any condition subject to which a licence is granted in accordance with the provisions of this Act is contravened or not complied with, the person to whom the licence was granted shall be guilty of an offence.

. . .

Definitions and Meanings
"*animals*": s.5(2).
"*keep a boarding establishment*": s.5(1).
"*local authority*": s.5(2).
"*veterinary practitioner*": s.5(2).
"*veterinary surgeon*": s.5(2).

Commentary
Subsections (1) and (8) make it an offence to keep a boarding establishment (kennels) for cats or dogs without a licence from the local authority.

Conditions may be attached to the licence, and the matters which may be governed by them are set out in subs.(3). The licence may be withheld if the authority considers that the requirements of those matters cannot be met, or if they have other grounds for refusal (subs.(3)).

An appeal may be made to a magistrates' court against refusal of a licence or a condition attached to it (subs.(4)).

Subsection (5) and (6) regulate the duration of licences. The meaning of these provisions is that the licence runs, at the applicant's choice, from the day it is granted to the end of the current year, or from the beginning of the next year to the end of that year.

Subsection (7) provides for the short-term continuation of a licence when the licensee dies.

Animal Boarding Establishments Act 1963

Further References
For the provisions about disqualification mentioned in subs.(2), see the following pages: for (a), s.3(3) of this Act at p.102; for (b), s.5(3) of the Pet Animals Act 1951 at p.237; for (f), ss.34(2), (3) and (4) of the Animal Welfare Act 2006 at p.310.

2. Inspection of boarding establishments for animals

(1) A local authority may authorise in writing any of its officers or any veterinary surgeon or veterinary practitioner to inspect (subject to compliance with such precautions as the authority may specify to prevent the spread among animals of infectious or contagious diseases) any premises in their area as respects which a licence granted in accordance with the the provisions of this Act is for the time being in force, and any person authorised under this section may, on producing his authority if so required, enter any such premises at all reasonable times and inspect them and any animals found thereon or any thing therein, for the purpose of ascertaining whether an offence has been or is being committed against this Act.

(2) Any person who wilfully obstructs or delays any person in the exercise of his powers of entry or inspection under this section shall be guilty of an offence.

Definitions
"*animals*", "*local authority*", "*veterinary practitioner*" and "*veterinary surgeon*": s.5(2).

Commentary
This section enables a local authority to authorise in writing any of its officers, and vets, to inspect boarding establishments for which a licence is in force; thus, no rights of entry exist before the issue of a licence or after it has expired (s.1(6)) or been cancelled (s.3(3)(4)).

Also, there is no right of entry unless the written authority is produced at the time, and the powers of inspection are limited to matters related to offences.

Obstructing or delaying an inspector is an offence (subs.(2)).

3. Offences and disqualifications

(1) Any person guilty of an offence under any provision of this Act shall be liable on summary conviction to a fine not exceeding level 2 on the standard scale.

(2) *Revoked.*

(3) Where a person is convicted of any offence under this Act or of any offence under the Protection of Animals Act, 1911, or the Protection of Animals (Scotland) Act, 1912, or the Pet Animals Act, 1951, or of any offence under sections 4, 5, 6(1) and (2), 7 to 9 and 11 of the Animal Welfare Act, 2006, the court by which he is convicted may cancel any licence held by him under this Act, and may, whether or not he is the holder of such a licence, disqualify him from keeping a boarding establishment for animals for such period as the court thinks fit.

(4) A court which has ordered the cancellation of a person's licence, or his disqualification, in pursuance of the last foregoing subsection may, if it thinks fit, suspend the operation of the order pending an appeal.

Definitions and Meanings
"*animals*": s.5(2).
"*keeping a boarding establishment for animals*": s.5(1).
"*level 2 on the standard scale*": currently £500.

Commentary
This section lays down the punishments available for offences under the Act, including cancellation of a licence and disqualification from keeping a boarding establishment. A disqualified person will be unable to obtain a licence for breeding kennels: see s.1(2) of the Breeding of Dogs Act 1973 at p.104.

An appeal against cancellation or disqualification lies to the Crown Court.

Further References
For the Pet Animals Act 1951, see pp.234–240; and for the Animal Welfare Act 2006, see pp.274–336.

4. Power of local authorities to prosecute

A local authority in England or Wales may prosecute proceedings for any offence under this Act committed in the area of the authority.

Animal Boarding Establishments Act 1963

Definition
"local authority": s.5(2).

5. Interpretation

(1) References in this Act to the keeping by any person of a boarding establishment for animals shall, subject to the following provisions of this section, be construed as references to the carrying on by him at premises of any nature (including a private dwelling) of a business of providing accommodation for other people's animals:
Provided that—
- (a) a person shall not be deemed to keep a boarding establishment for animals by reason only of his providing accommodation for other people's animals in connection with a business of which the provision of such accommodation is not the main activity; and
- (b) nothing in this Act shall apply to the keeping of an animal at any premises in pursuance of a requirement imposed under, or having effect by virtue of, the Animal Health Act 1981.

(2) In this Act, unless the context otherwise requires, the following expressions have the meanings hereby respectively assigned to them, that is to say:—

"animal" means any dog or cat;

"local authority" means the council of any county district, the council of a borough or the Common Council of the City of London . . .;

"veterinary practitioner" means a person who is for the time being registered in the Supplementary Veterinary Register;

"veterinary surgeon" means a person who is for the time being registered in the Register of Veterinary Surgeons.

Commentary
Of particular importance in this section is the interpretation to be given to the phrase "keeping a boarding establishment for animals" which is found in subs.(1) and upon which the need for a licence under s.1(1) depends. For comment on the meaning of "business" in that context see p.44.

In law, "premises" can include open land.

BREEDING OF DOGS ACT 1973

c. 60

Arrangement of sections

1. Licensing of breeding establishments for dogs
2. Inspection of breeding establishments for dogs
3. Offences and disqualifications

3A. Fees

4A. Breeding establishments for dogs

5. Interpretation

1. Licensing of breeding establishments for dogs

(1) No person shall keep a breeding establishment for dogs except under the authority of a licence granted in accordance with the provisions of this Act.

(2) Every local authority may, on application being made to them for that purpose by a person who is not for the time being disqualified—
  (a) from keeping a breeding establishment for dogs; or
  (b) under the Pet Animals Act 1951, from keeping a pet shop; or
  . . .
  (e) under the Protection of Animals (Amendment) Act 1954, from having the custody of animals; or
  (f) under the Animal Boarding Establishments Act 1963, from the boarding of animals; or
  (g) under section 34(2), (3) or (4) of the Animal Welfare Act 2006, . . .
grant a licence to that person to keep a breeding establishment for dogs at such premises in their area as may be specified in the application and subject to compliance with such conditions as may be specified in the licence.

(2A) On receipt of an application by a person to a local authority for the grant of a licence under this Act in respect of any premises—
  (a) if a licence under this Act has not previously been granted to the person in respect of the premises, the authority shall arrange for

Breeding of Dogs Act 1973

the inspection of the premises by a veterinary surgeon or veterinary practitioner and by an officer of the authority; and

(b) in any other case, the authority shall arrange for the inspection of the premises by a veterinary surgeon or veterinary practitioner or by an officer of the authority (or by both).

(2B) Where an inspection is arranged under subsection (2A) of this section, the local authority shall arrange for the making of a report about the premises, the applicant and any other relevant matter; and the authority shall consider the report before determining whether to grant a licence.

. . .

(4) In determining whether to grant a licence for the keeping of a breeding establishment for dogs by any person at any premises, a local authority shall in particular (but without prejudice to their discretion to withhold a licence on other grounds) have regard to the need for securing—

(a) that the dogs will at all times be kept in accommodation suitable as respects construction, size of quarters, number of occupants, exercising facilities, temperature, lighting, ventilation and cleanliness;

(b) that the dogs will be adequately supplied with suitable food, drink and bedding material, adequately exercised, and . . . visited at suitable intervals;

(c) that all reasonable precautions will be taken to prevent and control the spread among dogs of infectious or contagious diseases;

(d) that appropriate steps will be taken for the protection of the dogs in case of fire or other emergency;

(e) that all appropriate steps will be taken to secure that the dogs will be provided with suitable food, drink and bedding material and adequately exercised when being transported to or from the breeding establishment;

(f) that bitches are not mated if they are less than one year old;

(g) that bitches do not give birth to more than six litters of puppies each;

(h) that bitches do not give birth to puppies before the end of the period of twelve months beginning with the day on which they last gave birth to puppies; and

(i) that accurate records in a form prescribed by regulations are kept at the premises and made available for inspection there by any officer of the local authority, or any veterinary surgeon or

Breeding of Dogs Act 1973

veterinary practitioner, authorised by the local authority to inspect the premises;
and shall specify such conditions in the licence, if granted by them, as appear to the local authority necessary or expedient in the particular case for securing all the objects specified in paragraphs (a) to (i) of this subsection.

(4A) Regulations under paragraph (i) of subsection (4) of this section shall be made by the Secretary of State by statutory instrument; and a statutory instrument containing regulations made under that paragraph shall be subject to annulment in pursuance of a resolution of either House of Parliament.

(5) Any person aggrieved by the refusal of a local authority to grant such a licence, or by any condition subject to which such a licence is proposed to be granted, may appeal to a magistrates' court; and the court may on such an appeal give such directions with respect to the issue of a licence or, as the case may be, with respect to the conditions subject to which a licence is to be granted as it thinks proper.

(5A) A local authority shall determine whether to grant such a licence before the end of the period of three months beginning with the day on which the application for the licence is received.

(6) Any such licence shall come into force at the beginning of the day specified in the licence as the day on which it is to come into force; and that day shall be the later of—

(a) the day stated in the application as that on which the applicant wishes the licence to come into force; and

(b) the day on which the licence is granted.

(7) Subject to the provisions hereinafter contained with respect to cancellation, any such licence shall remain in force until the end of the period of one year beginning with the day on which it comes into force, and shall then expire.

(8) In the event of the death of a person who is keeping a breeding establishment for dogs at any premises under the authority of a licence granted under this Act, that licence shall be deemed to have been granted to his personal representatives in respect of those premises and shall, notwithstanding subsection (7) of this section (but subject to the provisions hereinafter contained with respect to cancellation), remain in force until the end of the period of three months beginning with the death and shall then expire:

Provided that the local authority by whom the licence was granted may from time to time, on the application of those representatives,

Breeding of Dogs Act 1973

extend or further extend the said period of three months if the authority are satisfied that the extension is necessary for the purpose of winding up the deceased's estate and that no other circumstances make it undesirable.

(9) Any person who contravenes the provisions of subsection (1) of this section shall be guilty of an offence; and if any condition subject to which a licence is granted in accordance with the provisions of this Act is contravened or not complied with, the person to whom the licence was granted shall be guilty of an offence.

. . .

Definitions
"keeping a breeding establishment for dogs": s.4A.
"local authority": s.5(2).

Commentary
This section is printed as substantially amended by ss.1–3 of the Breeding and Sale of Dogs (Welfare) Act 1999 at pp.184–187. The amendments came into force on December 30, 1999.

Subsection (1) and (9) make it an offence to keep a breeding establishment for dogs without a licence from the local authority.

Subsection (2A) and (2B), newly inserted, require that the premises for which a licence has been requested shall be inspected by a vet and/or an officer of the authority and that their reports shall be considered by the authority before they decide whether or not to grant a licence.

Conditions may be attached to the licence, and the matters which may be governed by them are set out in subs.(4). The licence may be withheld if the authority considers that the requirements of those matters cannot be met, or if they have other grounds for refusal. The prescribed form of records mentioned in subs.(4)(i) may be found in the Breeding of Dogs (Licensing of Records) Regulations 1999 at p.377.

An appeal may be made to a magistrates' court against refusal of a licence or a condition attached to it (subs.(5)).

The new subs.(5A) requires the local authority to make a decision on an application within three months of its receipt.

Amendments made by the 1999 Act to subss.(6) and (7) now provide that: a licence shall come into force on the date requested by the applicant or the date on which it is granted,

Breeding of Dogs Act 1973

whichever is the later; and a licence shall endure for one year unless cancelled under the provisions in s.3.

Subsection (8) provides for the short-term continuation of a licence when the licensee dies.

Further References
Home Office Circular 53/99, Annex A, paras 1–14, at pp.454–457.

For the provisions about disqualification mentioned in subs.(2) see the following sections of Acts and pages: for (a), s.3(3) of this Act at p.109; for (b), s.5(3) of the Pet Animals Act 1951 at p.237; s.3(3) of the Animal Boarding Establishments Act 1963 at p.102; for (g), s.34(2), (3) and (4) of the Animal Welfare Act 2006 at p.310.

2. Inspection of breeding establishments for dogs

(1) A local authority may authorise in writing any of its officers or any veterinary surgeon or veterinary practitioner to inspect (subject to compliance with such precautions as the authority may specify to prevent the spread among animals of infectious or contagious diseases) any premises in their area as respects which a licence granted in accordance with the provisions of this Act is for the time being in force, and any person authorised under this section may, on producing his authority if so required, enter any such premises at all reasonable times and inspect them and any animals found thereon or any thing therein, for the purpose of ascertaining whether an offence has been or is being committed against this Act.

(2) Any person who wilfully obstructs or delays any person in the exercise of his powers of entry or inspection under this section shall be guilty of an offence.

Definitions
"local authority", "veterinary practitioner" and *"veterinary surgeon":* s.5(2).

Commentary
This section enables the local authority to authorise in writing any of its officers, and vets, to inspect breeding establishments for which a licence is in force; thus, no rights of entry exist before the issue of a licence or after it has expired

Breeding of Dogs Act 1973

(subs.(7)) or been cancelled (s.3(3)). For further powers of entry, see below.

Also, there is no right of entry unless the written authority is produced at the time if required, and the powers of inspection are limited to matters related to offences.

Obstructing or delaying an inspector is an offence (subs.(2)) punishable as provided for in s.3(2).

Further References
Home Office Circular 53/1999, Annex A, para.16, at p.457.
For further powers of entry and inspection, see the Breeding of Dogs Act 1991 s.1, at p.138.

3. Offences and disqualifications

(1) Any person guilty of an offence under any provision of this Act other than the last foregoing section shall be liable on summary conviction to—
 (a) *Revoked*;
 (b) a fine not exceeding level 4 on the standard scale.

(2) Any person guilty of an offence under the last foregoing section shall be liable on summary conviction to a fine not exceeding level 3 on the standard scale.

(3) Where a person is convicted of any offence under this Act, the court by which he is convicted may (in addition to or in substitution for any penalty under subsection (1) or (2) of this section) make an order providing for any one or more of the following—
 (a) the cancellation of any licence held by him under this Act;
 (b) his disqualification, for such period as the court thinks fit, from keeping an establishment the keeping of which is required to be licensed under this Act; and
 (c) his disqualification, for such period as the court thinks fit, from having custody of any dog of a description specified in the order.

(4) A court which has made an order under this section may, if it thinks fit, suspend the operation of the order pending an appeal.

(5) Where a court makes an order under subsection (3)(c) of this section in relation to a description of dogs it may also make such order as it thinks fit in respect of any dog of that description which—
 (a) was in the offender's custody at the time when the offence was committed; or
 (b) has been in his custody at any time since that time.

(6) An order under subsection (5) of this section may (in particular)—
  (a) require any person who has custody of the dog to deliver it up to a specified person; and
  (b) (if it does) also require the offender to pay specified amounts to specified persons for the care of the dog from the time when it is delivered up in pursuance of the order until permanent arrangements are made for its care or disposal.

(7) A person who—
  (a) has custody of a dog in contravention of an order under subsection (3)(c) of this section; or
  (b) fails to comply with a requirement imposed on him under subsection (6) of this section,
shall be guilty of an offence.

(8) Where a court proposes to make an order under subsection (5) of this section in respect of a dog owned by a person other than the offender, the court shall notify the owner who may make representations to the court; and if an order is made the owner may, within the period of seven days beginning with the date of the order, appeal to—
  (a) in England and Wales, the Crown Court; or
  (b) in Scotland, the High Court of Justiciary,
against the order.

(9) A person who is subject to a disqualification by virtue of an order under subsection (3)(c) of this section may, at any time after the end of the period of one year beginning with the date of the order, apply to the court which made the order (or, in England and Wales, any magistrates' court acting in the same local justice area) for a direction terminating the disqualification from such date as the court considers appropriate.

(10) On an application under subsection (9) of this section the court—
  (a) shall notify the relevant local authority which may make representations to the court;
  (b) shall, having regard to the applicant's character and his conduct since the disqualification was imposed, any representations made by the relevant local authority and any other circumstances of the case, grant or refuse the application; and
  (c) may order the applicant to pay all or any part of the costs, or (in Scotland) expenses, of the application (including any costs, or expenses, of the relevant local authority in making representations);

Breeding of Dogs Act 1973

and in this subsection "the relevant local authority" means the local authority in whose area are situated the premises in relation to which the offence which led to the disqualification was committed.

(11) Where an application under subsection (9) of this section in respect of a disqualification is refused, no further application under that subsection in respect of that disqualification shall be entertained if made before the end of the period of one year beginning with the date of the refusal.

Definitions and Meanings
"keeping a breeding establishment for dogs": s.4A.
"levels 3 and 4 on the standard scale": currently £1,000 and £2,500.
"the relevant local authority": subs.(10).

Commentary
This section is printed as substantially amended by ss.4–6 of the Breeding and Sale of Dogs (Welfare) Act 1999 at pp.187–191.

Under subs.(1), offences under the Act, except those under s.2, can now be punished by a term of imprisonment. Further amendments to this section permit a court convicting a person for an offence under the Act to order his disqualification from having custody of named descriptions of dogs. The section also contains new provisions for a dog in an offender's custody to be delivered up to a named person, for rights of appeal and for disqualified persons to apply to a court for removal of their disqualification.

Further References
Home Office Circular 53/99, Annex A, para.18, at p.458.

3A. Fees

(1) The costs of inspecting premises under this Act and the Breeding of Dogs Act 1991 shall be met by the local authority concerned.

(2) A local authority may charge fees—
(a) in respect of applications for the grant of licences under this Act; and
(b) in respect of inspections of premises under section 1(2A) of this Act.

(3) A local authority may set the level of fees to be charged by virtue of subsection (2) of this section—

(a) with a view to recovering the reasonable costs incurred by them in connection with the administration and enforcement of this Act and the Breeding of Dogs Act 1991; and
(b) so that different fees are payable in different circumstances.

. . .

4A. Breeding establishments for dogs

(1) References in this Act to the keeping of a breeding establishment for dogs shall be construed in accordance with this section.

(2) A person keeps a breeding establishment for dogs at any premises if he carries on at those premises a business of breeding dogs for sale (whether by him or any other person).

(3) Subject to subsection (5) of this section, where—
(a) a person keeps a bitch at any premises at any time during any period of twelve months; and
(b) the bitch gives birth to a litter of puppies at any time during that period,

he shall be treated as carrying on a business of breeding dogs for sale at the premises throughout the period if a total of four or more other litters is born during the period to bitches falling within subsection (4) of this section.

(4) The bitches falling within this subsection are—
(a) the bitch mentioned in subsection (3)(a) and (b) of this section and any other bitches kept by the person at the premises at any time during the period;
(b) any bitches kept by any relative of his at the premises at any such time;
(c) any bitches kept by him elsewhere at any such time; and
(d) any bitches kept (anywhere) by any person at any such time under a breeding arrangement made with him.

(5) Subsection (3) of this section does not apply if the person shows that none of the puppies born to bitches falling within paragraph (a), (b) or (d) of subsection (4) of this section was in fact sold during the period (whether by him or any other person).

(6) In subsection (4) of this section "breeding arrangement" means a contract or other arrangement under which the person agrees that another person may keep a bitch of his on terms that, should the bitch give birth, the other person is to provide him with either—
(a) one or more of the puppies; or
(b) the whole or part of the proceeds of selling any of them;

Breeding of Dogs Act 1973

and "relative" means the person's parent or grandparent, child or grandchild, sibling, aunt or uncle or niece or nephew or someone with whom he lives as a couple.

(7) In this section "premises" includes a private dwelling.

. . .

Definitions and Meanings
"breeding arrangement" and *"relative":* subs.(6).
"premises": subs.(7).

Commentary
This section defines at length the meaning of the phrase "keeping a breeding establishment for dogs" upon which the requirement for a licence under s.1 depends.

Briefly, if the requirements of subss.(3) and (4) are met, there will be such a keeping of a breeding establishment, unless subs.(5) can be applied.

Subsections (6) and (7) define three terms used earlier in the section.

Further References
Home Office Circular 53/1999, Annex A, paras 21–24, at pp.459–460.

5. Interpretation

(1) Nothing in this Act shall apply to the keeping of a dog at any premises in pursuance of a requirement imposed under, or having effect by virtue of, the Diseases of Animals Act 1950.

(2) In this Act, unless the context otherwise requires, the following expressions have the meanings hereby respectively assigned to them, that is to say:—

. . .

"local authority" means in England the council of a London borough, the council of a district or the Common Council of the City of London and in Wales the council of a county or county borough; . . .

"veterinary practitioner" means a person who is for the time being registered in the supplementary veterinary register;

"veterinary surgeon" means a person who is for the time being registered in the register of veterinary surgeons.

Breeding of Dogs Act 1973

Commentary
The Diseases of Animals Act 1950 is now replaced by the Animal Health Act 1981.
The meaning of "keeping a breeding establishment for dogs" may be found in s.4A.

GUARD DOGS ACT 1975
c. 50

Arrangement of sections

1. Control of guard dogs
5. Offences, penalties and civil liability
7. Interpretation

1. Control of guard dogs

(1) A person shall not use or permit the use of a guard dog at any premises unless a person ("the handler") who is capable of controlling the dog is present on the premises and the dog is under the control of the handler at all times while it is being so used except while it is secured so that it is not at liberty to go freely about the premises.

(2) The handler of a guard dog shall keep the dog under his control at all times while it is being used as a guard dog at any premises except—
   (a) while another handler has control over the dog; or
   (b) while the dog is secured so that it is not at liberty to go freely about the premises.

(3) A person shall not use or permit the use of a guard dog at any premises unless a notice containing a warning that a guard dog is present is clearly exhibited at each entrance to the premises.

Definitions
"guard dog": s.7.
"handler" (of a guard dog): subs.(1).
"premises": s.7.

Commentary
Subsection (1) and s.5(1) make it an offence to use a guard dog unless the use complies with the terms of s.1.

5. Offences, penalties and civil liability

(1) A person who contravenes section 1 or 2 of this Act shall be guilty of an offence and liable on summary conviction to a fine not exceeding level 5 on the standard scale.

Guard Dogs Act 1975

(2) The provisions of this Act shall not be construed as—
(a) conferring a right of action in any civil proceedings (other than proceedings for the recovery of a fine . . .) in respect of any contravention of this Act. . . .
(b) derogating from any right of action or other remedy (whether civil or criminal) in proceedings instituted otherwise than by virtue of this Act.
. . .

Meanings
"level 5 on the standard scale": currently £5,000.

Commentary
Subsection (1) states the maximum fine for an offence under s.1.
Subsection (2) provides that the Act is not to affect other criminal or civil proceedings.

7. Interpretation
In this Act, unless the context otherwise requires—
"agricultural land" has the same meaning as in the Dogs (Protection of Livestock) Act 1953;
"guard dog" means a dog which is being used to protect—
(a) premises; or
(b) property kept on the premises; or
(c) a person guarding the premises or such property;
. . .
"local authority" means, in relation to England, a district council, a London borough council and the Common Council of the City of London and, in relation to Wales, a county council or county borough council; . . .
"premises" means land other than agricultural land and land within the curtilage of a dwelling-house, and buildings, including parts of buildings, other than dwelling-houses;
. . .

Commentary
The referred definition of "agricultural land" may be found at p.96. It is also used in the ensuing definition of "premises".
The curtilage of a dwelling house is, briefly, the garden and more immediate surrounds of the house.

ANIMAL HEALTH ACT 1981

c. 22

Arrangement of sections

PART I

GENERAL

Control of dogs

13. Orders as to dogs

PART V

ENFORCEMENT, OFFENCES AND PROCEEDINGS

Offences generally

72. Offences made and declared by and under this Act
73. General offences

Further provisions as to punishment of offences

74. Liability under the customs and excise Acts
75. Punishment for certain summary offences

PART VI

SUPPLEMENTAL

Interpretation, functions, and orders etc.

86. Ministers and their functions
87. Meaning of "animals" and "poultry"

Animal Health Act 1981

PART 1

GENERAL

Control of dogs

13. Orders as to dogs

(1) The Minister may make such orders as he thinks fit for prescribing and regulating—
(a) the muzzling of dogs, and the keeping of dogs under control; and
(b) so far as is supplemental to paragraph (a) above—
　(i) the seizure, detention, and disposal (including slaughter) of stray dogs and of dogs not muzzled, and of dogs not being kept under control; and
　(ii) the recovery from the owners of dogs of the expenses incurred in respect of their detention.

(2) The appropriate Minister may make such orders as he thinks fit—
(a) for prescribing and regulating the wearing by dogs, while in a highway or in a place of public resort, of a collar with the name and address of the owner inscribed on the collar or on a plate or a badge attached to it;
(b) with a view to the prevention of worrying of animals (including horses), for preventing dogs or any class of dogs from straying during all or any of the hours between sunset and sunrise;
(c) for providing that any dog in respect of which an offence is being committed against provisions made under either paragraph (a) or (b) above, may be seized and treated as a stray dog under the enactments relating to dogs;
(d) for prescribing and regulating—
　(i) the seizure, detention and disposal (including slaughter) of stray dogs and of dogs not muzzled; and
　(ii) the recovery from the owners of dogs of the expenses incurred in respect of their detention.

(3) An order under subsection (2)(a) above may include provision for the execution and enforcement of the order by the officers of local authorities (and not by the police force for any area).

(4) In subsection (3) above "local authority" and "officer" have the same meaning as in section 149 of the Environmental Protection Act 1990.

Animal Health Act 1981

Orders
The Control of Dogs Order 1992 (at p.366) was made under the provisions of this section.

Definitions
"*animals*": s.87(1)–(3).
"*appropriate Minister*": s.86(1)(b).
"*horse*": includes ass and mule (s.89(1)).
"*local authority*": see, by virtue of subs.(4), the Environmental Protection Act 1990 s.149(11), at p.134.
"*Minister*": s.86(1)(a).
"*officer*": see, by virtue of subs.(4), the Environmental Protection Act 1990 s.149(11), at p.134.

Commentary
This section provides Ministers with the powers to make a variety of orders controlling dogs; in many areas of control other legislation is already operative.

PART V

ENFORCEMENT, OFFENCES AND PROCEEDINGS

Offences generally

72. Offences made and declared by and under this act
A person is guilty of an offence against this Act who, without lawful authority or excuse, proof of which shall lie on him—
  (a) does or omits anything the doing or omission of which is declared by this Act or by an order of the Minister to be an offence by that person against this Act; or
  (b) does anything which by this Act or such an order is made or declared to be not lawful.

73. General offences
A person is guilty of an offence against this Act who, without lawful authority or excuse, proof of which shall lie on him—
  (a) does anything in contravention of this Act, or of an order of the Minister, or of a regulation of a local authority; or

Animal Health Act 1981

(b) fails to give, produce, observe or do any notice, licence, rule or thing which by this Act or such an order or regulation he is required to give, produce, observe or do.

Definitions
"local authority": generally, a county council, a London borough council, and the City Corporation of London (s.50).
"Minister": s.86(1)(a).

Commentary
Sections 72 and 73 declare that any breach of any Ministerial order shall be an offence against this Act. This will include the Rabies Order at p.346.
Punishments and other liability are set out in ss.74 and 75.

Further provisions as to punishment of offences

74. Liability under the customs and excise acts
A person who—
(a) lands or ships or attempts to land or ship or brings or attempts to bring through the tunnel system as defined in the Channel Tunnel Act 1987 an animal or thing, and
(b) by so doing is in contravention of this Act or of an order of the Minister,
is liable under and according to the customs and excise Acts to the penalties imposed on persons importing or exporting or attempting to import or export goods the importation or exportation of which is prohibited.
This section is without prejudice to any proceeding under this Act against such a person for an offence against this Act.

Definitions
"animal": s.87(1)–(3).
"Minister": s.86(1)(a).

Commentary
This section makes it clear that the illegal landing of animals will make the offender liable to customs and excise penalties in addition to sanctions under this Act.

Animal Health Act 1981

75. Punishment for certain summary offences

(1) This section applies to any offence under this Act for which no penalty is specified.

(2) A person guilty of an offence to which this section applies is liable on summary conviction to imprisonment for a term not exceeding six months or to a fine not exceeding level 5 on the standard scale.

Commentary
Level 5 on the standard scale is currently £5,000.

PART VI

SUPPLEMENTAL

Interpretation, functions, and orders etc.

86. Ministers and their functions
(1) In this Act—
(a) "the Minister" means, in relation to the whole of Great Britain, the Minister of Agriculture, Fisheries and Food, and "Ministry" shall be construed accordingly,
(b) "the appropriate Minister" means, in relation to England, the Minister of Agriculture, Fisheries and Food, and in relation to Scotland or to Wales, the Secretary of State. . . .

87. Meaning of "animals" and "poultry"
(1) In this Act, unless the context otherwise requires, "animals" means—
(a) cattle, sheep and goats, and
(b) all other ruminating animals and swine,
subject to subsections (2) and (3) below.

(2) The Ministers may by order for all or any of the purposes of this Act extend the definition of "animals" in subsection (1) above so that it shall for those or any of those purposes comprise—
(a) any kind of mammal except man; and
(b) any kind of four-footed beast which is not a mammal.

(3) The Ministers may by order for all or any of the purposes of this Act (except so far as it relates to disease) extend the definition of "animals" in subsection (1) so that it shall for those or any of those purposes comprise—

Animal Health Act 1981

(a) fish, reptiles, crustaceans, or
(b) other cold-blooded creatures of any species,
not being creatures in respect of which an order can be made under subsection (2) above.
. . .

Orders
A host of orders, too numerous to list here, have been made, or have effect as if made, under s.87.

Commentary
Sections 86 and 87(1)–(3) provide definitions for four terms used earlier in the Act.

The functions of the Secretary of State under the Act in relation to their exercise in Wales were transferred to the National Assembly for Wales by the National Assembly for Wales (Transfer of Functions) Order 2004 (SI 2004/3044), save in respect of functions under Sch.1 to the Act, none of which are relevant to this work.

ROAD TRAFFIC ACT 1988
c. 52

Arrangement of sections

PART I

PRINCIPAL ROAD SAFETY PROVISIONS

Other restrictions in interests of safety

27. Control of dogs on roads

PART VII

MISCELLANEOUS AND GENERAL

Duties in case of accident

170. Duty of driver to stop, report accident and give information or documents

Interpretation

185. Meaning of "motor vehicle" and other expressions relating to vehicles
189. Certain vehicles not to be treated as motor vehicles
192. General interpretation of Act

Road Traffic Act 1988

PART I

PRINCIPAL ROAD SAFETY PROVISIONS

Other restrictions in interests of safety

27. Control of dogs on roads

(1) A person who causes or permits a dog to be on a designated road without the dog being held on a lead is guilty of an offence.

(2) In this section "designated road" means a length of road specified by an order in that behalf of the local authority in whose area the length of road is situated.

(3) The powers which under subsection (2) above are exercisable by a local authority in England and Wales are, in the case of a road part of the width of which is in the area of one local authority and part in the area of another, exercisable by either authority with the consent of the other.

(4) An order under this section may provide that subsection (1) above shall apply subject to such limitations or exceptions as may be specified in the order, and (without prejudice to the generality of this subsection) subsection (1) above does not apply to dogs proved—
  (a) to be kept for driving or tending sheep or cattle in the course of a trade or business, or
  (b) to have been at the material time in use under proper control for sporting purposes.

(5) An order under this section shall not be made except after consultation with the chief officer of police.

(6) The Secretary of State may make regulations—
  (a) prescribing the procedure to be followed in connection with the making of orders under this section, and
  (b) requiring the authority making such an order to publish in such manner as may be prescribed by the regulations notice of the making and effect of the order.

(7) In this section "local authority" means—
  (a) in relation to England and Wales, the council of a county, metropolitan district or London borough or the Common Council of the City of London.

. . .

(8) The power conferred by this section to make an order includes power, exercisable in like manner and subject to the like conditions, to vary or revoke it.

Road Traffic Act 1988

Definitions
"*designated road*": subs.(2).
"*local authority*": subs.(7).
"*prescribed*": s.192(1).
"*road*": s.192(1).

Regulations and Orders
Orders made under subs.(4) are not made by Statutory Instrument and are not listed in this work.
As to subs.(6), the Control of Dogs on Roads Orders (Procedure) (England and Wales) Regulations 1995, p.370, prescribe the procedure to be followed in making orders under this section.

Commentary
This section enables a local authority by order to designate roads in its area on which it will be an offence to have a dog without a lead.
Subsection (3) provides for the situation where a road is in the area of two authorities.
Limitations and exceptions may be incorporated in the order, which will not apply in the cases at subs.(4)(a) and (b), and the police must be consulted before the order is made (subs.(4), (5)). An order may be later varied or revoked (subs.(8)).

PART VII

MISCELLANEOUS AND GENERAL

Duties in case of accident

170. Duty of driver to stop, report accident and give information or documents

(1) This section applies in a case where, owing to the presence of a mechanically propelled vehicle on a road, an accident occurs by which—

. . .

(b) damage is caused—

. . .

(ii) to an animal other than an animal in or on that mechanically propelled vehicle or a trailer drawn by that mechanically propelled vehicle.

. . .

(2) The driver of the mechanically propelled vehicle must stop and, if required to do so by any person having reasonable grounds for so requiring, give his name and address and also the name and address of the owner and the identification marks of the vehicle.

(3) If for any reason the driver of the mechanically propelled vehicle does not give his name and address under subsection (2) above, he must report the accident.

(4) A person who fails to comply with subsection (2) or (3) above is guilty of an offence.

. . .

(6) To comply with a duty under this section to report an accident . . . the driver—
 (a) must do so at a police station or to a constable, and
 (b) must do so as soon as is reasonably practicable and, in any case, within twenty-four hours of the occurrence of the accident.

. . .

(8) In this section "animal" means horse, cattle, ass, mule, sheep, pig, goat or dog.

Definitions
"animal": subs.(8).
"driver": s.192(1).
"owner": s.192(1).
"road": s.192(1).
"trailer": s.185(1).

Commentary
Subsection (1) describes the circumstances in which the driver of a mechanically propelled vehicle must stop after an accident and then give the information described in subs.(2). A driver should stop for such time as in the circumstances will enable any person entitled to do so to require the information from the driver personally (*Lee v Knapp* [1967] 2 Q.B. 442; [1966] 3 All E.R. 961).

Road Traffic Act 1988

If, for any reason, no person requires the information, subs.(3) obliges the driver to report the accident as described in subs.(6).

For comment on what may constitute "reasonable grounds for requiring the information", see p.15.

It has been decided that no offence is committed by a driver who does not stop, being unaware that an accident has happened (*Harding v Price* [1948] 1 K.B. 695; [1948] 1 All E.R. 283).

Failure to comply with subss.(2) or (3) is an offence (subs.(4)).

Interpretation

185. Meaning of "motor vehicle" and other expressions relating to vehicles

(1) In this Act—

. . .

"motor vehicle" means, subject to section 20 of the Chronically Sick and Disabled Persons Act 1970 (which makes special provision about invalid carriages, within the meaning of that Act), a mechanically propelled vehicle intended or adapted for use on roads, and

"trailer" means a vehicle drawn by a motor vehicle.

. . .

Commentary
This section provides definitions for the terms "motor vehicle" and "trailer" which are used in ss.170 and 185.

The former definition is qualified by s.189 below.

189. Certain vehicles not to be treated as motor vehicles

(1) For the purposes of the Road Traffic Acts—
(a) a mechanically propelled vehicle being an implement for cutting grass which is controlled by a pedestrian and is not capable of being used or adapted for any other purpose,
(b) any other mechanically propelled vehicle controlled by a pedestrian which may be specified by regulations made by the

Secretary of State for the purposes of this section and section 140 of the Road Traffic Regulation Act 1984, and

(c) an electrically assisted pedal cycle of such a class as may be prescribed by regulations so made,

is to be treated as not being a motor vehicle.

(2) In subsection (1) above "controlled by a pedestrian" means that the vehicle either—

(a) is constructed or adapted for use only under such control, or
(b) is constructed or adapted for use either under such control or under the control of a person carried on it, but is not for the time being in use under, or proceeding under, the control of a person carried on it.

Definitions
"controlled by a pedestrian": subs.(2).
"the Road Traffic Acts": s.192(1).

Regulations
To date, no regulations have been made under subs.(1)(b), but the Electrically Assisted Pedal Cycles Regulations 1983 have effect as if so made.

Commentary
This section qualifies the definition of "motor vehicle" given in s.185 by removing from it grass cutting vehicles controlled by pedestrians and other vehicles designated by regulations.

192. General interpretation of Act

(1) In this Act—

. . .

"driver", where a separate person acts as a steersman of a motor vehicle, includes (except for the purposes of section 1 of this Act) that person as well as any other person engaged in the driving of the vehicle, and "drive" is to be interpreted accordingly,

. . .

"owner", in relation to a vehicle which is the subject of a hiring agreement or hire-purchase agreement, means the person in possession of the vehicle under that agreement,

. . .

Road Traffic Act 1988

"prescribed" means prescribed by regulations made by the Secretary of State,

"road", in relation to England and Wales, means any highway and any other road to which the public has access, and includes bridges over which a road passes,

"the Road Traffic Acts" means the Road Traffic Offenders Act 1988, the Road Traffic (Consequential Provisions) Act 1988 (so far as it reproduces the effect of provisions repealed by that Act) and this Act,

. . .

Commentary
This section provides definitions for a number of terms used earlier in the Act.

DANGEROUS DOGS ACT 1989

c. 30

Arrangement of sections

1. Additional powers of court on complaint about dangerous dog

---

1. Additional powers of court on complaint about dangerous dog

(1) Where a magistrates' court makes an order under section 2 of the Dogs Act 1871 directing a dog to be destroyed it may also—
  (a) appoint a person to undertake its destruction and require any person having custody of the dog to deliver it up for that purpose; and
  (b) if it thinks fit, make an order disqualifying the owner for having custody of a dog for such period as is specified in the order.

(2) An appeal shall lie to the Crown Court against any order under section 2 of that Act or under subsection (1) above; and, unless the owner of a dog which is ordered to be delivered up and destroyed gives notice to the court that made the order that he does not intend to appeal against it, the dog shall not be destroyed pursuant to the order—
  (a) until the end of the period within which notice of appeal to the Crown Court against the order can be given; and
  (b) if notice of appeal is given within that period, until the appeal is determined or withdrawn.

(3) Any person who fails to comply with an order under section 2 of the said Act of 1871 to keep a dog under proper control or to deliver a dog up for destruction as required by an order under subsection (1)(a) above is guilty of an offence and liable on summary conviction to a fine not exceeding level 3 on the standard scale and the court may, in addition, make an order disqualifying him for having custody of a dog for such period as is specified in the order.

(4) A person who is disqualified for having custody of a dog by virtue of an order made under subsection (1)(b) or (3) above may, at any time

after the end of the period of one year beginning with the date of the order, apply to the court that made it (or any magistrates' court acting in the same local justice area as that court) for a direction terminating the disqualification.

(5) On an application under subsection (4) above the court may—
  (a) having regard to the applicant's character, his conduct since the disqualification was imposed and any other circumstances of the case, grant or refuse the application; and
  (b) order the applicant to pay all or any part of the costs of the application;

and where an application in respect of an order is refused no further application in respect of that order shall be entertained if made before the end of the period of one year beginning with the date of the refusal.

(6) Any person who has custody of a dog in contravention of an order made under subsection (1)(b) or (3) above is guilty of an offence and liable on summary conviction to a fine not exceeding level 5 on the standard scale.

...

Meanings
"levels 3 and 5 on the standard scale": currently £1,000 and £5,000.

Commentary
This section strengthens the powers of magistrates under the Dogs Act 1871 s.2 when making a destruction order by giving them the further powers described at subs.(1)(a) and (b).

Subsection (2) allows for appeals to the Crown Court against any Dogs Act 1871 s.2 order (including one made under subs.(1)), and provides for deferment of the execution of a destruction order whilst an appeal is being heard.

Non-compliance with a control order under s.2 of the 1871 Act or with a requirement under subs.(1)(a) of this Act will entitle magistrates to fine the accused and to disqualify him from having custody of a dog for as long as they think fit (subs.(3)). These powers to fine and disqualify are now available to the court for breach of any other s.2 order (Dangerous Dogs Act 1991 s.3(7), at p.147).

Subsections (4) and (5) set out the rules for removing a disqualification order. Breach of such an order is punishable by fine (subs.(6)).

Further References
Further provisions about s.2 orders under the Dogs Act 1871 may be found in the Dangerous Dogs Act 1991 s.3(5)–(7), at pp. 146–147, which Act contains further and more extensive legislation on dangerous dogs.

ENVIRONMENTAL PROTECTION ACT 1990

c. 43

Arrangement of sections

PART VIII

MISCELLANEOUS

Control of dogs

149. Seizure of stray dogs

150. Delivery of stray dogs to police or local authority officer

PART VIII

MISCELLANEOUS

Control of Dogs

149. Seizure of stray dogs

(1) Every local authority shall appoint an officer (under whatever title the authority may determine) for the purpose of discharging the functions imposed or conferred by this section for dealing with stray dogs found in the area of the authority.

(2) The officer may delegate the discharge of his functions to another person but he shall remain responsible for securing that the functions are properly discharged.

(3) Where the officer has reason to believe that any dog found in a public place or on any other land or premises is a stray dog, he shall (if practicable) seize the dog and detain it, but, where he finds it on land or premises which is not a public place, only with the consent of the owner or occupier of the land or premises.

(4) Where any dog seized under this section wears a collar having inscribed thereon or attached thereto the address of any person, or the

Environmental Protection Act 1990

owner of the dog is known, the officer shall serve on the person whose address is given on the collar, or on the owner, a notice in writing stating that the dog has been seized and where it is being kept and stating that the dog will be liable to be disposed of if it is not claimed within seven clear days after the service of the notice and the amounts for which he would be liable under subsection (5) below are not paid.

(5) A person claiming to be the owner of a dog seized under this section shall not be entitled to have the dog returned to him unless he pays all the expenses incurred by reason of its detention and such further amount as is for the time being prescribed.

(6) Where any dog seized under this section has been detained for seven clear days after the seizure or, where a notice has been served under subsection (4) above, the service of the notice and the owner has not claimed the dog and paid the amounts due under subsection (5) above the officer may dispose of the dog—
  (a) by selling it or giving it to a person who will, in his opinion, care properly for the dog;
  (b) by selling it or giving it to an establishment for the reception of stray dogs; or
  (c) by destroying it in a manner to cause as little pain as possible;
but no dog seized under this section shall be sold or given for the purposes of vivisection.

(7) Where a dog is disposed of under subsection (6)(a) or (b) above to a person acting in good faith, the ownership of the dog shall be vested in the recipient.

(8) The officer shall keep a register containing the prescribed particulars of or relating to dogs seized under this section and the register shall be available, at all reasonable times, for inspection by the public free of charge.

(9) The officer shall cause any dog detained under this section to be properly fed and maintained.

(10) Notwithstanding anything in this section, the officer may cause a dog detained under this section to be destroyed before the expiration of the period mentioned in subsection (6) above where he is of the opinion that this should be done to avoid suffering.

(11) In this section—
"local authority", in relation to England, means a district council, a London borough council, the Common Council of the City of London or the Council of the Isles of Scilly and, in relation to Wales, means a county council or a county borough council; . . .

"officer" means an officer appointed under subsection (1) above;
"prescribed" means prescribed in regulations made by the Secretary of State; and
"public place" means—
  (i) as respects England and Wales, any highway and any other place to which the public are entitled or permitted to have access;

...

and, for the purposes of section 160 below in its application to this section, the proper address of the owner of a dog which wears a collar includes the address given on the collar.

Definitions
"local authority", "officer", "prescribed" and *"public place"*: subs.(11).

Regulations
The Environmental Protection (Stray Dogs) Regulations 1992, which are reproduced at pp.362–365, contain the prescribed matters mentioned in subss.(5) and (8).

Commentary
Each local authority is to appoint an officer to deal with stray dogs (a dog warden) (subs.(1)); he may delegate his powers to another person (subs.(2)). Such dogs are to be seized by the dog warden (subs.(3)), and notice of seizure given to their owners where known; the notice will allow seven days for owners to claim their dogs (subs.(4)). Claims may not be met unless the expenses of their detention (and any further amount prescribed by regulations) are paid (subs.(5)). (The relevant regulations are those mentioned under "Regulations" above.)

When a stray dog is not claimed, it must be disposed of by the dog warden as detailed in subs.(6); the recipient will become the new owner of the dog (subs.(7)).

The dog warden must keep a register of dogs seized (subs.(8)), must properly feed and maintain them (subs.(9)), and may have a dog destroyed to avoid suffering (subs.(10)).

When is a dog a stray dog? It appears that there is no authoritative answer to this question. It is suggested that a dog may reasonably be treated as a stray if it is roaming freely and not

Environmental Protection Act 1990

under the control of any person, irrespective of whether it has a home.

The notice to be served under subs.(4) is to be served by delivering it to the addressee personally, by leaving it at his proper address, or by sending it by post to him at that address. The proper address is the person's last known address which includes the address on any collar worn by the dog (subs.(11) and s.160(1)(4)).

Further References
Defra Guidance Circular 2007 "Guidance on Stray Dogs", paras 9–16, 33–45, at pp.475–476, 479–481.

150. Delivery of stray dogs to police or local authority officer

(1) Any person (in this section referred to as "the finder") who takes possession of a stray dog shall forthwith either—
  (a) return the dog to its owner; or
  (b) take the dog—

  (i) to the officer of the local authority for the area in which the dog was found;

and shall inform the officer of the local authority where the dog was found.

(2) Where a dog has been taken under subsection (1) above to the officer of a local authority, then—
  (a) if the finder desires to keep the dog, he shall inform the officer of this fact and shall furnish his name and address and the officer shall, having complied with the procedure (if any) prescribed under subsection (6) below, allow the finder to remove the dog;
  (b) if the finder does not desire to keep the dog, the officer shall, unless he has reason to believe it is not a stray, treat it as if it had been seized by him under section 149 above.

(3) Where the finder of a dog keeps the dog by virtue of this section he must keep it for not less than one month.

. . .

(5) If the finder of a dog fails to comply with the requirements of subsection (1) or (3) above he shall be liable on summary conviction to a fine not exceeding level 2 on the standard scale.

Environmental Protection Act 1990

(6) The Secretary of State may, by regulations, prescribe the procedure to be followed under subsection (2)(a) above.

(7) In this section "local authority" and "officer" have the same meaning as in section 149 above.

Definitions and Meanings
"level 2 on the standard scale:" currently £500.
"local authority" and *"officer:"* see, by virtue of subs.(7), s.149(11).
"the finder": subs.(1).

Regulations
The Environmental Protection (Stray Dogs) Regulations 1992, which are reproduced at pp.362–365, were made under the powers contained in subs.(6) and other powers.

Commentary
This section lays down the rules about stray dogs found by persons other than dog wardens (for which see s.149) or by the police (for which see the Dogs Act 1906 s.3, at pp.90–92).

A finder must return the dog to its owner or take it to the local authority's dog warden (subs.(1)). When a dog is taken to a dog warden, the finder may keep it, following the procedure prescribed by the regulations mentioned under "Regulations" above; otherwise, unless the warden believes it is not a stray, it is treated as a stray under s.149 (subss.(2), (3)).

This section, unlike s.149(7), does not provide for ownership of the dog to be vested in the finder when he keeps it. The owner may therefore later assert his claim which would have to be determined under the general legal principles regarding ownership.

Further References
For comment on the meaning of "stray dog", see under "Commentary" to s.149 at pp.135–136.

Defra Guidance Circular 2007 "Guidance on Stray Dogs", paras 17–36, at pp.476–480.

BREEDING OF DOGS ACT 1991

c. 64

Arrangement of sections

1. Power to inspect premises not covered by licence under Breeding of Dogs Act 1973
2. Offence and disqualification

---

1. Power to inspect premises not covered by licence under Breeding of Dogs Act 1973.

(1) If a justice of the peace is satisfied by information on oath laid by any officer of a local authority authorised in writing for the purposes of this section by the authority, or any veterinary surgeon or veterinary practitioner so authorised, that there are reasonable grounds for suspecting that an offence against section 1(1) of the Breeding of Dogs Act 1973 (breeding establishments for dogs to be covered by a licence) has been or is being committed at any premises in the area of the authority, the justice may issue a warrant authorising any such officer, surgeon or practitioner to enter those premises, by reasonable force if need be, and inspect them and any animals or any thing found there.

(2) No warrant shall be issued under subsection (1) above authorising entry to any premises for the time being used as a private dwelling.

(3) The reference in subsection (2) above to premises for the time being used as a private dwelling does not include a reference to any garage, outhouse or other structure (whether or not forming part of the same building as the premises) which belongs to or is usually enjoyed with the premises.

(4) A warrant issued under subsection (1) above—
  (a) may authorise persons to accompany the person who is executing the warrant; and
  (b) shall continue in force for the period of one month commencing with the date of issue.

(5) The power of entry conferred by the warrant may be exercised at all reasonable times and any person entering the premises in exercise of that power shall—

Breeding of Dogs Act 1991

(a) produce the warrant if so required; and
(b) comply with such precautions (if any) as the justice of the peace may specify to prevent the spread among animals of infectious or contagious diseases.

. . .

(7) In this section "local authority", "veterinary practitioner" and "veterinary surgeon" have the same meanings as in the Breeding of Dogs Act 1973.

Definitions
"local authority", "veterinary practitioner" and "veterinary surgeon": see, by virtue of subs.(7), the Breeding of Dogs Act 1973, s.5(2), at p.113.

Commentary
The powers of entry to and inspection of breeding kennels given to local authority officers and vets by the Breeding of Dogs Act 1973 s.2, (see p.108) are limited to times when a licence is in force. Section 1 of the 1991 Act makes those powers available at any reasonable time whilst a warrant by a J.P. is in force, provided there are reasonable grounds for suspecting that an offence against s.1(1) of the 1973 Act has been or is being committed. Reasonable force to secure entry is now justified if the need arises.

Subsection (2) excludes a private dwelling from the kinds of premises which may be the subject of a warrant, but under subs.(3) certain parts of such a dwelling are not excluded. In law, "premises" may include land without buildings.

Subsections (4) and (5) contain further provisions about warrants and the powers of entry exercised thereunder respectively.

Further References
Home Office Circular 53/99, Annex C, paras 1–2, at p.462.

2. Offence and disqualification

(1) Any person who intentionally obstructs or delays any person in the exercise of his powers of entry or inspection under section 1 above is guilty of an offence and liable on summary conviction to a fine not exceeding level 3 on the standard scale.

Breeding of Dogs Act 1991

(2) Where a person is convicted of an offence under subsection (1) above, the court by which he is convicted may make an order providing for either or both of the following—
  (a) his disqualification, for such period as the court thinks fit, from keeping an establishment the keeping of which is required to be licensed under the Breeding of Dogs Act 1973; and
  (b) his disqualification, for such period as the court thinks fit, from having custody of any dog of a description specified in the order.

(2A) A court which has made an order under or by virtue of this section may, if it thinks fit, suspend the operation of the order pending an appeal.

(2B) Subsections (5) to (11) of section 3 of the Breeding of Dogs Act 1973 (provisions about disqualification) apply in relation to an order made under subsection (2)(b) above as they apply in relation to an order made under subsection (3)(c) of that section.

Meanings
"level 3 on the standard scale": currently £1,000.

Commentary
Subsection (1) creates an offence for obstructing or delaying the exercise of the powers of entry given by s.1(1).

Subsection (2) has been amended by the Breeding and Sale of Dogs (Welfare) Act 1999 to enable a court convicting under subs.(1) to disqualify the defendant from having custody of dogs as well as disqualifying him from keeping a dog breeding establishment.

Subsections (2A) and (2B) are newly added by the 1999 Act. Section 3 of the Breeding of Dogs Act 1973 may be found at p.109.

Further References
Home Office Circular 53/99, Annex C, para.3, at p.462.

DANGEROUS DOGS ACT 1991

c. 65

Arrangement of sections

1. Dogs bred for fighting
2. Other specially dangerous dogs
3. Keeping dogs under proper control
4. Destruction and disqualification orders

4A Contingent destruction orders

4B Destruction orders otherwise than on a conviction

5. Seizure, entry of premises and evidence
6. Dogs owned by young persons
7. Muzzling and leads
10. Short title, interpretation, commencement and extent

1. Dogs bred for fighting

(1) This section applies to—
   (a) any dog of the type known as the pit bull terrier;
   (b) any dog of the type known as the Japanese tosa; and
   (c) any dog of any type designated for the purposes of this section by an order of the Secretary of State, being a type appearing to him to be bred for fighting or to have the characteristics of a type bred for that purpose.

(2) No person shall—
   (a) breed, or breed from, a dog to which this section applies;
   (b) sell or exchange such a dog or offer, advertise or expose such a dog for sale or exchange;
   (c) make or offer to make a gift of such a dog or advertise or expose such a dog as a gift;
   (d) allow such a dog of which he is the owner or of which he is for the time being in charge to be in a public place without being muzzled and kept on a lead; or

(e) abandon such a dog of which he is the owner or, being the owner or for the time being in charge of such a dog, allow it to stray.

(3) After such day as the Secretary of State may by order appoint for the purposes of this subsection no person shall have any dog to which this section applies in his possession or custody except—
  (a) in pursuance of the power of seizure conferred by the subsequent provisions of this Act; or
  (b) in accordance with an order for its destruction made under those provisions;

but the Secretary of State shall by order make a scheme for the payment to the owners of such dogs who arrange for them to be destroyed before that day of sums specified in or determined under the scheme in respect of those dogs and the cost of their destruction.

(4) Subsection (2)(b) and (c) above shall not make unlawful anything done with a view to the dog in question being removed from the United Kingdom before the day appointed under subsection (3) above.

(5) The Secretary of State may by order provide that the prohibition in subsection (3) above shall not apply in such cases and subject to compliance with such conditions as are specified in the order and any such provision may take the form of a scheme of exemption containing such arrangements (including provision for the payment of charges or fees) as he thinks appropriate.

(6) A scheme under subsection (3) or (5) above may provide for specified functions under the scheme to be discharged by such persons or bodies as the Secretary of State thinks appropriate.

(7) Any person who contravenes this section is guilty of an offence and liable on summary conviction to imprisonment for a term not exceeding six months or a fine not exceeding level 5 on the standard scale or both except that a person who publishes an advertisement in contravention of subsection (2)(b) or (c)—
  (a) shall not on being convicted be liable to imprisonment if he shows that he published the advertisement to the order of someone else and did not himself devise it; and
  (b) shall not be convicted if, in addition, he shows that he did not know and had no reasonable cause to suspect that it related to a dog to which this section applies.

(8) An order under subsection (1)(c) above adding dogs of any type to those to which this section applies may provide that subsections (3) and (4) above shall apply in relation to those dogs with the substi-

Dangerous Dogs Act 1991

tution for the day appointed under subsection (3) of a later day specified in the order.

. . .

Definitions and Meanings
"*advertise*"; "*advertisement*": s.10(2).
"*kept on a lead*": s.7(1)(b).
"*level 5 on the standard scale*": currently £5,000.
"*muzzled*": s.7(1)(a).
"*owner*": s.6.
"*public place*": s.10(2).

Orders
The Dangerous Dogs (Designated Types) Order 1991, which is reproduced at p.352, made under subs.(1)(c) has added the dogs known as Dogos Argentinos and Fila Brazilieros to the named types of dog in subs.(1).

The Dangerous Dogs Compensation and Exemption Schemes Order 1991, which is reproduced at pp.353–359, made under subss. (3), (5) and (6) contains schemes for compensation and exemption under subss.(3) and (5) respectively.

Commentary
Subsection (1) designates the types of dog to which s.1 applies; to the types there named must be added the two further types mentioned in the first order listed under "Orders" above.

Subsection (2), which came into force on 12 August 1991, forbids a number of acts in relation to the designated types of dog ("designated types"), save that export of those dogs before November 30, 1991 is permitted (subs.(4)).

Subsection (3), which has been in operation since November 30, 1991, forbids custody or possession of a designated type except in three instances: when it is seized under s.5; when it is held under an order for its destruction under s.4; and when it is exempt under a subs.(5) scheme. Details of the scheme for compensation mentioned in subs.(3) may be found in the last order listed under "Orders" above.

The scheme for exemption under subs.(5) is contained in the last mentioned order. Under subs.(6) the Index of Exempted Dogs has been nominated to perform certain functions under the compensation and exemption schemes.

Dangerous Dogs Act 1991

Subsection (7) provides for sentences of imprisonment and fines to be imposed for contravention of s.1 and for some defences in the case of publishing an advertisement contrary to subs.(2)(b) and (c). Voluntary intoxication is no defence to a charge under subs.(7) (*DPP v Kellett* [1994] 158 J.P. 1138; [1994] Crim. L.R. 916).

Two cases in relation to the prohibition in subs.(2)(d) have been decided, as follows:

(a) The prohibition is absolute and accordingly the defence of necessity does not apply (*DPP v Fellowes* (1994) Crim. L.R. 918).

(b) A person having an unmuzzled dog in a car which is itself in a public place is a person in charge of the dog (*Bates v DPP* (1993) 157 J.P. 1004).

Further References

For a court decision describing which kinds of dog may be treated as pit bull terriers, see p.31.

For disqualification and detention orders which may be made on conviction for a s.1 offence, see s.4 at p.148.

For powers of seizure, powers of entry and search of premises, a J.P's power to order destruction of a dog, and the presumption in proceedings as to the type of a dog, see s.5 at p.154.

Home Office Circular 67/91, paras 4–32, at pp.417–424.

Home Office Circular 80/92, paras 2–5, at pp.444–445.

Home Office Circular 9/94, paras 2–6, at pp.448–449.

2. Other specially dangerous dogs

(1) If it appears to the Secretary of State that dogs of any type to which section 1 above does not apply present a serious danger to the public he may by order impose in relation to dogs of that type restrictions corresponding, with such modifications, if any, as he thinks appropriate, to all or any of those in subsection (2)(d) and (e) of that section.

(2) An order under this section may provide for exceptions from any restriction imposed by the order in such cases and subject to compliance with such conditions as are specified in the order.

(3) An order under this section may contain such supplementary or transitional provisions as the Secretary of State thinks necessary or expedient and may create offences punishable on summary conviction

Dangerous Dogs Act 1991

with imprisonment for a term not exceeding six months or a fine not exceeding level 5 on the standard scale or both.

(4) In determining whether to make an order under this section in relation to dogs of any type and, if so, what the provisions of the order should be, the Secretary of State shall consult with such persons or bodies as appear to him to have relevant knowledge or experience, including a body concerned with animal welfare, a body concerned with veterinary science and practice and a body concerned with breeds of dogs.

. . .

Meanings
"level 5 on the standard scale": currently £5,000.

Orders
To date, no orders have been made under subss.(1)–(3).

Commentary
This section allows the Secretary of State, by order, to impose restrictions on any type of dog, except one designated under s.1(1), which he believes presents a serious danger to the public. Before deciding on designation, he must consult with the persons and bodies named in subs.(4).

The restrictions to be so imposed must correspond to those mentioned in s.1(2)(d) and (e), though appropriate modifications and exceptions may be made (subss.(1), (2)). No other restrictions are permissible.

This procedure allows the Secretary of State to legislate for dogs which, though presenting a serious danger to the public, do not in his opinion warrant the more stringent measures available under other parts of s.1 for dealing with the designated types.

Further References
For disqualification and detention orders which may be made for a s.2 offence, see s.4 at pp.148–149.

For powers of seizure, powers of entry and search of premises, a J.P.'s powers to order destruction of a dog, and the presumption in proceedings as to the type of a dog, see s.5 at pp.154–155.

3. Keeping dogs under proper control

(1) If a dog is dangerously out of control in a public place—
(a) the owner; and
(b) if different, the person for the time being in charge of the dog,
is guilty of an offence, or, if the dog whilst so out of control injures any person, an aggravated offence, under this subsection.

(2) In proceedings for an offence under subsection (1) above against a person who is the owner of a dog but was not at the material time in charge of it, it shall be a defence for the accused to prove that the dog was at the material time in the charge of a person whom he reasonably believed to be a fit and proper person to be in charge of it.

(3) If the owner or, if different, the person for the time being in charge of a dog allows it to enter a place which is not a public place but where it is not permitted to be and whilst it is there—
(a) it injures any person; or
(b) there are grounds for reasonable apprehension that it will do so,
he is guilty of an offence, or, if the dog injures any person, an aggravated offence, under this subsection.

(4) A person guilty of an offence under subsection (1) or (3) above other than an aggravated offence is liable on summary conviction to imprisonment for a term not exceeding six months or a fine not exceeding level 5 on the standard scale or both; and a person guilty of an aggravated offence under either of those subsections is liable—
(a) on summary conviction, to imprisonment for a term not exceeding six months or a fine not exceeding the statutory maximum or both;
(b) on conviction on indictment, to imprisonment for a term not exceeding two years or a fine or both.

(5) It is hereby declared for the avoidance of doubt that an order under section 2 of the Dogs Act 1871 (order on complaint that dog is dangerous and not kept under proper control)—
(a) may be made whether or not the dog is shown to have injured any person; and
(b) may specify the measures to be taken for keeping the dog under proper control, whether by muzzling, keeping on a lead, excluding it from specified places or otherwise.

(6) If it appears to a court on a complaint under section 2 of the said Act of 1871 that the dog to which the complaint relates is a male and would be less dangerous if neutered the court may under that section make an order requiring it to be neutered.

Dangerous Dogs Act 1991

(7) The reference in section 1(3) of the Dangerous Dogs Act 1989 (penalties) to failing to comply with an order under section 2 of the said Act of 1871 to keep a dog under proper control shall include a reference to failing to comply with any other order made under that section; but no order shall be made under that section by virtue of subsection (6) above where the matters complained of arose before the coming into force of that subsection.

Definitions and Meanings
"aggravated offence": subss.(1), (3).
"dangerously out of control": s.10(3).
"keeping on a lead": s.7(1).
"level 5 on the standard scale": currently £5,000.
"muzzling": s.7(1).
"owner": s.6.
"public place": s.10(2).
"reasonable apprehension that [a dog] will injure any person": s.10(3).
"statutory maximum": currently £5,000.

Commentary
This section creates two offences:—

(1) Allowing a dog to be dangerously out of control in a public place. Both the owner and any other person in charge of the dog at the time are liable (subs.(1)), but the owner may have the defence provided by subs.(2). This offence is one of strict liability: see *R. v Bezzina* **[1994] 3 A.E.R. 964; [1994] 1 W.L.R. 1057, C.A.**

(2) Allowing a dog to enter a place which is not a public place but where it is not permitted to be and, while it is there, it injures any person or there are grounds for reasonable apprehension that it will do so. Both the owner and any other person in charge of the dog at the time are liable (subs.(3)), but no defence similar to that provided by subs.(2) is available to the owner.

In the case of both offences, if actual injury to any person is caused, the offence is treated as aggravated which makes the defendant liable to the more serious penalties described in subs.(4).

Subsections (5) and (6) strengthen the powers of magistrates when making an order under s.2 of the Dogs Act 1871, for which see p.85.

The effect of subs.(7), in association with s.1(3) of the Dangerous Dogs Act 1989 (at p.130), is to allow magistrates, on breach of any order made by them under s.2 of the Dogs Act 1871 (including orders under subss.(5) and (6)), to fine and disqualify the accused. But no neutering order under subs.(6) can be made if the matter of complaint arose before August 12, 1991, the date when the subsection came into force.

Further References
For disqualification and destruction orders which may be made for a s.3 offence, see s.4 below.

For powers of seizure and of entry and search of premises and a J.P.'s powers to order destruction of a dog, see s.5 at pp.154–155.

Home Office Circular 67/91, paras 33–43, 48–50, at pp.424–426, 427.

Home Office Circular 9/94, paras 7–8, at p.450.

4. Destruction and disqualification orders

(1) Where a person is convicted of an offence under section 1 or 3(1) or (3) above or of an offence under an order made under section 2 above the court—
   (a) may order the destruction of any dog in respect of which the offence was committed and, subject to subsection (1A) below, shall do so in the case of an offence under section 1 or an aggravated offence under section 3(1) or (3) above; and
   (b) may order the offender to be disqualified, for such period as the court thinks fit, for having custody of a dog.

(1A) Nothing in subsection (1)(a) above shall require the court to order the destruction of a dog if the court is satisfied—
   (a) that the dog would not constitute a danger to public safety; and
   (b) where the dog was born before 30th November 1991 and is subject to the prohibition in section 1(3) above, that there is a good reason why the dog has not been exempted from that prohibition.

(2) Where a court makes an order under subsection (1)(a) above for the destruction of a dog owned by a person other than the offender, the owner may appeal to the Crown Court against the order.

(3) A dog shall not be destroyed pursuant to an order under subsection (1)(a) above—
   (a) until the end of the period for giving notice of appeal against the conviction or against the order; and

Dangerous Dogs Act 1991

    (b) if notice of appeal is given within that period, until the appeal is determined or withdrawn,

unless the offender and, in a case to which subsection (2) above applies, the owner of the dog give notice to the court that made the order that there is to be no appeal.

    (4) Where a court makes an order under subsection (1)(a) above it may—
- (a) appoint a person to undertake the destruction of the dog and require any person having custody of it to deliver it up for that purpose; and
- (b) order the offender to pay such sum as the court may determine to be the reasonable expenses of destroying the dog and of keeping it pending its destruction.

    (5) Any sum ordered to be paid under subsection (4)(b) above shall be treated for the purposes of enforcement as if it were a fine imposed on conviction.

    (6) Any person who is disqualified for having custody of a dog by virtue of an order under subsection (1)(b) above may, at any time after the end of the period of one year beginning with the date of the order, apply to the court that made it (or a magistrates' court acting in the same local justice area as that court) for a direction terminating the disqualification.

    (7) On an application under subsection (6) above the court may—
- (a) having regard to the applicant's character, his conduct since the disqualification was imposed and any other circumstances of the case, grant or refuse the application; and
- (b) order the applicant to pay all or any part of the costs of the application;

and where an application in respect of an order is refused no further application in respect of that order shall be entertained if made before the end of the period of one year beginning with the date of the refusal.

    (8) Any person who—
- (a) has custody of a dog in contravention of an order under subsection (1)(b) above; or
- (b) fails to comply with a requirement imposed on him under subsection (4)(a) above,

is guilty of an offence and liable on summary conviction to a fine not exceeding level 5 on the standard scale.

    . . .

Dangerous Dogs Act 1991

Meanings
"level 5 on the standard scale": currently £5,000.

Commentary
This section was amended by s.1 of the Dangerous Dogs (Amendment) Act 1997 (at p.179) with effect from June 8, 1997.

Subsection (1) enables a convicting court, when the offence is one under ss.1 or 3(1) or (3) or under an order made under s.2, to order the destruction of the dog in respect of which the offence was committed and to disqualify the offender from having custody of any dog for as long as it thinks fit.

Formerly, the court was required to order the destruction of a dog for an offence under s.1 or an aggravated offence under s.3(1) or (3). As the result of the amendments made to s.4 as mentioned above, a destruction order is not now always obligatory.

Subsection (1A), newly added by the 1997 Amendment Act, allows the court to forbear making a destruction order if they feel that both the conditions in paras (a) and (b) of subs.(1A) are met. The court, first, has to judge whether the dog, if allowed to live, would constitute a danger to public safety. Secondly, they must be satisfied that there is a 'good reason' why the dog, if born before November 30, 1991 and if subject to the prohibition in s.1(3), has not been exempted from prohibition under arts 3–5 of the Dangerous Dogs Compensation and Exemption Schemes Order 1991 (at pp.354–356).

Subsection (2) and (3) provide for appeals to the Crown Court against destruction orders.

Subsection (4) contains supplementary powers available to magistrates when making a destruction order. A sum ordered to be paid under subs.(4)(b) is to be treated as a fine for the purpose of enforcing its recovery (subs.(5)).

Subsection (6) and (7) contain provisions for the removal by a court of a disqualification order made under subs.(1)(b).

Subsection (8) provides for fines to be levied on a person who has custody of a dog whilst disqualified or who fails to deliver it up for destruction when so ordered by the court.

Further References
For cases where proceedings were begun before June 8, 1997, see the Dangerous Dogs (Amendment) Act 1997 s.5, at p.182.

4A. Contingent destruction orders

(1) Where—
  (a) a person is convicted of an offence under section 1 above or an aggravated offence under section 3(1) or (3) above;
  (b) the court does not order the destruction of the dog under section 4(1)(a) above; and
  (c) in the case of an offence under section 1 above, the dog is subject to the prohibition in section 1(3) above,

the court shall order that, unless the dog is exempted from that prohibition within the requisite period, the dog shall be destroyed.

(2) Where an order is made under subsection (1) above in respect of a dog, and the dog is not exempted from the prohibition in section 1(3) above within the requisite period, the court may extend that period.

(3) Subject to subsection (2) above, the requisite period for the purposes of such an order is the period of two months beginning with the date of the order.

(4) Where a person is convicted of an offence under section 3(1) or (3) above, the court may order that, unless the owner of the dog keeps it under proper control, the dog shall be destroyed.

(5) An order under subsection (4) above—
  (a) may specify the measures to be taken for keeping the dog under proper control, whether by muzzling, keeping on a lead, excluding it from specified places or otherwise; and
  (b) if it appears to the court that the dog is a male and would be less dangerous if neutered, may require it to be neutered.

(6) Subsections (2) to (4) of section 4 above shall apply in relation to an order under subsection (1) or (4) above as they apply in relation to an order under subsection (1)(a) of that section.

Definitions
"*keeping on a lead*": s.7(1).
"*muzzling*": s.7(1).
"*requisite period*": subss.(2), (3).

Commentary
This section was added by s.2 of the Dangerous Dogs (Amendment) Act 1997 (at p.180) with effect from 8th June 1997.

This section applies in a case where the three conditions in subs.(1) are met. In that situation the court must order the destruction of the dog in question unless exemption from destruction is obtained within the 'requisite period'. This period is two months from the date of the order unless extended by the court. No guidance about an extension is given, so leaving it to the court to decide whether that should be done and, if so, the length of the extension. It appears that only one extension may be given.

The provisions about obtaining an exemption are in arts 3–5 of the Dangerous Dogs Compensation and Exemption Schemes Order 1991 at pp.354–355.

Where a person has been convicted under s.3(1) or (3), the court may order that, unless it is kept under proper control, the dog shall be destroyed (subs.(4)).

Subsection (5) gives additional powers to the court when making an order under subs.(4).

By subs.(6) the provisions in s.4(2)–(4) are applied to orders made under subss.(1) or (4) of s.4A.

Further References
For cases where proceedings were begun before June 8, 1997, see the Dangerous Dogs (Amendment) Act 1997 s.5, at p.182.

4B. Destruction orders otherwise than on a conviction

(1) Where a dog is seized under section 5(1) or (2) below and it appears to a justice of the peace . . . —
- (a) that no person has been or is to be prosecuted for an offence under this Act or an order under section 2 above in respect of that dog (whether because the owner cannot be found or for any other reason); or
- (b) that the dog cannot be released into the custody or possession of its owner without the owner contravening the prohibition in section 1(3) above,

he may order the destruction of the dog and, subject to subsection (2) below, shall do so if it is one to which section 1 above applies.

Dangerous Dogs Act 1991

(2) Nothing in subsection (1)(b) above shall require the justice ... to order the destruction of a dog if he is satisfied—
  (a) that the dog would not constitute a danger to public safety; and
  (b) where the dog was born before 30th November 1991 and is subject to the prohibition in section 1(3) above, that there is a good reason why the dog has not been exempted from that prohibition.

(3) Where in a case falling within subsection (1)(b) above the justice ... does not order the destruction of the dog, he shall order that, unless the dog is exempted from the prohibition in section 1(3) above within the requisite period, the dog shall be destroyed.

(4) Subsections (2) to (4) of section 4 above shall apply in relation to an order under subsection (1)(b) or (3) above as they apply in relation to an order under subsection (1)(a) of that section.

(5) Subsections (2) and (3) of section 4A above shall apply in relation to an order under subsection (3) above as they apply in relation to an order under subsection (1) of that section, except that the reference to the court in subsection (2) of that section shall be construed as a reference to the justice.

Commentary
This section was added by s.3(1) of the Dangerous Dogs (Amendment) Act 1997 (at p.181).

Subsection (1) enables a J.P. to order the destruction of a dog in either of the circumstances mentioned in paras (a) and (b) thereof. An order must be made if the dog is one of the dangerous breeds, for which see s.1(1) at p.141 and the first-mentioned order on p.143.

An order is not mandatory in the circumstances mentioned in paras (a) and (b) of subs.(2). However, in a case falling within subs.(1)(b) where a destruction order is not made, the J.P. must order the dog's destruction unless exemption from the prohibition in s.1(3) is obtained within 'the requisite period' (subs.(3)).

Provisions for exemption are to be found in arts 3–5 of the Dangerous Dogs Compensation and Exemption Schemes Order 1991 at pp.354–355.

As to 'the requisite period', this is presumably the period described in s.4A(3) though that is there said to relate only to a s.4A(2) order. Furthermore, it is not clear whether the period can be extended for the purposes of s.4B as it can for s.4A.

Dangerous Dogs Act 1991

Subsection (4) applies the provisions of s.4(2)–(4) to orders made under subss.(1)(b) or (3) of s.4B.

Subsection (5) applies, with a modification, the provisions of s.4A(2), (3) to orders made under subs.(3) of s.4B.

Further References

For cases where proceedings were begun before June 8, 1997, see the Dangerous Dogs (Amendment) Act 1997 s.5, at p.182.

5. Seizure, entry of premises and evidence

(1) A constable or an officer of a local authority authorised by it to exercise the powers conferred by this subsection may seize—

(a) any dog which appears to him to be a dog to which section 1 above applies and which is in a public place—

   (i) after the time when possession or custody of it has become unlawful by virtue of that section; or

   (ii) before that time, without being muzzled and kept on a lead;

(b) any dog in a public place which appears to him to be a dog to which an order under section 2 above applies and in respect of which an offence against the order has been or is being committed; and

(c) any dog in a public place (whether or not one to which that section or such an order applies) which appears to him to be dangerously out of control.

(2) If a justice of the peace is satisfied by information on oath . . . that there are reasonable grounds for believing—

(a) that an offence under any provision of this Act or of an order under section 2 above is being or has been committed; or

(b) that evidence of the commission of any such offence is to be found, on any premises he may issue a warrant authorising a constable to enter those premises (using such force as is reasonably necessary) and to search them and seize any dog or other thing found there which is evidence of the commission of such an offence.

. . .

(4) *Revoked.*

(5) If in any proceedings it is alleged by the prosecution that a dog is one to which section 1 or an order under section 2 above applies it shall be presumed that it is such a dog unless the contrary is shown by the accused by such evidence as the court considers sufficient; and the accused shall not be permitted to adduce such evidence unless he

has given the prosecution notice of his intention to do so not later than the fourteenth day before that on which the evidence is to be adduced.

Definitions
"*dangerously out of control*": s.10(3).
"*kept on a lead*": s.7(1)(b).
"*muzzled*": s.7(1)(a).
"*public place*": s.10(2).

Commentary
Subsection (1) confers on police officers and authorised local authority officers powers to seize dogs in respect of which offences in a public place under the Act are suspected. Paragraph (a) applies to dogs designated under s.1; the time when custody or possession became unlawful (subject to s.1(3)(5)) was November 30, 1991 — see the Commentary on that section at pp.143–144.

Paragraph (b) relates to dogs offending under a s.2 order. Para. (c) relates to dog appearing to an officer to be dangerously out of control.

Unusually, the term "local authority" is not defined in the Act. It is submitted that the term is intended to refer to district and unitary councils in England, county and county borough councils Wales and, in London, borough councils and the City Corporation.

Police officers, acting under the authority of a magistrate's warrant, are given wide powers of entry, search and seizure in investigating offences under the Act (subs.(2)). In law, "premises" can include land which is not built upon.

The repealed provisions of subs.(4) are now superseded by the provisions of s.4B of the Act at p.152.

Subsection (5) contains important evidential provisions for prosecutions under ss.1 and 2. For comment, see p.30.

Further References
Home Office Circular 67/91, paras 44–47, at pp.426–427.
Home Office Circular 80/92, para.6, at p.445.
As to access to and welfare of dogs which have been seized, see Home Office Circular 9/94, paras 6, 9–12, at pp.449–452.

Dangerous Dogs Act 1991

6. Dogs owned by young persons
Where a dog is owned by a person who is less than sixteen years old any reference to its owner in section 1(2)(d) or (e) or 3 above shall include a reference to the head of the household, if any, of which that person is a member . . .

Commentary
This section makes the head of a household liable for offences under the sections named when the owner of the dog in question is a member of his household and aged under 16. That member will also be liable.

For comment on the meaning of 'head of the household', see p.21.

7. Muzzling and leads
(1) In this Act—
(a) references to a dog being muzzled are to its being securely fitted with a muzzle sufficient to prevent it biting any person; and
(b) references to its being kept on a lead are to its being securely held on a lead by a person who is not less than sixteen years old.

(2) If the Secretary of State thinks it desirable to do so he may by order prescribe the kind of muzzle or lead to be used for the purpose of complying, in the case of a dog of any type, with section 1 or an order under section 2 above; and if a muzzle or lead of a particular kind is for the time being prescribed in relation to any type of dog the references in subsection (1) above to a muzzle or lead shall, in relation to any dog of that type, be construed as references to a muzzle or lead of that kind.
. . .

Orders
To date, no order has been made under subs.(2).

Commentary
Subsection (1) describes the meanings to be given to the muzzling of a dog and to its being kept on a lead when these expressions are used in earlier provisions of the Act. These meanings may later be modified under subs.(2).

10. Short title, interpretation, commencement and extent

(1) This Act may be cited as the Dangerous Dogs Act 1991.

(2) In this Act—

"advertisement" includes any means of bringing a matter to the attention of the public and "advertise" shall be construed accordingly;

"public place" means any street, road or other place (whether or not enclosed) to which the public have or are permitted to have access whether for payment or otherwise and includes the common parts of a building containing two or more separate dwellings.

(3) For the purposes of this Act a dog shall be regarded as dangerously out of control on any occasion on which there are grounds for reasonable apprehension that it will injure any person, whether or not it actually does so, but references to a dog injuring a person or there being grounds for reasonable apprehension that it will do so do not include references to any case in which the dog is being used for a lawful purpose by a constable or a person in the service of the Crown.

(4) Except for section 8, this Act shall not come into force until such day as the Secretary of State may appoint by an order made by statutory instrument and different days may be appointed for different provisions or different purposes.

. . .

Commentary

Subsections (2) and (3) interpret words and phrases used in earlier parts of the Act.

A public place will include theatres, shops, cinemas, public transport, public buildings and many other places to which the public customarily goes. The reference to common parts of a building is intended to cover such parts as passages, stairways and lifts in a block of flats and other shared residential buildings.

It has been decided that an "other place . . . to which the public . . . have access" in the definition of "public place" does not include a garden path (*DPP v Fellowes* (1993) Crim. L.R. 523).

A person having an unmuzzled pit bull terrier in a car which was in a public place has been held to be a person in charge of the dog in a public place (*Bates v DPP* (1993) 157 J.P. 1004).

In deciding for the purposes of s.3 whether a dog is dangerously out of control or whether there are grounds for reasonable

apprehension that it will injure a person, subs.(3) makes it clear that the lawful use of police dogs or those of Crown servants is to be excluded.

The phrase "dangerously out of control" sets an objective standard of reasonable apprehension unrelated to the state of mind of the dog owner (*R. v Bezzina* [1994] 3 A.E.R. 964; [1994] 1 W.L.R. 1057, CA).

As to subs.(4), the whole of this Act, except s.8, came into force on August 12, 1991.

PROTECTION OF BADGERS ACT 1992
c. 51

Arrangement of sections

Offences

1. Taking, injuring or killing badgers
2. Cruelty
3. Interfering with badger setts

Exceptions and licences

6. General exceptions
7. Exceptions from s.1
8. Exceptions from s.3
10. Licences

Enforcement and penalties

11. Powers of constables
12. Penalties and forfeiture
13. Powers of court where dog used or present at commission of offence
14. Interpretation

Offences

1. Taking, injuring or killing badgers

(1) A person is guilty of an offence if, except as permitted by or under this Act, he wilfully kills, injures or takes, or attempts to kill, injure or take, a badger.

Protection of Badgers Act 1992

(2) If, in any proceedings for an offence under subsection (1) above consisting of attempting to kill, injure or take a badger, there is evidence from which it could be reasonably concluded that at the material time the accused was attempting to kill, injure or take a badger, he shall be presumed to have been attempting to kill, injure or take a badger unless the contrary is shown.

. . .

Definition
"*badger*": s.14.

Commentary
The involvement of a dog in the commission of this offence enables the convicting court to exercise the sanctions described in s.13.

Sections 6, 7 and 10 provide possible defences for this offence.

2. Cruelty

(1) A person is guilty of an offence if—
 (a) he cruelly ill-treats a badger;
 (b) he uses any badger tongs in the course of killing or taking, or attempting to kill or take, a badger;
 (c) except as permitted by or under this Act, he digs for a badger; or
 (d) he uses for the purpose of killing or taking a badger any firearm other than a smooth bore weapon of not less than 20 bore or a rifle using ammunition having a muzzle energy not less than 160 footpounds and a bullet weighing not less than 38 grains.

(2) If in any proceedings for an offence under subsection (1)(c) above there is evidence from which it could reasonably be concluded that at the material time the accused was digging for a badger he shall be presumed to have been digging for a badger unless the contrary is shown.

Definitions
"*ammunition*", "*badger*" and "*firearm*": s.14.

Commentary
The involvement of a dog in the commission of any of these offences enables the convicting court to exercise the sanctions described in s.13.

Protection of Badgers Act 1992

Sections 6 and 10 provide possible defences to a prosecution.

3. Interfering with badger setts

A person is guilty of an offence if, except as permitted by or under this Act, he interferes with a badger sett by doing any of the following things—

(a) damaging a badger sett or any part of it;
(b) destroying a badger sett;
(c) obstructing access to, or any entrance of, a badger sett;
(d) causing a dog to enter a badger sett; or
(e) disturbing a badger when it is occupying a badger sett,

intending to do any of those things or being reckless as to whether his actions would have any of those consequences.

. . .

Definitions
"badger" and "badger sett": s.14.

Commentary
The involvement of a dog in the commission of any of these offences enables the convicting court to exercise the sanctions described in s.13.

Sections 6 and 10 provide possible defences to any prosecution under this section.

Exceptions and licences

6. General exceptions

A person is not guilty of an offence under this Act by reason only of—

(a) taking or attempting to take a badger which has been disabled otherwise than by his act and is taken or to be taken solely for the purpose of tending it;
(b) killing or attempting to kill a badger which appears to be so seriously injured or in such a condition that to kill it would be an act of mercy;
(c) unavoidably killing or injuring a badger as an incidental result of a lawful action;
(d) doing anything which is authorised under the Animals (Scientific Procedures) Act 1986.

Definition
"badger": s.14.

Commentary
This section provides four defences which may be available for any prosecution under this Act.
An example of the defence at para.(c) would be an accident between a vehicle and a badger on the road.
The Animals (Scientific Procedures) Act 1986 may be found at p.267.

7. Exceptions from s.1

(1) Subject to subsection (2) below, a person is not guilty of an offence under section 1(1) above by reason of—
   (a) killing or taking, or attempting to kill or take, a badger; or
   (b) injuring a badger in the course of taking it or attempting to kill or take it,
if he shows that his action was necessary for the purpose of preventing serious damage to land, crops, poultry or any other form of property.

(2) The defence provided by subsection (1) above does not apply in relation to any action taken at any time if it had become apparent, before that time, that the action would prove necessary for the purpose there mentioned and either—
   (a) a licence under section 10 below authorising that action had not been applied for as soon as reasonably practicable after that fact had become apparent; or
   (b) an application for such a licence had been determined.

Definition
"badger": s.14.

Commentary
This section contains the particular defence which may be available in a prosecution under s.1(1). Other defences may be found in ss.6 and 10.
The wording of subs.(2), which describes the circumstances in which the defence is not available, is somewhat convoluted. It appears that it is only necessary to apply for a licence in good time and that the outcome of the application is irrelevant.

Protection of Badgers Act 1992

8. Exceptions from s.3

(1) Subject to subsection (2) below, a person is not guilty of an offence under section 3 above if he shows that his action was necessary for the purpose of preventing serious damage to land, crops, poultry or any other form of property.

(2) Subsection (2) of section 7 above applies to the defence in subsection (1) above as it applies to the defence in subsection (1) of that section.

(3) A person is not guilty of an offence under section 3(a), (c) or (e) above if he shows that his action was the incidental result of a lawful operation and could not reasonably have been avoided.

. . .

Definitions
"*badger sett*": s.14.
"*recognised Hunt*": subs.(9).

Commentary
This section contains a number of defences which may be available in a prosecution under s.3. Subsections (1) and (2) apply to any offence under s.3; subs.(3) only applies to s.3(a), (c) and (e).
Other defences may be found in ss.6 and 10.
As to subs.(2), see the Commentary on s.7.

10. Licences

(1) A licence may be granted to any person by the appropriate conservation body authorising him, notwithstanding anything in the foregoing provisions of this Act, but subject to compliance with any conditions specified in the licence—
  (a) for scientific or educational purposes or for the conservation of badgers—
    (i) to kill or take, within an area specified in the licence by any means so specified, or to sell, or to have in his possession, any number of badgers so specified; or
    (ii) to interfere with any badger sett within an area specified in the licence by any means so specified;

Protection of Badgers Act 1992

(b) for the purpose of any zoological gardens or collection specified in the licence, to take within an area specified in the licence by any means so specified, or to sell, or to have in his possession, any number of badgers so specified;

(c) for the purpose of ringing and marking, to take badgers within an area specified in the licence, to mark such badgers or to attach to them any ring, tag or other marking device as specified in the licence;

(d) for the purpose of any development as defined in section 55(1) of the Town and Country Planning Act 1990 . . . to interfere with a badger sett within an area specified in the licence by any means so specified;

(e) for the purpose of the preservation, or archaeological investigation, of a monument scheduled under section 1 of the Ancient Monuments and Archaeological Areas Act 1979, to interfere with a badger sett within an area specified in the licence by any means so specified;

(f) for the purpose of investigating whether any offence has been committed or gathering evidence in connection with proceedings before any court, to interfere with a badger sett within an area specified in the licence by any means so specified.

(2) A licence may be granted to any person by the appropriate Minister authorising him, notwithstanding anything in the foregoing provisions of this Act, but subject to compliance with any conditions specified in the licence—

(a) for the purpose of preventing the spread of disease, to kill or take badgers, or to interfere with a badger sett, within an area specified in the licence by any means so specified;

(b) for the purpose of preventing serious damage to land, crops, poultry or any other form of property, to kill or take badgers, or to interfere with a badger sett, within an area specified in the licence by any means so specified;

(c) for the purpose of any agricultural or forestry operation, to interfere with a badger sett within an area specified in the licence by any means so specified;

(d) for the purpose of any operation (whether by virtue of the Land Drainage Act 1991 or otherwise) to maintain or improve any existing watercourse or drainage works, or to construct new works required for the drainage of any land, including works for the purpose of defence against sea water or tidal water, to

Protection of Badgers Act 1992

interfere with a badger sett within an area specified in the licence by any means so specified.

(3) A licence may be granted to any person either by the appropriate conservation body or the appropriate Minister authorising that person, notwithstanding anything in the foregoing provisions of this Act, but subject to compliance with any conditions specified in the licence, to interfere with a badger sett within an area specified in the licence by any means so specified for the purpose of controlling foxes in order to protect livestock, game or wild life.

(4) In this section "the appropriate conservation body" means, in relation to a licence for an area—
(a) in England, Natural England;
(b) in Wales, the Countryside Council for Wales;
. . .
(5) In this section "the appropriate Minister" means in relation to a licence for an area—
(a) in England, the Secretary of State; and
(b) in Wales . . . the Secretary of State.

(6) The appropriate Minister shall from time to time consult with the appropriate conservation body as to the exercise of his functions under subsection (2)(b), (c) or (d) above and shall not grant a licence of any description unless he has been advised by the appropriate conservation body as to the circumstances in which, in that body's opinion, licences of that description should be granted.
. . .
(8) A licence granted under this section may be revoked at any time by the authority by whom it was granted, and without prejudice to any other liability to a penalty which he may have incurred under this or any other Act, a person who contravenes or fails to comply with any condition imposed on the grant of a licence under this section is guilty of an offence.

(9) A licence under this section shall not be unreasonably withheld or revoked.

(10) It shall be a defence in proceedings for an offence under section 8(b) of the Protection of Animals Act 1911 . . . (each of which restricts the placing on land of poison and poisonous substances) to show that—
  (a) the act alleged to constitute the offence was done under the authority of a licence granted under subsection (2)(a) above; and
  (b) any conditions specified in the licence were complied with.

Protection of Badgers Act 1992

Definitions
"*appropriate Conservancy Council*": subs.(4).
"*appropriate Minister*": subs.(5).
"*badger*" and "*badger sett*": s.14.

Commentary
This section provides for licences to be granted, by a Minister or Conservancy Council, to licensees enabling them to carry out several acts in relation to badgers and their setts which might otherwise constitute offences under the Act, provided any conditions of the licence are fulfilled (subss.(1)–(5)).
Subsections (6)–(10) contain supplementary provisions.

Enforcement and penalties

11. Powers of constables
Where a constable has reasonable grounds for suspecting that a person is committing an offence under the foregoing provisions of this Act, or has committed an offence under those provisions or those of the Badgers Act 1973 and that evidence of the commission of the offence is to be found on that person or any vehicle or article he may have with him, the constable may—
  (a) without warrant stop and search that person and any vehicle or article he may have with him;
  (b) seize and detain for the purposes of proceedings under any of those provisions anything which may be evidence of the commission of the offence or may be liable to be forfeited under section 12(4) below;

. . .

Commentary
This section confers on constables powers to stop, search, seize and detain as described. As well as police constables, including special police constables, the word "constable" will include others holding that office, e.g. harbour constables.
  The Badgers Act 1973 was repealed on October 15, 1992 (s.15(2) and Sch.), the date on which the present Act came into force (s.15(3)).

Protection of Badgers Act 1992

12. Penalties and forfeiture

(1) A person guilty of an offence under section 1(1) or (3), 2 or 3 above is liable on summary conviction to imprisonment for a term not exceeding six months or a fine not exceeding level 5 on the standard scale or both; and a person guilty of an offence under section 4, 5 or 10(8) above or 13(7) below is liable on summary conviction to a fine not exceeding that level.

(2) Where an offence was committed in respect of more than one badger the maximum fine which may be imposed under subsection (1) above shall be determined as if the person convicted had been convicted of a separate offence in respect of each badger.

(3) A person guilty of an offence under section 1(5) above is liable on summary conviction to a fine not exceeding level 3 on the standard scale.

(4) The court by which a person is convicted of an offence under this Act shall order the forfeiture of any badger or badger skin in respect of which the offence was committed and may, if they think fit, order the forfeiture of any weapon or article in respect of or by means of which the offence was committed.

. . .

Definitions and Meanings
"*badger*": s.14.
"*level 3 on the standard scale*": currently £1,000.
"*level 5 on the standard scale*": currently £5,000.

Commentary
Subsections (1)–(3) prescribe the maximum punishments which may be imposed for offences under the Act.

Subsection (4) makes it mandatory for the convicting court, in addition to other punishments, to order forfeiture of the articles there described.

13. Powers of court where dog used or present at commission of offence

(1) Where a dog has been used in or was present at the commission of an offence under sections 1(1), 2 or 3 above, the court, on convicting the offender, may, in addition to or in substitution for any other punishment, make either or both of the following orders—

(a) an order for the destruction or other disposal of the dog;

Protection of Badgers Act 1992

(b) an order disqualifying the offender, for such period as it thinks fit, for having custody of a dog.

(2) Where the court makes an order under subsection (l)(a) above, it may—
   (a) appoint a person to undertake the destruction or other disposal of the dog and require any person having custody of the dog to deliver it up for that purpose; and
   (b) order the offender to pay such sum as the court may determine to be the reasonable expenses of destroying or otherwise disposing of the dog and of keeping it pending its destruction or disposal.

(3) Where an order under subsection (l)(a) above is made in relation to a dog owned by a person other than the offender, the owner of the dog may appeal to the Crown Court against the order.

(4) A dog shall not be destroyed pursuant to an order under subsection (l)(a) above—
   (a) until the end of the period within which notice of appeal to the Crown Court against the order can be given; and
   (b) if notice of appeal is given in that period, until the appeal is determined or withdrawn,

unless the owner of the dog gives notice to the court which made the order that he does not intend to appeal against it.

(5) A person who is disqualified for having custody of a dog by virtue of an order made under subsection (l)(b) above may, at any time after the end of the period of one year beginning with the date of the order, apply to the court that made it (or any magistrates' court acting in the same local justice area as that court) for a direction terminating the disqualification.

(6) On an application under subsection (5) above the court may—
   (a) having regard to the applicant's character, his conduct since the disqualification was imposed and any other circumstances of the case, grant or refuse the application; and
   (b) order the applicant to pay all or any part of the costs of the application;

and where an application in respect of an order is refused no further application in respect of that order shall be entertained if made before the end of the period of one year beginning with the date of the refusal.

(7) Any person who—

Protection of Badgers Act 1992

(a) has custody of a dog in contravention of an order under subsection (l)(b) above; or
(b) fails to comply with a requirement imposed on him under subsection (2)(a) above,

is guilty of an offence.

(8) A sum ordered to be paid by an order under subsection (2)(b) above shall be recoverable summarily as a civil debt.

. . .

Commentary
This section contains the principal provisions of the Act about dogs, enabling a convicting court to order destruction or disposal of a dog or disqualification of an offender for having custody of a dog, or both, for offences under ss.1(1), 2 or 3.

Such orders may be made instead of, or in addition to, other available punishments, for which see s.12.

The section applies to dogs used in the commission of an offence or present at it.

Rights of appeal to the Crown Court exist: (a) against a destruction order if the dog is not owned by the offender; and (b) against actual destruction by the offender if he owns the dog (subss.(3) and (4)).

A person who is disqualified for having custody of a dog may apply after one year to have the disqualification order terminated and, if unsuccessful, may re-apply after a further year, and so on (subss.(5) and (6)).

Failure to deliver up a dog for destruction and having a dog while disqualified are made offences by subs.(7). For the maximum punishments, see s.12(1).

14. Interpretation
In this Act—
"ammunition" has the same meaning as in the Firearms Act 1968;
"badger" means any animal of the species *Meles meles*;
"badger sett" means any structure or place which displays signs indicating current use by a badger;
"firearm" has the same meaning as in the Firearms Act 1968;

. . .

Commentary
Section 14 supplies definitions for a number of terms used earlier in the Act.
The two terms defined by reference to the Firearms Act 1968 are so described in s.57 thereof as to include all ordinary kinds of firearms and ammunition.

DOGS (FOULING OF LAND) ACT 1996[1]

c. 20

Arrangement of sections

1. Land to which Act applies.
2. Designation of such land.
3. Offence.
4. Fixed penalty notices.
5. Orders and regulations by Secretary of State.
6. Effect of Act on byelaws.
7. Interpretation.
8. Short title, commencement and extent.

1. Land to which Act applies

(1) Subject to subsections (2) to (4) below, this Act applies to any land which is open to the air and to which the public are entitled or permitted to have access (with or without payment).

(2) This Act does not apply to land comprised in or running alongside a highway which comprises a carriageway unless the driving of motor vehicles on the carriageway is subject, otherwise than temporarily, to a speed limit of 40 miles per hour or less.

(3) This Act does not apply to land of any of the following descriptions, namely—
   (a) land used for agriculture or for woodlands;
   (b) land which is predominantly marshland, moor or heath; and
   (c) common land to which the public are entitled or permitted to have access otherwise than by virtue of section 193(1) of the Law of Property Act 1925 (right of access to urban common land).

---

1 See Commentary on p.178 regarding the repeal of this Act.

Dogs (Fouling of Land) Act 1996

(4) Where a private Act confers powers for the regulation of any land, the person entitled to exercise those powers may, by notice in writing given to the local authority in whose area the land is situated, exclude the application of this Act to that land.

(5) For the purposes of this section, any land which is covered shall be treated as land which is "open to the air" if it is open to the air on at least one side.

(6) In this section—

"agriculture" includes horticulture, fruit growing, seed growing, dairy farming and livestock breeding and keeping, and the use of land as grazing land, meadow land, osier land, market gardens and nursery grounds;

"carriageway" has the same meaning as in the Highways Act 1980;

"common land" has the same meaning as in the Commons Registration Act 1965;

"speed limit" means a speed limit imposed or having effect as if imposed under the Road Traffic Regulation Act 1984.

Definitions
"agriculture": subs.(6).
"carriageway": subs.(6).
"common land": subs.(6).
"open air": subs.(5).
"speed limit": subs.(6).

Commentary
Subsection (1) broadly describes the type of land which may be the subject of a designation order under s.2. Lands which are excluded from that description are shown in subss.(2)–(4).

2. Designation of such land

(1) A local authority may by order designate for the purposes of this Act any land in their area which is land to which this Act applies; and in this Act "designated land" means land to which this Act applies which is for the time being so designated.

(2) The power conferred by subsection (1) above includes power to designate land either specifically or by description, and to revoke or amend orders previously made.

(3) The Secretary of State shall by regulations prescribe the form of orders under subsection (1) above, and the procedure to be followed in the making of such orders.

(4) Such regulations shall in particular include provision requiring local authorities to publicise the making and effect of such orders.

Definition
"local authority": s.7.

Commentary
Subsections (1) and (2) enable a local authority by order to designate land to which s.1 applies either specifically or by description and to revoke and amend orders.

Subsections (3) and (4) authorise the Government to make regulations about how orders are to be made. Regulations so made are mentioned under the heading "Regulations" above.

3. Offence

(1) If a dog defecates at any time on designated land and a person who is in charge of the dog at that time fails to remove the faeces from the land forthwith, that person shall be guilty of an offence unless—
  (a) he has a reasonable excuse for failing to do so; or
  (b) the owner, occupier or other person or authority having control of the land has consented (generally or specifically) to his failing to do so.

(2) A person who is guilty of an offence under this section shall be liable on summary conviction to a fine not exceeding level 3 on the standard scale.

(3) Nothing in this section applies to a person registered as a blind person in a register compiled under section 29 of the National Assistance Act 1948.

(4) For the purposes of this section—
  (a) a person who habitually has a dog in his possession shall be taken to be in charge of the dog at any time unless at that time some other person is in charge of the dog;

(b) placing the faeces in a receptacle on the land which is provided for the purpose, or for the disposal of waste, shall be a sufficient removal from the land; and

(c) being unaware of the defecation (whether by reason of not being in the vicinity or otherwise), or not having a device for or other suitable means of removing the faeces, shall not be a reasonable excuse for failing to remove the faeces.

Definitions and Meanings
"designated land": s.2(1).
"level 3 on the standard scale": currently £1,000.

Commentary
The basic offence under this section is allowing a dog to defecate on designated land and not removing its faeces, but the following defences are available:

(1) Having a reasonable excuse, but being unaware of the defecation or not having suitable means for removing t he faeces are not reasonable excuses (subss.(1)(a) and (4)(c)).

(2) Consent of the owner, occupier or other person having control of the land to the faeces not being removed (subs.(1)(b)).

(3) Being a registered blind person (subs.(3)).

(4) If the defendant habitually has the dog in his possession, that he can show that at the time some other person was in charge of the dog (subs.(4)(a)).

(5) Placing the faeces in a receptacle on the land (subs.(4)(b)).

Note that the person primarily liable to prosecution is the person who habitually has the dog in his possession. He may escape prosecution if he can show that another person was in charge of it at the time, when that person will be liable (subss.(1), (4)(a)).

4. Fixed penalty notices

(1) Where on any occasion an authorised officer of a local authority finds a person who he has reason to believe has on that occasion committed an offence under section 3 above in the area of that authority,

Dogs (Fouling of Land) Act 1996

he may give that person a notice offering him the opportunity of discharging any liability to conviction for that offence by payment of a fixed penalty.

(2) Subsections (2) to (8) of section 88 of the Environmental Protection Act 1990 shall apply for the purposes of this section as they apply for the purposes of that section but as if references to a litter authority were references to a local authority.

(3) In subsection (8) of that section as it applies for the purposes of this section "chief finance officer", in relation to a local authority, means the person having responsibility for the financial affairs of the authority.

(4) In this section "authorised officer", in relation to a local authority, means any employee of the authority who is authorised in writing by the authority for the purpose of issuing notices under this section.

(5) In subsection (4) above, the reference to any employee of the authority includes references to—
- (a) any person by whom, in pursuance of arrangements made with the authority, any functions relating to the enforcement of this Act fall to be discharged; and
- (b) any employee of any such person.

Definitions
"*authorised officer*": subs.(4).
"*chief finance officer*": subs.(3).
"*employee of the local authority*": subs.(5).
"*local authority*": s.7.

Commentary
This section enables an offender under s.3 to discharge his liability by paying a fixed penalty when served with a notice by an authorised officer of the local authority.

No proceedings for the offence can be started within 14 days of the date of the notice, and payment of the fixed penalty within that time will avoid conviction for the offence (Environmental Protection Act 1990, s.88(2)).

5. Orders and regulations by Secretary of State
(1) Any power of the Secretary of State to make an order or regulations under this Act shall be exercisable by statutory instrument.

Dogs (Fouling of Land) Act 1996

(2) A statutory instrument containing an order or regulations under this Act shall be subject to annulment in pursuance of a resolution of either House of Parliament.

6. Effect of Act on byelaws

(1) Subsections (2) and (3) below apply to any byelaw made by a local authority which has the effect of making any person in charge of a dog guilty of an offence if—
   (a) he permits the dog to defecate on any land; or
   (b) in a case where the dog defecates on any land, he fails to remove the faeces from the land.

(2) In so far as any byelaw to which this subsection applies would, apart from this subsection, have effect in relation to any designated land, the byelaw—
   (a) shall cease to have effect in relation to the land; or
   (b) where it is made after the order under section 2(1) above, shall not have effect in relation to the land.

(3) In so far as any byelaw to which this subsection applies still has effect at the end of the period of 10 years beginning with the day on which this Act comes into force, it shall cease to have effect at the end of that period in relation to any land to which this Act applies.

(4) Where any omission would, apart from this subsection, constitute an offence both under section 3 above and under any byelaw other than one to which subsections (2) and (3) above apply, the omission shall not constitute an offence under the byelaw.

Definitions
"*designated land*": s.2(1).
"*local authority*": s.7.

Commentary
Local authority byelaws making it an offence to allow a dog to defecate on land or for failing to remove its faeces are to cease to have effect on any land designated under s.2 and are to be ineffectual if made after a designation (subss.(1) and (2)).

Byelaws as described above affecting land to which the Act applies under s.1 ceased to have effect after 10 years from the

Dogs (Fouling of Land) Act 1996

date on which the Act came into force: August 17, 1996 (subs.(3), s.8(2)). Other byelaws as described above which do not affect land to which the Act applies are to continue in force unless specifically revoked.

Omissions constituting offences are dealt with in subs.(4).

7. Interpretation

(1) In this Act "local authority"—
(a) in relation to England, means any unitary authority or any district council so far as they are not a unitary authority; and
(b) in relation to Wales, means the council of any county or county borough.

(2) The following are unitary authorities for the purposes of subsection (1)(a) above, namely—
(a) any county council so far as they are the council for an area for which there are no district councils;
(b) the council of any district comprised in an area for which there is no county council;
(c) any London borough council;
(d) the Common Council of the City of London; and
(e) the Council of the Isles of Scilly.

8. Short title, commencement and extent

(1) This Act may be cited as the Dogs (Fouling of Land) Act 1996.

(2) This Act shall come into force at the end of the period of two months beginning with the day on which it is passed.

(3) This Act extends to England and Wales only.

Commentary

By virtue of subs.(2), the Act came into force on August 17, 1996.

The whole Act has been repealed by s.107 of and Pt 5 of Sch.5 to the Clean Neighbourhoods and Environment Act 2005. Nevertheless, the Act will continue to apply to land designated under it until a dog control order is made over the land or the land ceases to be designated (art.4, Environmental Offences

Dogs (Fouling of Land) Act 1996

(Fixed Penalties) (Miscellaneous Provisions) Regulations 2006 (SI 2006/783) – England, and art.4, of the Clean Neighbourhoods and Environment Act 2005 (Commencement No. 2, Transitional Provisions and Savings) (Wales) Order 2006 (SI 2006/2797)).

DANGEROUS DOGS (AMENDMENT) ACT 1997

c. 53

Arrangement of sections

1. Destruction orders
2. Contingent destruction orders
3. Destruction orders otherwise than on a conviction
4. Extended application of 1991 Order
5. Transitional provisions
6. Short title, commencement and extent

1. Destruction orders

(1) In paragraph (a) of subsection (1) of section 4 (destruction and disqualification orders) of the Dangerous Dogs Act 1991 ("the 1991 Act"), after the words "committed and" there shall be inserted the words ", subject to subsection (1A) below,".

(2) After that subsection there shall be inserted the following subsection—
   "(1A) Nothing in subsection (1)(a) above shall require the court to order the destruction of a dog if the court is satisfied—
      (a) that the dog would not constitute a danger to public safety; and
      (b) where the dog was born before 30th November 1991 and is subject to the prohibition in section 1(3) above, that there is a good reason why the dog has not been exempted from that prohibition."

(3) In subsection (2) of that section, the words "then, unless the order is one that the court is required to make" shall cease to have effect.

(4) In subsection (3)(a) of that section, the words ", where the order was not one that the court was required to make" shall cease to have effect.

Dangerous Dogs (Amendment) Act 1997

Commentary
This section amends subss.(1), (2) and (3) of s.4 of the Dangerous Dogs Act 1991 and inserts a new subs.(1A) in s.4.

These amendments are incorporated in the text of s.4 at pp.148–149, and a commentary thereon is given on p.150.

2. Contingent destruction orders
After section 4 of the 1991 Act there shall be inserted the following section—

"**4A. Contingent destruction orders**
  (1) Where—
    (a) a person is convicted of an offence under section 1 above or an aggravated offence under section 3(1) or (3) above;
    (b) the court does not order the destruction of the dog under section 4(1)(a) above; and
    (c) in the case of an offence under section 1 above, the dog is subject to the prohibition in section 1(3) above,
  the court shall order that, unless the dog is exempted from that prohibition within the requisite period, the dog shall be destroyed.

  (2) Where an order is made under subsection (1) above in respect of a dog, and the dog is not exempted from the prohibition in section 1(3) above within the requisite period, the court may extend that period.

  (3) Subject to subsection (2) above, the requisite period for the purposes of such an order is the period of two months beginning with the date of the order.

  (4) Where a person is convicted of an offence under section 3(1) or (3) above, the court may order that, unless the owner of the dog keeps it under proper control, the dog shall be destroyed.

  (5) An order under subsection (4) above—
    (a) may specify the measures to be taken for keeping the dog under proper control, whether by muzzling, keeping on a lead, excluding it from specified places or otherwise; and
    (b) if it appears to the court that the dog is a male and would be less dangerous if neutered, may require it to be neutered.

  (6) Subsections (2) to (4) of section 4 above shall apply in relation to an order under subsection (1) or (4) above as they apply in relation to an order under subsection (1)(a) of that section."

Dangerous Dogs (Amendment) Act 1997

Commentary
This section inserts s.4A in the Dangerous Dogs Act 1991 which is incorporated in the text of that Act at p.151.
A commentary on the section is given on p.152.

3. Destruction orders otherwise than on a conviction

(1) After section 4A of the 1991 Act there shall be inserted the following section—

"**4B. Destruction orders otherwise than on a conviction**

(1) Where a dog is seized under section 5(1) or (2) below and it appears to a justice of the peace . . . —

(a) that no person has been or is to be prosecuted for an offence under this Act or an order under section 2 above in respect of that dog (whether because the owner cannot be found or for any other reason); or

(b) that the dog cannot be released into the custody or possession of its owner without the owner contravening the prohibition in section 1(3) above,

he may order the destruction of the dog and, subject to subsection (2) below, shall do so if it is one to which section 1 above applies.

(2) Nothing in subsection (1)(b) above shall require the justice . . . to order the destruction of a dog if he is satisfied—

(a) that the dog would not constitute a danger to public safety; and

(b) where the dog was born before 30th November 1991 and is subject to the prohibition in section 1(3) above, that there is a good reason why the dog has not been exempted from that prohibition.

(3) Where in a case falling within subsection (1)(b) above the justice . . . does not order the destruction of the dog, he shall order that, unless the dog is exempted from the prohibition in section 1(3) above within the requisite period, the dog shall be destroyed.

(4) Subsections (2) to (4) of section 4 above shall apply in relation to an order under subsection (1)(b) or (3) above as they apply in relation to an order under subsection (1)(a) of that section.

(5) Subsections (2) and (3) of section 4A above shall apply in relation to an order under subsection (3) above as they apply in relation to an order under subsection (1) of that section, except that the reference to the court in subsection (2) of that section shall be construed as a reference to the justice . . ."

(2) In section 5 of the 1991 Act (seizure, entry of premises and evidence), subsection (4) (which is superseded by this section) shall cease to have effect.

Commentary
Subsection (1) of this section inserts s.4B in the Dangerous Dogs Act 1991 which is incorporated in the text of that Act at p.152.

A commentary on the section is given on p.153.

Subsection (2) revokes s.5(4) of the Dangerous Dogs Act 1991 whose provisions have been superseded by those in the new s.4B.

4. Extended application of 1991 Order

(1) Where an order is made under section 4A(1) or 4B(3) of the 1991 Act, Part III of the Dangerous Dogs Compensation and Exemption Schemes Order 1991 (exemption scheme) shall have effect as if—
- (a) any reference to the appointed day were a reference to the end of the requisite period within the meaning of section 4A or, as the case may be, section 4B of the 1991 Act;
- (b) paragraph (a) of Article 4 and Article 6 were omitted; and
- (c) the fee payable to the Agency under Article 9 were a fee of such amount as the Secretary of State may by order prescribe.

(2) The power to make an order under this section shall be exercisable by statutory instrument which shall be subject to annulment in pursuance of a resolution of either House of Parliament.

Commentary
Subsection (1) makes amendments to Part III of the Dangerous Dogs Compensation and Exemption Schemes Order 1991 (at pp.353–359) in cases where an order is made under the new ss.4A(1) or 4B(3).

Under subs.(1)(c), a fee of £20 plus VAT has been prescribed by the Dangerous Dogs (Fees) Order 1997 (SI 1997/1152).

5. Transitional provisions

(1) This Act shall apply in relation to cases where proceedings have been instituted before, as well as after, the commencement of this Act.

(2) In a case where, before the commencement of this Act—

Dangerous Dogs (Amendment) Act 1997

(a) the court has ordered the destruction of a dog in respect of which an offence under section 1, or an aggravated offence under section 3(1) or (3), of the 1991 Act has been committed, but

(b) the dog has not been destroyed,

that destruction order shall cease to have effect and the case shall be remitted to the court for reconsideration.

(3) Where a case is so remitted, the court may make any order in respect of the dog which it would have power to make if the person in question had been convicted of the offence after the commencement of this Act.

Commentary
Subsection (1) states that the 1997 Act is also to apply to cases where proceedings have been begun before the commencement of the Act (June 8, 1997).

Subsection (2) provides that where, before the Act's commencement, a court has ordered the destruction of a dog for an offence under s.1 or for an aggravated offence under s.3(1) or (3) of the Dangerous Dogs Act 1991, and the dog has not been destroyed, the destruction order shall cease to have effect and the court must reconsider the case.

On a re-hearing, the court may make any order which could have been made if the person in question had been convicted after the Act's commencement (subs.(3)).

6. Short title, commencement and extent

(1) This Act may be cited as the Dangerous Dogs (Amendment) Act 1997.

(2) This Act does not extend to Northern Ireland.

(3) This Act shall come into force on such day as the Secretary of State may by order made by statutory instrument appoint.

Commentary
By virtue of the Dangerous Dogs (Amendment) Act 1997 (Commencement) Order 1997 (SI 1997/1151) the whole Act came into force on June 8, 1997.

BREEDING AND SALE OF DOGS (WELFARE) ACT 1999

c. 11

Arrangement of sections

1. Inspection and report before grant of licence
2. Licence conditions
3. Commencement and duration of licence
4. Imprisonment for keeping unlicensed establishment etc.
5. Disqualification
6. Fees
7. Definition of establishments

Sale of dogs

8. Sale of dogs
9. Penalties

Supplementary

10. Repeals
11. Short title, commencement and extent

Schedule – Repeals

---

1. Inspection and report before grant of licence
In the Breeding of Dogs Act 1973 ("the 1973 Act"), after subsection (2) of section 1 insert—
"(2A) On receipt of an application by a person to a local authority for the grant of a licence under this Act in respect of any premises—

Breeding and Sale of Dogs (Welfare) Act 1999

(a) if a licence under this Act has not previously been granted to the person in respect of the premises, the authority shall arrange for the inspection of the premises by a veterinary surgeon or veterinary practitioner and by an officer of the authority; and

(b) in any other case, the authority shall arrange for the inspection of the premises by a veterinary surgeon or veterinary practitioner or by an officer of the authority (or by both).

(2B) Where an inspection is arranged under subsection (2A) of this section, the local authority shall arrange for the making of a report about the premises, the applicant and any other relevant matter; and the authority shall consider the report before determining whether to grant a licence."

Definitions
"local authority", "veterinary practitioner" and *"veterinary surgeon"*: s.5(2) of the 1973 Act at p.113.

Commentary
This section adds two subsections to s.1 of the Breeding of Dogs Act 1973. These amendments are included in the text of that section at pp.104–105.

2. Licence conditions

(1) In subsection (4) of section 1 of the 1973 Act (matters to which a local authority shall have regard in determining whether to grant a licence and about which conditions must be included in the licence), in paragraph (b) (dogs to be visited at suitable intervals, so far as necessary), omit "(so far as necessary)".

(2) In that subsection, after paragraph (e) insert—

"(f) that bitches are not mated if they are less than one year old;

(g) that bitches do not give birth to more than six litters of puppies each;

(h) that bitches do not give birth to puppies before the end of the period of twelve months beginning with the day on which they last gave birth to puppies; and

(i) that accurate records in a form prescribed by regulations are kept at the premises and made available for inspection there by any officer of the local authority, or any veterinary surgeon or

Breeding and Sale of Dogs (Welfare) Act 1999

veterinary practitioner, authorised by the local authority to inspect the premises;",
and for "paragraphs (a) to (e)" substitute "paragraphs (a) to (i)".

(3) After that subsection insert—

"(4A) Regulations under paragraph (i) of subsection (4) of this section shall be made by the Secretary of State by statutory instrument; and a statutory instrument containing regulations made under that paragraph shall be subject to annulment in pursuance of a resolution of either House of Parliament."

Regulations
The Breeding of Dogs (Licensing Records) Regulations 1999 (at p.377) were made under the provisions of subss.(4)(i) and (4A).

Definitions
"local authority", "veterinary practitioner" and "veterinary surgeon": Breeding of Dogs Act 1973, s.5(2), at p.113.
"the 1973 Act": s.1.

Commentary
This section amends subs.(4) of, and adds a subsection to, s.1 of the Breeding of Dogs Act 1973.

These amendments are included in the text of that section at pp.105–106.

3. Commencement and Duration of Licence

(1) After subsection (5) of section 1 of the 1973 Act insert—

"(5A) A local authority shall determine whether to grant such a licence before the end of the period of three months beginning with the day on which the application for the licence is received."

(2) In subsection (6) of that section (commencement of licences), for the words from ("according" to the end substitute "come into force at the beginning of the day specified in the licence as the day on which it is to come into force; and that day shall be the later of—

(a) the day stated in the application as that on which the applicant wishes the licence to come into force; and

(b) the day on which the licence is granted."

(3) In subsection (7) of that section (period of licence), for "year to which it relates" substitute "period of one year beginning with the day on which it comes into force".

Breeding and Sale of Dogs (Welfare) Act 1999

(4) Subsection (1) does not apply in relation to any application for a licence received before the day on which this Act comes into force; and subsections (2) and (3) do not apply in relation to a licence granted before that day.

Definitions and Meanings
"day on which this Act comes into force": the Act was passed on June 30, 1999 and therefore, by virtue of s.11(2), came into force on December 30, 1999.

Commentary
This section amends subss.(6) and (7) of, and adds a subsection to, s.1 of the Breeding of Dogs Act 1973.

These amendments are included in the text of that section at pp.105–106.

4. Imprisonment for keeping unlicensed establishment etc.

(1) In subsection (1) of section 3 of the 1973 Act (offence of keeping an unlicensed establishment etc.), for the words from "to" to the end substitute "to—
  (a) imprisonment for a term not exceeding three months; or
  (b) a fine not exceeding level 4 on the standard scale,
or to both."

(2) Subsection (1) does not apply in relation to an offence committed before this Act comes into force.

Meanings
"day on which this Act came into force": the Act was passed on June 30, 1999 and therefore, by virtue of s.11(2), came into force on December 30, 1999.
"level 4 on the standard scale": currently £2,500.

Commentary
The amendments made by this section to s.3(1) of the Breeding of Dogs Act 1973 are incorporated in the text of that section at p.109.

By virtue of s.280(1) of the Criminal Justice Act 2003, a summary offence under this section is not punishable by imprisonment.

Breeding and Sale of Dogs (Welfare) Act 1999

5. Disqualification

(1) In subsection (3) of section 3 of the 1973 Act (cancellation of licences and disqualification), for the words from "or of any offence" to the end substitute, "the court by which he is convicted may (in addition to or in substitution for any penalty under subsection (1) or (2) of this section) make an order providing for any one or more of the following—
  (a) the cancellation of any licence held by him under this Act;
  (b) his disqualification, for such period as the court thinks fit, from keeping an establishment the keeping of which is required to be licensed under this Act; and
  (c) his disqualification, for such period as the court thinks fit, from having custody of any dog of a description specified in the order."

(2) In subsection (4) of that section (suspension of cancellation or disqualification pending appeal), for "ordered the cancellation of a person's licence, or his disqualification, in pursuance of the last foregoing subsection" substitute "made an order under this section".

(3) After that subsection insert—

"(5) Where a court makes an order under subsection (3)(c) of this section in relation to a description of dogs it may also make such order as it thinks fit in respect of any dog of that description which—
  (a) was in the offender's custody at the time when the offence was committed; or
  (b) has been in his custody at any time since that time.

(6) An order under subsection (5) of this section may (in particular)—
  (a) require any person who has custody of the dog to deliver it up to a specified person; and
  (b) (if it does) also require the offender to pay specified amounts to specified persons for the care of the dog from the time when it is delivered up in pursuance of the order until permanent arrangements are made for its care or disposal.

(7) A person who—
  (a) has custody of a dog in contravention of an order under subsection (3)(c) of this section; or
  (b) fails to comply with a requirement imposed on him under subsection (6) of this section,
shall be guilty of an offence.

(8) Where a court proposes to make an order under subsection (5) of this section in respect of a dog owned by a person other than the offender, the court shall notify the owner who may make representations to the

Breeding and Sale of Dogs (Welfare) Act 1999

court; and if an order is made the owner may, within the period of seven days beginning with the date of the order, appeal to—
  (a) in England and Wales, the Crown Court; or
  (b) in Scotland, the High Court of Justiciary,
against the order.

(9) A person who is subject to a disqualification by virtue of an order under subsection (3)(c) of this section may, at any time after the end of the period of one year beginning with the date of the order, apply to the court which made the order (or, in England and Wales, any magistrates' court acting for the same petty sessions area) for a direction terminating the disqualification from such date as the court considers appropriate.

(10) On an application under subsection (9) of this section the court—
  (a) shall notify the relevant local authority which may make representations to the court;
  (b) shall, having regard to the applicant's character and his conduct since the disqualification was imposed, any representations made by the relevant local authority and any other circumstances of the case, grant or refuse the application; and
  (c) may order the applicant to pay all or any part of the costs, or (in Scotland) expenses, of the application (including any costs, or expenses, of the relevant local authority in making representations);
and in this subsection "the relevant local authority" means the local authority in whose area are situated the premises in relation to which the offence which led to the disqualification was committed.

(11) Where an application under subsection (9) of this section in respect of a disqualification is refused, no further application under that subsection in respect of that disqualification shall be entertained if made before the end of the period of one year beginning with the date of the refusal."

(4) In subsection (2) of section 2 of the Breeding of Dogs Act 1991 (disqualification for offence of obstruction etc. of inspector of premises not covered by a licence under the 1973 Act), for the words from "disqualify him" to the end substitute "make an order providing for either or both of the following—
  (a) his disqualification, for such period as the court thinks fit, from keeping an establishment the keeping of which is required to be licensed under the Breeding of Dogs Act 1973; and

Breeding and Sale of Dogs (Welfare) Act 1999

    (b) his disqualification, for such period as the court thinks fit, from having custody of any dog of a description specified in the order."
  (5) After that subsection insert—
    "(2A) A court which has made an order under or by virtue of this section may, if it thinks fit, suspend the operation of the order pending an appeal.
    (2B) Subsections (5) to (11) of section 3 of the Breeding of Dogs Act 1973 (provisions about disqualification) apply in relation to an order made under subsection (2)(b) above as they apply in relation to an order made under subsection (3)(c) of that section."
  (6) This section does not apply in relation to an offence committed before this Act comes into force.

Definitions and Meanings
"the 1973 Act": s.1.
"the relevant local authority": subs.(10).
"this Act comes into force": the Act was passed on June 30, 1999 and therefore, by virtue of s.11(2), came into force on December 30, 1999.

Commentary
This section amends s.3 of the Breeding of Dogs Act 1973 and s.2 of the Breeding of Dogs Act 1991. These amendments are incorporated in the texts of those two sections at, respectively, pp.109 and 139.

6. Fees
After section 3 of the 1973 Act insert—
  "**Fees**
    3A—(1) The costs of inspecting premises under this Act and the Breeding of Dogs Act 1991 shall be met by the local authority concerned.
    (2) A local authority may charge fees—
        (a) in respect of applications for the grant of licences under this Act; and
        (b) in respect of inspections of premises under section 1(2A) of this Act.
    (3) A local authority may set the level of fees to be charged by virtue of subsection (2) of this section—

Breeding and Sale of Dogs (Welfare) Act 1999

(a) with a view to recovering the reasonable costs incurred by them in connection with the administration and enforcement of this Act and the Breeding of Dogs Act 1991; and
(b) so that different fees are payable in different circumstances."

Definitions
"*local authority*": Breeding of Dogs Act 1973, s.5(2), at p.113.

Commentary
This section adds s.3A to the Breeding of Dogs Act 1973. This addition is incorporated in the text of that Act at pp.111–112.

7. Definition of establishments
Before section 5 of the 1973 Act insert—
  "**Breeding establishments for dogs**
  4A—(1) References in this Act to the keeping of a breeding establishment for dogs shall be construed in accordance with this section.
  (2) A person keeps a breeding establishment for dogs at any premises if he carries on at those premises a business of breeding dogs for sale (whether by him or any other person).
  (3) Subject to subsection (5) of this section, where—
    (a) a person keeps a bitch at any premises at any time during any period of twelve months; and
    (b) the bitch gives birth to a litter of puppies at any time during that period,
  he shall be treated as carrying on a business of breeding dogs for sale at the premises throughout the period if a total of four or more other litters is born during the period to bitches falling within subsection (4) of this section.
  (4) The bitches falling within this subsection are—
    (a) the bitch mentioned in subsection (3)(a) and (b) of this section and any other bitches kept by the person at the premises at any time during the period;
    (b) any bitches kept by any relative of his at the premises at any such time;
    (c) any bitches kept by him elsewhere at any such time; and
    (d) any bitches kept (anywhere) by any person at any such time under a breeding arrangement made with him.

(5) Subsection (3) of this section does not apply if the person shows that none of the puppies born to bitches falling within paragraph (a), (b) or (d) of subsection (4) of this section was in fact sold during the period (whether by him or any other person).

(6) In subsection (4) of this section "breeding arrangement" means a contract or other arrangement under which the person agrees that another person may keep a bitch of his on terms that, should the bitch give birth, the other person is to provide him with either—
  (a) one or more of the puppies; or
  (b) the whole or part of the proceeds of selling any of them;
and "relative" means the person's parent or grandparent, child or grandchild, sibling, aunt or uncle or niece or nephew or someone with whom he lives as a couple.

(7) In this section "premises" includes a private dwelling."
. . .

Definitions
"breeding arrangement" and *"relative":* s.4A(6).
"premises": s.4A(7).

Commentary
This section adds s.4A to the Breeding of Dogs Act 1973 which is incorporated in the text of the 1973 Act at p.112.

8. Sale of dogs
(1) The keeper of a licensed breeding establishment is guilty of an offence if—
  (a) he sells a dog otherwise than at a licensed breeding establishment, a licensed pet shop or a licensed Scottish rearing establishment,
  (b) he sells a dog otherwise than to the keeper of a licensed pet shop or a licensed Scottish rearing establishment knowing or believing that the person who buys it intends that it should be sold (by him or any other person),
  (c) he sells a dog which is less than eight weeks old otherwise than to the keeper of a licensed pet shop or a licensed Scottish rearing establishment,

Breeding and Sale of Dogs (Welfare) Act 1999

(d) he sells to the keeper of a licensed pet shop or a licensed Scottish rearing establishment a dog which was not born at a licensed breeding establishment, or

(e) he sells to the keeper of a licensed pet shop or a licensed Scottish rearing establishment a dog which, when delivered, is not wearing a collar with an identifying tag or badge.

. . .

(3) The keeper of a licensed pet shop is guilty of an offence if he sells a dog which, when delivered to him, was wearing a collar with an identifying tag or badge but is not wearing such a collar when delivered to the person to whom he sells it.

(4) In proceedings against any person for an offence under this section it shall be a defence for that person to show that he took all reasonable steps and exercised all due diligence to avoid committing the offence.

(5) In this section—

"identifying tag or badge", in relation to a dog, means a tag or badge which clearly displays information indicating the licensed breeding establishment at which it was born and any other information required by regulations,

"licensed breeding establishment" means a breeding establishment for dogs the keeping of which by its keeper (or, where more than one, each of its keepers) is licensed under the 1973 Act,

"licensed pet shop" means a pet shop the keeping of which by its keeper (or, where more than one, each of its keepers) is licensed under the Pet Animals Act 1951,

"licensed Scottish rearing establishment" means a rearing establishment for dogs the keeping of which by its keeper (or, where more than one, each of its keepers) is licensed under the 1973 Act (as it applies in relation to Scotland), and

"regulations" means regulations made by the Secretary of State by statutory instrument;

and a statutory instrument containing regulations made under this section shall be subject to annulment in pursuance of a resolution of either House of Parliament.

Regulations

The Sale of Dogs (Identification Tag) Regulations 1999 (at p.376) were made under the provisions of subs.(5).

Breeding and Sale of Dogs (Welfare) Act 1999

Definitions
"*identifying tag or badge*", "*licensed breeding establishment*", "*licensed pet shop*", "*licensed Scottish rearing establishment*" and "*regulations*": subs.(5).

Commentary
Subsections (1) and (3) place wide-ranging restrictions on the sale of dogs by the keeper of a licensed dog breeding establishment. The breach of any restriction is an offence punishable as provided for in s.9.
 In relation to para.(e) of subs.(1) and subs.(3), further information is to be displayed attached to dogs' collars in accordance with the regulations noted under "Regulations" above.
 Subsection (4) provides a defence against a prosecution under the section's provisions.
 Subsection (5) defines a number of terms used in the section.

Further References
Home Office Circular 53/99, Annex B, paras 1–5 at pp.460–462.
 For the licensing of pet shops, see the Pet Animals Act 1951 at p.234.

9. Penalties

(1) A person guilty of an offence under section 8 is liable on summary conviction to—
 (a) *revoked*;
 (b) a fine not exceeding level 4 on the standard scale.

(2) Where a person is convicted of an offence under section 8(1) or (2), the court before which he is convicted may (in addition to or in substitution for any penalty under subsection (1)) make an order providing for any one or more of the following—
 (a) the cancellation of any licence held by him under the 1973 Act,
 (b) his disqualification, for such period as the court thinks fit, from keeping an establishment the keeping of which is required to be licensed under the 1973 Act, and
 (c) his disqualification, for such period as the court thinks fit, from having custody of any dog of a description specified in the order.

(3) A court which has made an order under this section may, if it thinks fit, suspend the operation of the order pending an appeal.

(4) Where a court makes an order under subsection (2)(c) in relation to a description of dogs it may also make such order as it thinks fit in respect of any dog of that description which—
- (a) was in the offender's custody at the time when the offence was committed, or
- (b) has been in his custody at any time since that time.

(5) An order under subsection (4) may (in particular)—
- (a) require any person who has custody of the dog to deliver it up to a specified person, and
- (b) (if it does) also require the offender to pay specified amounts to specified persons for the care of the dog from the time when it is delivered up in pursuance of the order until permanent arrangements are made for its care or disposal.

(6) A person who—
- (a) has custody of a dog in contravention of an order under subsection (2)(c), or
- (b) fails to comply with a requirement imposed on him under subsection (5),

is guilty of an offence.

(7) A person guilty of an offence under subsection (6) is liable on summary conviction to—
- (a) *revoked*;
- (b) a fine not exceeding level 4 on the standard scale.

(8) Where a court proposes to make an order under subsection (4) in respect of a dog owned by a person other than the offender, the court shall notify the owner who may make representations to the court; and if an order is made the owner may, within the period of seven days beginning with the date of the order, appeal to—
- (a) in England and Wales, the Crown Court, or
- (b) in Scotland, the High Court of Justiciary,

against the order.

(9) A person who is subject to a disqualification by virtue of an order under subsection (2)(c) may, at any time after the end of the period of one year beginning with the date of the order, apply to the court which made the order (or, in England and Wales, any magistrates' court acting in the same local justice area) for a direction terminating the disqualification from such date as the court considers appropriate.

(10) On an application under subsection (9) the court shall, having regard to—
- (a) the applicant's character,

Breeding and Sale of Dogs (Welfare) Act 1999

 (b) his conduct since the disqualification was imposed, and
 (c) any other circumstances of the case,
grant or refuse the application; and where an application under subsection (9) in respect of a disqualification is refused, no further application under that subsection in respect of that disqualification shall be entertained if made before the end of the period of one year beginning with the date of the refusal.

Definitions
"level 4 on the standard scale": currently £2,500.
"the 1973 Act": s.1.

Commentary
In addition to the punishments of a fine and imprisonment which may be imposed for for offences under s.8 by s.9(1), a convicting court may make any one or more of the following orders:
 (a) an order cancelling the defendant's licence to keep a dog breeding establishment;
 (b) an order disqualifying him from keeping such an establishment which requires licensing; and
 (c) an order disqualifying him from keeping a dog of a kind described in the order (subss.(2), (4)).

Any order made is appealable to the Crown Court and may be suspended pending an appeal (subs.(3)).

An order under subs.(2)(c) (para.(c) above) may contain provisions about the future custody of a dog in the defendant's care and payment for its upkeep (subs.(5)). Subsections (6) and (7) create offences for contravention of an order under subss.(2)(c) or (5) and lay down maximum punishments.

Subsection (8) deals with situations where a dog which is the subject of an order under subs.(4) is not owned by the convicted person.

Subsections (9) and (10) specify the procedures to be adopted where a person disqualified under subs.(2)(c) applies to the court to terminate the disqualification.

Further References
Home Office Circular 53/99, Annex B, para.6, at pp.461–462.

10. Repeals
The Schedule (repeals, including repeals of spent enactments) has effect.

11. Short title, commencement and extent
(1) This Act may be cited as the Breeding and Sale of Dogs (Welfare) Act 1999.

(2) This Act shall come into force at the end of the period of six months beginning with the day on which it was passed.

(3) This Act does not extend to Northern Ireland.

Commentary
The Act was passed on June 30, 1999 and therefore came into force on December 30, 1999.

Schedule – Repeals
Chapter
1973 c. 60.

Short title
The Breeding of Dogs Act 1973.

Extent of repeal
In section 1, in subsection (2), the words "under this Act" and the words from "and on payment" to "determine" and, in subsection (4)(b), the words "(so far as necessary)".

In section 5, in subsection (1), the words from the beginning to "Provided that" and, in subsection (2), the definitions of "breeding establishment" and, in Scotland, "breeding or rearing establishment".
Section 6.

. . .

Chapter
1991 c. 64.

Short title
The Breeding of Dogs Act 1991.

Extent of repeal
Section 2(3).

HUNTING ACT 2004

c. 37

Arrangement of sections

PART 1

Offences

1. Hunting wild mammals with dogs
2. Exempt hunting
3. Hunting: assistance
4. Hunting: defence
5. Hare coursing

PART 2

Enforcement

6. Penalty
7. Arrest
8. Search and seizure
9. Forfeiture
10. Offence by body corporate

PART 3

General

11. Interpretation

Schedule 1: Exempt Hunting

Hunting Act 2004

PART 1 – OFFENCES

1. Hunting wild mammals with dogs
A person commits an offence if he hunts a wild mammal with a dog, unless his hunting is exempt.

Definition
"*wild mammal*": s.11.

Commentary
This section creates the offence of hunting a wild mammal, unless the hunting is exempt (see Sch.1 and commentary below).

The question of the burden of proof in establishing whether or not an offence has been committed under the section was raised in *DPP v Wright; R. (on the application of Scott) v Taunton Deane Magistrates' Court* **[2009] EWHC 105 (Admin)**.

2. Exempt hunting
(1) Hunting is exempt if it is within a class specified in Schedule 1.
(2) The Secretary of State may by order amend Schedule 1 so as to vary a class of exempt hunting.

Commentary
Subsection (1) determines which types of hunting are exempt by reference to Sch. 1, and subs.(2) empowers the Secretary of State (at present, for Environment, Food and Rural Affairs) to vary the classes of exempt hunting.

3. Hunting: assistance
(1) A person commits an offence if he knowingly permits land which belongs to him to be entered or used in the course of the commission of an offence under section 1.
(2) A person commits an offence if he knowingly permits a dog which belongs to him to be used in the course of the commission of an offence under section 1.

Commentary
Subsection (1) makes a person who knowingly allows land which belongs to him to be entered or used for the commission of an offence under s.1 himself guilty of an offence.

"Knowingly" is not defined but implies actual knowledge of what is going on. Section 11 defines what is meant by land belonging to a person.

4. Hunting: defence

It is a defence for a person charged with an offence under section 1 in respect of hunting to show that he reasonably believed that the hunting was exempt.

Commentary

Section 4 provides that a reasonable belief that hunting is exempt is a defence to a charge of committing an offence under s.1. What is reasonable will vary with the circumstances and will be for the court to decide.

5. Hare coursing

(1) A person commits an offence if he—
 (a) participates in a hare coursing event,
 (b) attends a hare coursing event,
 (c) knowingly facilitates a hare coursing event, or
 (d) permits land which belongs to him to be used for the purposes of a hare coursing event.

(2) Each of the following persons commits an offence if a dog participates in a hare coursing event—
 (a) any person who enters the dog for the event,
 (b) any person who permits the dog to be entered, and
 (c) any person who controls or handles the dog in the course of or for the purposes of the event.

(3) A "hare coursing event" is a competition in which dogs are, by the use of live hares, assessed as to skill in hunting hares.

Definition

"hare coursing event": subs.(3).

Commentary

Section 5 has the effect of rendering hare coursing illegal and any person doing anything specified in subss.(2) and (3) commits an offence.

Hunting Act 2004

PART 2 – ENFORCEMENT

6. Penalty

A person guilty of an offence under this Act shall be liable on summary conviction to a fine not exceeding level 5 on the standard scale.

Definition
"level 5 on the standard scale": currently £5000.

Commentary
Section 6 prescribes the maximum penalty for conviction of an offence under Part 1 of the Act. The current level 5 fine is £5,000.

7. Arrest

A constable without a warrant may arrest a person whom he reasonably suspects—
 (a) to have committed an offence under section 1 or 5(1)(a), (b) or (2),
 (b) to be committing an offence under any of those provisions, or
 (c) to be about to commit an offence under any of those provisions.

Commentary
Section 7 gives a police constable power to arrest a person whom he reasonably believes has committed, is committing or is about to commit an offence under ss.1, 5(1)(a) or (b) or 5(2).

8. Search and seizure

(1) This section applies where a constable reasonably suspects that a person ("the suspect") is committing or has committed an offence under Part 1 of this Act.

(2) If the constable reasonably believes that evidence of the offence is likely to be found on the suspect, the constable may stop the suspect and search him.

(3) If the constable reasonably believes that evidence of the offence is likely to be found on or in a vehicle, animal or other thing of which the suspect appears to be in possession or control, the constable may stop and search the vehicle, animal or other thing.

(4) A constable may seize and detain a vehicle, animal or other thing if he reasonably believes that—

(a) it may be used as evidence in criminal proceedings for an offence under Part 1 of this Act, or
(b) it may be made the subject of an order under section 9.

(5) For the purposes of exercising a power under this section a constable may enter—
(a) land;
(b) premises other than a dwelling;
(c) a vehicle.

(6) The exercise of a power under this section does not require a warrant.

Commentary
Section 8 gives powers to a constable to search for, seize and detain evidence relating to the commission of an offence under Part 1. No search warrant is required.

9. Forfeiture

(1) A court which convicts a person of an offence under Part 1 of this Act may order the forfeiture of any dog or hunting article which—
(a) was used in the commission of the offence, or
(b) was in the possession of the person convicted at the time of his arrest.

(2) A court which convicts a person of an offence under Part 1 of this Act may order the forfeiture of any vehicle which was used in the commission of the offence.

(3) In subsection (1) "hunting article" means anything designed or adapted for use in connection with—
(a) hunting a wild mammal, or
(b) hare coursing.

(4) A forfeiture order—
(a) may include such provision about the treatment of the dog, vehicle or article forfeited as the court thinks appropriate, and
(b) subject to provision made under paragraph (a), shall be treated as requiring any person who is in possession of the dog, vehicle or article to surrender it to a constable as soon as is reasonably practicable.

(5) Where a forfeited dog, vehicle or article is retained by or surrendered to a constable, the police force of which the constable is a member shall ensure that such arrangements are made for its destruction or disposal—

(a) as are specified in the forfeiture order, or
(b) where no arrangements are specified in the order, as seem to the police force to be appropriate.

(6) The court which makes a forfeiture order may order the return of the forfeited dog, vehicle or article on an application made—
(a) by a person who claims to have an interest in the dog, vehicle or article (other than the person on whose conviction the order was made), and
(b) before the dog, vehicle or article has been destroyed or finally disposed of under subsection (5).

(7) A person commits an offence if he fails to—
(a) comply with a forfeiture order, or
(b) co-operate with a step taken for the purpose of giving effect to a forfeiture order.

Definition
"hunting article": subs.(3).

Commentary
Section 9 empowers a court which convicts a person of an offence under Part 1 to forfeit any dog or hunting article used in the commission of the offence or in the possession of the convicted person at the time of his arrest. The court may also order the forfeiture of any vehicle used in the commission of the offence. Subsection (3) defines a "hunting article" as anything designed or adapted for use in connection with hunting a wild mammal or hare coursing. Subsections (4) to (6) make detailed provisions about the destruction or disposal of forfeited articles. Subsection (7) makes it an offence to fail to comply with a forfeiture order or to co-operate in the execution of a forfeiture order.

10. Offence by body corporate

(1) This section applies where an offence under this Act is committed by a body corporate with the consent or connivance of an officer of the body.

(2) The officer, as well as the body, shall be guilty of the offence.

(3) In subsection (1) a reference to an officer of a body corporate includes a reference to—
(a) a director, manager or secretary,

Hunting Act 2004

(b) a person purporting to act as a director, manager or secretary, and
(c) if the affairs of the body are managed by its members, a member.

Commentary
Section 10 provides that, where a corporate body commits an offence under Part 1, an officer (director, manager or secretary or a person acting in that capacity, or a member if the body is managed by its members) is also guilty of an offence if he consents to, or connives at the commission of, the offence.

PART 3 – GENERAL

11. Interpretation

(1) In this Act "wild mammal" includes, in particular—
(a) a wild mammal which has been bred or tamed for any purpose,
(b) a wild mammal which is in captivity or confinement,
(c) a wild mammal which has escaped or been released from captivity or confinement, and
(d) any mammal which is living wild.

(2) For the purposes of this Act a reference to a person hunting a wild mammal with a dog includes, in particular, any case where—
(a) a person engages or participates in the pursuit of a wild mammal, and
(b) one or more dogs are employed in that pursuit (whether or not by him and whether or not under his control or direction).

(3) For the purposes of this Act land belongs to a person if he—
(a) owns an interest in it,
(b) manages or controls it, or
(c) occupies it.

(4) For the purposes of this Act a dog belongs to a person if he—
(a) owns it,
(b) is in charge of it, or
(c) has control of it.

. . .

Commentary
Section 11 provides for interpretation of terms and phrases in the Act.

Hunting Act 2004

SCHEDULE 1

Section 2   EXEMPT HUNTING

Stalking and flushing out

1.—(1) Stalking a wild mammal, or flushing it out of cover, is exempt hunting if the conditions in this paragraph are satisfied.

(2) The first condition is that the stalking or flushing out is undertaken for the purpose of—
- (a) preventing or reducing serious damage which the wild mammal would otherwise cause—
  - (i) to livestock,
  - (ii) to game birds or wild birds (within the meaning of section 27 of the Wildlife and Countryside Act 1981 (c. 69)),
  - (iii) to food for livestock,
  - (iv) to crops (including vegetables and fruit),
  - (v) to growing timber,
  - (vi) to fisheries,
  - (vii) to other property, or
  - (viii) to the biological diversity of an area (within the meaning of the United Nations Environmental Programme Convention on Biological Diversity of 1992),
- (b) obtaining meat to be used for human or animal consumption, or
- (c) participation in a field trial.

(3) In subparagraph (2)(c) "field trial" means a competition (other than a hare coursing event within the meaning of section 5) in which dogs—
- (a) flush animals out of cover or retrieve animals that have been shot (or both), and
- (b) are assessed as to their likely usefulness in connection with shooting.

(4) The second condition is that the stalking or flushing out takes place on land—
- (a) which belongs to the person doing the stalking or flushing out, or
- (b) which he has been given permission to use for the purpose by the occupier or, in the case of unoccupied land, by a person to whom it belongs.

(5) The third condition is that the stalking or flushing out does not involve the use of more than two dogs.

(6) The fourth condition is that the stalking or flushing out does not involve the use of a dog below ground otherwise than in accordance with paragraph 2 below.

(7) The fifth condition is that—
- (a) reasonable steps are taken for the purpose of ensuring that as soon as possible after being found or flushed out the wild mammal is shot dead by a competent person, and
- (b) in particular, each dog used in the stalking or flushing out is kept under sufficiently close control to ensure that it does not prevent or obstruct achievement of the objective in paragraph (a).

Use of dogs below ground to protect birds for shooting

2.—(1) The use of a dog below ground in the course of stalking or flushing out is in accordance with this paragraph if the conditions in this paragraph are satisfied.

(2) The first condition is that the stalking or flushing out is undertaken for the purpose of preventing or reducing serious damage to game birds or wild birds (within the meaning of section 27 of the Wildlife and Countryside Act 1981 (c. 69)) which a person is keeping or preserving for the purpose of their being shot.

(3) The second condition is that the person doing the stalking or flushing out—
- (a) has with him written evidence—
  - (i) that the land on which the stalking or flushing out takes place belongs to him, or
  - (ii) that he has been given permission to use that land for the purpose by the occupier or, in the case of unoccupied land, by a person to whom it belongs, and
- (b) makes the evidence immediately available for inspection by a constable who asks to see it.

(4) The third condition is that the stalking or flushing out does not involve the use of more than one dog below ground at any one time.

(5) In so far as stalking or flushing out is undertaken with the use of a dog below ground in accordance with this paragraph, paragraph 1 shall have effect as if for the condition in paragraph 1(7) there were substituted the condition that—
- (a) reasonable steps are taken for the purpose of ensuring that as soon as possible after being found the wild mammal is flushed out from below ground,

(b) reasonable steps are taken for the purpose of ensuring that as soon as possible after being flushed out from below ground the wild mammal is shot dead by a competent person,
(c) in particular, the dog is brought under sufficiently close control to ensure that it does not prevent or obstruct achievement of the objective in paragraph (b),
(d) reasonable steps are taken for the purpose of preventing injury to the dog, and
(e) the manner in which the dog is used complies with any code of practice which is issued or approved for the purpose of this paragraph by the Secretary of State.

Rats

3. The hunting of rats is exempt if it takes place on land—
   (a) which belongs to the hunter, or
   (b) which he has been given permission to use for the purpose by the occupier or, in the case of unoccupied land, by a person to whom it belongs.

Rabbits

4. The hunting of rabbits is exempt if it takes place on land—
   (a) which belongs to the hunter, or
   (b) which he has been given permission to use for the purpose by the occupier or, in the case of unoccupied land, by a person to whom it belongs.

Retrieval of hares

5. The hunting of a hare which has been shot is exempt if it takes place on land—
   (a) which belongs to the hunter, or
   (b) which he has been given permission to use for the purpose of hunting hares by the occupier or, in the case of unoccupied land, by a person to whom it belongs.

Falconry

6. Flushing a wild mammal from cover is exempt hunting if undertaken—
   (a) for the purpose of enabling a bird of prey to hunt the wild mammal, and

(b) on land which belongs to the hunter or which he has been given permission to use for the purpose by the occupier or, in the case of unoccupied land, by a person to whom it belongs.

Recapture of wild mammal

7.—(1) The hunting of a wild mammal which has escaped or been released from captivity or confinement is exempt if the conditions in this paragraph are satisfied.

(2) The first condition is that the hunting takes place—
(a) on land which belongs to the hunter,
(b) on land which he has been given permission to use for the purpose by the occupier or, in the case of unoccupied land, by a person to whom it belongs, or
(c) with the authority of a constable.

(3) The second condition is that—
(a) reasonable steps are taken for the purpose of ensuring that as soon as possible after being found the wild mammal is recaptured or shot dead by a competent person, and
(b) in particular, each dog used in the hunt is kept under sufficiently close control to ensure that it does not prevent or obstruct achievement of the objective in paragraph (a).

(4) The third condition is that the wild mammal—
(a) was not released for the purpose of being hunted, and
(b) was not, for that purpose, permitted to escape.

Rescue of wild mammal

8.—(1) The hunting of a wild mammal is exempt if the conditions in this paragraph are satisfied.

(2) The first condition is that the hunter reasonably believes that the wild mammal is or may be injured.

(3) The second condition is that the hunting is undertaken for the purpose of relieving the wild mammal's suffering.

(4) The third condition is that the hunting does not involve the use of more than two dogs.

(5) The fourth condition is that the hunting does not involve the use of a dog below ground.

(6) The fifth condition is that the hunting takes place—
(a) on land which belongs to the hunter,
(b) on land which he has been given permission to use for the purpose by the occupier or, in the case of unoccupied land, by a person to whom it belongs, or

(c) with the authority of a constable.

(7) The sixth condition is that—
(a) reasonable steps are taken for the purpose of ensuring that as soon as possible after the wild mammal is found appropriate action (if any) is taken to relieve its suffering, and
(b) in particular, each dog used in the hunt is kept under sufficiently close control to ensure that it does not prevent or obstruct achievement of the objective in paragraph (a).

(8) The seventh condition is that the wild mammal was not harmed for the purpose of enabling it to be hunted in reliance upon this paragraph.

Research and observation

9.—(1) The hunting of a wild mammal is exempt if the conditions in this paragraph are satisfied.

(2) The first condition is that the hunting is undertaken for the purpose of or in connection with the observation or study of the wild mammal.

(3) The second condition is that the hunting does not involve the use of more than two dogs.

(4) The third condition is that the hunting does not involve the use of a dog below ground.

(5) The fourth condition is that the hunting takes place on land—
(a) which belongs to the hunter, or
(b) which he has been given permission to use for the purpose by the occupier or, in the case of unoccupied land, by a person to whom it belongs.

(6) The fifth condition is that each dog used in the hunt is kept under sufficiently close control to ensure that it does not injure the wild mammal.

. . .

Commentary
Schedule 1 defines exempt hunting in great detail.
The question of the burden of proof in establishing whether or not an exemption applies was raised in *DPP v Wright; R. (on the application of Scott) v Taunton Deane Magistrates' Court* [2009] EWHC 105 (Admin).

CLEAN NEIGHBOURHOODS AND ENVIRONMENT ACT 2005

c. 16

Arrangement of sections

PART 6 – DOGS

Chapter 1: Controls on dogs

Dog control orders

55. Power to make dog control orders
56. Dog control orders: supplementary
57. Land to which Chapter 1 applies
58. Primary and secondary authorities

Fixed penalty notices

59. Fixed penalty notices
60. Amount of fixed penalties
61. Power to require name and address
62. Community support officers etc

Supplementary

63. Overlapping powers
64. Byelaws
65. Dogs (Fouling of Land) Act 1996

General

66. "Appropriate person"

Clean Neighbourhoods and Environment Act 2005

67. Regulations and orders

Chapter 2: Stray dogs

68. Termination of police responsibility for stray dogs

---

55. Power to make dog control orders

(1) A primary or secondary authority may in accordance with this Chapter make an order providing for an offence or offences relating to the control of dogs in respect of any land in its area to which this Chapter applies.

(2) An order under subsection (1) is to be known as a "dog control order".

(3) For the purposes of this Chapter an offence relates to the control of dogs if it relates to one of the following matters—
  (a) fouling of land by dogs and the removal of dog faeces;
  (b) the keeping of dogs on leads;
  (c) the exclusion of dogs from land;
  (d) the number of dogs which a person may take on to any land.

(4) An offence provided for in a dog control order must be an offence which is prescribed for the purposes of this section by regulations made by the appropriate person.

(5) Regulations under subsection (4) may in particular—
  (a) specify all or part of the wording to be used in a dog control order for the purpose of providing for any offence;
  (b) permit a dog control order to specify the times at which, or periods during which, an offence is to apply;
  (c) provide for an offence to be defined by reference to failure to comply with the directions of a person of a description specified in the regulations.

(6) A dog control order may specify the land in respect of which it applies specifically or by description.

(7) A dog control order may be revoked or amended by the authority which made it; but this Chapter applies in relation to any amendment of a dog control order as if it were the making of a new order.

Definitions

"*appropriate person*": s.66.
"*dog control order*": subs.(2).
"*land*": s.57.
"*primary or secondary authority*": s.58.

Commentary

This section empowers primary and secondary authorities to make dog control orders which create offences relating to the fouling of land by dogs, the removal of dog faeces, the keeping of dogs on leads, the exclusion of dogs from land and the number of dogs a person may take on to any land. The area or areas of land to which an order applies are specified by the order-making authority. The offences are prescribed by the "appropriate person" (the Secretary of State in England and the National Assembly in Wales) in regulations.

The provisions of this section effectively supersede the Dogs (Fouling of Land) Act 1996 (which is repealed) and the powers of local authorities to make byelaws relating to the control of dogs.

56. Dog control orders: supplementary

(1) The appropriate person must by regulations prescribe the penalties, or maximum penalties, which may be provided for in a dog control order in relation to any offence.

(2) Regulations under subsection (1) may not in any case permit a dog control order to provide for a penalty other than a fine not exceeding level 3 on the standard scale in relation to any offence.

(3) The appropriate person must by regulations prescribe such other requirements relating to the content and form of a dog control order as the appropriate person thinks fit.

(4) The appropriate person must by regulations prescribe the procedure to be followed by a primary or secondary authority before and after making a dog control order.

(5) Regulations under subsection (4) must in particular include provision as to—
- (a) consultation to be undertaken before a dog control order is made;
- (b) the publicising of a dog control order after it has been made.

Clean Neighbourhoods and Environment Act 2005

Definitions
"appropriate person": s.66.
"dog control order": s.55(2).
"primary or secondary authority": s.58.

Commentary
This section makes supplementary provision for dog control orders by giving the "appropriate person" (the Secretary of State in England and the National Assembly in Wales) power to make regulations relating, among other matters, to the form and content of the orders.

57. Land to which Chapter 1 applies

(1) Subject to this section, this Chapter applies to any land which is open to the air and to which the public are entitled or permitted to have access (with or without payment).

(2) For the purposes of this section, any land which is covered is to be treated as land which is "open to the air" if it is open to the air on at least one side.

(3) The appropriate person may by order designate land as land to which this Chapter does not apply (generally or for such purposes as may be specified in the order).

(4) Land may be designated under subsection (3) specifically or by description.

(5) Where a private Act confers powers on a person other than a primary or secondary authority for the regulation of any land, that person may, by notice in writing given to the primary and secondary authorities in whose area the land is situated, exclude the application of this Chapter to that land.

Definitions
"primary or secondary authority": s.58.

Commentary
This section defines the land to which Chapter 1 of Part 6 of the Act (ss.55–67) applies. In effect, the definition comprises land in the open air to which the public are entitled or allowed to have access, with or without payment. Land is still in the open air so long as one side is uncovered.

Where a person has powers under a private Act to control dogs, he may exclude the area over which he has control from designation under Chapter 1 by giving written notice to the primary or secondary authority.

58. Primary and secondary authorities

(1) Each of the following is a "primary authority" for the purposes of this Chapter—
  (a) a district council in England;
  (b) a county council in England for an area for which there is no district council;
  (c) a London borough council;
  (d) the Common Council of the City of London;
  (e) the Council of the Isles of Scilly;
  (f) a county or county borough council in Wales.

(2) Each of the following is a "secondary authority" for the purposes of this Chapter—
  (a) a parish council in England;
  (b) a community council in Wales.

(3) The appropriate person may by order designate any person or body exercising functions under an enactment as a secondary authority for the purposes of this Chapter in respect of an area specified in the order.

Commentary

This section defines the local authorities which are primary and secondary authorities for the purposes of Chapter 1 of Part 6 of the Act. The "appropriate person" (the Secretary of State in England and the National Assembly in Wales) may designate a person or body exercising functions under statutory powers as a secondary authority for the purposes of the Chapter in respect of an area of land specified in the order.

59. Fixed penalty notices

(1) This section applies where on any occasion—
  (a) an authorised officer of a primary or secondary authority has reason to believe that a person has committed an offence under a dog control order made by that authority; or
  (b) an authorised officer of a secondary authority has reason to believe that a person has in its area committed an offence under a dog control order made by a primary authority.

Clean Neighbourhoods and Environment Act 2005

(2) The authorised officer may give that person a notice offering him the opportunity of discharging any liability to conviction for the offence by payment of a fixed penalty.

(3) A fixed penalty payable under this section is payable to the primary or secondary authority whose officer gave the notice.

(4) Where a person is given a notice under this section in respect of an offence—
  (a) no proceedings may be instituted for that offence before the expiration of the period of fourteen days following the date of the notice; and
  (b) he may not be convicted of that offence if he pays the fixed penalty before the expiration of that period.

(5) A notice under this section must give such particulars of the circumstances alleged to constitute the offence as are necessary for giving reasonable information of the offence.

(6) A notice under this section must also state—
  (a) the period during which, by virtue of subsection (4), proceedings will not be taken for the offence;
  (b) the amount of the fixed penalty; and
  (c) the person to whom and the address at which the fixed penalty may be paid.

(7) Without prejudice to payment by any other method, payment of the fixed penalty may be made by pre-paying and posting a letter containing the amount of the penalty (in cash or otherwise) to the person mentioned in subsection (6)(c) at the address so mentioned.

(8) Where a letter is sent in accordance with subsection (7) payment is to be regarded as having been made at the time at which that letter would be delivered in the ordinary course of post.

(9) The form of a notice under this section is to be such as the appropriate person may by order prescribe.

(10) In any proceedings a certificate which—
  (a) purports to be signed on behalf of the chief finance officer of a primary or secondary authority, and
  (b) states that payment of a fixed penalty was or was not received by a date specified in the certificate,
is evidence of the facts stated.

(11) In this section—
"authorised officer", in relation to a primary or secondary authority, means—

(a) an employee of the authority who is authorised in writing by the authority for the purpose of giving notices under this section;
(b) any person who, in pursuance of arrangements made with the authority, has the function of giving such notices and is authorised in writing by the authority to perform that function; and
(c) any employee of such a person who is authorised in writing by the authority for the purpose of giving such notices;
"chief finance officer", in relation to a primary or secondary authority, means the person having responsibility for the financial affairs of the authority.

(12) The appropriate person may by regulations prescribe conditions to be satisfied by a person before a secondary authority may authorise him in writing for the purpose of giving notices under this section.

Definitions
"appropriate person": s.66.
"authorised officer": subs.(11).
"chief finance officer": subs.(11).
"dog control order": s.55(2).
"primary or secondary authority": s.58.

Commentary
This section makes provision for the issue of a fixed penalty notice by an authorised officer of a primary or secondary authority where he has reason to believe that an offence under a dog control order has been committed. The section also sets out the procedure to be followed and empowers the "appropriate person" (the Secretary of State in England and the National Assembly in Wales) to prescribe the form of a fixed penalty notice. Subsection (12) empowers the appropriate person to prescribe conditions which must be satisfied by a person before a secondary authority may authorise him in writing to give fixed penalty notices.

60. Amount of fixed penalties

(1) The amount of a fixed penalty payable to a primary or secondary authority in pursuance of a notice under section 59 in respect of an offence under a dog control order—
(a) is the amount specified by the authority which made the order;
(b) if no amount is so specified, is £75.

Clean Neighbourhoods and Environment Act 2005

(2) A primary or secondary authority may under subsection (1)(a) specify different amounts in relation to different offences.

(3) A primary or secondary authority may make provision for treating a fixed penalty payable to that authority in pursuance of a notice under section 59 as having been paid if a lesser amount is paid before the end of a period specified by the authority.

(4) The appropriate person may by regulations make provision in connection with the powers conferred on primary and secondary authorities under subsections (1)(a) and (3).

(5) Regulations under subsection (4) may (in particular)—
 (a) require an amount specified under subsection (1)(a) to fall within a range prescribed in the regulations;
 (b) restrict the extent to which, and the circumstances in which, a primary or secondary authority can make provision under subsection (3).

(6) The appropriate person may by order substitute a different amount for the amount for the time being specified in subsection (1)(b).

Definition
"*appropriate person*": s.66.
"*primary or secondary authority*": s.58.

Commentary
Section 60 makes provision for setting the amount of a fixed penalty for breach of a dog control order. The maximum is the amount specified by the order-making authority or, if no such amount is specified, £75. Subsection (3) enables the order-making authority to offer a discount for prompt payment. Subsection (5) empowers the "appropriate person" (the Secretary of State in England and the National Assembly in Wales) to specify the range within which the amount of a fixed penalty must fall and to restrict the extent to which, and circumstances within which, the order-making authority can offer a prompt payment discount.

61. Power to require name and address

(1) If an authorised officer of a primary or secondary authority proposes to give a person a notice under section 59, the officer may require the person to give him his name and address.

(2) A person commits an offence if—

(a) he fails to give his name and address when required to do so under subsection (1), or
(b) he gives a false or inaccurate name or address in response to a requirement under that subsection.

(3) A person guilty of an offence under subsection (2) is liable on summary conviction to a fine not exceeding level 3 on the standard scale.

(4) In this section "authorised officer" has the same meaning as in section 59.

Definitions
"authorised officer": s.59 and subs.(4).
"level 3 on the standard scale": currently £1,000.
"primary or secondary authority": s.58.

Commentary
Section 61 empowers an authorised officer of an order-making authority to require a person on whom the officer proposes to serve a fixed penalty notice to give his name and address and prescribes the penalty for failing to do so, or for giving a false or inaccurate name or address.

62. Community support officers etc

(1) The Police Reform Act 2002 (c. 30) is amended as follows.

(2) In Schedule 4 (community support officers), in paragraph 1(2), after paragraph (d) insert
   "and
   (e) the power of an authorised officer of a primary or secondary authority, within the meaning of section 59 of the Clean Neighbourhoods and Environment Act 2005, to give a notice under that section (fixed penalty notices in respect of offences under dog control orders)."

(3) In Schedule 5 (accredited persons), in paragraph 1(2), after paragraph (c) insert "and (d) the power of an authorised officer of a primary or secondary authority, within the meaning of section 59 of the Clean Neighbourhoods and Environment Act 2005, to give a notice under that section (fixed penalty notices in respect of offences under dog control orders)."

Clean Neighbourhoods and Environment Act 2005

Definitions
"*accredited person*": s.41 and Part 5, Sch. 4, Police Reform Act 2002.
"*authorised officer*": s.59.
"*community support officer*": s.38 and Part 1, Sch. 4, Police Reform Act 2002.
"*primary or secondary authority*": s.58.

Commentary
This section confers on a community support officer and an accredited person the powers exercisable by an authorised officer of a primary or secondary authority under s.59 of the Act relating to fixed penalty notices.

63. Overlapping powers

(1) Where a primary authority makes a dog control order providing for an offence relating to a matter specified in any of paragraphs (a) to (d) of section 55(3) as respects any land—
   (a) a secondary authority may not make a dog control order providing for any offence which relates to the matter specified in that paragraph as respects that land;
   (b) any dog control order previously made by a secondary authority providing for any offence which relates to the matter specified in that paragraph shall, to the extent that it so provides, cease to have effect.

(2) Where the area of an authority designated as a secondary authority under section 58(3) is to any extent the same as that of a parish or community council, subsection (1) applies in relation to orders made by the designated authority and that council as if the council were a primary authority.

Definitions
"*dog control order*": s.55(2).
"*primary or secondary authority*": s.58.

Commentary
Section 63 contains provisions to avoid overlapping dog control orders being made by primary and secondary authorities. Where a primary authority has made an order, a secondary authority may not do so in respect of the same land and any existing order made by the latter authority over

that land ceases to have effect. The same applies to an order made by an authority designated as a secondary authority under s.58.

64. Byelaws

(1) Where, apart from this subsection, a primary or secondary authority has at any time power to make a byelaw in relation to any matter specified in any of paragraphs (a) to (d) of section 55(3) as respects any land, it may not make such a byelaw if at that time it has power under this Chapter to make a dog control order as respects that land in relation to the matter specified in that paragraph.

(2) Subsection (1) does not affect any byelaw which the authority had power to make at the time it was made.

(3) Where a dog control order is made in relation to any matter specified in any of paragraphs (a) to (d) of section 55(3) as respects any land, any byelaw previously made by a primary or secondary authority which has the effect of making a person guilty of any offence in relation to the matter specified in that paragraph as respects that land shall cease to have that effect.

(4) Where any act or omission would, apart from this subsection, constitute an offence under a dog control order and any byelaw, the act or omission shall not constitute an offence under the byelaw.

Definitions
"dog control order": s.55(2).
"primary or secondary authority": s.58.

Commentary
Section 64 provides that an order-making authority may not make a byelaw in relation to anything specified in s.55(3)(a)–(d) in respect of which it has power to make a dog control order. Subsections (3) and (4) provide, in effect, that any penal provision in a byelaw which is covered by a dog control order ceases to have effect.

The converse of these provisions is that non-penal clauses in a byelaw will continue to apply in an area subject to a dog control order unless and until the local authority revokes or amends those clauses.

65. Dogs (Fouling of Land) Act 1996
The Dogs (Fouling of Land) Act 1996 (c. 20) shall cease to have effect.

Commentary
This section repeals the Dogs (Fouling of Land) Act 1996.

66. "Appropriate person"
In this Chapter, "appropriate person" means—
  (a) the Secretary of State, in relation to England;
  (b) the National Assembly for Wales, in relation to Wales.

Commentary
This section defines "appropriate person" as the Secretary of State (at present for Environment, Food and Rural Affairs) in England and the National Assembly in Wales.

67. Regulations and orders
(1) Any power conferred by this Chapter on the Secretary of State or National Assembly for Wales to make regulations or an order includes—
  (a) power to make different provision for different purposes (including different provision for different authorities or different descriptions of authority);
  (b) power to make consequential, supplementary, incidental and transitional provision and savings.

(2) Any power conferred by this Chapter on the Secretary of State or National Assembly for Wales to make regulations or an order is exercisable by statutory instrument.

(3) The Secretary of State may not make a statutory instrument containing regulations under section 55(4) or 56(1) unless a draft of the instrument has been laid before, and approved by a resolution of, each House of Parliament.

(4) A statutory instrument containing—
  (a) regulations made by the Secretary of State under this Chapter to which subsection (3) does not apply, or
  (b) an order made by the Secretary of State under this Chapter,
is subject to annulment in pursuance of a resolution of either House of Parliament.

Clean Neighbourhoods and Environment Act 2005

Commentary
This section confers on the Secretary of State and the National Assembly for Wales power to make regulations and orders.

68. Termination of police responsibility for stray dogs

(1) Section 3 of the Dogs Act 1906 (c. 32) (seizure of stray dogs by police) shall, subject to subsection (2), cease to have effect.

(2) The repeal in subsection (1) does not apply for the purposes of section 2(2) and (3) of the Dogs (Protection of Livestock) Act 1953 (c. 28).

(3) In section 150 of the Environmental Protection Act 1990 (c. 43) (delivery of stray dogs to police or local authority officer), in subsection (1)—

(a) in paragraph (b), omit sub-paragraph (ii) and the preceding "or";
(b) omit the words from "or the police officer" to "as the case may be,".

(4) In the heading to that section, omit "police or".

. . .

Commentary
This section terminates the police responsibility for stray dogs except in relation to dogs detained for worrying livestock under the Dogs (Protection of Livestock) Act 1953. The section came into force on April 6, 2008 by virtue of the Clean Neighbourhoods and Environment Act 2005 (Commencement No. 5) Order 2008 (SI 2008/956).

Part III

Acts of Parliament Relating to Animals Generally

Performing Animals (Regulation) Act 1925 ss.1–5, 7 225

Cinematograph Films (Animals) Act 1937 s.1 232

Pet Animals Act 1951 ss.1, 4–7 234

Veterinary Surgeons Act 1966 ss.19, 27, Schedule 3 241

Theft Act 1968 ss.1–6, 22, 23, 34 247

Animals Act 1971 ss.2, 3, 5, 6, 8, 9, 11 253

Criminal Damage Act 1971 ss.1, 5, 10 261

Public Health (Control of Disease) Act 1984 ss.55, 74 265

Animals (Scientific Procedures) Act 1986 ss.1, 2, 5, 7, 10, 16, 30, Schedule 1 267

Animal Welfare Act 2006 ss.1–45, 51–62, 68, Schedule 2 274

Fraud Act 2006 ss.1–5 337

Part III

Acts of Parliament Relative to Annesley Generally

PERFORMING ANIMALS (REGULATION) ACT 1925

c. 38

Arrangement of sections

1. Restriction on exhibition and training of performing animals
2. Power of courts to prohibit or restrict exhibition and training of performing animals
3. Power to enter premises
4. Offences and legal proceedings
5. Interpretation, rules, and expenses
7. Exceptions from application of Act

---

1. Restriction on exhibition and training of performing animals

(1) No person shall exhibit or train any performing animal unless he is registered in accordance with this Act.

(2) Every local authority shall keep a register for the purpose of this Act, and any person who exhibits or trains animals as aforesaid on making an application in the prescribed form to the local authority of the district in which he resides, or if he has no fixed place of residence in Great Britain, to the local authority of such one of the prescribed districts as he may choose, and on payment of such fee as appears to the local authority to be appropriate shall be registered under this Act, unless he is a person, who, in pursuance of an order of the court made under this Act, is prohibited from being so registered.

(3) Any application for registration under this Act shall contain such particulars as to the animals and as to the general nature of the performances in which the animals are to be exhibited or for which they are to be trained as may be prescribed, and the particulars so given shall be entered in the register.

(4) The local authority shall give to every person whose name appears on the register kept by them a certificate of registration

in the prescribed form containing the particulars entered in the register.

(5) Every register kept under this Act shall at all reasonable times be open for inspection, and any person shall be entitled to take copies thereof or make extracts therefrom.

(6) Any person entered on the register shall, subject to the provisions of any order made under this Act by any court, be entitled, on making application for the purpose, to have the particulars entered in the register with respect to him varied, and where any such particulars are so varied the existing certificate shall be cancelled and a new certificate issued.

(7) A copy of every certificate of registration issued by a local authority shall be transmitted by the authority to the Secretary of State and shall be available for inspection at all reasonable times.

(8) A local authority may charge such fees as appear to them to be appropriate for inspection of the register, for taking copies thereof or making extracts therefrom or for inspection of copies of certificates of registration issued by them.

Definitions and Meanings
"animal", "exhibit", "local authority", "prescribed" and *"train"*: s.5(1).
"the Secretary of State": the Secretary of State for Environment, Food and Rural Affairs.

Commentary
An exhibitor or trainer of a performing animal is required by this section, but subject to s.7, to register with the local authority. It appears that the authority has no discretion to refuse registration unless the applicant is disqualified from registration under s.4(2) or the application is deficient under the terms of subs.(3).

Registration may be cancelled under s.4(2) and may be affected by a magistrates' order under s.2(1).

A certificate of registration is to be issued (subs.(4)), the register and copies of certificates are to be open to inspection by the public (subss.(5), (7)), and provision is made for variation of the registered particulars (subs.(6)).

Appropriate fees for various matters mentioned in this section may be charged by the local authority (subs.(8)). Other

Performing Animals (Regulation) Act 1925

fees are prescribed by the Performing Animals Rules 1925, art.9, at p.344.

The registration of animals is now provided for in the Animal Welfare Act 2006 s.13(8) of which empowers the appropriate national authority to repeal the section; see p.274 for the 2006 Act.

Further References
For "prescribed districts" (subs.(2)) and "prescribed form" (subs.(4)), see the Performing Animals Rules 1925, arts 2 and 1, at p.343.

2. Power of courts to prohibit or restrict exhibition and training of performing animals

(1) Where it is proved to the satisfaction of a court of summary jurisdiction on a complaint made by a constable or an officer of a local authority that the training or exhibition of any performing animal has been accompanied by cruelty and should be prohibited or allowed only subject to conditions, the court may make an order against the person in respect of whom the complaint is made prohibiting the training or exhibition or imposing such conditions thereon as may be specified by the order.

(2) If any person is aggrieved by the making of such an order or a refusal to make such an order, he may appeal to the Crown Court.

(3) An order made under this Act shall not come into force until seven days after it is made, or, if an appeal has been entered within that period, until the determination of the appeal.

(4) Any court by which an order is made under this section shall cause a copy of the order to be sent as soon as may be after the order comes into force to the local authority by which the person against whom the order is made is registered and to the Secretary of State, and shall cause the particulars of the order to be endorsed upon the certificate held by that person, and that person shall produce his certificate on being so required by the court for the purposes of endorsement. A local authority to which a copy of an order is sent under this section shall enter the particulars of the order on the register.

Definitions and Meanings
"animal", "exhibition", "local authority" and "training": s.5(1).
"the Secretary of State": the Secretary of State for Environment, Food and Rural Affairs.

Performing Animals (Regulation) Act 1925

Commentary
Subsection (1) authorises magistrates, when satisfied that the training or exhibition of performing animals has been accompanied by cruelty, to make an order prohibiting that training or exhibition or imposing conditions on them.

There is a right of appeal to the Crown Court against the order (subs.(2)), copies of it are to be sent to the local authority and to the Secretary of State, and particulars of it are to be endorsed on the registration certificate and entered in the local authority's register (subs.(4)).

3. Power to enter premises

(1) Any officer of a local authority duly authorised in that behalf by the local authority and any constable may—
  (a) enter at all reasonable times and inspect any premises in which any performing animals are being trained or exhibited, or kept for training or exhibition, and any such animals found therein; and
  (b) require any person who he has reason to believe is a trainer or exhibitor of performing animals to produce his certificate.

(2) No constable or such officer as aforesaid shall be entitled under this section to go on or behind the stage during a public performance of performing animals.

Definitions
"animals", "exhibited", "exhibitor", "local authority", "trained" and "trainer": s.5(1).

Commentary
Subsection (1) enables police officers and authorised local authority officers to enter and inspect places where performing animals are being trained or exhibited, and to require production of registration certificates, subject to the proviso in subs.(2).

In law, "premises" will include land which is not built upon.

4. Offences and legal proceedings

(1) If any person—
  (a) not being registered under this Act exhibits or trains any performing animal; or

(b) being registered under this Act exhibits or trains any performing animal with respect to which or in a manner with respect to which he is not registered; or

(c) being a person against whom an order by a court of summary jurisdiction has been made on complaint under this Act, contravenes or fails to comply with the order in any part of Great Britain, whether within or without the area of jurisdiction of that court; or

(d) obstructs or wilfully delays any constable or officer of a local authority in the execution of his powers under this Act as to entry or inspection; or

(e) conceals any animal with a view to avoiding such inspection; or

(f) being a person registered under this Act, on being duly required in pursuance of this Act to produce his certificate under this Act fails without reasonable excuse so to do; or

(g) applies to be registered under this Act when prohibited from being so registered;

he shall be guilty of an offence against this Act and shall be liable on summary conviction upon a complaint made by a constable or an officer of a local authority to a fine not exceeding level 3 on the standard scale.

(2) Where a person is convicted of an offence against this Act, or against the Protection of Animals Act, 1911, as amended by any subsequent enactment, or of an offence under any of sections 4, 5, 6(1) and (2), 7 to 9 and 11 of the Animal Welfare Act 2006, the court before which he is convicted may in addition to or in lieu of imposing any other penalty—

(a) if such person is registered under this Act order that his name be removed from the register;

(b) order that such person shall either permanently or for such time as may be specified in the order be disqualified for being registered under this Act;

and where such an order is made, the provisions of subsections (2), (3) and (4) of section two of this Act shall apply to the order as they apply to an order made under that section.

Definitions and Meanings
"animal", "exhibits", "local authority" and *"trains"*: s.5(1).
"level 3 on the standard scale": currently £1,000.

Commentary

Subsection (1) lists the several acts and omissions for which offences under the Act are created, and prescribes a maximum fine.

Subsection (2) enables a convicting court, in addition to fining an offender, to order removal of his name from the local authority's register and to disqualify him from being registered for as long as it thinks fit. The provisions of s.2(2)–(4) apply to such orders.

Further References

For the provisions of the Animal Welfare Act 2006, see pp.274–336. The Protection of Animals Act 1911 was almost wholly repealed by the 2006 Act. The reference in subs.(2) remains necessary to cover offences under the 1911 Act which were committed before the repeal on April 6, 2007.

5. Interpretation, rules, and expenses

(1) For the purposes of this Act—

The expression "animal" does not include invertebrates:

The expression "exhibit" means exhibit at any entertainment to which the public are admitted, whether on payment of money or otherwise, and the expression "train" means train for the purpose of any such exhibition, and the expressions "exhibitor" and "trainer" have respectively the corresponding meanings:

The expression "local authority" means—

As respects the City of London, the common council;

As respects any London borough, the council of the borough;

As respects any county or metropolitan district, the council of the county or district;

The expression "prescribed" means prescribed by rules made by the Secretary of State.

(2) The Secretary of State may make rules for prescribing anything which is to be prescribed under this Act, and as to the execution and performance by local authorities of their powers and duties under this Act, and generally for carrying this Act into effect.

(3) Any expenses of a local authority under this Act, so far as not covered by fees, shall be defrayed in the case of the council of a county, out of the county fund, and in the case of the council of a metropolitan district or London borough, out of the general rate fund.

Performing Animals (Regulation) Act 1925

Rules
The Performing Animals Rules 1925, for which see pp.343–345, were made under the powers given in subs.(2).

Commentary
Subsection (1) defines a number of terms used earlier in the Act. The subs.(2) rules are referred to above.

7. Exceptions from application of Act
This Act shall not apply to the training of animals for bona fide military, police, agricultural or sporting purposes, or the exhibition of any animals so trained.

Definitions
"animals", "exhibition", "trained" and *"training":* s.5(1)

Commentary
By this section the types of training and exhibition of animals there described are totally excluded from the operation of the Act.

CINEMATOGRAPH FILMS (ANIMALS) ACT 1937

c. 59

Arrangement of sections

1. Prohibition of films involving cruelty to animals

1. Prohibition of films involving cruelty to animals

(1) No person shall exhibit to the public, or supply to any person for public exhibition (whether by him or by another person), any cinematograph film (whether produced in Great Britain or elsewhere) if in connection with the production of the film any scene represented in the film was organised or directed in such a way as to involve the cruel infliction of pain or terror on any animal or the cruel goading of any animal to fury.

(2) In any proceedings brought under this Act in respect of any film, the court may (without prejudice to any other mode of proof) infer from the film as exhibited to the public or supplied for public exhibition, as the case may be, that a scene represented in the film as so exhibited or supplied was organised or directed in such a way as to involve the cruel infliction of pain or terror on an animal or the cruel goading of an animal to fury, but (whether the court draws such an inference or not) it shall be a defence for the defendant to prove that he believed, and had reasonable cause to believe, that no scene so represented was so organised or directed.

(3) Any person contravening the provisions of this section shall be liable on summary conviction to a fine not exceeding level 3 on the standard scale, or to imprisonment for a term not exceeding 51 weeks or to both such fine and such imprisonment.

(4) For the purposes of this Act—

(a) a cinematograph film shall be deemed to be exhibited to the public when, and only when, it is exhibited in a place to which for the time being members of the general public as such have access, whether on payment of money or otherwise, and the expression "public exhibition" shall be construed accordingly; and

(b) in relation to England and Wales, the expression "animal" means a protected animal within the meaning of the Animal Welfare Act 2006.

Definitions and Meanings

"animal": see, by virtue of subs.(4)(b), the Animal Welfare Act 2006 s.2, at p.278.
"exhibited to the public": subs.(4)(a).
"level 3 on the standard scale": currently £1,000.
"public exhibition": subs.(4)(a).

Commentary

Subsection (1) prohibits the public exhibition and supply of films in the making of which cruelty was inflicted on animals.

Subsection (2) allows the court before which a prosecution is brought to make an inference of cruelty from scenes depicted in the film. It also provides the defendant with a defence based on a reasonable belief that cruelty was absent.

Subsection (3) sets out the maximum punishments for contravening subs.(1), and subs.(4) defines a number of terms used earlier in the Act.

"51 weeks" is substituted for "three months" in s.1(3) by para.9 of Sch.26 to the Criminal Justice Act 2003, from a day to be appointed.

PET ANIMALS ACT 1951

c. 35

Arrangement of sections

1. Licensing of pet shops
4. Inspection of pet shops
5. Offences and disqualifications
6. Power of local authority to prosecute
7. Interpretation

1. Licensing of pet shops

(1) No person shall keep a pet shop except under the authority of a licence granted in accordance with the provisions of this Act.

(2) Every local authority may, on application being made to them for that purpose by a person who is not for the time being disqualified from keeping a pet shop, and on payment of such fee as may be determined by the local authority, grant a licence to that person to keep a pet shop at such premises in their area as may be specified in the application and subject to compliance with such conditions as may be specified in the licence.

(3) In determining whether to grant a licence for the keeping of a pet shop by any person at any premises, a local authority shall in particular (but without prejudice to their discretion to withhold a licence on other grounds) have regard to the need for securing—
  (a) that animals will at all times be kept in accommodation suitable as respects size, temperature, lighting, ventilation and cleanliness;
  (b) that animals will be adequately supplied with suitable food and drink and (so far as necessary) visited at suitable intervals;
  (c) that animals, being mammals, will not be sold at too early an age;
  (d) that all reasonable precautions will be taken to prevent the spread among animals of infectious diseases;
  (e) that appropriate steps will be taken in case of fire or other emergency;

Pet Animals Act 1951

and shall specify such conditions in the licence, if granted by them, as appear to the local authority necessary or expedient in the particular case for securing all or any of the objects specified in paragraphs (a) to (e) of this subsection.

(3A) No condition may be specified under subsection (3) of this section in so far as it relates to any matter in relation to which requirements or prohibitions are or could be imposed by or under the Regulatory Reform (Fire Safety) Order 2005.

(4) Any person aggrieved by the refusal of a local authority to grant such a licence, or by any condition subject to which such a licence is proposed to be granted, may appeal to a court of summary jurisdiction having jurisdiction in the place in which the premises are situated; and the court may on such an appeal give such directions with respect to the issue of a licence or, as the case may be, with respect to the conditions subject to which a licence is to be granted as they think proper.

(5) Any such licence shall (according to the applicants' requirements) relate to the year in which it is granted or to the next following year. In the former case, the licence shall come into force at the beginning of the day on which it is granted, and in the latter case it shall come into force at the beginning of the next following year.

(6) Subject to the provisions hereinafter contained with respect to cancellation, any such licence shall remain in force until the end of the year to which it relates and shall then expire.

(7) Any person who contravenes the provisions of subsection (1) of this section shall be guilty of an offence; and if any condition subject to which a licence is granted in accordance with the provisions of this Act is contravened or not complied with the person to whom the licence was granted shall be guilty of an offence.

. . .

Definitions
"*animals*": s.7(3).
"*keep a pet shop*": s.7(1).
"*local authority*": s.7(3).

Commentary
This section makes it an offence to keep a pet shop without a licence from the local authority (subs.(1), (7)). The conditions which may be attached to a licence are set out in subs.(3);

contravention of conditions is also an offence (subs.(7)). Punishments for offences are regulated by s.5.

Subsection (4) provides rights of appeal against refusal of a licence or conditions attached to it.

Subsections (5) and (6) regulate the duration of licences; the meaning of these provisions is that a licence runs, at the applicant's choice, from the day it is granted to the end of the current year, or from the beginning of the next year to the end of that year.

For instances where a person will be disqualified from keeping a pet shop, and will thereby be ineligible for a licence under subs.(2), see s.5(3) below. A person disqualified under this Act will also be prevented from obtaining licences under the Animal Boarding Establishments Act 1963 (s.1(2), at p.98) or the Breeding of Dogs Act 1973 (s.1(2) at p.104).

4. Inspection of pet shops

(1) A local authority may authorise in writing any of its officers or any veterinary surgeon or veterinary practitioner to inspect (subject to compliance with such precautions as the authority may specify to prevent the spread among animals of infectious diseases) any premises in their area as respects which a licence granted in accordance with the provisions of this Act is for the time being in force, and any person authorised under this section may, on producing his authority if so required, enter any such premises at all reasonable times and inspect them and any animals found thereon or any thing therein, for the purpose of ascertaining whether an offence has been or is being committed against this Act.

(2) Any person who wilfully obstructs or delays any person in the exercise of his powers of entry or inspection under this section shall be guilty of an offence.

Definitions
"animal", "local authority", "veterinary practitioner" and "veterinary surgeon": s.7(3).

Commentary
This section enables the local authority to authorise in writing any of its officers, and vets., to inspect premises for which a licence is in force; thus, no rights of entry exist before the issue

Pet Animals Act 1951

of a licence or after it has expired (s.2(5), (6)) or been cancelled (s.5(3)). In law, "premises" includes land which is not built upon.

Also, there is no right of entry unless the written authority is produced at the time if required, and the powers of inspection are limited to matters related to offences.

Obstructing or delaying an inspector is an offence (subs.(2)), the punishment for which is given in s.5(2) below.

5. Offences and disqualifications

(1) Any person guilty of an offence under any provision of this Act shall be liable on summary conviction to a fine not exceeding level 2 on the standard scale.

(2) Any person guilty of an offence under the last foregoing section shall be liable on summary conviction to a fine not exceeding level 2 on the standard scale.

(3) Where a person is convicted of any offence under this Act or of any offence under the Protection of Animals Act, 1911, or the Protection of Animals (Scotland) Act, 1912, or of any offence under any of sections 4, 5, 6(1) and (2), 7 to 9 and 11 of the Animal Welfare Act, 2006, the court by which he is convicted may cancel any licence held by him under this Act, and may, whether or not he is the holder of such a licence, disqualify him from keeping a pet shop for such period as the court thinks fit.

(4) A court which has ordered the cancellation of a person's licence, or his disqualification, in pursuance of the last foregoing subsection may, if it thinks fit, suspend the operation of the order pending an appeal.

Definitions and Meanings
"keeping a pet shop": s.7(1).
"level 2 on the standard scale": currently £500.

Commentary
This section lays down the punishments available for offences under the Act, including cancellation of a licence and disqualification from keeping a pet shop (subss.(1)–(3)). Cancellation and disqualification may be suspended pending the hearing of any appeal (subs.(4)) which may be made to the Crown Court.

In subs.1 "other than the last foregoing section" and the words from "or to imprisonment" to the end are repealed by

Pet Animals Act 1951

Part 9 of Sch.37 to the Criminal Justice Act 2003, from a day to be appointed.

Further References
For the provisions of the Animal Welfare Act 2006, see pp.274–336.

6. Power of local authority to prosecute
A local authority in England or Wales may prosecute proceedings for any offence under this Act committed in the area of the authority.

Definitions
"local authority": s.7(3).

7. Interpretation
(1) References in this Act to the keeping of a pet shop shall, subject to the following provisions of this section, be construed as references to the carrying on at premises of any nature (including a private dwelling) of a business of selling animals as pets, and as including references to the keeping of animals in any such premises as aforesaid with a view to their being sold in the course of such a business, whether by the keeper thereof or by any other person:
Provided that—
(a) a person shall not be deemed to keep a pet shop by reason only of his keeping or selling pedigree animals bred by him, or the offspring of an animal kept by him as a pet;
(b) where a person carries on a business of selling animals as pets in conjunction with a business of breeding pedigree animals, and the local authority are satisfied that the animals so sold by him (in so far as they are not pedigree animals bred by him) are animals which were acquired by him with a view to being used, if suitable, for breeding or show purposes but have subsequently been found by him not to be suitable or required for such use, the local authority may if they think fit direct that the said person shall not be deemed to keep a pet shop by reason only of his carrying on the first-mentioned business.

(2) References in this Act to the selling or keeping of animals as pets shall be construed in accordance with the following provisions, that is to say—

Pet Animals Act 1951

(a) as respects cats and dogs, such references shall be construed as including references to selling or keeping, as the case may be, wholly or mainly for domestic purposes; and

(b) as respects any animal, such references shall be construed as including references to selling or keeping, as the case may be, for ornamental purposes.

(3) In this Act, unless the context otherwise requires, the following expressions have the meanings hereby respectively assigned to them, that is to say:—

"animal" includes any description of vertebrate;

"local authority" means the council of any county district, the council of a borough or the Common Council of the City of London;

"pedigree animal" means an animal of any description which is by its breeding eligible for registration with a recognised club or society keeping a register of animals of that description;

. . .

"veterinary surgeon" means a person who is for the time being registered in the Register of Veterinary Surgeons;

"veterinary practitioner" means a person who is for the time being registered in the Supplementary Veterinary Register.

Commentary

This section interprets a number of words and phrases used in the earlier parts of the Act.

Of particular importance is the definition in subs.(1) of the phrase "keeping a pet shop" upon which the need for a licence under s.1(1) depends. Note especially:

(1) The description of "premises" as given in subs.(1). As a matter of general law, the word can also include open land.

(2) In law, an activity does not necessarily have to be profitable in order to be described as a business. It is suggested that any continuous activity of selling pets will be a business.

(3) A person who keeps pets at premises which are sold as a business by him elsewhere, or by another person there or elsewhere, will be deemed to be keeping a pet shop (subs.(1) and the case cited below).

(4) Provisos (a) and (b) to subs.(1) provide exemption for breeders of pedigree animals, which are defined in subs.(3).

(5) The meaning of "selling or keeping animals as pets" in subs.(2).

Pet Animals Act 1951

A person keeping animals on premises for short periods (48 hours in this particular case) for the purpose of exporting them nevertheless keeps a pet shop within the definition, even though the public did not go to the premises to buy animals (*Chalmers v Diwell* (1975) 74 L.G.R. 173; [1976] Crim. L.R. 134, D.C.)

VETERINARY SURGEONS ACT 1966

c. 36

Arrangement of sections

Restriction on practice of veterinary surgery

19. Restriction on practice of veterinary surgery by unqualified persons

Miscellaneous and general

27. Interpretation

Schedule 3: Exemption from restrictions on practice of veterinary surgery

Part I – Treatments and operations which may be given or carried out by unqualified persons

Part II – Exclusions from provisions of Part I

Restriction on practice of veterinary surgery

19. Restriction on practice of veterinary surgery by unqualified persons

(1) Subject to the following provisions of this section, no individual shall practise, or hold himself out as practising or as being prepared to practise, veterinary surgery unless he is registered in the register of veterinary surgeons or the supplementary veterinary register, and an individual who acts in contravention of this subsection shall be liable—

(a) on summary conviction to a fine not exceeding the prescribed sum;
(b) on conviction on indictment to a fine.

. . .

(3) The Council may make regulations exempting from subsection (1) of this section the carrying out or performance of any veterinary treatment, test or operation prescribed by the regulations, subject to

Veterinary Surgeons Act 1966

compliance with prescribed conditions, by students of veterinary surgery of any prescribed class.

(4) Subsection (1) of this section shall not prohibit—
  (a) the carrying out of any procedure duly authorised under the Animals (Scientific Procedures) Act 1986;
  (b) the doing of anything specified in Part I of Schedule 3 to this Act and not excluded by Part II of that Schedule;
  (c) the performance by a registered medical practitioner of an operation on an animal for the purpose of removing an organ or tissue for use in the treatment of human beings;
  (d) the carrying out or performance of any treatment, test or operation by a registered medical practitioner or a registered dentist at the request of a person registered in the register of veterinary surgeons or the supplementary veterinary register;
  (e) the carrying out or performance of any minor treatment, test or operation specified in an order made by the Ministers after consultation with the Council, so long as any conditions so specified are complied with.

(5) The Ministers may, after consultation with the Council and with persons appearing to the Ministers to represent interests so appearing to be substantially affected, by order amend the provisions of Schedule 3 to this Act.

(6) Any order under subsection (4) or (5) of this section may be varied or revoked by a subsequent order of the Ministers under that subsection made after the like consultation.

. . .

Definitions and Meanings
"animal", "Council", "the Ministers" and *"veterinary surgery":* s.27(1).
"prescribed sum": currently £5,000.

Orders
Schedule 3 has been amended by a number of orders made under subss.(5) and (6). That Schedule, at p.244, is printed as currently amended.

Commentary
The purpose of this section is to prevent the practice of veterinary surgery by unregistered persons, but with the exceptions given in subs.(4) and Sch.3.

Veterinary Surgeons Act 1966

Regulations may be made by the Royal College of Veterinary Surgeons allowing students to perform veterinary treatment, etc. in accordance with those regulations (subs.(3)).

Further References
For the Animals (Scientific Procedures) Act 1986, see pp.267–273.

Miscellaneous and general

27. Interpretation

(1) In this Act, except so far as the context otherwise requires—
"animals" includes birds and reptiles;
"College" means the Royal College of Veterinary Surgeons;
. . .
"Council" means the Council of the College;
. . .
"the Ministers" means the Minister of Agriculture, Fisheries and Food, the Secretary of State for Scotland and the Secretary of State for Wales and the Minister of Agriculture for Northern Ireland acting jointly;
. . .
"veterinary surgery" means the art and science of veterinary surgery and medicine and, without prejudice to the generality of the foregoing, shall be taken to include—
(a) the diagnosis of diseases in, and injuries to, animals including tests performed on animals for diagnostic purposes;
(b) the giving of advice based upon such diagnosis;
(c) the medical or surgical treatment of animals; and
(d) the performance of surgical operations on animals.
. . .
(3) References in this Act to any other enactment shall be construed as references thereto as amended, and as including references thereto as extended, by or under any subsequent enactment.
. . .

Commentary
This section supplies definitions for a number of terms used in s.19 and Sch.3.

Veterinary Surgeons Act 1966

SCHEDULE 3
EXEMPTIONS FROM RESTRICTIONS ON PRACTICE OF VETERINARY SURGERY

PART I

Treatment and operations which may be given or carried out by unqualified persons

1. Any minor medical treatment given to an animal by its owner, by another member of the household of which the owner is a member or by a person in the employment of the owner.

. . .

3. The rendering in an emergency of first aid for the purpose of saving life or relieving pain or suffering.

4. The performance by any person of or over the age of eighteen of any of the following operations, that is to say—
   (a) the castration of a male animal or the caponising of an animal, whether by chemical means or otherwise;

. . .

   (d) the amputation of the dew claws of a dog before its eyes are open.

5. The performance, by any person of the age of seventeen undergoing instruction in animal husbandry, of any operation mentioned in paragraph 4(a) . . . above and the disbudding of a calf by any such person or by a person of or over the age of eighteen undergoing such instruction, if, in each case, either of the following conditions is complied with, that is to say—
   (a) the instruction in animal husbandry is given by a person registered in the register of veterinary surgeons or the supplementary veterinary register and the operation is performed under his direct personal supervision;
   (b) the instruction in animal husbandry is given at a recognised institution and the operation is performed under the direct personal supervision of a person appointed to give such instruction at the institution.

In the foregoing paragraph "recognised institution" means—
   (i) as respects Great Britain, an institution maintained or assisted (in England and Wales) by a local education authority or (in Scotland) by an education authority or in either case an institution for the giving of further education as respects which

Veterinary Surgeons Act 1966

a grant is paid by the Secretary of State or an institution recognised for the purposes of this paragraph by the Secretary of State;
(i) an institution within the further education sector within the meanings of section 91(3) of the Further and Higher Education Act 1992;
(ii) as respects Northern Ireland, an agricultural college maintained by the Department of Agriculture for Northern Ireland.

6. Any medical treatment or any minor surgery (not involving entry into a body cavity) to any animal by a veterinary nurse if the following conditions are complied with, that is to say—
(a) the animal is, for the time being, under the care of a registered veterinary surgeon or veterinary practitioner and the medical treatment or minor surgery is carried out by the veterinary nurse at his direction;
(b) the registered veterinary surgeon or veterinary practitioner is the employer or is acting on behalf of the employer of the veterinary nurse;
(c) the registered veterinary surgeon or veterinary practitioner directing the medical treatment or minor surgery is satisfied that the veterinary nurse is qualified to carry out the treatment or surgery.

In this paragraph—
"veterinary nurse" means a nurse whose name is entered in the list of veterinary nurses maintained by the college.

PART II

Exclusions from provisions of Part I

Nothing in section 19(4)(b) of this Act shall authorise—
(a) the castration of a male animal being—

 . . .

 (iv) a cat or dog;
(b) the spaying of a cat or dog;

. . .

Definitions
"animal" and *"college"*: s.27(1).
"recognised institution": Sch.3, para.5.
"companion animal" and *"veterinary nurse"*: Sch.3, para.6.

Veterinary Surgeons Act 1966

Commentary

Under the terms of s.19 of this Act, the treatment and operations listed in Part I of Sch.3 are permitted to be carried out by unqualified persons, i.e. those not registered in a veterinary register, unless the treatment or operation is caught by Part II of the Schedule.

Prior to July 1993, the docking of a dog's tail by an unqualified person was permitted.

Further References

For operations and the use of anaesthetics on animals generally, see pp.51–52.

THEFT ACT 1968
c. 60

Arrangement of sections

Definition of "theft"

1. Basic definition of theft
2. "Dishonestly"
3. "Appropriates"
4. "Property"
5. "Belonging to another"
6. "With the intention of permanently depriving the other of it"

Offences relating to goods stolen etc.

22. Handling stolen goods
23. Advertising rewards for return of goods stolen or lost

Supplementary

34. Interpretation

Definition of "theft"

1. Basic definition of theft

(1) A person is guilty of theft if he dishonestly appropriates property belonging to another with the intention of permanently depriving the other of it; and "thief" and "steal" shall be construed accordingly.

(2) It is immaterial whether the appropriation is made with a view to gain, or is made for the thief's own benefit.

(3) The five following sections of this Act shall have effect as regards the interpretation and operation of this section (and, except as otherwise provided by this Act, shall apply only for purposes of this section).

Theft Act 1968

Definitions
"*appropriates*": s.3.
"*belonging to another*": s.5.
"*dishonestly*": s.2.
"*gain*": s.34(2).
"*permanently depriving*": s.6.
"*property*": s.4(1).

Commentary
Subsection (1) contains the basic definition of theft. Explanations of the component parts of the definition are to be found in subs.(2) and ss.2–6 following.

2. "Dishonestly"

(1) A person's appropriation of property belonging to another is not to be regarded as dishonest—

  (a) if he appropriates the property in the belief that he has in law the right to deprive the other of it, on behalf of himself or of a third person; or

  (b) if he appropriates the property in the belief that he would have the other's consent if the other knew of the appropriation and the circumstances of it; or

  (c) (except where the property came to him as trustee or personal representative) if he appropriates the property in the belief that the person to whom the property belongs cannot be discovered by taking reasonable steps.

(2) A person's appropriation of property belonging to another may be dishonest notwithstanding that he is willing to pay for the property.

Definitions
"*appropriates*": s.3.
"*belonging to another*": s.5.
"*property*": s.4.

Commentary
In explanation of s.1(1), this section provides three instances when appropriation of property is not to be regarded as dishonest (subs.(1)) and one instance when appropriation may be dishonest (subs.(2)).

Theft Act 1968

3. "Appropriates"

(1) Any assumption by a person of the rights of an owner amounts to an appropriation, and this includes, where he has come by the property (innocently or not) without stealing it, any later assumption of a right to it by keeping or dealing with it as owner.

(2) Where property or a right or interest in property is or purports to be transferred for value to a person acting in good faith, no later assumption by him of rights which he believed himself to be acquiring shall, by reason of any defect in the transferor's title, amount to theft of the property.

Definitions
"*property*": s.4(1).

Commentary
This section supplies the meaning to be given to "appropriates" in s.1(1).

4. "Property"

(1) "Property" includes money and all other property, real or personal, including things in action and other intangible property.

. . .

Commentary
Subsection (1) contains the definition of "property" for the purposes of s.1(1). It includes dogs.

5. "Belonging to another"

(1) Property shall be regarded as belonging to any person having possession or control of it, or having in it any proprietary right or interest (not being an equitable interest arising only from an agreement to transfer or grant an interest).

(2) Where property is subject to a trust, the persons to whom it belongs shall be regarded as including any person having a right to enforce the trust, and an intention to defeat the trust shall be regarded accordingly as an intention to deprive of the property any person having that right.

(3) Where a person receives property from or on account of another, and is under an obligation to the other to retain and deal with that property or its proceeds in a particular way, the property or proceeds shall be regarded (as against him) as belonging to the other.

(4) Where a person gets property by another's mistake, and is under an obligation to make restoration (in whole or in part) of the property or its proceeds or of the value thereof, then to the extent of that obligation the property or proceeds shall be regarded (as against him) as belonging to the person entitled to restoration, and an intention not to make restoration shall be regarded accordingly as an intention to deprive that person of the property or proceeds.

(5) Property of a corporation sole shall be regarded as belonging to the corporation notwithstanding a vacancy in the corporation.

Definitions
"*property*": s.4(1).

Commentary
This section details the circumstances in which, for the purposes of s.1(1), property is to be regarded as belonging to another person.

6. "With the intention of permanently depriving the other of it"

(1) A person appropriating property belonging to another without meaning the other permanently to lose the thing itself is nevertheless to be regarded as having the intention of permanently depriving the other of it if his intention is to treat the thing as his own to dispose of regardless of the other's rights; and a borrowing or lending of it may amount to so treating it if, but only if, the borrowing or lending of it is for a period and in circumstances making it equivalent to an outright taking or disposal.

(2) Without prejudice to the generality of subsection (1) above, where a person, having possession or control (lawfully or not) of property belonging to another, parts with the property under a condition as to its return which he may not be able to perform, this (if done for purposes of his own and without the other's authority) amounts to treating the property as his own to dispose of regardless of the other's rights.

Definitions
"*belonging to another*": s.5.
"*property*": s.4(1).

Theft Act 1968

Commentary
This section, the last of the explanatory sections linked to s.1(1), describes particular circumstances in which there will be an intention permanently to deprive another person of property for the purposes of s.1(1).

Offences relating to goods stolen etc.

22. Handling stolen goods

(1) A person handles stolen goods if (otherwise than in the course of the stealing) knowing or believing them to be stolen goods he dishonestly receives the goods, or dishonestly undertakes or assists in their retention, removal, disposal or realisation by or for the benefit of another person, or if he arranges to do so.

(2) A person guilty of handling stolen goods shall on conviction on indictment be liable to imprisonment for a term not exceeding fourteen years.

Definitions
"*goods*": s.34(2)(b).

Commentary
This section describes the offence commonly known as receiving. Dogs are within the definition of "goods" in s.34(2)(b) and can be the subject of this offence.

23. Advertising rewards for return of goods stolen or lost

Where any public advertisement of a reward for the return of any goods which have been stolen or lost uses any words to the effect that no questions will be asked, or that the person producing the goods will be safe from apprehension or inquiry, or that any money paid for the purchase of the goods or advanced by way of loan on them will be repaid, the person advertising the reward and any person who prints or publishes the advertisement shall on summary conviction be liable to a fine not exceeding level 3 on the standard scale.

Definitions and Meanings
"*goods*": s.34(2)(b).
"*level 3 on the standard scale*": currently £1,000.

Theft Act 1968

Commentary
The inclusion of any of the stated words in a public advertisement for lost or stolen goods is made an offence by this section. The printer or publisher of the advertisement, as well as the advertiser, will be liable.

Dogs fall within the definition of "goods".

Supplementary

34. Interpretation

(1) Sections 4(1) and 5(1) of this Act shall apply generally for purposes of this Act as they apply for purposes of section 1.

(2) For purposes of this Act—
(a) "gain" and "loss" are to be construed as extending only to gain or loss in money or other property, but as extending to any such gain or loss whether temporary or permanent; and—
   (i) "gain" includes a gain by keeping what one has, as well as a gain by getting what one has not;
   . . .
(b) "goods", except in so far as the context otherwise requires, includes money and every other description of property except land, and includes things severed from the land by stealing.

Definitions
"property": s.4(1).

Commentary
This section defines the words "gain" and "goods" which are used in the earlier provisions of the Act.

ANIMALS ACT 1971

c. 22

Arrangement of sections

Strict liability for damage done by animals

2. Liability for damage done by dangerous animals

3. Liability for injury done by dogs to livestock

5. Exceptions from liability under sections 2 to 4

6. Interpretation of certain expressions used in sections 2 to 5

Animals straying on to highway

8. Duty to take care to prevent damage from animals straying on to the highway

Protection of livestock against dogs

9. Killing of or injury to dogs worrying livestock

Supplemental

11. General interpretation

Strict liability for damage done by animals

2. Liability for damage done by dangerous animals

(1) Where any damage is caused by an animal which belongs to a dangerous species, any person who is a keeper of the animal is liable for the damage, except as otherwise provided by this Act.

(2) Where damage is caused by an animal which does not belong to a dangerous species, a keeper of the animal is liable for the damage, except as otherwise provided by this Act, if—

(a) the damage is of a kind which the animal, unless restrained, was likely to cause or which, if caused by the animal, was likely to be severe; and
(b) the likelihood of the damage or of its being severe was due to characteristics of the animal which are not normally found in animals of the same species or are not normally so found except at particular times or in particular circumstances; and
(c) those characteristics were known to that keeper or were at any time known to a person who at that time had charge of the animal as the keeper's servant or, where that keeper is the head of a household, were known to another keeper of the animal who is a member of that household and under the age of sixteen.

Definitions
"*damage*": s.11.
"*dangerous species*": s.6(2).
"*keeper of an animal*": s.6(3).
"*species*": s.11.

Commentary
The definition of "dangerous species" in s.6(2) excludes any dog which is commonly domesticated in this country. Thus, pit bull terriers are not within this description, but other dogs not commonly domesticated and which have the dangerous attributes described in s.6(2)(b) will be.

Under subs.(2) the keepers of dogs not belonging to a dangerous species are liable for the damage caused by their dogs if all the conditions in that subs. are met, provided no defence under s.5(1)–(3) is available.

Interpretation of these conditions is difficult. Whether characteristics displayed by a dog are judged to be normal will often be crucial. The propensity of a dog to attack people carrying bags is not a normal characteristic of dogs (*Kite v Napp* (1982), *The Times*, June 1, 1982). But the keeper of a dog with a known propensity to attack other dogs is liable to a plaintiff injured in the course of an attack on the plaintiff's dog (*Smith v Ainger* (1990), *The Times*, June 5, 1990, CA).

As to subs.(2)(a), it is not necessary to show that an animal has abnormal characteristics making it likely that if the animal

Animals Act 1971

does cause damage that that damage will be severe. (*Curtis v Betts* [1990] 1 All E.R. 769; [1990] 1 W.L.R. 459, CA.)

Further References
For other legislation dealing specifically with dangerous dogs, see the Dogs Act 1871 s.2, at p.85 and the Dangerous Dogs Act 1991 at pp.141–158.

3. Liability for injury done by dogs to livestock

Where a dog causes damage by killing or injuring livestock, any person who is a keeper of the dog is liable for the damage, except as otherwise provided by this Act.

Definitions
"*damage*": s.11.
"*keeper*": s.6(2).
"*livestock*": s.11.

Commentary
Liability in the circumstances here described can only be avoided if the case can be brought within s.5(1) or (4).

Earlier cases indicate that injuring in this contest can include indirect injury: dog barking at foals which injured themselves (*Campbell v Wilkinson* (1909) 43 I.L.T. 327); poultry ceasing to lay as a result of shock caused by dogs (*Ives v Brewer* (1951) 95 S.J. 286).

Another earlier case decided that, where damage is caused by two or more dogs acting together, the keeper of each dog can be held responsible for the whole of the damage (*Arneil v Paterson* [1931] A.C. 560).

5. Exceptions from liability under sections 2 to 4

(1) A person is not liable under sections 2 to 4 of this Act for any damage which is due wholly to the fault of the person suffering it.

(2) A person is not liable under section 2 of this Act for any damage suffered by a person who has voluntarily accepted the risk thereof.

(3) A person is not liable under section 2 of this Act for any damage caused by an animal kept on any premises or structure to a person trespassing there, if it is proved either—

(a) that the animal was not kept there for the protection of persons or property; or
(b) (if the animal was kept there for the protection of persons or property) that keeping it there for that purpose was not unreasonable.

(4) A person is not liable under section 3 of this Act if the livestock was killed or injured on land on to which it had strayed and either the dog belonged to the occupier or its presence on the land was authorised by the occupier.

. . .

Definitions
"damage", *"fault"* and *"livestock":* s.11.

Commentary
This section contains the several defences available to actions for damage by animals under ss.2 and 3.

The defence at subs.(2) is qualified by the provisions in s.6(5).

The defence at subs.(3) is concerned with the protection of persons or property by dogs. The defendant to an action under s.2 must show that the keeping of a dog for such protection was not unreasonable; this is a question of fact in each case. For example, it has been suggested that it is unreasonable to keep a fierce dog at a house in circumstances where innocent visitors might be injured by it (*Sarch v Blackburn* (1830) 4 C. & P. 297 at 300; Mood & M. 505).

Further References
For specific legislation about guard dogs, see the Guard Dogs Act 1975 at pp.115–116.

6. Interpretation of certain expressions used in sections 2 to 5

(1) The following provisions apply to the interpretation of sections 2 to 5 of this Act.

(2) A dangerous species is a species—
(a) which is not commonly domesticated in the British Islands; and
(b) whose fully grown animals normally have such characteristics that they are likely, unless restrained, to cause severe damage or that any damage they may cause is likely to be severe.

(3) Subject to subsection (4) of this section, a person is a keeper of an animal if—
  (a) he owns the animal or has it in his possession; or
  (b) he is the head of a household of which a member under the age of sixteen owns the animal or has it in his possession;
and if at any time an animal ceases to be owned by or to be in the possession of a person, any person who immediately before that time was a keeper thereof by virtue of the preceding provisions of this subsection continues to be a keeper of the animal until another person becomes a keeper thereof by virtue of those provisions.

(4) Where an animal is taken into and kept in possession for the purpose of preventing it from causing damage or of restoring it to its owner, a person is not a keeper of it by virtue only of that possession.

(5) Where a person employed as a servant by a keeper of an animal incurs a risk incidental to his employment he shall not be treated as accepting it voluntarily.

Definitions
"damage" and *"species"*: s.11.

Commentary
This section contains the definitions of "dangerous species" of an animal (which is relevant to s.2) and of the expression "keeper of an animal" which is used in ss.2 and 3. For comment about the identity of the head of a household, see p.21.

Subsection (5) relates to the defence to s.2 claims described at s.5(2).

Animals straying on to highway

8. Duty to take care to prevent damage from animals straying on to the highway

(1) So much of the rules of the common law relating to liability for negligence as excludes or restricts the duty which a person might owe to others to take such care as is reasonable to see that damage is not caused by animals straying on to a highway is hereby abolished.

(2) Where damage is caused by animals straying from unfenced land to a highway a person who placed them on the land shall not be regarded as having committed a breach of the duty to take care by reason only of placing them there if—

Animals Act 1971

(a) the land is common land, or is land situated in an area where fencing is not customary, or is a town or village green; and

(b) he had a right to place the animals on that land.

Definitions
"common land", "damage", "fencing" and *"town or village green":* s.11.

Commentary
Formerly, owners of animals were generally not obliged to take steps to prevent their animals straying on to a road and causing damage. Subsection (1) has the effect of reversing that situation and obliging owners to take reasonable care under the Common Law rules of negligence to prevent straying, unless subs.(2) applies.

What is reasonable will depend upon the particular circumstances of each case. It is suggested, for example, that greater care is needed when the adjoining road is heavily trafficked than when the road is a little frequented country lane. It has been decided that, if a fence, though not 100 percent secure, is reasonably adequate to prevent the animal in question from straying, the duty is fulfilled (*Smith v Sudron and Coulson* (1981), Ct. of App. Transcripts 140, April 10, 1981).

Though intended primarily to deal with cases of straying livestock, this section also applies to dogs.

Protection of livestock against dogs

9. Killing of or injury to dogs worrying livestock

(1) In any civil proceedings against a person (in this section referred to as the defendant) for killing or causing injury to a dog it shall be a defence to prove—

(a) that the defendant acted for the protection of any livestock and was a person entitled to act for the protection of that livestock; and

(b) that within forty-eight hours of the killing or injury notice thereof was given by the defendant to the officer in charge of a police station.

(2) For the purposes of this section a person is entitled to act for the protection of any livestock if, and only if—

(a) the livestock or the land on which it is belongs to him or to any person under whose express or implied authority he is acting; and

Animals Act 1971

(b) the circumstances are not such that liability for killing or causing injury to the livestock would be excluded by section 5(4) of this Act.

(3) Subject to subsection (4) of this section, a person killing or causing injury to a dog shall be deemed for the purposes of this section to act for the protection of any livestock if, and only if, either—
 (a) the dog is worrying or is about to worry the livestock and there are no other reasonable means of ending or preventing the worrying; or
 (b) the dog has been worrying livestock, has not left the vicinity and is not under the control of any person and there are no practicable means of ascertaining to whom it belongs.

(4) For the purposes of this section the condition stated in either of the paragraphs of the preceding subsection shall be deemed to have been satisfied if the defendant believed that it was satisfied and had reasonable ground for that belief.

(5) For the purposes of this section—
 (a) an animal belongs to any person if he owns it or has it in his possession; and
 (b) land belongs to any person if he is the occupier thereof.

. . .

Definitions

"*act for the protection of livestock*": subss.(3), (4).
"*belongs to*": (in relation to animals and land), subs.(5).
"*defendant*": subs.(1).
"*livestock*": s.11.

Commentary

This section provides some immunity for the owner of livestock who feels compelled to kill or injure a dog which is attacking it.

To secure immunity, the conditions in subs.1(a) and (b) must be met. As to subs.(1)(a), the circumstances in which an owner can be said to be entitled to act for the protection of livestock, and those in which he will be deemed to be so acting, are set out in subs.(2) and subss.(3) and (4), respectively.

There is no definition in the Act of the expression "worrying livestock" which is used in subs.(3). The definition in the Dogs (Protection of Livestock) Act 1953 s.1(2)–(4), at pp.93–94, though not applied to the 1971 Act, may be useful as a guide.

Animals Act 1971

Further References
This section relates to the civil law only. For the criminal law relating to the killing of dogs, see the Criminal Damage Act 1971 at pp.261–264.

Supplemental

11. General interpretation
In this Act—
   "common land", and "town or village green" have the same meanings as in the Commons Registration Act 1965;
   "damage" includes the death of, or injury to, any person (including any disease and any impairment of physical or mental condition);
   . . .
   "fencing" includes the construction of any obstacle designed to prevent animals from straying;
   "livestock" means cattle, horses, asses, mules, hinnies, sheep, pigs, goats and poultry, and also deer not in the wild state and, in sections 3 and 9, also, while in captivity, pheasants, partridges and grouse;
   "poultry" means the domestic varieties of the following, that is to say, fowls, turkeys, geese, ducks, guinea-fowls, pigeons, peacocks and quails; and
   "species" includes sub-species and variety.

Commentary
This section defines a number of terms used earlier in the Act.
   "Common land": the definition above is substituted by para.2 of Sch.5 to the Commons Act 2006 from a day to be appointed, as follows:
   "common land" means—
   (a) land registered as a common in a register of common land kept under Part I of the Commons Act 2006;
   (b) land to which Part I of that Act does not apply and which is subject to rights of common within the
   meaning of that Act;
   "town or village green" means land registered as a town or village green in a register of town or village
   greens kept under Part I of the Commons Act 2006.
   "Fencing" will include ditches if made to prevent animals from straying.

CRIMINAL DAMAGE ACT 1971

c. 48

Arrangement of sections

1. Destroying or damaging property
5. "Without lawful excuse"
10. Interpretation

1. Destroying or damaging property

(1) A person who without lawful excuse destroys or damages any property belonging to another intending to destroy or damage any such property or being reckless as to whether any such property would be destroyed or damaged shall be guilty of an offence.

(2) A person who without lawful excuse destroys or damages any property, whether belonging to himself or another—
- (a) intending to destroy or damage any property or being reckless as to whether any property would be destroyed or damaged; and
- (b) intending by the destruction or damage to endanger the life of another or being reckless as to whether the life of another would be thereby endangered;

shall be guilty of an offence.

. . .

Definitions
"belonging to (property)": s.10(2)–(4).
"property": s.10(1).
"without lawful excuse": s.5.

Commentary
Subsection (1) states the simple offence of destroying or damaging property belonging to another. The definition of "property" in s.10(1) will include dogs, and therefore this section may be read as applying to the killing or injuring of dogs.

Subsection (2) creates the aggravated offence of causing damage or destruction and thereby endangering the life of another.

Further References
For the civil law about the killing or injuring of another person's dog, see the Animals Act 1971 at pp.253–262.

5. "Without lawful excuse"

(1) This section applies to any offence under section 1(1) above and any offence under section 2 or 3 above other than one involving a threat by the person charged to destroy or damage property in a way which he knows is likely to endanger the life of another or involving an intent by the person charged to use or cause or permit the use of something in his custody or under his control so to destroy or damage property.

(2) A person charged with an offence to which this section applies shall, whether or not he would be treated for the purposes of this Act as having a lawful excuse apart from this subsection, be treated for those purposes as having a lawful excuse—
- (a) if at the time of the act or acts alleged to constitute the offence he believed that the person or persons whom he believed to be entitled to consent to the destruction of or damage to the property in question had so consented, or would have so consented to it if he or they had known of the destruction or damage and its circumstances; or
- (b) if he destroyed or damaged or threatened to destroy or damage the property in question or, in the case of a charge of an offence under section 3 above, intended to use or cause or permit the use of something to destroy or damage it, in order to protect property belonging to himself or another or a right or interest in property which was or which he believed to be vested in himself or another, and at the time of the act or acts alleged to constitute the offence he believed—
  - (i) that the property, right or interest was in immediate need of protection; and
  - (ii) that the means of protection adopted or proposed to be adopted were or would be reasonable having regard to all the circumstances.

(3) For the purposes of this section it is immaterial whether a belief is justified or not if it is honestly held.

(4) For the purposes of subsection (2) above a right or interest in property includes any right or privilege in or over land, whether created by grant, licence or otherwise.

(5) This section shall not be construed as casting doubt on any defence recognised by law as a defence to criminal charges.

Definitions
"*belonging to (property)*": s.10(2)–(4).
"*property*": s.10(1).

Commentary
No offence will be committed under s.1 if the defendant can show that he had a lawful excuse when destroying or damaging another's property. Section 5 sets out at length the circumstances in which such an excuse will exist.

10. Interpretation

(1) In this Act "property" means property of a tangible nature, whether real or personal, including money and—
  (a) including wild creatures which have been tamed or are ordinarily kept in captivity, and any other wild creatures or their carcasses if, but only if, they have been reduced into possession which has not been lost or abandoned or are in the course of being reduced into possession; but
  (b) not including mushrooms growing wild on any land or flowers, fruit or foliage of a plant growing wild on any land.

For the purposes of this subsection "mushroom" includes any fungus and "plant" includes any shrub or tree.

(2) Property shall be treated for the purposes of this Act as belonging to any person—
  (a) having the custody of it;
  (b) having in it any proprietary right or interest (not being an equitable interest arising only from an agreement to transfer or grant an interest); or
  (c) having a charge on it.

(3) Where property is subject to a trust, the persons to whom it belongs shall be so treated as including any person having a right to enforce the trust.

(4) Property of a corporation sole shall be so treated as belonging to the corporation notwithstanding a vacancy in the corporation.

Criminal Damage Act 1971

Commentary
This section defines "property" for the purposes of earlier sections of the Act, and describes the circumstances in which for the purposes of those sections property is to be regarded as belonging to a person.

PUBLIC HEALTH (CONTROL OF DISEASE) ACT 1984

c. 22

Arrangement of sections

PART V

MISCELLANEOUS

55. Inducements offered by dealers in rags and old clothes

PART VI

GENERAL

74. Interpretation

PART V

MISCELLANEOUS

55. Inducements offered by dealers in rags and old clothes

(1) No person who collects or deals in rags, old clothes or similar articles, and no person assisting or acting on behalf of any such person, shall—
 (a) in or from any shop or premises used for or in connection with the business of a dealer in any such articles, or
 (b) while engaged in collecting any such articles,
sell or deliver, whether gratuitously or not—
 (i) any article of food or drink to any person, or
 (ii) any article whatsoever to a person under the age of 14 years.

(2) In subsection (1)(ii) above, "article" includes any animal, fish, bird or other living thing.

Public Health (Control of Disease) Act 1984

(3) A person who contravenes any of the provisions of this section shall be liable on summary conviction to a fine not exceeding level 1 on the standard scale.

Definitions and Meanings
"article": subs.(2).
"level 1 on the standard scale": currently £200.
"premises": s.74.

Commentary
So far as dogs are concerned, this section has the effect of prohibiting old clothes dealers or their assistants from selling or giving a dog to a child under 14 while they are operating from a dealer's shop or other place of business or while they are collecting any of the articles described at the beginning of the section.

PART VI

GENERAL

74. Interpretation
In this Act, unless the context otherwise requires—

. . .

"premises" including buildings, lands, easements and hereditaments of any tenure;

. . .

Commentary
This section provides a definition for the word "premises" which is used in s.55 above.

ANIMALS (SCIENTIFIC PROCEDURES) ACT 1986

c. 14

Arrangement of sections

Preliminary

1. Protected animals
2. Regulated procedures

Personal and project licences

5. Project licences

Designated establishments

7. Breeding and supplying establishments

Licences and designation certificates: general provisions

10. Conditions

Additional controls

16. Prohibition of public displays

Miscellaneous and supplementary

30. Short title, interpretation and commencement

Schedule 1: Appropriate methods of humane killing

Preliminary

1. Protected animals

(1) Subject to the provisions of this section, "a protected animal" for the purposes of this Act means any living vertebrate other than man.

Animals (Scientific Procedures) Act 1986

(2) Any such vertebrate in its foetal, larval or embryonic form is a protected animal only from the stage of its development when—
   (a) in the case of a mammal, bird or reptile, half the gestation or incubation period for the relevant species has elapsed; and
   (b) in any other case, it becomes capable of independent feeding.

(3) The Secretary of State may by order—
   (a) extend the definition of protected animal so as to include invertebrates of any description;
   (b) alter the stage of development specified in subsection (2) above;
   (c) make provision in lieu of subsection (2) above as respects any animal which becomes a protected animal by virtue of an order under paragraph (a) above.

(4) For the purposes of this section an animal shall be regarded as continuing to live until the permanent cessation of circulation or the destruction of its brain.

(5) In this section "vertebrate" means any animal of the Sub-phylum Vertebrata of the Phylum Chordata and "invertebrate" means any animal not of that Sub-phylum.

Orders
To date, no orders relevant to this book have been made under subs.(3).

Commentary
This section defines the term "protected animal" when used in later provisions of the Act.

2. Regulated procedures

(1) Subject to the provisions of this section, "a regulated procedure" for the purposes of this Act means any experimental or other scientific procedure applied to a protected animal which may have the effect of causing that animal pain, suffering, distress or lasting harm.

(2) An experimental or other scientific procedure applied to an animal is also a regulated procedure if—
   (a) it is part of a series or combination of such procedures (whether the same or different) applied to the same animal; and
   (b) the series or combination may have the effect mentioned in the subsection (1) above; and
   (c) the animal is a protected animal throughout the series or combination or in the course of it attains the stage of its development when it becomes such an animal.

Animals (Scientific Procedures) Act 1986

(3) Anything done for the purpose of, or liable to result in, the birth or hatching of a protected animal is also a regulated procedure if it may as respects that animal have the effect mentioned in subsection (1) above.

(4) In determining whether any procedure may have the effect mentioned in subsection (1) above the use of an anaesthetic or analgesic, decerebration and any other procedure for rendering an animal insentient shall be disregarded; and the administration of an anaesthetic or analgesic to a protected animal, or decerebration or any other such procedure applied to such an animal, for the purposes of any experimental or other scientific procedure shall itself be a regulated procedure.

(5) The ringing, tagging or marking of an animal, or the application of any other humane procedure for the sole purpose of enabling an animal to be identified, is not a regulated procedure if it causes only momentary pain or distress and no lasting harm.

(6) The administration of any substance or article to an animal is not a regulated procedure if the substance or article is administered in accordance with an animal test certificate granted under the Veterinary Medicines Regulations 2006.

(7) Killing a protected animal is a regulated procedure only if it is killed for experimental or other scientific use, the place where it is killed is a designated establishment and the method employed is not one appropriate to the animal under Schedule 1 of this Act.

(8) In this section references to a scientific procedure do not include references to any recognised veterinary, agricultural or animal husbandry practice.

(9) Schedule 1 to this Act may be amended by orders made by the Secretary of State.

Orders

The Animals (Scientific Procedures) Act 1986 (Appropriate Methods of Humane Killing) Order 1996 was made under the provisions of subs.(9).

Definitions

"*protected animal*": includes a dog by virtue of ss.1, 30(2).

Commentary

This section describes at length the meaning to be given to the term "regulated procedure" which is relevant to s.16 following.

Animals (Scientific Procedures) Act 1986

The 1996 order cited above amends Schedule 1 to the Act. That Schedule, as so amended, and so far as applicable to dogs, appears on p.273.

Personal and project licences

5. Project licences

(1) A project licence is a licence granted by the Secretary of State specifying a programme of work and authorising the application, as part of that programme, of specified regulated procedures to animals of specified descriptions at a specified place or specified places.

. . .

Definitions
"regulated procedures": ss.2, 30(2).

Commentary
This section describes the meaning to be given to the term "project licence" which is relevant to s.10 following.

Designated establishments

7. Breeding and supplying establishments

(1) A person shall not at any place breed for use in regulated procedures (whether there or elsewhere) protected animals of a description specified in Schedule 2 to this Act unless that place is designated by a certificate issued by the Secretary of State under this section as a breeding establishment.

(2) A person shall not at any place keep any such protected animals which have not been bred there but are to be supplied for use elsewhere in regulated procedures unless that place is designated by a certificate issued by the Secretary of State under this section as a supplying establishment.

(3) An application for a certificate in respect of a breeding or supplying establishment shall be made to the Secretary of State in such form and shall be supported by such information as he may reasonably require.

(4) A certificate shall not be issued under this section unless the application nominates for inclusion in the certificate pursuant to subsection (5) below a person or persons appearing to the Secretary of State to be suitable for that purpose.

Animals (Scientific Procedures) Act 1986

(5) A certificate under this section shall specify—
  (a) a person to be responsible for the day-to-day care of the animals bred or kept for breeding at the establishment or, as the case may be, kept there for the purpose of being supplied for use in regulated procedures; and
  (b) a veterinary surgeon or other suitably qualified person to provide advice on their health and welfare;
and the same person may, if the Secretary of State thinks fit, be specified under both paragraphs of this subsection.

(6) If it appears to any person specified in a certificate pursuant to subsection (5) above that the health or welfare of any such animal as is mentioned in that subsection gives rise to concern he shall take steps to ensure that it is cared for and, if it is necessary for it to be killed, that it is killed by a method appropriate under Schedule 1 to this Act or approved by the Secretary of State.

. . .

Definitions
"protected animals": includes a dog by virtue of ss.1, 30(2).
"regulated procedures": ss.2, 30(2).

Commentary
This section describes the meanings to be applied to designated "breeding establishments" and "supply establishments" which are relevant to s.10 following.

Dogs are listed in Schedule 2 to the Act.

Licences and designation certificates: general provisions

10. Conditions

(1) Subject to the provisions of this section, a licence or certificate under this Act may contain such conditions as the Secretary of State thinks fit.

. . .

(3) The conditions of a project licence shall, unless the Secretary of State considers that an exception is justified, include a condition to the effect—
  (a) that no cat or dog shall be used under the licence unless it has been bred at and obtained from a designated breeding establishment;
  . . .

Animals (Scientific Procedures) Act 1986

but no exception shall be made from the condition required by paragraph (a) above unless the Secretary of State is satisfied that no animal suitable for the purpose of the programme specified in the licence can be obtained in accordance with that condition.

. . .

Definitions
"*designated breeding establishment*": ss.7(1), 30(2).
"*designated supplying establishment*": ss.7(2), 30(2).
"*project licence*": ss.5(1), 30(2).
"*protected animal*": includes a dog by virtue of ss.1, 30(2).

Commentary
Subsection (3) gives dogs used for experimental or scientific purposes some measure of protection by ensuring that they shall only be available from a designated breeding establishment.

Additional controls

16. Prohibition of public displays

(1) No person shall carry out any regulated procedure as an exhibition to the general public or carry out any such procedure which is shown live on television for general reception.

(2) No person shall publish a notice or advertisement announcing the carrying out of any regulated procedure in a manner that would contravene subsection (1) above.

Definitions
"*regulated procedure*": ss.2, 30(2).

Commentary
This section bans experiments, etc. on animals as an exhibition to the general public, and prohibits the advertising of such an exhibition.

Miscellaneous and supplementary

30. Short title, interpretation and commencement

. . .

(2) In this Act—

"designated", in relation to an establishment, means designated by a certificate under section 6 or 7 above;
...

"place" includes any place within the seaward limits of the territorial waters of the United Kingdom, including any vessel other than a ship which is not a British ship;

"project licence" means a licence granted under section 5 above;

"protected animal" has the meaning given in section 1 above but subject to any order under subsection (3) of that section;

"regulated procedure" has the meaning given in section 2 above.
...

Commentary

This section provides definitions of terms used in the earlier provisions of the Act.

SCHEDULE 1

APPROPRIATE METHODS OF HUMANE KILLING

2. ...
A. Methods for animals other than foetal larva and embryonic forms
Animals for which appropriate

1. Overdose of an anaesthetic using a route and an anaesthetic agent appropriate for the size and species of animal.	All animals

ANIMAL WELFARE ACT 2006

c. 45

Arrangement of sections

Introductory

1. Animals to which the Act applies
2. "Protected animal"
3. Responsibility for animals

Prevention of harm

4. Unnecessary suffering
5. Mutilation
6. Docking of dogs' tails
7. Administration of poisons etc.
8. Fighting etc.

Promotion of welfare

9. Duty of person responsible for animal to ensure welfare
10. Improvement notices
11. Transfer of animals by way of sale or prize to persons under 16
12. Regulations to promote welfare

Licensing and registration

13. Licensing or registration of activities involving animals

Animal Welfare Act 2006

Codes of practice

14. Codes of practice
15. Making and approval of codes of practice: England
16. Making of codes of practice: Wales
17. Revocation of codes of practice

Animals in distress

18. Powers in relation to animals in distress
19. Power of entry for section 18 purposes
20. Orders in relation to animals taken under section 18(5)
21. Orders under section 20: appeals

Enforcement powers

22. Seizure of animals involved in fighting offences
23. Entry and search under warrant in connection with offences
24. Entry for purposes of arrest
25. Inspection of records required to be kept by holder of licence
26. Inspection in connection with licences
27. Inspection in connection with registration
28. Inspection of farm premises
29. Inspection relating to community obligations

Prosecutions

30. Power of local authority to prosecute offences
31. Time limits for prosecutions

Animal Welfare Act 2006

Post-conviction powers

32. Imprisonment or fine
33. Deprivation
34. Disqualification
35. Seizure of animals in connection with disqualification
36. Section 35: supplementary
37. Destruction in the interests of the animal
38. Destruction of animals involved in fighting offences
39. Reimbursement of expenses relating to animals involved in fighting offences
40. Forfeiture of equipment used in offences
41. Orders under section 33, 35, 37, 38 or 40: pending appeals
42. Orders with respect to licences
43. Termination of disqualification under section 34 or 42
44. Orders made on conviction for reimbursement of expenses
45. Orders for reimbursement of expenses: right of appeal for non-offenders

General

51. Inspectors
52. Conditions for grant of warrant
53. Powers of entry, inspection and search: supplementary
54. Power to stop and detain vehicles
55. Power to detain vessels, aircraft and hovercraft
56. Obtaining of documents in connection with carrying out orders etc.
57. Offences by bodies corporate
58. Scientific research

59. Fishing

60. Crown application

61. Orders and regulations

62. General interpretation

68. Commencement

SCHEDULES

Schedule 2: Powers of entry, inspection and search: supplementary

Introductory

1. Animals to which the Act applies

(1) In this Act, except subsections (4) and (5), "animal" means a vertebrate other than man.

(2) Nothing in this Act applies to an animal while it is in its foetal or embryonic form.

(3) The appropriate national authority may by regulations for all or any of the purposes of this Act—
- (a) extend the definition of "animal" so as to include invertebrates of any description;
- (b) make provision in lieu of subsection (2) as respects any invertebrates included in the definition of "animal";
- (c) amend subsection (2) to extend the application of this Act to an animal from such earlier stage of its development as may be specified in the regulations.

(4) The power under subsection (3)(a) or (c) may only be exercised if the appropriate national authority is satisfied, on the basis of scientific evidence, that animals of the kind concerned are capable of experiencing pain or suffering.

(5) In this section, "vertebrate" means any animal of the Sub-phylum Vertebrata of the Phylum Chordata and "invertebrate" means any animal not of that Subphylum.

Definitions
"appropriate national authority": s.62(1).
"suffering": s.62(1).

Animal Welfare Act 2006

Commentary
At the time of going to press, no regulations had been made under the section.

2. "Protected animal"
An animal is a "protected animal" for the purposes of this Act if—
  (a) it is of a kind which is commonly domesticated in the British Islands,
  (b) it is under the control of man whether on a permanent or temporary basis, or
  (c) it is not living in a wild state.

Definitions
"animal": ss.1(1) and 62(1).

Commentary
The British Islands are the United Kingdom, the Channel Islands and the Isle of Man.

3. Responsibility for animals
(1) In this Act, references to a person responsible for an animal are to a person responsible for an animal whether on a permanent or temporary basis.

(2) In this Act, references to being responsible for an animal include being in charge of it.

(3) For the purposes of this Act, a person who owns an animal shall always be regarded as being a person who is responsible for it.

(4) For the purposes of this Act, a person shall be treated as responsible for any animal for which a person under the age of 16 years of whom he has actual care and control is responsible.

Definitions
"animal": ss.1(1) and 62(1).

Prevention of harm

4. Unnecessary suffering
  (1) A person commits an offence if—
  (a) an act of his, or a failure of his to act, causes an animal to suffer,

Animal Welfare Act 2006

(b) he knew, or ought reasonably to have known, that the act, or failure to act, would have that effect or be likely to do so,
(c) the animal is a protected animal, and
(d) the suffering is unnecessary.
(2) A person commits an offence if—
(a) he is responsible for an animal,
(b) an act, or failure to act, of another person causes the animal to suffer,
(c) he permitted that to happen or failed to take such steps (whether by way of supervising the other person or otherwise) as were reasonable in all the circumstances to prevent that happening, and
(d) the suffering is unnecessary.

(3) The considerations to which it is relevant to have regard when determining for the purposes of this section whether suffering is unnecessary include—
  (a) whether the suffering could reasonably have been avoided or reduced;
  (b) whether the conduct which caused the suffering was in compliance with any relevant enactment or any relevant provisions of a licence or code of practice issued under an enactment;
  (c) whether the conduct which caused the suffering was for a legitimate purpose, such as—
    (i) the purpose of benefiting the animal, or
    (ii) the purpose of protecting a person, property or another animal;
  (d) whether the suffering was proportionate to the purpose of the conduct concerned;
  (e) whether the conduct concerned was in all the circumstances that of a reasonably competent and humane person.

(4) Nothing in this section applies to the destruction of an animal in an appropriate and humane manner.

Definitions
"*animal*": ss.1(1) and 62(1).
"*protected animal*": ss.2 and 62(1).
"*responsible for an animal*": ss.3 and 62(1).

Commentary
The section creates two offences:

Animal Welfare Act 2006

(a) acting, or failing to act, in such a way that unnecessary suffering is caused to a protected animal;
(b) being responsible for an animal, permitting or culpably failing to prevent another person causing unnecessary suffering to that animal.

The section also sets out relevant considerations which apply when determining whether suffering is unnecessary. It should be noted that these considerations are not conclusive; the courts are entitled to have regard to any other relevant considerations.

5. Mutilation

(1) A person commits an offence if—
(a) he carries out a prohibited procedure on a protected animal;
(b) he causes such a procedure to be carried out on such an animal.
(2) A person commits an offence if—
(a) he is responsible for an animal,
(b) another person carries out a prohibited procedure on the animal, and
(c) he permitted that to happen or failed to take such steps (whether by way of supervising the other person or otherwise) as were reasonable in all the circumstances to prevent that happening.

(3) References in this section to the carrying out of a prohibited procedure on an animal are to the carrying out of a procedure which involves interference with the sensitive tissues or bone structure of the animal, otherwise than for the purpose of its medical treatment.

(4) Subsections (1) and (2) do not apply in such circumstances as the appropriate national authority may specify by regulations.

(5) Before making regulations under subsection (4), the appropriate national authority shall consult such persons appearing to the authority to represent any interests concerned as the authority considers appropriate.

(6) Nothing in this section applies to the removal of the whole or any part of a dog's tail.

Definitions

"*animal*": ss.1(1) and 62(1).
"*protected animal*": ss.2 and 62(1).
"*responsible for an animal*": ss.3 and 62(1).
"*suffering*": s.62(1).

Commentary
The section creates three offences:
  (a) carrying out a "prohibited procedure" (defined below) on a protected animal;
  (b) causing such a procedure to be carried out on a protected animal;
  (c) being responsible for an animal, permitting or culpably failing to prevent another person carrying out a prohibited procedure on an animal.

A prohibited procedure is one which involves interference with the sensitive tissues or bone structure of the animal otherwise than for medical treatment. However, the docking of a dog's tail is not covered by the foregoing offences; this is treated separately in s.6 (see below).

The appropriate national authority (for definition, see Abbreviations and Explanatory Notes) may by regulations specify circumstances in which the foregoing actions are not classed as offences.

The following regulations have been made under subs.(4): the Mutilations (Permitted Procedures) (England) Regulations 2007 (SI 2007/1100) and the Mutilations (Permitted Procedures) (Wales) Regulations 2007 (SI 2007/1029).

6. Docking of dogs' tails

(1) A person commits an offence if—
  (a) he removes the whole or any part of a dog's tail, otherwise than for the purpose of its medical treatment;
  (b) he causes the whole or any part of a dog's tail to be removed by another person, otherwise than for the purpose of its medical treatment.

(2) A person commits an offence if—
  (a) he is responsible for a dog,
  (b) another person removes the whole or any part of the dog's tail, otherwise than for the purpose of its medical treatment, and
  (c) he permitted that to happen or failed to take such steps (whether by way of supervising the other person or otherwise) as were reasonable in all the circumstances to prevent that happening.

(3) Subsections (1) and (2) do not apply if the dog is a certified working dog that is not more than 5 days old.

Animal Welfare Act 2006

(4) For the purposes of subsection (3), a dog is a certified working dog if a veterinary surgeon has certified, in accordance with regulations made by the appropriate national authority, that the first and second conditions mentioned below are met.

(5) The first condition referred to in subsection (4) is that there has been produced to the veterinary surgeon such evidence as the appropriate national authority may by regulations require for the purpose of showing that the dog is likely to be used for work in connection with—
- (a) law enforcement,
- (b) activities of Her Majesty's armed forces,
- (c) emergency rescue,
- (d) lawful pest control, or
- (e) the lawful shooting of animals.

(6) The second condition referred to in subsection (4) is that the dog is of a type specified for the purposes of this subsection by regulations made by the appropriate national authority.

(7) It is a defence for a person accused of an offence under subsection (1) or (2) to show that he reasonably believed that the dog was one in relation to which subsection (3) applies.

(8) A person commits an offence if—
- (a) he owns a subsection (3) dog, and
- (b) fails to take reasonable steps to secure that, before the dog is 3 months old, it is identified as a subsection (3) dog in accordance with regulations made by the appropriate national authority.

(9) A person commits an offence if—
- (a) he shows a dog at an event to which members of the public are admitted on payment of a fee,
- (b) the dog's tail has been wholly or partly removed (in England and Wales or elsewhere), and
- (c) removal took place on or after the commencement day.

(10) Where a dog is shown only for the purpose of demonstrating its working ability, subsection (9) does not apply if the dog is a subsection (3) dog.

(11) It is a defence for a person accused of an offence under subsection (9) to show that he reasonably believed—
- (a) that the event was not one to which members of the public were admitted on payment of an entrance fee,
- (b) that the removal took place before the commencement day, or
- (c) that the dog was one in relation to which subsection (10) applies.

Animal Welfare Act 2006

(12) A person commits an offence if he knowingly gives false information to a veterinary surgeon in connection with the giving of a certificate for the purposes of this section.

(13) The appropriate national authority may by regulations make provision about the functions of inspectors in relation to—
   (a) certificates for the purposes of this section, and
   (b) the identification of dogs as subsection (3) dogs.

(14) Power to make regulations under this section includes power—
   (a) to make different provision for different cases, and
   (b) to make incidental, supplementary, consequential or transitional provision or savings.

(15) Before making regulations under this section, the appropriate national authority shall consult such persons appearing to the authority to represent any interests concerned as the authority considers appropriate.

(16) In this section—
"commencement day" means the day on which this section comes into force;
"subsection (3) dog" means a dog whose tail has, on or after the commencement day, been wholly or partly removed without contravening subsection (1), because of the application of subsection (3).

Definitions
"*animal*": ss.1(1) and 62(1).
"*protected animal*": ss.2 and 62(1).
"*responsible for an animal*": ss.3 and 62(1).

Commentary
The section creates five offences, to which statutory defences apply:
   (a) **removing, or causing to be removed by another person, the whole or part of a dog's tail, except for medical treatment;**
   (b) **being responsible for a dog, permitting or culpably failing to prevent another person from removing the whole or part of the dog's tail, except for medical treatment;**
   (c) **being the owner of a "subsection (3) dog)" (a term defined below), failing to take reasonable steps before the dog is three months old to ensure that the dog is a subs.(3) dog in accordance with regulations made by the appropriate national authority;**

(d) after the commencement of s.6, showing a dog from which the tail has been wholly or partly removed at an event to which members of the public are admitted on payment of a fee;
(e) knowingly giving false information to a veterinary surgeon in relation to the certification of a dog as a subs.(3) dog.

The statutory defences are as follows:
(i) no offence under (a) or (b) above is committed where the dog is a certified working dog (i.e. a subs.(3) dog) that is not more than five days old. A dog is certified if a veterinary surgeon certifies that, in accordance with regulations made by the appropriate national authority, the following conditions are met:
— evidence is produced to the vet that the dog is likely to be used in connection with law enforcement, the armed forces, emergency rescue, lawful pest control or the lawful shooting of animals;
— the dog is of a type specified for the purposes of the legislation by regulations made by the appropriate national authority.
(ii) a reasonable belief by a person accused of an offence under (a) or (b) above that the dog was a subs.(3) dog;
(iii) showing a dog in public contrary to (d) above is not an offence if the dog is shown solely to demonstrate its working abilities;
(iv) in relation to an offence under (d) above, a reasonable belief that the event was not one to which the public paid for admittance, the event took place before the legislation commenced or the dog was a subs.(3) dog.

The section gives the appropriate national authority power to make regulations for the purposes of the section. The Secretary of State has made the Docking of Working Dogs' Tails (England) Regulations 2007 (SI 2007/1120) in relation to England only. No regulations have so far been made in Wales.

7. Administration of poisons etc.

(1) A person commits an offence if, without lawful authority or reasonable excuse, he—

(a) administers any poisonous or injurious drug or substance to a protected animal, knowing it to be poisonous or injurious, or
(b) causes any poisonous or injurious drug or substance to be taken by a protected animal, knowing it to be poisonous or injurious.

(2) A person commits an offence if—
(a) he is responsible for an animal,
(b) without lawful authority or reasonable excuse, another person administers a poisonous or injurious drug or substance to the animal or causes the animal to take such a drug or substance, and
(c) he permitted that to happen or, knowing the drug or substance to be poisonous or injurious, he failed to take such steps (whether by way of supervising the other person or otherwise) as were reasonable in all the circumstances to prevent that happening.

(3) In this section, references to a poisonous or injurious drug or substance include a drug or substance which, by virtue of the quantity or manner in which it is administered or taken, has the effect of a poisonous or injurious drug or substance.

Commentary
The section creates three offences:
   (a) without lawful authority or excuse, administering poison or injurious drug to a protected animal (see above for definition), knowing the substance to be poisonous or injurious;
   (b) causing a protected animal to take poison or an injurious drug, knowing the substance to be poisonous or injurious;
   (c) being responsible for an animal, without lawful authority or reasonable excuse, permitting or culpably failing to prevent another person from administering a poisonous or injurious drug to that animal.

8. Fighting etc.

(1) A person commits an offence if he—
(a) causes an animal fight to take place, or attempts to do so;
(b) knowingly receives money for admission to an animal fight;
(c) knowingly publicises a proposed animal fight;
(d) provides information about an animal fight to another with the intention of enabling or encouraging attendance at the fight;

Animal Welfare Act 2006

(e) makes or accepts a bet on the outcome of an animal fight or on the likelihood of anything occurring or not occurring in the course of an animal fight;

(f) takes part in an animal fight;

(g) has in his possession anything designed or adapted for use in connection with an animal fight with the intention of its being so used;

(h) keeps or trains an animal for use for in connection with an animal fight;

(i) keeps any premises for use for an animal fight.

(2) A person commits an offence if, without lawful authority or reasonable excuse, he is present at an animal fight.

(3) A person commits an offence if, without lawful authority or reasonable excuse, he—

(a) knowingly supplies a video recording of an animal fight,

(b) knowingly publishes a video recording of an animal fight,

(c) knowingly shows a video recording of an animal fight to another, or

(d) possesses a video recording of an animal fight, knowing it to be such a recording, with the intention of supplying it.

(4) Subsection (3) does not apply if the video recording is of an animal fight that took place—

(a) outside Great Britain, or

(b) before the commencement date.

(5) Subsection (3) does not apply—

(a) in the case of paragraph (a), to the supply of a video recording for inclusion in a programme service;

(b) in the case of paragraph (b) or (c), to the publication or showing of a video recording by means of its inclusion in a programme service;

(c) in the case of paragraph (d), by virtue of intention to supply for inclusion in a programme service.

(6) Provision extending the application of an offence under subsection (3), so far as relating to the provision of information society services, may be made under section 2(2) of the European Communities Act 1972 (c. 68) (powers to implement Community obligations by regulations) notwithstanding the limits imposed by paragraph 1(1)(d) of Schedule 2 to that Act on the penalties with which an offence may be punishable on summary conviction.

(7) In this section—

"animal fight" means an occasion on which a protected animal is placed with an animal, or with a human, for the purpose of fighting, wrestling or baiting;
' "commencement date" means the date on which subsection (3) comes into force;
"information society services" has the meaning given in Article 2(a) of Directive 2000/31/EC of the European Parliament and of the Council of 8 June 2000 on certain legal aspects of information society services, in particular electronic commerce in the Internal Market (Directive on electronic commerce);
"programme service" has the same meaning as in the Communications Act 2003 (c. 21);
"video recording" means a recording, in any form, from which a moving image may by any means be reproduced and includes data stored on a computer disc or by other electronic means which is capable of conversion into a moving image.
(8) In this section—
(a) references to supplying or publishing a video recording are to supplying or publishing a video recording in any manner, including, in relation to a video recording in the form of data stored electronically, by means of transmitting such data;
(b) references to showing a video recording are to showing a moving image reproduced from a video recording by any means.

Definitions
"*animal*": ss.1(1) and 62(1).
"*premises*": s.62(1).
"*protected animal*": ss.2 and 62(1).

Commentary
This section creates a number of offences related to fighting, wrestling or baiting involving animals and animals and humans:
  (a) causing or attempting to cause an animal fight to take place;
  (b) knowingly receiving money for admission to an animal fight;
  (c) knowingly publicising an animal fight;
  (d) providing information about an animal fight to another person with the intention of enabling or encouraging attendance at such a fight;

Animal Welfare Act 2006

(e) making or accepting bets on the outcome of an animal fight, or of anything occurring during an animal fight;
(f) taking part in an animal fight;
(g) having possession of anything designed to be used in connection with an animal fight with the intention that it is used in a fight;
(h) keeping or training an animal for use in an animal fight;
(i) keeping premises for use in an animal fight;
(j) knowingly supplying a video recording of an animal fight;
(k) knowingly publishing such a recording;
(l) knowingly showing such a recording to another person;
(m) possessing such a recording, knowing it to be a recording of an animal fight and with the intention of supplying it.

However, no offence is committed in relation to (j) to (m) above if the event took place outside Great Britain or before s.8 came into force. There are also exceptions to liability in relation to (j), (k) and (l) above in relation to video recordings included in a programme service (as defined in s.405 of the Communications Act 2003).

There is provision to extend the offences in (j) to (m) above to other member states of the European Union.

Promotion of welfare

9. Duty of person responsible for animal to ensure welfare

(1) A person commits an offence if he does not take such steps as are reasonable in all the circumstances to ensure that the needs of an animal for which he is responsible are met to the extent required by good practice.

(2) For the purposes of this Act, an animal's needs shall be taken to include—
  (a) its need for a suitable environment,
  (b) its need for a suitable diet,
  (c) its need to be able to exhibit normal behaviour patterns,
  (d) any need it has to be housed with, or apart from, other animals, and
    (e) its need to be protected from pain, suffering, injury and disease.

(3) The circumstances to which it is relevant to have regard when applying Subsection (1) include, in particular—

(a) any lawful purpose for which the animal is kept, and

(b) any lawful activity undertaken in relation to the animal.

(4) Nothing in this section applies to the destruction of an animal in an appropriate and humane manner.

Definitions
"animal": ss.1(1) and 62(1).
"animal for which he is responsible": ss.3 and 62(1).
"suffering": s.62(1).

Commentary
Section 9 makes it an offence not to take, in all the circumstances specified in the section, reasonable steps to ensure that the needs of an animal for which one is responsible are met to the extent required by good practice. The specified circumstances are any lawful purpose for which the animal is kept and any lawful activity undertaken in relation to the animal. The needs of an animal are taken to include:

(a) a suitable environment;

(b) a suitable diet;

(c) being able to exhibit normal behaviour patterns;

(d) being housed with, or apart from, other animals; and

(e) being protected from pain, suffering, injury and disease.

Nothing in s.9 applies to the destruction of an animal in an appropriate and humane manner.

Section 10 below describes the action that can be taken following contravention of s.9(1).

10. Improvement notices

(1) If an inspector is of the opinion that a person is failing to comply with section 9(1), he may serve on the person a notice which—

(a) states that he is of that opinion,

(b) specifies the respects in which he considers the person is failing to comply with that provision,

(c) specifies the steps he considers need to be taken in order to comply with the provision,

(d) specifies a period for the taking of those steps, and

(e) explains the effect of subsections (2) and (3).

(2) Where a notice under subsection (1) ("an improvement notice") is served, no proceedings for an offence under section 9(1) may be

instituted before the end of the period specified for the purposes of subsection (1)(d) ("the compliance period") in respect of—
  (a) the non-compliance which gave rise to the notice, or
  (b) any continuation of that non-compliance.

(3) If the steps specified in an improvement notice are taken at any time before the end of the compliance period, no proceedings for an offence under section 9(1) may be instituted in respect of—
  (a) the non-compliance which gave rise to the notice, or
  (b) any continuation of that non-compliance prior to the taking of the steps specified in the notice.

(4) An inspector may extend, or further extend, the compliance period specified in an improvement notice.

Definitions
"*inspector*": s.51(1).

11. Transfer of animals by way of sale or prize to persons under 16

(1) A person commits an offence if he sells an animal to a person whom he has reasonable cause to believe to be under the age of 16 years.

(2) For the purposes of subsection (1), selling an animal includes transferring, or agreeing to transfer, ownership of the animal in consideration of entry by the transferee into another transaction.

(3) Subject to subsections (4) to (6), a person commits an offence if—
  (a) he enters into an arrangement with a person whom he has reasonable cause to believe to be under the age of 16 years, and
  (b) the arrangement is one under which that person has the chance to win an animal as a prize.

(4) A person does not commit an offence under subsection (3) if—
  (a) he enters into the arrangement in the presence of the person with whom the arrangement is made, and
  (b) he has reasonable cause to believe that the person with whom the arrangement is made is accompanied by a person who is not under the age of 16 years.

(5) A person does not commit an offence under subsection (3) if—
  (a) he enters into the arrangement otherwise than in the presence of the person with whom the arrangement is made, and
  (b) he has reasonable cause to believe that a person who has actual care and control of the person with whom the arrangement is made has consented to the arrangement.

Animal Welfare Act 2006

(6) A person does not commit an offence under subsection (3) if he enters into the arrangement in a family context.

Definitions
"*animal*": ss.1(1) and 62(1).

Commentary
It is an offence under this section:
  (a) to sell an animal to a person whom the seller reasonably believes to be under 16; and
  (b) to enter into an arrangement with such a person under which that person has an opportunity to win the animal as a prize.

No offence is committed where the arrangement is made in the presence of the person under 16 and that person is accompanied by a person over that age, nor where the person under 16 is not present but the transferor has reason to believe that the consent of the person who has care or control over the person under 16 (e.g. a parent or legal guardian) has been given.

No offence is committed under the section where the arrangement takes place in a family context (e.g. transfer from parent to child).

12. Regulations to promote welfare

(1) The appropriate national authority may by regulations make such provision as the authority thinks fit for the purpose of promoting the welfare of animals for which a person is responsible, or the progeny of such animals.

(2) Without prejudice to the generality of the power under subsection (1), regulations under that subsection may, in particular—
  (a) make provision imposing specific requirements for the purpose of securing that the needs of animals are met;
  (b) make provision to facilitate or improve co-ordination in relation to the carrying out by different persons of functions relating to the welfare of animals;
  (c) make provision for the establishment of one or more bodies with functions relating to advice about the welfare of animals.

(3) Power to make regulations under subsection (1) includes power—
  (a) to provide that breach of a provision of the regulations is an offence;

Animal Welfare Act 2006

(b) to apply a relevant post-conviction power in relation to conviction for an offence under the regulations;

(c) to make provision for fees or other charges in relation to the carrying out of functions under the regulations;

(d) to make different provision for different cases or areas;

(e) to provide for exemptions from a provision of the regulations, either subject to specified conditions or without conditions;

(f) to make incidental, supplementary, consequential or transitional provision or savings.

(4) Power to make regulations under subsection (1) does not include power to create an offence triable on indictment or punishable with—

(a) imprisonment for a term exceeding 51 weeks, or

(b) a fine exceeding level 5 on the standard scale.

(5) Regulations under subsection (1) may provide that a specified offence under the regulations is to be treated as a relevant offence for the purposes of section 23.

(6) Before making regulations under subsection (1), the appropriate national authority shall consult such persons appearing to the authority to represent any interests concerned as the authority considers appropriate.

(7) In this section, "specified" means specified in regulations under subsection (1).

Definitions

"*animal*": ss.1(1) and 62(1).
"*animals for which a person is responsible*": ss.3 and 62(1).
"*appropriate national authority*": s.62(1).
"*relevant post-conviction power*": s.62(6).

Commentary

This section empowers the appropriate national authority to make regulations for the promotion of the welfare of animals (and their progeny) for which a person is responsible (thus excluding wild animals).

The regulations may cover, for example:

(a) specific requirements for meeting the needs of animals;

(b) facilitating or improving co-ordination between those with responsibilities relating to the welfare of animals;

(c) establishing a body or bodies to give advice about the welfare of animals.

Licensing and registration

13. Licensing or registration of activities involving animals

(1) No person shall carry on an activity to which this subsection applies except under the authority of a licence for the purposes of this section.

(2) Subsection (1) applies to an activity which—
(a) involves animals for which a person is responsible, and
(b) is specified for the purposes of the subsection by regulations made by the appropriate national authority.

(3) No person shall carry on an activity to which this subsection applies unless registered for the purposes of this section.

(4) Subsection (3) applies to an activity which—
(a) involves animals for which a person is responsible, and
(b) is specified for the purposes of the subsection by regulations made by the appropriate national authority.

(5) Regulations under subsection (2) or (4) may only be made for the purpose of promoting the welfare of animals for which a person is responsible, or the progeny of such animals.

(6) A person commits an offence if he contravenes subsection (1) or (3).

(7) The appropriate national authority may by regulations make provision about licences or registration for the purposes of this section.

(8) The appropriate national authority may by regulations repeal any of the following enactments (which impose licence or registration requirements in relation to activities involving animals)—
(a) section 1(1) of the Performing Animals (Regulation) Act 1925 (c. 38);
(b) section 1(1) of the Pet Animals Act 1951 (c. 35);
(c) section 1(1) of the Animal Boarding Establishments Act 1963 (c. 43);
(d) section 1(1) of the Riding Establishments Act 1964 (c. 70);
(e) section 1(1) of the Breeding of Dogs Act 1973 (c. 60).

(9) Before making regulations under this section, the appropriate national authority shall consult such persons appearing to the authority to represent any interests concerned as the authority considers appropriate.

(10) Schedule 1 (which makes provision about regulations under this section) has effect.

Definitions
"*animal*": ss.1(1) and 62(1).
"*animals for which a person is responsible*": ss.3 and 62(1).
"*appropriate national authority*": s.62(1).
"*relevant post-conviction power*": s.62(6).

Commentary
This section empowers the appropriate national authority to make regulations covering the licensing and registration of activities involving animals. The authority is given power t o repeal or amend the licensing or registration provisions in the Performing Animals (Regulation) Act 1925 (see pp.61 and 225), the Animal Boarding Establishments Act 1963 (see pp.44 and 98) and the Breeding of Dogs Act 1973 (see pp.44 and 98).

Schedule 1 to the 2006 Act (not reproduced in this text) makes detailed provision about the making of regulations.

The Welfare of Racing Greyhounds Regulations 2010 (SI 2010/543) have been made under the section. They apply only in England.

Codes of practice

14. Codes of practice

(1) The appropriate national authority may issue, and may from time to time revise, codes of practice for the purpose of providing practical guidance in respect of any provision made by or under this Act.

(2) The authority responsible for issuing a code of practice under subsection (1) shall publish the code, and any revision of it, in such manner as it considers appropriate.

(3) A person's failure to comply with a provision of a code of practice issued under this section shall not of itself render him liable to proceedings of any kind.

(4) In any proceedings against a person for an offence under this Act or an offence under regulations under section 12 or 13—
- (a) failure to comply with a relevant provision of a code of practice issued under this section may be relied upon as tending to establish liability, and
- (b) compliance with a relevant provision of such a code of practice may be relied upon as tending to negative liability.

Definitions
"*appropriate national authority*": s.62(1).

Commentary
A Code of Practice for the Welfare of Dogs was published by Defra in April 2010. This relates to England and can be viewed on the Defra website.

The Welsh Assembly Government issued a Code of Practice for the Welfare of Dogs for Wales in October 2008. This can be viewed on the Welsh Assembly Government website.

15. Making and approval of codes of practice: England

(1) Where the Secretary of State proposes to issue (or revise) a code of practice under section 14, he shall—
   (a) prepare a draft of the code (or revised code),
   (b) consult about the draft such persons appearing to him to represent any interests concerned as he considers appropriate, and
   (c) consider any representations made by them.

(2) If following consultation under subsection (1) the Secretary of State decides to proceed with a draft (either in its original form or with such modifications as he thinks fit), he shall lay a copy of it before Parliament.

(3) If, within the 40-day period, either House of Parliament resolves not to approve a draft laid under subsection (2), the Secretary of State shall take no further steps in relation to it.

(4) If, within the 40-day period, neither House resolves not to approve a draft laid under subsection (2), the Secretary of State shall issue (or revise) the code in the form of the draft.

(5) A code (or revised code) shall come into force on such day as the Secretary of State may by order appoint.

(6) Subsection (3) does not prevent a new draft of a code (or revised code) from being laid before Parliament.

(7) An order under subsection (5) may include transitional provision or savings.

(8) In this section, "the 40-day period", in relation to a draft laid under subsection (2), means—
   (a) if the draft is laid before the Houses on different days, the period of 40 days beginning with the later of the two days, and

(b) in any other case, the period of 40 days beginning with the day on which the draft is laid before each House, no account being taken of any period during which Parliament is dissolved or prorogued or during which both Houses are adjourned for more than four days.

16. Making of codes of practice: Wales

(1) Where the National Assembly for Wales proposes to issue (or revise) a code of practice under section 14, it shall—
   (a) prepare a draft of the code (or revised code),
   (b) consult about the draft such persons appearing to it to represent any interests concerned as it considers appropriate, and
   (c) consider any representations made by them.

(2) The Assembly may issue (or revise) a code either in the form of the draft prepared under subsection (1)(a) or with such modification as it thinks fit.

(3) A code (or revised code) shall come into force in accordance with its provisions.

(4) A code (or revised code) may include transitional provision or savings.

17. Revocation of codes of practice

(1) The appropriate national authority may by order revoke a code of practice issued by it under section 14.

(2) An order under subsection (1) may include transitional provision or savings.

(3) Before making an order under subsection (1), the appropriate national authority shall consult such persons appearing to the authority to represent any interests concerned as the authority considers appropriate.

(4) Subsection (3) does not apply in relation to an order revoking a code of practice in connection with its replacement by a new one.

Definitions
"*appropriate national authority*": s.62(1).

Animal Welfare Act 2006

Animals in distress

18. Powers in relation to animals in distress

(1) If an inspector or a constable reasonably believes that a protected animal is suffering, he may take, or arrange for the taking of, such steps as appear to him to be immediately necessary to alleviate the animal's suffering.

(2) Subsection (1) does not authorise destruction of an animal.

(3) If a veterinary surgeon certifies that the condition of a protected animal is such that it should in its own interests be destroyed, an inspector or a constable may—
- (a) destroy the animal where it is or take it to another place and destroy it there, or
- (b) arrange for the doing of any of the things mentioned in paragraph (a).

(4) An inspector or a constable may act under subsection (3) without the certificate of a veterinary surgeon if it appears to him—
- (a) that the condition of the animal is such that there is no reasonable alternative to destroying it, and
- (b) that the need for action is such that it is not reasonably practicable to wait for a veterinary surgeon.

(5) An inspector or a constable may take a protected animal into possession if a veterinary surgeon certifies—
- (a) that it is suffering, or
- (b) that it is likely to suffer if its circumstances do not change.

(6) An inspector or a constable may act under subsection (5) without the certificate of a veterinary surgeon if it appears to him—
- (a) that the animal is suffering or that it is likely to do so if its circumstances do not change, and
- (b) that the need for action is such that it is not reasonably practicable to wait for a veterinary surgeon.

(7) The power conferred by subsection (5) includes power to take into possession dependent offspring of an animal taken into possession under that subsection.

(8) Where an animal is taken into possession under subsection (5), an inspector or a constable may—
- (a) remove it, or arrange for it to be removed, to a place of safety;
- (b) care for it, or arrange for it to be cared for—
  - (i) on the premises where it was being kept when it was taken into possession, or

Animal Welfare Act 2006

(ii) at such other place as he thinks fit;
(c) mark it, or arrange for it to be marked, for identification purposes.

(9) A person acting under subsection (8)(b)(i), or under an arrangement under that provision, may make use of any equipment on the premises.

(10) A veterinary surgeon may examine and take samples from an animal for the purpose of determining whether to issue a certificate under subsection (3) or (5) with respect to the animal.

(11) If a person exercises a power under this section otherwise than with the knowledge of a person who is responsible for the animal concerned, he must, as soon as reasonably practicable after exercising the power, take such steps as are reasonable in the circumstances to bring the exercise of the power to the notice of such a person.

(12) A person commits an offence if he intentionally obstructs a person in the exercise of power conferred by this section.

(13) A magistrates' court may, on application by a person who incurs expenses in acting under this section, order that he be reimbursed by such person as it thinks fit.

(14) A person affected by a decision under subsection (13) may appeal against the decision to the Crown Court.

Definitions
"animal": ss.1(1) and 62(1).
"inspector": s.51(1).
"premises": s.62(1).
"protected animal": ss.2 and 62(1).
"suffering": s.62(1).
"veterinary surgeon": s.62(1).

Commentary
This section:
- **(a) empowers an inspector or a constable who reasonably believes that a protected animal is suffering to take immediate steps (other than destruction) to alleviate the animal's suffering;**
- **(b) empowers an inspector or a constable to destroy a protected animal when a veterinary surgeon certifies that the animal should in its own interests be destroyed;**

(c) empowers an inspector or a constable to destroy a protected animal where there appears to be no reasonable alternative because of the animal's condition and it is not reasonably practicable to wait for a vet;
(d) empowers an inspector or a constable to take a protected animal into possession if a vet certifies that the animal is suffering;
(e) empowers an inspector or a constable to take a protected animal into possession where it is suffering and it is not reasonably practicable to wait for a vet;
(f) empowers an inspector or a constable acting under (d) above to arrange for the animal to be cared for at a place of safety;
(g) makes it an offence deliberately to obstruct a person exercising the foregoing powers;
(h) entitles those exercising the foregoing powers to apply to a magistrates' court for an order to reimburse their expenses and for a person so ordered to appeal to the Crown Court.

19. Power of entry for section 18 purposes

(1) An inspector or a constable may enter premises for the purpose of searching for a protected animal and of exercising any power under section 18 in relation to it if he reasonably believes—
(a) that there is a protected animal on the premises, and
(b) that the animal is suffering or, if the circumstances of the animal do not change, it is likely to suffer.

(2) Subsection (1) does not authorise entry to any part of premises which is used as a private dwelling.

(3) An inspector or a constable may (if necessary) use reasonable force in exercising the power conferred by subsection (1), but only if it appears to him that entry is required before a warrant under subsection (4) can be obtained and executed.

(4) Subject to subsection (5), a justice of the peace may, on the application of an inspector or constable, issue a warrant authorising an inspector or a constable to enter premises for the purpose mentioned in subsection (1), if necessary using reasonable force.

(5) The power to issue a warrant under subsection (4) is exercisable only if the justice of the peace is satisfied—

Animal Welfare Act 2006

(a) that there are reasonable grounds for believing that there is a protected animal on the premises and that the animal is suffering or is likely to suffer if its circumstances do not change, and
(b) that section 52 is satisfied in relation to the premises.

Definitions
"animal": ss.1(1) and 62(1).
"inspector": s.51(1).
"premises": s.62(1).
"premises used as a private dwelling": s.62(3).
"protected animal": ss.2 and 62(1).
"suffering": s.62(1).

Commentary
This section gives powers of entry for the purposes specified in s.18.

20. Orders in relation to animals taken under section 18(5)

(1) A magistrates' court may order any of the following in relation to an animal taken into possession under section 18(5)—
  (a) that specified treatment be administered to the animal;
  (b) that possession of the animal be given up to a specified person;
  (c) that the animal be sold;
  (d) that the animal be disposed of otherwise than by way of sale;
  (e) that the animal be destroyed.

(2) If an animal is taken into possession under section 18(5) when it is pregnant, the power conferred by subsection (1) shall also be exercisable in relation to any offspring that results from the pregnancy.

(3) The power conferred by subsection (1) shall be exercisable on application by—
  (a) the owner of the animal, or
  (b) any other person appearing to the court to have a sufficient interest in the animal.

(4) A court may not make an order under subsection (1) unless—
  (a) it has given the owner of the animal an opportunity to be heard, or
  (b) it is satisfied that it is not reasonably practicable to communicate with the owner.

(5) Where a court makes an order under subsection (1), it may—

Animal Welfare Act 2006

(a) appoint a person to carry out, or arrange for the carrying out, of the order;
(b) give directions with respect to the carrying out of the order;
(c) confer additional powers (including power to enter premises where the animal is being kept) for the purpose of, or in connection with, the carrying out of the order;
(d) order a person to reimburse the expenses of carrying out the order.

(6) In determining how to exercise its powers under this section, the court shall have regard, amongst other things, to the desirability of protecting the animal's value and avoiding increasing any expenses which a person may be ordered to reimburse.

(7) A person commits an offence if he intentionally obstructs a person in the exercise of any power conferred by virtue of this section.

(8) If the owner of the animal is subject to a liability by virtue of section 18(13) or subsection (5)(d) above, any amount to which he is entitled as a result of sale of the animal may be reduced by an amount equal to that liability.

Definitions
"*animal*": ss.1(1) and 62(1).

Commentary
This section empowers a magistrates' court to authorise the provision of treatment to, the sale or other disposal of, or the destruction of an animal taken into possession in accordance with s.18(6).

21. Orders under section 20: appeals

(1) Where a court makes an order under section 20(1), the owner of the animal to which the order relates may appeal against the order to the Crown Court.

(2) Nothing may be done under an order under section 20(1) unless—
(a) the period for giving notice of appeal against the order has expired, and
(b) if the order is the subject of an appeal, the appeal has been determined or withdrawn.

(3) Where the effect of an order is suspended under subsection (2)—

(a) no directions given in connection with the order shall have effect, but
(b) the court may give directions about how any animal to which the order applies is to be dealt with during the suspension.

(4) Directions under subsection (3)(b) may, in particular—
(a) appoint a person to carry out, or arrange for the carrying out, of the directions;
(b) require any person who has possession of the animal to deliver it up for the purposes of the directions;
(c) confer additional powers (including power to enter premises where the animal is being kept) for the purpose of, or in connection with, the carrying out of the directions;
(d) provide for the recovery of any expenses which are reasonably incurred in carrying out the directions.

(5) Where a court decides on an application under section 20(3)(a) not to exercise the power conferred by subsection (1) of that section, the applicant may appeal against the decision to the Crown Court.

(6) Where a court makes an order under section 20(5)(d), the person against whom the order is made may appeal against the order to the Crown Court.

Definitions
"*animal*": ss.1(1) and 62(1).
"*premises*": s.62(1).

Commentary
This section provides for appeals to the Crown Court against orders made under s.20.

Enforcement powers

22. Seizure of animals involved in fighting offences

(1) A constable may seize an animal if it appears to him that it is one in relation to which an offence under section 8(1) or (2) has been committed.

(2) A constable may enter and search premises for the purpose of exercising the power under subsection (1) if he reasonably believes—
(a) that there is an animal on the premises, and
(b) that the animal is one in relation to which the power under subsection (1) is exercisable.

(3) Subsection (2) does not authorise entry to any part of premises which is used as a private dwelling.

(4) Subject to subsection (5), a justice of the peace may, on the application of a constable, issue a warrant authorising a constable to enter and search premises, if necessary using reasonable force, for the purpose of exercising the power under subsection (1).

(5) The power to issue a warrant under subsection (4) is exercisable only if the justice of the peace is satisfied—
- (a) that there are reasonable grounds for believing that there is on the premises an animal in relation to which an offence under section 8(1) or (2) has been committed, and
- (b) that section 52 is satisfied in relation to the premises.

(6) In this section, references to an animal in relation to which an offence under section 8(1) or (2) has been committed include an animal which took part in an animal fight in relation to which such an offence was committed.

Definitions
"*animal*": ss.1(1) and 62(1).
"*premises*": s.62(1).
"*premises used as a private dwelling*": s.62(3).

Commentary
This section empowers a constable to seize animals involved in fighting offences.

23. Entry and search under warrant in connection with offences

(1) Subject to subsection (2), a justice of the peace may, on the application of an inspector or constable, issue a warrant authorising an inspector or a constable to enter premises, if necessary using reasonable force, in order to search for evidence of the commission of a relevant offence.

(2) The power to issue a warrant under subsection (1) is exercisable only if the justice of the peace is satisfied—
- (a) that there are reasonable grounds for believing—
  - (i) that a relevant offence has been committed on the premises, or
  - (ii) that evidence of the commission of a relevant offence is to be found on the premises, and

(b) that section 52 is satisfied in relation to the premises.

(3) In this section, "relevant offence" means an offence under any of sections 4 to 9, 13(6) and 34(9).

Definitions
"inspector": s.51(1).
"premises": s.62(1).

Commentary
This section gives powers of entry and search under warrant for the purposes of relevant offences, as defined in subs.(3).

24. Entry for purposes of arrest

In section 17(1)(c) of the Police and Criminal Evidence Act 1984 (c. 60) (power of constable to enter and search premises for purpose of arresting a person for offence under specified enactments), at end insert—

"(v) any of sections 4, 5, 6(1) and (2), 7 and 8(1) and (2) of the Animal Welfare Act 2006 (offences relating to the prevention of harm to animals);".

Commentary
This section amends the Police and Criminal Evidence Act 1984 to cover entry of premises for the purposes of arrest in accordance with the relevant provisions of the 2006 Act.

25. Inspection of records required to be kept by holder of licence

(1) An inspector may require the holder of a licence to produce for inspection any records which he is required to keep by a condition of the licence.

(2) Where records which a person is so required to keep are stored in electronic form, the power under subsection (1) includes power to require the records to be made available for inspection—

(a) in a visible and legible form, or
(b) in a form from which they can readily be produced in a visible and legible form.

(3) An inspector may inspect and take copies of any records produced for inspection in pursuance of a requirement under this section.

Definitions
"inspector": s.51(1).
"licence": ss.13 and 62(1).

26. Inspection in connection with licences

(1) An inspector may carry out an inspection in order to check compliance with—
  (a) the conditions subject to which a licence is granted;
  (b) provision made by or under this Act which is relevant to the carrying on of an activity to which a licence relates.

(2) An inspector may, for the purpose of carrying out an inspection under subsection (1), enter—
  (a) premises specified in a licence as premises on which the carrying on of an activity is authorised;
  (b) premises on which he reasonably believes an activity to which a licence relates is being carried on.

(3) Subsection (2) does not authorise entry to any part of premises which is used as a private dwelling unless 24 hours' notice of the intended entry is given to the occupier.

Definitions
"inspector": s.51(1).
"licence": ss.13 and 62(1).
"occupier": s.62(2).
"premises": s.62(1).
"premises which is used as a private dwelling": s.62(5).

27. Inspection in connection with registration

(1) An inspector may carry out an inspection in order to check compliance with provision made by or under this Act which is relevant to the carrying on of an activity to which a registration for the purposes of section 13 relates.

(2) An inspector may, for the purpose of carrying out an inspection under subsection (1), enter premises on which he reasonably believes a person registered for the purposes of section 13 is carrying on an activity to which the registration relates.

(3) Subsection (2) does not authorise entry to any part of premises which is used as a private dwelling unless 24 hours' notice of the intended entry is given to the occupier.

Animal Welfare Act 2006

Definitions
"inspector": s.51(1).
"occupier": s.62(2).
"premises": s.62(1).
"premises which is used as a private dwelling": s.62(5).

28. Inspection of farm premises

(1) An inspector may carry out an inspection in order to—
  (a) check compliance with regulations under section 12 which relate to animals bred or kept for farming purposes;
  (b) ascertain whether any offence under or by virtue of this Act has been or is being committed in relation to such animals.

(2) An inspector may enter premises which he reasonably believes to be premises on which animals are bred or kept for farming purposes in order to carry out an inspection under subsection (1).

(3) Subsection (2) does not authorise entry to any part of premises which is used as a private dwelling.

(4) Subject to subsection (5), a justice of the peace may, on the application of an inspector, issue a warrant authorising an inspector to enter premises, if necessary using reasonable force, in order to carry out an inspection under subsection (1).

(5) The power to issue a warrant under subsection (4) is exercisable only if the justice of the peace is satisfied—
  (a) that it is reasonable to carry out an inspection on the premises, and
  (b) that section 52 is satisfied in relation to the premises.

Definitions
"animals": ss.1(1) and 62(1).
"inspector": s.51(1).
"occupier": s.62(2).
"premises": s.62(1).
"premises which is used as a private dwelling": s.62(5).

29. Inspection relating to community obligations

(1) An inspector may carry out an inspection in order to check compliance with regulations under section 12 which implement a Community obligation.

(2) An inspector may enter any premises in order to carry out an inspection under subsection (1).

(3) Subsection (2) does not authorise entry to any part of premises which is used as a private dwelling.

Definitions
"*animals*": ss.1(1) and 62(1).
"*inspector*": s.51(1).
"*occupier*": s.62(2).
"*premises*": s.62(1).
"*premises which is used as a private dwelling*": s.62(5).

Prosecutions

30. Power of local authority to prosecute offences
A local authority in England or Wales may prosecute proceedings for any offence under this Act.

Definitions
"*local authority*": s.62(1).

31. Time limits for prosecutions
(1) Notwithstanding anything in section 127(1) of the Magistrates' Courts Act 1980 (c. 43), a magistrates' court may try an information relating to an offence under this Act if the information is laid—
 (a) before the end of the period of three years beginning with the date of the commission of the offence, and
 (b) before the end of the period of six months beginning with the date on which evidence which the prosecutor thinks is sufficient to justify the proceedings comes to his knowledge.
(2) For the purposes of subsection (1)(b)—
 (a) a certificate signed by or on behalf of the prosecutor and stating the date on which such evidence came to his knowledge shall be conclusive evidence of that fact, and
 (b) a certificate stating that matter and purporting to be so signed shall be treated as so signed unless the contrary is proved.

Commentary
This section sets out time limits for prosecutions. The limit is three years from the date of the commission of the offence and six months from the date when the prosecutor thinks there is sufficient evidence to justify proceedings.

Animal Welfare Act 2006

Post-conviction powers

32. Imprisonment or fine

(1) A person guilty of an offence under any of sections 4, 5, 6(1) and (2), 7 and 8 shall be liable on summary conviction to—
 (a) imprisonment for a term not exceeding 51 weeks, or
 (b) a fine not exceeding £20,000,
or to both.

(2) A person guilty of an offence under section 9, 13(6) or 34(9) shall be liable on summary conviction to—
 (a) imprisonment for a term not exceeding 51 weeks, or
 (b) a fine not exceeding level 5 on the standard scale,
or to both.

(3) A person guilty of an offence under regulations under section 12 or 13 shall be liable on summary conviction to such penalty by way of imprisonment or fine as may be provided by regulations under that section.

(4) A person guilty of any other offence under this Act shall be liable on summary conviction to—
 (a) imprisonment for a term not exceeding 51 weeks, or
 (b) a fine not exceeding level 4 on the standard scale,
or to both.

(5) In relation to an offence committed before the commencement of section 281(5) of the Criminal Justice Act 2003 (c. 44), the reference in each of subsections (1)(a), (2)(a) and (4)(a) to 51 weeks is to be read as a reference to 6 months.

33. Deprivation

(1) If the person convicted of an offence under any of sections 4, 5, 6(1) and (2), 7, 8 and 9 is the owner of an animal in relation to which the offence was committed, the court by or before which he is convicted may, instead of or in addition to dealing with him in any other way, make an order depriving him of ownership of the animal and for its disposal.

(2) Where the owner of an animal is convicted of an offence under section 34(9) because ownership of the animal is in breach of a disqualification under section 34(2), the court by or before which he is convicted may, instead of or in addition to dealing with him in any other way, make an order depriving him of ownership of the animal and for its disposal.

Animal Welfare Act 2006

(3) Where the animal in respect of which an order under subsection (1) or (2) is made has any dependent offspring, the order may include provision depriving the person to whom it relates of ownership of the offspring and for its disposal.

(4) Where a court makes an order under subsection (1) or (2), it may—
  (a) appoint a person to carry out, or arrange for the carrying out of, the order;
  (b) require any person who has possession of an animal to which the order applies to deliver it up to enable the order to be carried out;
  (c) give directions with respect to the carrying out of the order;
  (d) confer additional powers (including power to enter premises where an animal to which the order applies is being kept) for the purpose of, or in connection with, the carrying out of the order;
  (e) order the offender to reimburse the expenses of carrying out the order.

(5) Directions under subsection (4)(c) may—
  (a) specify the manner in which an animal is to be disposed of, or
  (b) delegate the decision about the manner in which an animal is to be disposed of to a person appointed under subsection (4)(a).

(6) Where a court decides not to make an order under subsection (1) or (2) in relation to an offender, it shall—
  (a) give its reasons for the decision in open court, and
  (b) if it is a magistrates' court, cause them to be entered in the register of its proceedings.

(7) Subsection (6) does not apply where the court makes an order under section 34(1) in relation to the offender.

(8) In subsection (1), the reference to an animal in relation to which an offence was committed includes, in the case of an offence under section 8, an animal which took part in an animal fight in relation to which the offence was committed.

(9) In this section, references to disposing of an animal include destroying it.

Definitions
"animal": ss.1(1) and 62(1).

Commentary
This section enables the owner of an animal who is convicted of an offence under ss.4, 5, 6(1) and (2), 7, 8 or 9 to be deprived

of ownership of the animal instead of, or in addition to, being fined or imprisoned.

34. Disqualification

(1) If a person is convicted of an offence to which this section applies, the court by or before which he is convicted may, instead of or in addition to dealing with him in any other way, make an order disqualifying him under any one or more of subsections (2) to (4) for such period as it thinks fit.

(2) Disqualification under this subsection disqualifies a person—
 (a) from owning animals,
 (b) from keeping animals,
 (c) from participating in the keeping of animals, and
 (d) from being party to an arrangement under which he is entitled to control or influence the way in which animals are kept.

(3) Disqualification under this subsection disqualifies a person from dealing in animals.

(4) Disqualification under this subsection disqualifies a person—
 (a) from transporting animals, and
 (b) from arranging for the transport of animals.

(5) Disqualification under subsection (2), (3) or (4) may be imposed in relation to animals generally, or in relation to animals of one or more kinds.

(6) The court by which an order under subsection (1) is made may specify a period during which the offender may not make an application under section 43(1) for termination of the order.

(7) The court by which an order under subsection (1) is made may—
 (a) suspend the operation of the order pending an appeal, or
 (b) where it appears to the court that the offender owns or keeps an animal to which the order applies, suspend the operation of the order, and of any order made under section 35 in connection with the disqualification, for such period as it thinks necessary for enabling alternative arrangements to be made in respect of the animal.

(8) Where a court decides not to make an order under subsection (1) in relation to an offender, it shall—
 (a) give its reasons for the decision in open court, and
 (b) if it is a magistrates' court, cause them to be entered in the register of its proceedings.

(9) A person who breaches a disqualification imposed by an order under subsection (1) commits an offence.

(10) This section applies to an offence under any of sections 4, 5, 6(1) and (2), 7, 8, 9 and 13(6) and subsection (9).

Definitions
"animals": ss.1(1) and 62(1).

Commentary
This section enables a person convicted of an offence under ss.4, 5, 6 (1) and (2), 7, 8, 9, 13(6) or 34(9) (breach if a disqualification order) to be disqualified from owning, keeping or participating in the keeping of animals, or being party to an arrangement whereby he is able to control or influence the way in which animals are kept. The disqualification extends to transporting animals or arranging for their transport. Breach of a disqualification order is an offence.

35. Seizure of animals in connection with disqualification

(1) Where—
  (a) a court makes an order under section 34(1), and
  (b) it appears to the court that the person to whom the order applies owns or keeps any animal contrary to the disqualification imposed by the order,
it may order that all animals he owns or keeps contrary to the disqualification be taken into possession.

(2) Where a person is convicted of an offence under section 34(9) because of owning or keeping an animal in breach of disqualification under section 34(2), the court by or before which he is convicted may order that all animals he owns or keeps in breach of the disqualification be taken into possession.

(3) An order under subsection (1) or (2), so far as relating to any animal owned by the person subject to disqualification, shall have effect as an order for the disposal of the animal.

(4) Any animal taken into possession in pursuance of an order under subsection (1) or (2) that is not owned by the person subject to disqualification shall be dealt with in such manner as the appropriate court may order.

(5) A court may not make an order for disposal under subsection (4) unless—

(a) it has given the owner of the animal an opportunity to be heard, or
(b) it is satisfied that it is not reasonably practicable to communicate with the owner.

(6) Where a court makes an order under subsection (4) for the disposal of an animal, the owner may—
(a) in the case of an order made by a magistrates' court, appeal against the order to the Crown Court;
(b) in the case of an order made by the Crown Court, appeal against the order to the Court of Appeal.

(7) In subsection (4), the reference to the appropriate court is to—
(a) the court which made the order under subsection (1) or (2), or
(b) in the case of an order made by a magistrates' court, to a magistrates' court for the same local justice area as that court.

(8) In this section, references to disposing of an animal include destroying it.

Definitions
"*animal*": ss.1(1) and 62(1).

Commentary
This section empowers the court which makes a disqualification order under s.34 to order the seizure of an animal which is owned or kept in breach of the disqualification order.

36. Section 35: supplementary

(1) The court by which an order under section 35 is made may—
(a) appoint a person to carry out, or arrange for the carrying out of, the order;
(b) require any person who has possession of an animal to which the order applies to deliver it up to enable the order to be carried out;
(c) give directions with respect to the carrying out of the order;
(d) confer additional powers (including power to enter premises where an animal to which the order applies is being kept) for the purpose of, or in connection with, the carrying out of the order;
(e) order the person subject to disqualification, or another person, to reimburse the expenses of carrying out the order.

(2) Directions under subsection (1)(c) may—
(a) specify the manner in which an animal is to be disposed of, or
(b) delegate the decision about the manner in which an animal is to be disposed of to a person appointed under subsection (1)(a).

(3) In determining how to exercise its powers under section 35 and this section, the court shall have regard, amongst other things, to—
  (a) the desirability of protecting the value of any animal to which the order applies, and
  (b) the desirability of avoiding increasing any expenses which a person may be ordered to reimburse.

(4) In determining how to exercise a power delegated under subsection (2)(b), a person shall have regard, amongst other things, to the things mentioned in subsection (3)(a) and (b).

(5) If the owner of an animal ordered to be disposed of under section 35 is subject to a liability by virtue of subsection (1)(e), any amount to which he is entitled as a result of sale of the animal may be reduced by an amount equal to that liability.

Definitions
"animal": ss.1(1) and 62(1).
"premises": s.62(1).

37. Destruction in the interests of the animal

(1) The court by or before which a person is convicted of an offence under any of sections 4, 5, 6(1) and (2), 7, 8(1) and (2) and 9 may order the destruction of an animal in relation to which the offence was committed if it is satisfied, on the basis of evidence given by a veterinary surgeon, that it is appropriate to do so in the interests of the animal.

(2) A court may not make an order under subsection (1) unless—
  (a) it has given the owner of the animal an opportunity to be heard, or
  (b) it is satisfied that it is not reasonably practicable to communicate with the owner.

(3) Where a court makes an order under subsection (1), it may—
  (a) appoint a person to carry out, or arrange for the carrying out of, the order;
  (b) require a person who has possession of the animal to deliver it up to enable the order to be carried out;
  (c) give directions with respect to the carrying out of the order (including directions about how the animal is to be dealt with until it is destroyed);
  (d) confer additional powers (including power to enter premises where the animal is being kept) for the purpose of, or in connection with, the carrying out of the order;

(e) order the offender or another person to reimburse the expenses of carrying out the order.

(4) Where a court makes an order under subsection (1), each of the offender and, if different, the owner of the animal may—
  (a) in the case of an order made by a magistrates' court, appeal against the order to the Crown Court;
  (b) in the case of an order made by the Crown Court, appeal against the order to the Court of Appeal.

(5) Subsection (4) does not apply if the court by which the order is made directs that it is appropriate in the interests of the animal that the carrying out of the order should not be delayed.

(6) In subsection (1), the reference to an animal in relation to which an offence was committed includes, in the case of an offence under section 8(1) or (2), an animal which took part in an animal fight in relation to which the offence was committed.

Definitions
"animal": ss.1(1) and 62(1).
"premises": s.62(1).
"veterinary surgeon": s.62(1).

Commentary
Where a person is convicted of an offence under ss.4, 5, 6(1) and (2), 7, 8(1) and (2) or 9 of the 2006 Act, this section empowers the court, on the evidence of a vet, to order the destruction of an animal in relation to which the offence was committed.

38. Destruction of animals involved in fighting offences

(1) The court by or before which a person is convicted of an offence under section 8(1) or (2) may order the destruction of an animal in relation to which the offence was committed on grounds other than the interests of the animal.

(2) A court may not make an order under subsection (1) unless—
  (a) it has given the owner of the animal an opportunity to be heard, or
  (b) it is satisfied that it is not reasonably practicable to communicate with the owner.

(3) Where a court makes an order under subsection (1), it may—

(a) appoint a person to carry out, or arrange for the carrying out of, the order;
(b) require a person who has possession of the animal to deliver it up to enable the order to be carried out;
(c) give directions with respect to the carrying out of the order (including directions about how the animal is to be dealt with until it is destroyed);
(d) confer additional powers (including power to enter premises where the animal is being kept) for the purpose of, or in connection with, the carrying out of the order;
(e) order the offender or another person to reimburse the expenses of carrying out the order.

(4) Where a court makes an order under subsection (1) in relation to an animal which is owned by a person other than the offender, that person may—
(a) in the case of an order made by a magistrates' court, appeal against the order to the Crown Court;
(b) in the case of an order made by the Crown Court, appeal against the order to the Court of Appeal.

(5) In subsection (1), the reference to an animal in relation to which the offence was committed includes an animal which took part in an animal fight in relation to which the offence was committed.

Definitions
"animal": ss.1(1) and 62(1).
"premises": s.62(1).

Commentary
This section makes similar provision to that in the previous section in relation to animals involved in fighting offences.

39. Reimbursement of expenses relating to animals involved in fighting offences

(1) The court by or before which a person is convicted of an offence under section 8(1) or (2) may order the offender or another person to reimburse any expenses incurred by the police in connection with the keeping of an animal in relation to which the offence was committed.

(2) In subsection (1), the reference to an animal in relation to which the offence was committed includes an animal which took part in a fight in relation to which the offence was committed.

Animal Welfare Act 2006

Definitions
"animal": ss.1(1) and 62(1).
"premises": s.62(1).

Commentary
This section empowers the court to order a person convicted of an offence under s.8(1) or (2), or another person, to reimburse the expenses of the police in looking after the animal.

40. Forfeiture of equipment used in offences

(1) Where a person is convicted of an offence under any of sections 4, 5, 6(1) and (2), 7 and 8, the court by or before which he is convicted may order any qualifying item which is shown to the satisfaction of the court to relate to the offence to be—
  (a) forfeited, and
  (b) destroyed or dealt with in such manner as may be specified in the order.
(2) The reference in subsection (1) to any qualifying item is—
  (a) in the case of a conviction for an offence under section 4, to anything designed or adapted for causing suffering to an animal;
  (b) in the case of a conviction for an offence under section 5, to anything designed or adapted for carrying out a prohibited procedure on an animal;
  (c) in the case of a conviction for an offence under section 6(1) or (2), to anything designed or adapted for removing the whole or any part of a dog's tail;
  (d) in the case of a conviction for an offence under section 7, to anything designed or adapted for administering any drug or substance to an animal;
  (e) in the case of a conviction for an offence under section 8(1) or (2), to anything designed or adapted for use in connection with an animal fight;
  (f) in the case of a conviction for an offence under section 8(3), to a video recording of an animal fight, including anything on or in which the recording is kept.
(3) The court shall not order anything to be forfeited under subsection (1) if a person claiming to be the owner of it or otherwise interested in it applies to be heard by the court, unless he has been given an opportunity to show cause why the order should not be made.

(4) An expression used in any of paragraphs (a) to (f) of subsection (2) has the same meaning as in the provision referred to in that paragraph.

Definitions
"*animal*": ss.1(1) and 62(1).
"*suffering*": s.62(1).

Commentary
Under this section, a person convicted of an offence under ss.4, 5, 6(1) and (2), 7 or 8 may be required by the court to forfeit a "qualifying item", defined in subs.(2), which may be destroyed or otherwise dealt with as specified in the order.

41. Orders under section 33, 35, 37, 38 or 40: pending appeals

(1) Nothing may be done under an order under section 33, 35, 37 or 38 with respect to an animal or an order under section 40 unless—
- (a) the period for giving notice of appeal against the order has expired,
- (b) the period for giving notice of appeal against the conviction on which the order was made has expired, and
- (c) if the order or conviction is the subject of an appeal, the appeal has been determined or withdrawn.

(2) Subsection (1) does not apply to an order under section 37(1) if the order is the subject of a direction under subsection (5) of that section.

(3) Where the effect of an order is suspended under subsection (1)—
- (a) no requirement imposed or directions given in connection with the order shall have effect, but
- (b) the court may give directions about how any animal to which the order applies is to be dealt with during the suspension.

(4) Directions under subsection (3)(b) may, in particular—
- (a) authorise the animal to be taken into possession;
- (b) authorise the removal of the animal to a place of safety;
- (c) authorise the animal to be cared for either on the premises where it was being kept when it was taken into possession or at some other place;
- (d) appoint a person to carry out, or arrange for the carrying out, of the directions;
- (e) require any person who has possession of the animal to deliver it up for the purposes of the directions;

Animal Welfare Act 2006

(f) confer additional powers (including power to enter premises where the animal is being kept) for the purpose of, or in connection with, the carrying out of the directions;

(g) provide for the recovery of any expenses in relation to removal or care of the animal which are incurred in carrying out the directions.

(5) Any expenses a person is directed to pay under subsection (4)(g) shall be recoverable summarily as a civil debt.

(6) Where the effect of an order under section 33 is suspended under subsection (1) the person to whom the order relates may not sell or part with any animal to which the order applies.

(7) Failure to comply with subsection (6) is an offence.

Definitions
"*animal*": ss.1(1) and 62(1).
"*premises*": s.62(1).

Commentary
This section provides that nothing may be done under ss.33, 35, 37, 38 or 40 until the time for making an appeal has expired or an appeal has been determined or withdrawn.

42. Orders with respect to licences

(1) If a person is convicted of an offence under any of sections 4, 5, 6(1) and (2), 7 to 9, 11 and 13(6), the court by or before which he is convicted may, instead of or in addition to dealing with him in any other way—

(a) make an order cancelling any licence held by him;

(b) make an order disqualifying him, for such period as it thinks fit, from holding a licence.

(2) Disqualification under subsection (1)(b) may be imposed in relation to licences generally or in relation to licences of one or more kinds.

(3) The court by which an order under subsection (1)(b) is made may specify a period during which the offender may not make an application under section 43(1) for termination of the order.

(4) The court by which an order under subsection (1) is made may suspend the operation of the order pending an appeal.

Definitions
"*licence*": ss.13 and 62(1).

Commentary
This section provides that a person convicted of an offence under ss.4, 5, 6(1) and (2), 7 to 9, 11 or 13(6) may have his licence cancelled and he may be disqualified from holding a licence for a period specified by the court.

43. Termination of disqualification under section 34 or 42

(1) A person who is disqualified by virtue of an order under section 34 or 42 may apply to the appropriate court for the termination of the order.

(2) No application under subsection (1) may be made—
   (a) before the end of the period of one year beginning with the date on which the order is made,
   (b) where a previous application under that subsection has been made in relation to the same order, before the end of the period of one year beginning with the date on which the previous application was determined, or
   (c) before the end of any period specified under section 34(6), 42(3) or subsection (5) below in relation to the order.

(3) On an application under subsection (1), the court may—
   (a) terminate the disqualification,
   (b) vary the disqualification so as to make it less onerous, or
   (c) refuse the application.

(4) When determining an application under subsection (1), the court shall have regard to the character of the applicant, his conduct since the imposition of the disqualification and any other circumstances of the case.

(5) Where the court refuses an application under subsection (1), it may specify a period during which the applicant may not make a further application under that subsection in relation to the order concerned.

(6) The court may order an applicant under subsection (1) to pay all or part of the costs of the application.

(7) In subsection (1), the reference to the appropriate court is to—
   (a) the court which made the order under section 34 or 42, or
   (b) in the case of an order made by a magistrates' court, to a magistrates' court acting for the same local justice area as that court.

Commentary
This section enables a person disqualified under ss.34 or 43 to apply to the court for the disqualification to be lifted. At least one year must pass after the disqualification was imposed before an application can be made.

44. Orders made on conviction for reimbursement of expenses

Where an order is made under section 33(4)(e), 36(1)(e), 37(3)(e), 38(3)(e) or 39(1), the expenses that are required by the order to be reimbursed shall not be regarded for the purposes of the Magistrates' Courts Act 1980 (c. 43) as a sum adjudged to be paid by a summary conviction, but shall be recoverable summarily as a civil debt.

Commentary
This section provides that, where a person is required on conviction to reimburse the expenses of looking after an animal, those expenses are recoverable as a civil debt.

45. Orders for reimbursement of expenses: right of appeal for non-offenders

(1) Where a court makes an order to which this section applies, the person against whom the order is made may—
  (a) in the case of an order made by a magistrates' court, appeal against the order to the Crown Court;
  (b) in the case of an order made by the Crown Court, appeal against the order to the Court of Appeal.
(2) This section applies to—
(a) an order under section 36(1)(e) against a person other than the person subject to disqualification, and
(b) an order under section 37(3)(e), 38(3)(e) or 39(1) against a person other than the offender.
. . .

Commentary
This section provides that a non-offender may appeal against the imposition of an order to reimburse expenses.

Animal Welfare Act 2006

General

51. Inspectors

(1) In this Act, "inspector", in the context of any provision, means a person appointed to be an inspector for the purposes of that provision by—

(a) the appropriate national authority, or

(b) a local authority.

(2) In appointing a person to be an inspector for purposes of this Act, a local authority shall have regard to guidance issued by the appropriate national authority.

(3) The appropriate national authority may, in connection with guidance under subsection (2), draw up a list of persons whom the authority considers suitable for appointment by a local authority to be an inspector for purposes of this Act.

(4) A person may be included in a list under subsection (3) as suitable for appointment as an inspector for all the purposes of this Act or only for such one or more of those purposes as may be specified in the list.

(5) An inspector shall not be liable in any civil or criminal proceedings for anything done in the purported performance of his functions under this Act if the court is satisfied that the act was done in good faith and that there were reasonable grounds for doing it.

(6) Relief from liability of an inspector under subsection (5) shall not affect any liability of any other person in respect of the inspector's act.

Definitions
"*appropriate national authority*": s.62(1).
"*local authority*": s.62(1).

Commentary
This section defines an inspector as a person so appointed by the appropriate national authority (for definition see Abbreviations and Explanatory Notes) or the local authority. The appropriate national authority may issue guidance, to which a local authority must have regard. An inspector is not liable in civil or criminal proceedings for anything done in purported performance of his functions under the Act if he acted in good faith and had reasonable grounds for so acting.

52. Conditions for grant of warrant

(1) This section is satisfied in relation to premises if any of the following four conditions is met.

(2) The first condition is that the whole of the premises is used as a private dwelling and the occupier has been informed of the decision to apply for a warrant.

(3) The second condition is that any part of the premises is not used as a private dwelling and that each of the following applies to the occupier of the premises—
- (a) he has been informed of the decision to seek entry to the premises and of the reasons for that decision;
- (b) he has failed to allow entry to the premises on being requested to do so by an inspector or a constable;
- (c) he has been informed of the decision to apply for a warrant.

(4) The third condition is that—
- (a) the premises are unoccupied or the occupier is absent, and
- (b) notice of intention to apply for a warrant has been left in a conspicuous place on the premises.

(5) The fourth condition is that it is inappropriate to inform the occupier of the decision to apply for a warrant because—
- (a) it would defeat the object of entering the premises, or
- (b) entry is required as a matter of urgency.

Definitions
"inspector": s.51(1).
"occupier": s.62(2).
"premises": s.62(1).
"premises . . . used as a private dwelling": s.62(3).

Commentary
This section specifies the conditions which must apply before a warrant of entry to premises can be granted.

53. Powers of entry, inspection and search: supplementary

Schedule 2 (which makes supplementary provision in relation to powers of entry, inspection and search) has effect.

54. Power to stop and detain vehicles

(1) A constable in uniform or, if accompanied by such a constable, an inspector may stop and detain a vehicle for the purpose of entering and searching it in the exercise of a power conferred—

(a) by section 19(1), or

(b) by a warrant under section 19(4) or 23(1).

(2) A constable in uniform may stop and detain a vehicle for the purpose of entering and searching it in the exercise of a power conferred—

(a) by section 22(2), or

(b) by a warrant under section 22(4).

(3) If accompanied by a constable in uniform, an inspector may stop and detain a vehicle for the purpose of entering it and carrying out an inspection in the exercise of a power conferred—

(a) by section 26(2), 27(2), 28(2) or 29(2), or

(b) by a warrant under section 28(4).

(4) A vehicle may be detained for as long as is reasonably required to permit a search or inspection to be carried out (including the exercise of any related power under this Act) either at the place where the vehicle was first detained or nearby.

Definitions
"inspector": s.51(1).

Commentary
This section gives powers to a constable, or an inspector accompanied by a constable, to stop and detain vehicles in exercise of powers under specified sections of the Act.

55. Power to detain vessels, aircraft and hovercraft

(1) Where an inspector appointed by the appropriate national authority certifies in writing that he is satisfied that an offence under or by virtue of this Act is being or has been committed on board a vessel in port, the vessel may be detained.

(2) A certificate under subsection (1) shall—

(a) specify each offence to which it relates, and

(b) set out the inspector's reasons for being satisfied that each offence to which it relates is being or has been committed.

(3) Section 284 of the Merchant Shipping Act 1995 (c. 21) (which provides for enforcement of the detention of a ship under that

Act by specified officers) shall apply as if the power of detention under subsection (1) were conferred by that Act.

(4) An officer who detains a vessel in reliance on a certificate under subsection (1) shall as soon as is reasonably practicable give a copy of it to the master or person in charge of the vessel.

(5) A vessel may be detained under subsection (1) until the appropriate national authority otherwise directs.

(6) The appropriate national authority may by regulations—
  (a) apply this section to aircraft or hovercraft, with such modifications as the authority thinks fit, or
  (b) make such other provision for the detention of aircraft or hovercraft in relation to offences under or by virtue of this Act as the authority thinks fit.

Definitions
"appropriate national authority": s.62(1).
"inspector": s.51(1).

Commentary
This section gives powers to an inspector to detain vessels, aircraft and hovercraft where he certifies in writing that he is satisfied that an offence under the Act has been committed on board a vessel in port. The section also empowers the appropriate national authority to make regulations extending the section to aircraft and hovercraft. At the time of going to press no regulations had been made.

56. Obtaining of documents in connection with carrying out orders etc.

(1) Where—
  (a) an order under section 20(1), 33(1) or (2), 35(1) or (2) or 37(1) has effect, and
  (b) the owner of an animal to which the order relates has in his possession, or under his control, documents which are relevant to the carrying out of the order or any directions given in connection with it,

the owner shall, if so required by a person authorised to carry out the order, deliver the documents to that person as soon as practicable and in any event before the end of the period of 10 days beginning with the date on which he is notified of the requirement.

(2) Where—
(a) directions under section 41(3)(b) have effect, and
(b) the owner of an animal to which the directions relate has in his possession, or under his control, documents which are relevant to the carrying out of the directions,

the owner shall, if so required by a person authorised to carry out the directions, deliver the documents to that person as soon as practicable and in any event before the end of the period of 10 days beginning with the date on which he is notified of the requirement.

(3) A person who fails without reasonable excuse to comply with subsection (1) or (2) commits an offence.

Definitions
"animal": ss.1(1) and 62(1).

Commentary
This section enables relevant documents to be obtained from the owner of an animal in relation to orders under specified sections of the Act.

57. Offences by bodies corporate

(1) Where an offence under this Act is committed by a body corporate and is proved to have been committed with the consent or connivance of or to be attributable to any neglect on the part of—
(a) any director, manager, secretary or other similar officer of the body corporate, or
(b) any person who was purporting to act in any such capacity,

he (as well as the body corporate) commits the offence and shall be liable to be proceeded against and punished accordingly.

(2) Where the affairs of a body corporate are managed by its members, subsection (1) applies in relation to the acts and defaults of a member in connection with his functions of management as if he were a director of the body corporate.

58. Scientific research

(1) Nothing in this Act applies to anything lawfully done under the Animals (Scientific Procedures) Act 1986 (c. 14).

(2) No power of entry, inspection or search conferred by or under this Act, except for any such power conferred by section 28, may be exercised in relation to a place which is—

(a) designated under section 6 of the Animals (Scientific Procedures) Act 1986 as a scientific procedure establishment, or

(b) designated under section 7 of that Act as a breeding establishment or as a supplying establishment.

(3) Section 9 does not apply in relation to an animal which—

(a) is being kept, at a place designated under section 6 of the Animals (Scientific Procedures) Act 1986 as a scientific procedure establishment, for use in regulated procedures,

(b) is being kept, at a place designated under section 7 of that Act as a breeding establishment, for use for breeding animals for use in regulated procedures,

(c) is being kept at such a place, having been bred there for use in regulated procedures, or

(d) is being kept, at a place designated under section 7 of that Act as a supplying establishment, for the purpose of being supplied for use elsewhere in regulated procedures.

(4) In subsection (3), "regulated procedure" has the same meaning as in the Animals (Scientific Procedures) Act 1986.

Definitions
"*animal*": ss.1(1) and 62(1).

Commentary
For the Animals (Scientific Procedures) Act 1986 see p.267.

59. Fishing
Nothing in this Act applies in relation to anything which occurs in the normal course of fishing.

60. Crown application
(1) Subject to the provisions of this section, this Act and regulations and orders made under it shall bind the Crown.

(2) No contravention by the Crown of any provision made by or under this Act shall make the Crown criminally liable; but the High Court may declare unlawful any act or omission of the Crown which constitutes such a contravention.

(3) Notwithstanding subsection (2), the provisions of this Act and of regulations and orders made under it shall apply to persons in the service of the Crown as they apply to other persons.

(4) If the Secretary of State certifies that it appears to him appropriate in the interests of national security that powers of entry conferred by or under this Act should not be exercisable in relation to Crown premises specified in the certificate, those powers shall not be exercisable in relation to those premises.

(5) In subsection (4), "Crown premises" means premises held, or used, by or on behalf of the Crown.

(6) No power of entry conferred by or under this Act may be exercised in relation to land belonging to Her Majesty in right of Her private estates.

(7) In subsection (6), the reference to Her Majesty's private estates shall be construed in accordance with section 1 of the Crown Private Estates Act 1862 (c. 37).

Definitions
"*premises*": s.62(1).

61. Orders and regulations

(1) Any power of the Secretary of State, the National Assembly for Wales or the Scottish Ministers to make orders or regulations under this Act, except the power under section 17(1) of the National Assembly for Wales, is exercisable by statutory instrument.

(2) No regulations under section 1(3), 5(4), 6, 12 or 13 shall be made by the Secretary of State unless a draft of the instrument containing the regulations has been laid before, and approved by a resolution of, each House of Parliament.

(3) No order under section 17(1) shall be made by the Secretary of State unless a draft of the instrument containing the order has been laid before Parliament.

(4) Subsection (3) does not apply in relation to an order revoking a code of practice in connection with its replacement by a new one.

(5) A statutory instrument containing regulations under section 55(6) made by the Secretary of State shall be subject to annulment in pursuance of a resolution of either House of Parliament.

62. General interpretation

(1) In this Act—
"animal" has the meaning given by section 1(1);
   "appropriate national authority" means—
   (a) in relation to England, the Secretary of State;

(b) in relation to Wales, the National Assembly for Wales;

"enactment" includes an enactment contained in subordinate legislation (within the meaning of the Interpretation Act 1978 (c. 30));

"licence" means a licence for the purposes of section 13;

"local authority" means—

(a) in relation to England, a county council, a district council, a London borough council, the Common Council of the City of London or the Council of the Isles of Scilly;

(b) in relation to Wales, a county council or a county borough council;

"premises" includes any place and, in particular, includes—

(a) any vehicle, vessel, aircraft or hovercraft;

(b) any tent or movable structure;

"protected animal" has the meaning given by section 2;

"suffering" means physical or mental suffering and related expressions shall be construed accordingly;

"veterinary surgeon" means a person registered in the register of veterinary surgeons, or the supplementary veterinary register, kept under the Veterinary Surgeons Act 1966 (c. 36).

(2) In this Act, references to the occupier of premises, in relation to any vehicle, vessel, aircraft or hovercraft, are to the person who appears to be in charge of the vehicle, vessel, aircraft or hovercraft, and "unoccupied" shall be construed accordingly.

(3) In this Act, references to a part of premises which is used as a private dwelling include any yard, garden, garage or outhouse which is used for purposes in connection with it.

(4) In this Act, references to responsibility, in relation to an animal, are to be read in accordance with section 3.

(5) In this Act, references to the needs of an animal are to be read in accordance with section 9(2).

(6) In this Act, references to a "relevant post-conviction power" are to a power conferred by—

(a) section 33, 34, 37 or 42 of this Act,

(b) section 4(2) of the Performing Animals (Regulation) Act 1925 (c. 38) (power to remove name from register under Act and disqualify from registration),

(c) section 5(3) of the Pet Animals Act 1951 (c. 35) (power to cancel licence under Act and disqualify from carrying on licensable activity),

(d) section 3(3) of the Animal Boarding Establishments Act 1963 (c. 43) (provision corresponding to that mentioned in paragraph (c) above),

(e) section 4(3) of the Riding Establishments Act 1964 (c. 70) (further corresponding provision),

(f) section 3(4) of the Guard Dogs Act 1975 (c. 50) (power to cancel licence under Act),

(g) section 6(2) of the Dangerous Wild Animals Act 1976 (c. 38) (power to cancel licence under Act and disqualify from carrying on licensable activity), or

(h) section 4(4) of the Zoo Licensing Act 1981 (c. 37) (power to refuse licence under Act for conviction for an offence).

. . .

68. Commencement

(1) This section and sections 61, 67 and 69 shall come into force on the day on which this Act is passed.

(2) Sections 46 to 50 shall come into force on such day as the Scottish Ministers may by order appoint.

(3) The remaining provisions of this Act—

(a) so far as relating to England, Scotland or Northern Ireland, shall come into force on such day as the Secretary of State may by order appoint, and

(b) so far as relating to Wales, shall come into force on such day as the National Assembly for Wales may by order appoint.

(4) Power under subsection (3) includes power to appoint different days for different purposes.

Commentary
The whole of the Act, except ss.8(3) to (6), 14–16, 46–50 (which apply only to Scotland), para.3(1) of Sch.3 and in Sch.4 the entries relating to (i) s.2 of the Pet Animals Act 1951; (ii) ss.2, 3, 6, 7 and 8 of the Agriculture (Miscellaneous Provisions) Act 1968; (iii) ss.37–39 of the Animal Health Act 1981 and para.8 of Sch.5 to that Act, was brought into force as follows:

In England, by the Animal Welfare Act 2006 (Commencement No. 1) (England) Order 2007 (SI 2007/499); in Wales, by the Animal Welfare Act 2006 (Commencement No. 1) (Wales) Order 2007 (SI 2007/1030).

The provisions in (ii) and (iii) above were brought into force in England by the Animal Welfare Act (Commencement No. 2 and Saving and Transitional Provisions) (England) Order 2007 (SI 2007/2711) and in Wales by the Animal Welfare Act (Commencement No. 2 and Saving and Transitional Provisions) (Wales) Order 2007 (SI 2007/3065).

Animal Welfare Act 2006

SCHEDULES

SCHEDULE 2

Section 53

POWERS OF ENTRY, INSPECTION AND SEARCH: SUPPLEMENTARY

Safeguards etc. in connection with powers of entry conferred by warrant

1.—(1) Sections 15 and 16 of the Police and Criminal Evidence Act 1984 (c. 60) shall have effect in relation to the issue of a warrant under section 19(4) or 23(1) to an inspector as they have effect in relation to the issue of a warrant under that provision to a constable.

(2) In their application in relation to the issue of a warrant under section 19(4) or 23(1), sections 15 and 16 of that Act shall have effect with the following modifications.

(3) In section 15—
(a) in subsection (2), omit the words from the end of paragraph (a)(ii) to the end of paragraph (b);
(b) omit subsections (2A) and (5A);
(c) in subsection (5), omit the words from "unless" to the end;
(d) in subsection (6)(a), omit the words from the end of sub-paragraph (iii) to the end of sub-paragraph (iv);
(e) in subsection (7), omit the words from "(see" to the end.

(4) In section 16—
(a) omit subsections (3A) and (3B);
(b) in subsection (9), omit the words after paragraph (b).

2.—(1) This paragraph and paragraph 3 have effect in relation to the issue to inspectors of warrants under section 28(4); and an entry on premises under such a warrant is unlawful unless it complies with this paragraph and paragraph 3.

(2) Where an inspector applies for a warrant, he shall—
(a) state the ground on which he makes the application,
(b) state the enactment under which the warrant would be issued, and
(c) specify the premises which it is desired to enter.

(3) An application for a warrant shall be made without notice and supported by an information in writing.

Animal Welfare Act 2006

(4) The inspector shall answer on oath any question that the justice of the peace hearing the application asks him.

(5) A warrant shall authorise an entry on one occasion only.

(6) A warrant shall specify—
  (a) the name of the person who applies for it,
  (b) the date on which it is issued, and
  (c) the enactment under which it is issued.

(7) Two copies shall be made of a warrant.

(8) The copies shall be clearly certified as copies.

3.—(1) A warrant may be executed by any inspector.

(2) A warrant may authorise persons to accompany any inspector who is executing it.

(3) A person authorised under sub-paragraph (2) has the same powers as the inspector whom he accompanies in respect of the execution of the warrant, but may exercise those powers only in the company, and under the supervision, of an inspector.

(4) Execution of a warrant must be within three months from the date of its issue.

(5) Execution of a warrant must be at a reasonable hour unless it appears to the inspector executing it that the purpose of entry may be frustrated on an entry at a reasonable hour.

(6) Where the occupier of premises which are to be entered under a warrant is present at the time when an inspector seeks to execute it, the inspector shall—
  (a) identify himself to the occupier and shall produce to him documentary evidence that he is an inspector,
  (b) produce the warrant to him, and
  (c) supply him with a copy of it.

(7) Where—
  (a) the occupier of premises which are to be entered under a warrant is not present when an inspector seeks to execute it, but
  (b) some other person who appears to the inspector to be in charge of the premises is present,
sub-paragraph (6) shall have effect as if any reference to the occupier were a reference to that other person.

(8) If there is no person present who appears to the inspector to be in charge of the premises, he shall leave a copy of the warrant in a prominent place on the premises.

(9) A warrant which—
  (a) has been executed, or

Animal Welfare Act 2006

(b) has not been executed within the time authorised for its execution,

shall be returned to the designated officer for the local justice area in which the justice of the peace who issued the warrant was acting when he issued it.

(10) A warrant which is returned under sub-paragraph (9) shall be retained by the officer to whom it is returned for 12 months from its return.

(11) If during the period for which a warrant is to be retained the occupier of the premises to which it relates asks to inspect it, he shall be allowed to do so.

Duty to produce evidence of identity

4.—(1) This paragraph applies to a power of entry conferred by section 19(1), 22(2), 26(2), 27(2), 28(2) or 29(2).

(2) A person may only exercise a power of entry to which this paragraph applies if on request—
  (a) he produces evidence of his identity and of his entitlement to exercise the power;
  (b) he outlines the purpose for which the power is exercised.

Power to take persons onto premises

5. In exercising a power to which paragraph 4 applies, a person may take with him onto the premises such persons as he thinks appropriate.

Duty to exercise power of entry at reasonable time

6. Entry under a power to which paragraph 4 applies shall be at a reasonable time, unless it appears to the person exercising the power that the purpose for which he is exercising the power would be frustrated on entry at a reasonable time.

Power to require assistance

7.—(1) This paragraph applies to a power of entry conferred by—
  (a) section 19(1), 22(2), 26(2), 27(2), 28(2) or 29(2), or
  (b) a warrant under section 19(4), 22(4), 23(1) or 28(4).

(2) Where a person enters premises in the exercise of a power of entry to which this paragraph applies, he may require any qualifying

Animal Welfare Act 2006

person on the premises to give him such assistance as he may reasonably require for the purpose for which entry is made.

(3) The reference in sub-paragraph (2) to a qualifying person is to—
  (a) the occupier of the premises;
  (b) any person who appears to the person exercising the power to be responsible for animals on the premises;
  (c) any person who appears to the person exercising the power to be under the direction or control of a person mentioned in paragraph (a) or (b).

(4) In the case of a power under section 26(2), the reference in sub-paragraph (2) to a qualifying person also includes the holder of a licence—
  (a) specifying the premises as premises on which the carrying on of an activity is authorised, or
  (b) relating to an activity which is being carried on on the premises.

Power to take equipment onto premises

8. In exercising a power to which paragraph 7 applies, a person may take with him such equipment and materials as he thinks appropriate.

Duty to leave premises secured

9. If, in the exercise of a power of entry to which paragraph 7 applies, a person enters premises which are unoccupied, he shall leave them as effectively secured against entry as he found them.

Functions in connection with inspection and search

10.—(1) This paragraph applies to—
  (a) a power of inspection conferred by section 26(1), 27(1), 28(1) or 29(1),
    and
  (b) a power of search conferred by a warrant under section 23(1).
(2) A person exercising a power to which this paragraph applies may—
  (a) inspect an animal found on the premises;
  (b) inspect any other thing found on the premises, including a document or record (in whatever form it is held);
  (c) carry out a measurement or test (including a measurement or test of an animal found on the premises);

(d) take a sample (including a sample from an animal found on the premises or from any substance on the premises which appears to be intended for use as food for such an animal);
(e) mark an animal found on the premises for identification purposes;
(f) remove a carcass found on the premises for the purpose of carrying out a post-mortem examination on it;
(g) take copies of a document or record found on the premises (in whatever form it is held);
(h) require information stored in an electronic form and accessible from the premises to be produced in a form in which it can be taken away and in which it is visible and legible or from which it can readily be produced in a visible and legible form;
(i) take a photograph of anything on the premises;
(j) seize and detain or remove anything which the person exercising the power reasonably believes to be evidence of any non-compliance, or of the commission of any offence, relevant to the purpose for which the inspection or search is made.

(3) A person taken onto premises under paragraph 5 may exercise any power conferred by sub-paragraph (2) if he is in the company, and under the supervision, of a person exercising a power to which this paragraph applies.

11. A person who takes a sample from an animal pursuant to paragraph 10(2)(d) shall give a part of the sample, or a similar sample, to any person appearing to be responsible for the animal, if, before the sample is taken, he is requested to do so by that person.

12.—(1) Paragraph 10(2)(j) does not include power to seize an item which the person exercising the power has reasonable grounds for believing to be subject to legal privilege (within the meaning of section 10 of the Police and Criminal Evidence Act 1984 (c. 60)).

(2) A person who seizes anything in exercise of the power under paragraph 10(2)(j) shall on request provide a record of the thing seized to a person showing himself—
(a) to be the occupier of premises on which it was seized, or
(b) to have had possession or control of it immediately before its seizure.

(3) Subject to sub-paragraph (4), anything which has been seized in the exercise of a power under paragraph 10(2)(j) may be retained so long as is necessary in all the circumstances and in particular—
(a) for use as evidence at a trial for a relevant offence, or
(b) for forensic examination or for investigation in connection with a relevant offence.

Animal Welfare Act 2006

(4) Nothing may be retained for either of the purposes mentioned in subparagraph (3) if a photograph or a copy would be sufficient for that purpose.

13. As soon as reasonably practicable after having exercised a power to which paragraph 10 applies, the person who exercised the power shall—
  (a) prepare a written report of the inspection or search, and
  (b) if requested to do so by the occupier of the premises, give him a copy of the report.

14.—(1) A person exercising a power of search conferred by a warrant under section 23(1) may (if necessary) use reasonable force in the exercise of powers under paragraph 10 in connection with the execution of the warrant.

(2) A person carrying out an inspection under section 28(1) on premises which he is authorised to enter by a warrant under section 28(4) may (if necessary) use reasonable force in the exercise of powers under paragraph 10 in connection with the inspection.

Functions in connection with entry under section 19

15.—(1) Where a person enters premises in exercise of a power of entry conferred by section 19(1), or by a warrant under section 19(4), he may—
  (a) inspect an animal found on the premises;
  (b) remove a carcass found on the premises for the purposes of carrying out a post-mortem examination on it;
  (c) remove for those purposes the carcass of an animal destroyed on the premises in exercise of power conferred by section 18(3) or (4);
  (d) take a photograph of anything on the premises.

(2) Where a person exercising a power of entry under section 19(1) takes another person with him under paragraph 5, the other person may exercise any power conferred by sub-paragraph (1) if he is in the company, and under the supervision, of the person exercising the power of entry.

Offences

16. A person commits an offence if he—
  (a) intentionally obstructs a person in the lawful exercise of a power to which paragraph 7 or 10 applies;
  (b) intentionally obstructs a person in the lawful exercise of a power conferred by this Schedule;

(c) fails without reasonable excuse to give any assistance which he is required to give under paragraph 7.

Definitions
"*animal*": ss.1(1) and 62(1).
"*enactment*": s.62(1).
"*inspector*": s.51(1).
"*licence*": s.62(1).
"*occupier of premises*": s.62(2).
"*premises*": s.62(1).
"*responsible for animals*": ss.3 and 62(1).

FRAUD ACT 2006

c. 35

Arrangement of sections

Fraud

1. Fraud
2. Fraud by false representation
3. Fraud by failing to disclose information
4. Fraud by abuse of position
5. "Gain" and "loss"

Fraud

1. Fraud

(1) A person is guilty of fraud if he is in breach of any of the sections listed in subsection (2) (which provide for different ways of committing the offence).

(2) The sections are—
(a) section 2 (fraud by false representation),
(b) section 3 (fraud by failing to disclose information), and
(c) section 4 (fraud by abuse of position).

(3) A person who is guilty of fraud is liable—
(a) on summary conviction, to imprisonment for a term not exceeding 12 months or to a fine not exceeding the statutory maximum (or to both);
(b) on conviction on indictment, to imprisonment for a term not exceeding 10 years or to a fine (or to both).

(4) Subsection (3)(a) applies in relation to Northern Ireland as if the reference to 12 months were a reference to 6 months.

Definitions
"gain": s.5(1)–(3).
"loss": s.5(1), (2), (4).

Fraud Act 2006

Commentary
This section contains the basic definition of fraud, the component parts of which are set out in ss.2, 3 and 4. In all cases, it is possible that dogs can be the subject of fraud.

2. Fraud by false representation
(1) A person is in breach of this section if he—
(a) dishonestly makes a false representation, and
(b) intends, by making the representation—
   (i) to make a gain for himself or another, or
   (ii) to cause loss to another or to expose another to a risk of loss.
(2) A representation is false if—
(a) it is untrue or misleading, and
(b) the person making it knows that it is, or might be, untrue or misleading.
(3) "Representation" means any representation as to fact or law, including a representation as to the state of mind of—
(a) the person making the representation, or
(b) any other person.
(4) A representation may be express or implied.
(5) For the purposes of this section a representation may be regarded as made if it (or anything implying it) is submitted in any form to any system or device designed to receive, convey or respond to communications (with or without human intervention).

Definitions
"*gain*": s.5(1)–(3).
"*loss*": s.5(1), (2), (4).

3. Fraud by failing to disclose information
A person is in breach of this section if he—
(a) dishonestly fails to disclose to another person information which he is under a legal duty to disclose, and
(b) intends, by failing to disclose the information—
   (i) to make a gain for himself or another, or
   (ii) to cause loss to another or to expose another to a risk of loss.

Definitions
"*gain*": s.5(1)–(3).
"*loss*": s.5(1), (2), (4).

Fraud Act 2006

4. Fraud by abuse of position

(1) A person is in breach of this section if he—
   (a) occupies a position in which he is expected to safeguard, or not to act against, the financial interests of another person,
   (b) dishonestly abuses that position, and
   (c) intends, by means of the abuse of that position—
      (i) to make a gain for himself or another, or
      (ii) to cause loss to another or to expose another to a risk of loss.

(2) A person may be regarded as having abused his position even though his conduct consisted of an omission rather than an act.

Definitions
"gain": s.5(1)–(3).
"loss": s.5(1), (2), (4).

5. "Gain" and "loss"

(1) The references to gain and loss in sections 2 to 4 are to be read in accordance with this section.

(2) "Gain" and "loss"—
   (a) extend only to gain or loss in money or other property;
   (b) include any such gain or loss whether temporary or permanent;
   and "property" means any property whether real or personal (including things in action and other intangible property).

(3) "Gain" includes a gain by keeping what one has, as well as a gain by getting what one does not have.

(4) "Loss" includes a loss by not getting what one might get, as well as a loss by parting with what one has.

Part IV

Statutory Orders and Regulations

Performing Animals Rules 1925	343
Rabies (Control) Order 1974	346
Motorways Traffic (England and Wales) Regulations 1982	350
Dangerous Dogs (Designated Types) Order 1991	352
Dangerous Dogs Compensation and Exemption Schemes Order 1991	353
Litter (Animal Droppings) Order 1991	360
Environmental Protection (Stray Dogs) Regulations 1992	362
Control of Dogs Order 1992	366
Control of Dogs on Roads Orders (Procedure) (England and Wales) Regulations 1995	369
Sale of Dogs (Identification Tag) Regulations 1999	376
Breeding of Dogs (Licensing Records) Regulations 1999	377
Non Commercial Movement of Pet Animals (England) Regulations 2004	379
Controls on Dogs (Non-application to Designated Land) Order 2006	390
Dog Control Orders (Procedures) Regulations 2006	393
Dog Control Orders (Prescribed Offences and Penalties, etc.) Regulations 2006	398
Controls on Dogs (Non-application to Designated Land) Order 2009	413

SI 1925/1219
ANIMAL
Performing Animals Rules 1925

THE PERFORMING ANIMALS RULES, 1925, DATED DECEMBER 3, 1925, MADE BY THE SECRETARY OF STATE FOR THE HOME DEPARTMENT, UNDER SECTION 5(2) OF THE PERFORMING ANIMALS (REGULATION) ACT, 1925 (15 & 16 GEO. 5. C. 38).

In pursuance of Section 5(2) of the Performing Animals (Regulation) Act 1925, hereinafter referred to as the Act, I hereby make the following Rules:—

Form of application for registration (section 1)
1. Every application for registration under the Act shall be made in writing in the form, and shall contain the particulars, set out in the First Schedule hereto.

Application by person having no fixed place of residence in Great Britain (section 1(2))
2. If the applicant has no fixed place of residence in Great Britain he shall make his application for registration to the local authority of one of the following districts:—
    In England and Wales:— The City of London, the County of London; the Cities of Birmingham, Bristol, Cardiff, Kingston-upon-Hull, Leeds, Liverpool, Manchester and Newcastle-on-Tyne; and the County Boroughs of Plymouth and Southampton. . . .

Form of register (section 1(2))
3. The register which the local authority is required to keep for the purpose of the Act shall be in the form set out in the Second Schedule hereto. Each registration shall be given a serial number according to the order in which it is made, and the serial number shall be inserted in the certificate of registration issued to the applicant.

Performing Animals Rules 1925

4. The local authority shall either arrange the names of the registered persons alphabetically or shall keep as part of the register an alphabetical index of the names of persons registered.

Form of certificate of registration (section 1(4))
5. The certificate of registration which the local authority is required to issue to each registered person shall be in the form set out in the Third Schedule hereto.

Application for variation of registered particulars (section 1(6))
6. Applications for the variation of the registered particulars shall be made in the form set out in the Fourth Schedule hereto.

Certified copy of certificate of registration
7. A local authority may issue a certified copy of any certificate of registration issued by them if satisfied that the original has been destroyed or lost, and may charge therefore the fee hereinafter prescribed; provided that such certified copy shall be issued only to the person to whose registration it relates.

Inspection of register entries (section 1(5))
8. The copy of the certificate of registration sent by the local authority to the Home Office shall be open to inspection on payment of the prescribed fee on each day other than Saturday on which the office is open between the hours of 11 and 12 in the morning and 3 and 4 in the afternoon.

Fees (sections 1(2), (5), (7) and 5(3))
9. The following fees shall be payable to the land authority;—
    For each registration £3
    For the issue of a copy of a certificate of registration under
    Rule 7 ....5s. (now 25p)

Short title
10. These rules may be cited as the Performing Animals Rules, 1925.

W. Joynson-Hicks
One of His Majesty's
Principal Secretaries of State.

SI 1925/1219

Home Office,
Whitehall.
3rd December, 1925.

Commentary

The Performing Animals (Regulation) Act 1925, s.5(2) (at p.230), provides for the Secretary of State to prescribe by rules the details for certain matters under the Act.

These 1925 Rules, so made and later amended by the Performing Animals Rules 1968, in arts 1, 3–6 and four Schedules prescribe the forms to be used in operating the Act (not reproduced here), and in art.2 name the local authorities to which applications for registration are to be made when the applicant has no fixed place of residence.

Articles 7–9 provide for the issue of copies of certificates of registration, the inspection of the local authority's register, and the fees to be charged for these services.

Further References

The local authorities involved are described in s.5(1) of the 1925 Act at p.230.

SI 1974/2212

ANIMALS

DISEASES OF ANIMALS

The Rabies (Control) Order 1974

Made .... *31st December 1974*
Coming into Operation .... *5th February 1975*

The Minister of Agriculture, Fisheries and Food and the Secretary of State, acting jointly, in exercise of the powers conferred by sections 1, 8(3), 10, 11, 17(2), 20, 77(3), 84(3)(a) and 85(1) of the Diseases of Animals Act 1950, as extended in the case of the said section 10 by sections 1 and 2 of the Rabies Act 1974, and now vested in them, and of all their other enabling powers, hereby order as follows:—

. . .

2. Interpretation

(1) In this order, unless the context otherwise requires—

"the Act" means the Diseases of Animals Act 1950, as amended and extended by the Rabies Act 1974;

"animal" means an animal (other than man) belonging to any of the orders of mammals specified in Schedule 1 to this order;

. . .

"inspector" means a person appointed to be an inspector for the purposes of the Act by the Minister or by a local authority, and, when used in relation to an inspector of the Ministry, includes a veterinary inspector;

"licence" means a licence granted under this order, and includes any permit, approval or other form of authorisation;

"the Minister" and "the Ministry" mean respectively the Minister and Ministry of Agriculture, Fisheries and Food;

. . .

"premises" includes land, with or without buildings, and where a person occupies land which comprises two or more non-adjacent areas, each of those areas shall be deemed to be separate premises for the purposes of this order;

SI 1974/2212

"veterinary inspector" means a veterinary inspector appointed by the Minister.

. . .

4. Notice of rabies or suspected rabies

(1) Subject to paragraph (4) below, a person who knows or suspects that an animal (whether in captivity or not) is affected with rabies, or was at the time of its death so affected, shall with all practicable speed give notice of that fact to an inspector or to a police constable, unless he believes on reasonable grounds that another person has given notice under this paragraph in respect of that animal.

(2) Without prejudice to paragraph (1) above, a person who knows or suspects that an animal in his possession or under his charge is, or was at the time of its death, affected with rabies shall, as far as practicable, keep that animal or, as the case may be, the carcass of that animal separate from any other animal.

. . .

(4) Paragraphs (1) and (2) above shall not apply in such cases as may be prescribed by an order made under section 1 of the Act for the purpose of regulating the keeping, importation or use of rabies virus.

. . .

6. Veterinary inquiry as to the existence of rabies

(1) Where by reason of information received, whether under Articles 4 and 5 above or otherwise, a veterinary inspector has grounds for suspecting that rabies exists, or has within the preceding 56 days existed at any premises, or that there is an animal thereat which has been or which may have been exposed to the infection of that disease, he shall with all practicable speed inquire as to the correctness of such information, and examine any animal or the carcass of any animal found at the premises. The opinion of the veterinary inspector as to the existence or previous existence of rabies at the premises shall be subject to confirmation by or on behalf of the Chief Veterinary Officer of the Ministry.

(2) For the purpose of discharging his functions under this Article, a veterinary inspector may—
  (a) enter on any part of the premises;
  (b) remove or cause to be removed from the premises any animal affected with or suspected of being affected with rabies, or any animal which has been in contact with an animal so affected or

suspected, or the carcass of any such animal, to a place where the animal can conveniently be kept under veterinary observation by or on behalf of the Ministry, or to a place where the animal or carcass can be subjected to diagnostic tests; and

(c) take such samples as may be required for the purpose of diagnosis from any animal on the premises, whether or not such animal is affected with or suspected of being affected with rabies, or has been in contact with an animal so affected or suspected;

and the occupier of the premises and the persons in his employment shall render such reasonable assistance to the veterinary inspector as may be required for the purposes of this Article.

(3) The occupier of any premises on which there is or has been an animal affected with or suspected of being affected with rabies, or the carcass of any such animal, or an animal or the carcass of an animal which has been in contact with an animal so affected or suspected, and the veterinary surgeon (if any) who has been attending or has been consulted respecting the animal or carcass, and any person who has been in charge of the animal or carcass or in any manner in contact with it, shall give all reasonable facilities for an inquiry under this Article, and for the removal of any animal or carcass and the taking of samples.

(4) Any such occupier, veterinary surgeon or person as aforesaid shall, if so required by an officer of the Ministry, give such information as he possesses as to the animal or carcass, as to the location or movements of any other animal in his possession or under his charge, and as to any other animal with which any such animal may have been in contact.

. . .

In Witness whereof the Official Seal of the Minister of Agriculture, Fisheries and Food is hereunto affixed on 23rd December 1974.

Frederick Peart,
Minister of Agriculture,
Fisheries and Food.
William Ross,
Secretary of State for Scotland.

31st December 1974.

Definitions
"animal", "inspector", "licence", "premises", "the Act", "the Minister" and *"veterinary inspector":* art.2(1).

Commentary

Article 4(1)(2) requires that immediate notice be given to an inspector or the police when an animal is known to be, or suspected to be, suffering from rabies, and that animal must be separated from others.

Article 6 sets out the duties of a Ministry veterinary inspector when there is a threat of rabies. Others involved are required to give assistance, information and facilities.

The word "animal" includes a dog by virtue of Sch.1.

The Diseases of Animals Act 1950 and the Rabies Act 1974 are now replaced by the Animal Health Act 1981.

Further References

For details about offences, see the Animal Health Act 1981, ss.72–75, at pp.119–121.

SI 1982/1163

ROAD TRAFFIC

SPECIAL ROADS

The Motorways Traffic (England and Wales) Regulations 1982

Made .... 11th August 1982
Laid before Parliament .... 24th August 1982
Coming into Operation .... 15th September 1982

The Secretary of State for Transport (as respects England) and the Secretary of State for Wales (as respects Wales), in exercise of the powers conferred by Section 13(2) and (3) of the Road Traffic Regulation Act 1967 and now vested in them, and of all other enabling powers, and after consultation with representative organisations in accordance with the provisions of section 107(2) of that Act, hereby make the following Regulations:—

. . .

3. Interpretation

(1) In these Regulations, the following expressions have the meanings hereby respectively assigned to them:—

. . .

(f) "motorway" means any road or part of a road to which these Regulations apply by virtue of Regulation 4;

(g) "verge" means any part of a motorway which is not a carriageway, a hard shoulder, or a central reservation.

. . .

(4) In these Regulations references to numbered classes of traffic are references to the classes of traffic set out in Schedule 4 to the Highways Act 1980.

4. Application

These Regulations apply to every special road or part of a special road which can only be used by traffic of Classes I or II, but shall not apply to any part of any such road until such date as may be declared in accordance with the provisions of section 1(7) of the Act of 1967 to be the date on which it is open for use as a special road.

. . .

14. Restrictions affecting animals carried in vehicles

The person in charge of any animal which is carried by a vehicle using a motorway shall, so far as is practicable, secure that—
   (a) the animal shall not be removed from or permitted to leave the vehicle while the vehicle is on a motorway, and
   (b) if it escapes from, or it is necessary for it to be removed from, or permitted to leave, the vehicle—
      (i) it shall not go or remain on any part of the motorway other than a hard shoulder, and
      (ii) it shall whilst it is not on or in the vehicle be held on a lead or otherwise kept under proper control.

. . .

David Howell,
Secretary of State for Transport.

4th August 1982.

Michael Roberts
Parliamentary Under Secretary of State, Welsh Office.

Signed by authority of
the Secretary of State
11th August 1982.

Definitions
"hard shoulder": reg.3(1)(e).
"motorway": regs 3(1)(f), 4.

Commentary
Regulation 14 of these Regulations sets out the rules affecting dogs when carried in a vehicle on a motorway.

SI 1991/1743

DOGS

The Dangerous Dogs (Designated Types) Order 1991

Made .... 25th July 1991
Laid before Parliament .... 26th July 1991
Coming into force .... 12th August 1991

In exercise of the powers conferred upon me by section 1(1)(c) of the Dangerous Dogs Act 1991, I hereby make the following Order:

1. This Order may be cited as the Dangerous Dogs (Designated Types) Order 1991 and shall come into force on 12th August 1991.

2. There are hereby designated for the purposes of section 1 of the Dangerous Dogs Act 1991 dogs of the following types, being types appearing to be bred for fighting or to have the characteristics of types bred for that purpose, namely:

(a) any dog of the type known as the Dogo Argentino; and
(b) any dog of the type known as the Fila Braziliero.

Kenneth Baker
One of her Majesty's Principal Secretaries of State

Home Office
25th July 1991

Commentary

Section 1(1) of the Dangerous Dogs Act 1991 (at p.141) lists two breeds of fighting dogs which are to be subject to the restrictions set out in the following provisions of the Act, and empowers the Secretary of State by order to add further breeds to that listing.

By this order, the first of its kind to be made, the dogs known as Dogo Argentinos and Fila Brazilieros are added to the listing.

SI 1991/1744

DOGS

The Dangerous Dogs Compensation and Exemption Schemes Order 1991

Made . . . . *25th July 1991*
Laid before Parliament . . . . *26th July 1991*
Coming into force . . . . *12th August 1991*

In exercise of the powers conferred upon me by subsections (3), (5) and (6) of section 1 of the Dangerous Dogs Act 1991, I hereby make the following Order:

PART 1

PRELIMINARY

1. (1) This Order may be cited as the Dangerous Dogs Compensation and Exemption Schemes Order 1991 and shall come into force on 12th August 1991.

(2) In this Order—
  (a) "the Act" means the Dangerous Dogs Act 1991;
  (b) "the Agency" means the person or body for the time being designated by the Secretary of State to discharge those functions under this Order, which, in pursuance thereof, are functions falling to be discharged by the Agency;
  (c) "the appointed day" means the day appointed for the purposes of section 1(3) of the Act; and
  (d) unless the context otherwise requires, any reference to an article is to an article of this Order and any reference in an article to a paragraph is to a paragraph of that article.

PART II

COMPENSATION SCHEME

2. (1) The owner of a dog to which section 1 of the Act applies who has arranged for it to be destroyed before the appointed day shall be paid

by the Secretary of State the sums mentioned in paragraphs (2) and (3), if, after complying with article 6 (provision of information to the police), he makes written application to the Agency in such form, containing such particulars and supported by such evidence as the Agency may reasonably require for the purpose of satisfying themselves—
  (a) that the dog is one to which section 1 applies;
  (b) that the applicant is the owner of the dog;
  (c) that he has complied with article 6; and
  (d) that the dog has been destroyed,
and the Agency are satisfied as aforesaid.

(2) The sum payable in respect of dogs in relation to which the Agency are so satisfied shall be—
  (a) in the case of a pit bull terrier £25;
  (b) in the case of a Japanese Tosa £100; and
  (c) in the case of a dog of a type designated in an order under section 1(1)(c) of the Act £100.

(3) The sum payable in respect of the cost of destruction of a dog in relation to which the Agency are so satisfied shall be £25.

PART III

EXEMPTION SCHEME

3. The prohibition contained in subsection (3) of section 1 of the Act (no person to have in his possession or custody after the appointed day a dog to which that section applies) shall not apply to a dog born before the appointed day in respect of which the conditions specified in article 4, or as the case may be, article 5 are complied with.

Conditions for adult dogs

4. In the case of a dog which is over the age of six months on the appointed day, the conditions referred to in article 3 are—
  (a) that article 6 has been complied with;
  (b) that the requirements of article 7 have been complied with;
  (c) that there is in force in respect of the dog third party insurance which complies with article 8;
  (d) that the fee specified in article 9 has been paid;
  (e) that a certificate of exemption issued in accordance with article 10 is in force; and

(f) that the requirements specified in the certificate, in accordance with article 10, are complied with.

Conditions for puppies

5. In the case of a dog which is under the age of six months on the appointed day, the conditions referred to in article 3 are those specified in article 4 except that the conditions contained in paragraphs (b) to (f) of article 4 need not be complied with until after the appointed day as long as they are complied with within one month of the dog's attaining the age of six months.

Reporting to the police

6. The owner of a dog to which section 1 of the Act applies who wishes to claim compensation in accordance with Part II of this Order and a person who wishes such a dog to be exempt from the provisions of section 1(3) of the Act shall, in the case of a dog to which article 4 applies, before 12th October 1991, and in the case of a dog to which article 5 applies, before the appointed day, report to a police station and provide the police with such information concerning the dog as may reasonably be required by the Secretary of State for the purpose of establishing—
   (a) that the dog is one to which section 1 of the Act applies; and
   (b) the address at which the dog is kept; and
   (c) the name, age and gender of the dog.

Neutering and identification

7. (1) A male dog which is to be exempted from the provisions of section 1(3) of the Act shall be castrated, and a female dog which is to be so exempted shall be spayed, in either case by a veterinary surgeon or registered veterinary practitioner and the dog shall be provided with permanent identification in such form as may be prescribed by the Agency in order that it may be readily ascertained that the relevant operation has been performed on it.

(2) A person wishing to claim exemption shall provide the Agency with such evidence as they may require of the fact that the requirements of paragraph (1) have been met.

Third party insurance

8. (1) There shall be in force in respect of a dog which is to be exempted from the provisions of section 1(3) of the Act a policy of insurance

which subject to such terms, conditions, limitations and exclusions as may be contained in the policy, insures the person specified in the policy (the policyholder) in respect of the death of, or bodily injury to, any person caused by the dog other than the death of, or bodily injury to, a member of the policyholder's family who resides permanently with him or a person in respect of whom the policyholder is required to maintain a policy of insurance by virtue of the Employers' Liability (Compulsory Insurance) Act 1969.

(2) A person wishing to claim exemption shall provide the Agency with such evidence as they may require of the fact that the dog is insured in accordance with paragraph (1).

The fee
9. The fee payable to the Agency in respect of a certificate of exemption shall be £20 and value added tax thereon.

Certificate of exemption
10.(1) If satisfied that the conditions referred to in paragraphs (a) to (d) of article 4 have been met, the Agency shall issue a certificate of exemption in respect of the dog.

(2) Such a certificate shall contain the following requirements:
(a) a requirement to notify the Agency of any change of address at which the dog to which it relates is kept for a period in excess of 30 days;
(b) a requirement to notify the Agency of the death or export of the dog;
(c) a requirement, on request by a person specified in section 5(1) of the Act, to produce the certificate to such a person within five days of being requested to do so;
(d) a requirement, on request by a person specified in section 5(1) of the Act, to display the dog's permanent identification pursuant to article 7 to such a person;
(e) a requirement to satisfy the Agency that a policy of insurance which complies with article 8 continues in force;
(f) a requirement to keep the dog to which it relates in sufficiently secure conditions to prevent its escape;
(g) a requirement to keep the dog to which it relates muzzled and on a lead when in a public place;
(h) a requirement to provide the Agency before 1st March 1992 with such evidence as they may require that (in addition to the

permanent identification required by Article 7(1)) the dog has been tattooed in such manner as may be prescribed by them;
  (i) a requirement, on request on or after 1st March 1992 by a person specified in s.5(1)(a) of the Act, to display the dog's tattoo pursuant to paragraph (h) to such a person.

(3) Such a certificate may also contain such additional requirements, including the imposition of time limits, as the Agency may reasonably require for the purpose of ensuring that the requirements of this article are complied with.

11. The Secretary of State shall make such payments to the Agency in respect of the discharge by them of functions under this Order as are agreed between them or, in default of agreement, as appear to him appropriate.

Kenneth Baker
One of Her Majesty's Principal Secretaries of State

Home Office
25th July 1991

Definitions
"*muzzled*": Dangerous Dogs Act 1991, s.7(1)(a).
"*on a lead*": Dangerous Dogs Act 1991, s.7(1)(b).
"*public place*": Dangerous Dogs Act 1991, s.10(4).
"*the Act*": art.1(2)(a).
"*the Agency*": art.1(2)(b).
"*the appointed day*": art.1(2)(c) (November 30, 1991).

Commentary
This order is printed here as amended by two Amendment Orders (SI 1991/2297 and SI 1991/2636).

   This order falls into two main parts:

PART II OF THE ORDER
Part II provides a compensation scheme for owners of pit bull terriers, Japanese tosas, Dogo Argentinos and Fila Brazilieros who have arranged for their dogs to be destroyed before November 30, 1991 (the appointed day). Payment of compensation is made subject to the following conditions being met:

(1) The owner reporting particulars of his dog to a police station in accordance with art.6.

(2) The owner making a written application to the Agency in the terms of art.2(1). (The Secretary of State has appointed the Index of Exempted Dogs as the Agency for the purpose of this Order.)

(3) The Agency being satisfied about the particulars at art.2(1)(a)–(d) given to them about the dog.

The compensation payable is of two kinds: for loss of the dog, £25 for a pit bull terrier and £100 for other breeds; for the cost of the dog's destruction, £25 in all cases (art.2(2), (3)).

It will be seen that compensation is dependent upon the stipulated timetable (dates for reporting to the police in art.6, and destruction before November 30, 1991) being followed. Otherwise no compensation is payable.

PART III OF THE ORDER

The effect of s.1(3), (5) of the Dangerous Dogs Act 1991 (at p.142) is to make illegal the possession or custody of any of the four breeds of fighting dogs named by or under s.1(1) after November 30, 1991, subject only to powers of seizure and orders for destruction (under s.4(1), (4)) and to exemption under the Secretary of State's order.

Part III sets out the conditions for such exemption. These are listed in art.4 in the case of adult dogs and in art.5 in the case of dogs under six months old on November 30, 1991.

Article 4 lists six conditions, the details of the first four of which are to be found in arts 6–9. If the appointed Agency (the Index of Exempted Dogs) is satisfied that these four conditions have been met, they will issue a certificate of exemption under art.10 which will contain the requirements there mentioned; the specified person referred to in art.10(2)(i) is a police officer or an authorised officer of a local authority.

Exemption will only continue in force for as long as those requirements are being met (art.4(f)).

The conditions of exemption for puppies under art.5 are the same as those for adult dogs, except that conditions (b) to (f) of art.4 need not be met until the dog is seven months old.

Breeding from the four named breeds of fighting dogs has been prohibited since August 12, 1991 (Dangerous Dogs Act 1991, s.1(2)(a), at p.141), and no puppies born after November 30, 1991 can be exempted.

SI 1991/1744

It will be seen that, in both cases, exemption depends upon compliance with the requirements for reporting to the police under art.6 by October 12, 1991 or, in the case of puppies, November 30, 1991 (the appointed day). Unless this has been done, no exemption can be given.

However, when an order has been made under s.4A(1) or 4B(3) of the Dangerous Dogs Act 1991, Part III of the Order is to be differently interpreted. In those cases, the words "the end of the requisite period" are to be substituted for the words "the appointed day" where they appear in arts 3–5 and arts 4(a) and 6 are to be omitted. The term "the requisite period" is to have the respective meanings assigned to it by ss.4A and 4B of the 1991 Act (Dangerous Dogs (Amendment) Act 1997, s.4(1)(a), (b)).

The fee payable under art.9 was, from June 8, 1997, increased to £20 plus VAT by the Dangerous Dogs (Fees) Order 1997 (SI 1997/1152).

Further references
For the exemption scheme and exempted dogs, see Home Office Circular 67/91, paras 10–26, at pp.418–423, and Home Office Circular 80/92, paras 10–14, at pp.446–447.

SI 1991/961
ENVIRONMENTAL PROTECTION
The Litter (Animal Droppings) Order 1991

Made .... *9th April 1991*
Laid before Parliament .... *10th April 1991*
Coming into force .... *1st May 1991*

The Secretary of State for the Environment, as respects England, the Secretary of State for Wales, as respects Wales, and the Secretary of State for Scotland, as respects Scotland, in exercise of the powers conferred on them by section 86(14) and (15) of the Environmental Protection Act 1990, and of all other powers enabling them in that behalf, hereby make the following Order:—

1. This Order may be cited as the Litter (Animal Droppings) Order 1991 and shall come into force on 1st May 1991.

2. The provisions of Part IV of the Environmental Protection Act 1990 which apply to refuse shall apply to dog faeces on land of the following descriptions which is not heath or woodland or used for the grazing of animals:

any public walk or pleasure ground;

any land, whether inclosed or not, on which there are no buildings or of which no more than one-twentieth part is covered with buildings, and the whole or the remainder of which is laid out as a garden or is used for the purposes of recreation;

any part of the seashore (that is to say every cliff, bank, barrier, dune, beach, flat or other land adjacent to and about the place to which the tide flows at mean high water springs) which is—

frequently used by large numbers of people, and

managed by the person having direct control of it as a tourist resort or recreational facility;

any esplanade or promenade which is above the place to which the tide flows at mean high water springs;

any land not forming part of the highway . . .;

a trunk road picnic area provided by the Minister under section 112 of the Highways Act 1980 . . .;

a picnic site provided by a local planning authority under section 10(2) of the Countryside Act 1968 . . .;

land (whether above or below ground and whether or not consisting of or including buildings) forming or used in connection with off-street parking places provided in accordance with section 32 of the Road Traffic Regulation Act 1984.

Michael Heseltine
Secretary of State for the Environment

4th April 1991

David Hunt
Secretary of State for Wales

9th April 1991

James Douglas-Hamilton
Parliamentary Under Secretary of State, Scottish Office

8th April 1991

Commentary

The Environmental Protection Act 1990 s.89 obliges designated authorities, bodies and other persons to keep land under their control clear of litter and refuse. Section 86(14) and (15) of that Act authorises the Secretary of State by order to define the circumstances in which animal droppings are to be treated as refuse for the purposes of s.89.

This order, made under those powers, declares that dog faeces are to be so treated when deposited on the types of land described in art.2 of the order, but excepting heath, woodland and animal grazing land.

SI 1992/288

ENVIRONMENTAL PROTECTION

The Environmental Protection (Stray Dogs) Regulations 1992

Made . . . .*19th February 1992*
Laid before Parliament . . . .*19th February 1992*
Coming into force . . . .*1st April 1992*

The Secretary of State for the Environment as respects England, the Secretary of State for Scotland as respects Scotland, and the Secretary of State for Wales as respects Wales, in exercise of their powers under sections 149(5), (8) and (11), 150(2) and (6), and 161 of the Environmental Protection Act 1990, and of all other powers enabling them in that behalf, hereby make the following Regulations:

1. Title, commencement and interpretation
(1) These Regulations may be cited as the Environmental Protection (Stray Dogs) Regulations 1992 and shall come into force on 1st April 1992.

(2) In these Regulations, "the Act" means the Environmental Protection Act 1990, and "seized dog" means a dog seized pursuant to section 149 of that Act.

2. Prescribed amount to be paid by owner of seized dog
For the purposes of section 149(5) of the Act, the sum of £25 (twenty-five pounds) is hereby prescribed as the further amount (additional to all expenses) to be paid by a person claiming to be the owner of a seized dog before he is entitled to have the dog returned to him.

3. Register of seized dogs — prescribed particulars
For the purposes of section 149(8) of the Act, the following are the prescribed particulars to be contained in the register of seized dogs which is kept by the officer—
  (a) a brief description of each dog, including its breed (if known), and any distinctive physical characteristics or markings, tattoos or scars;
  (b) any information which is recorded on a tag or collar worn by, or which is otherwise carried by, the dog;

SI 1992/288

(c) the date, time and place of the seizure;
(d) where a notice has been served pursuant to section 149(4), the date of service of the notice, and the name and address of the person on whom it has been served;
(e) where the officer disposes of the dog pursuant to section 149(6)—
   (i) the date of disposal;
   (ii) whether disposal was by destruction, gift or sale, and if by sale, the price obtained;
   (iii) the name and address of the purchaser, donee or person effecting the destruction; and
(f) where the dog was returned to a person claiming to be its owner, the name and address of that person, and the date of return.

4. Procedure where finder desires to keep a stray dog

(1) This regulation prescribes the procedure to be followed by the officer for the purposes of section 150(2)(a) before a finder desiring to keep a stray dog is allowed to remove it.

(2) The officer shall make a clear and accurate record of the following matters in a permanent form suitable for reference purposes—
(a) a brief description of the dog, including its breed (if known), and any distinctive physical characteristics or markings, tattoos or scars;
(b) any information which is recorded on a tag or collar worn by, or which is otherwise carried by, the dog;
(c) the date, time and place of the finding of the dog; and
(d) the name and address of the finder.

(3) Where the owner of the dog can be identified and can readily be contacted, the officer shall make reasonable attempts to contact him, and, if appropriate in the circumstances of the case, afford him forthwith a reasonable opportunity to collect the dog.

(4) The officer shall make all such enquiries as he considers appropriate in the circumstances of the case to ascertain that the finder is a fit and proper person to keep the dog, and that he is able to feed and care for it.

(5) The officer shall inform the finder both verbally and in writing that the finder is obliged under section 150(3) to keep the dog (if

unclaimed by the owner) for not less than one month, and that failure to comply with that obligation is a criminal offence.

Michael Heseltine
Secretary of State for the Environment

17th February 1992

Ian Lang
Secretary of State for Scotland

19th February 1992

David Hunt
Secretary of State for Wales

17th February 1992

Definitions
"seized dog" and *"the Act":* art.1(2). (The Environmental Protection Act 1990 s.149 is reproduced at pp.133–135).

Commentary
Sections 149 and 150 of the Environmental Protection Act 1990 (at pp.133–137) provide for three matters connected with the seizure and disposal of stray dogs to be prescribed by regulations made by the Secretaries of State. These regulations, so made, provide for those matters.

An owner reclaiming his dog which has been seized must pay to the local authority a fixed sum of £25 in addition to the expenses of its detention before he is entitled to have the dog returned to him (art.2).

The local authority's officer, i.e. dog warden, must keep a register of dogs held and disposed of by him. Article 3 lists the particulars to be recorded.

Section 150(2)(a) of the 1990 Act provides for the return to the finder of a stray dog which he takes to the local authority. The dog warden must first record the particulars shown in art.4(2). He must then try to contact the owner of the dog, if known, and, if appropriate in the circumstances, give him an opportunity to collect it (art.4(3)). Failing such collection, the finder may take the dog if enquiries about him are satisfactory, i.e. if he is found to be a suitable person to keep the dog, and he has been warned of the obligation to keep the dog for at least one month. (Failure to do so is an offence under s.150(5) of the 1990 Act.)

The foregoing procedure, while appearing to be fair and reasonable, may present dog wardens with a number of difficulties. For example: to what lengths must they go to contact the owner? What circumstances would make it inappropriate for them to give the owner an opportunity to reclaim his dog? How much time must the owner be given to do that? Legislation cannot hope to cover all circumstances, and a dog warden can only act with common sense within the guidelines above.

Further References
As to the ownership of a dog kept by its finder, see under "Commentary" to s.150 of the 1990 Act at p.137.

SI 1992/901

DOGS

CONTROL OF DOGS

The Control of Dogs Order 1992

Made .... *19th March 1992*
Coming into force .... *1st April 1992*

The Minister of Agriculture, Fisheries and Food, in relation to England, the Secretary of State for Scotland in relation to Scotland, and the Secretary of State for Wales in relation to Wales, in exercise of the powers conferred on them by sections 13(2) and (3) and 72 of the Animal Health Act 1981 and of all other powers enabling them in that behalf, hereby make the following Order:

1. Title and commencement
This Order may be cited as the Control of Dogs Order 1992 and shall come into force on 1st April 1992.

2. Wearing of collars by dogs
(1) Subject to paragraph (2) below, every dog while in a highway or in a place of public resort shall wear a collar with the name and address of the owner inscribed on the collar or on a place or badge attached to it.

(2) Paragraph (1) above shall not apply to—
(a) any pack of hounds,
(b) any dog while being used for sporting purposes,
(c) any dog while being used for the capture or destruction of vermin,
(d) any dog while being used for the driving or tending of cattle or sheep,
(e) any dog while being used on official duties by a member of Her Majesty's Armed Forces or Her Majesty's Customs and Excise or the police force for any area,
(f) any dog while being used in emergency rescue work, or
(g) any dog registered with the Guide Dogs for the Blind Association.

3. Offences

The owner of a dog or the person in charge of a dog who, without lawful authority or excuse, proof of which shall lie on him, causes or permits the dog to be in a highway or in a place of public resort not wearing a collar as prescribed in article 2(1) above shall be guilty of an offence against the Animal Health Act 1981.

4. Seizure of dogs

Any dog in respect of which an offence is being committed against this Order may be seized and treated as a stray dog under section 3 of the Dogs Act 1906 or under section 149 of the Environmental Protection Act 1990.

5. Enforcement

(1) This Order shall be executed and enforced by the officers of a local authority (and not by the police force for any area).

(2) In this article "local authority" and "officer" have the same meaning as in section 149 of the Environmental Protection Act 1990.

. . .

In witness whereof the Official Seal of the Minister of Agriculture, Fisheries and Food is hereunto affixed on 16th March 1992.

John Selwyn Gummer
Minister of Agriculture, Fisheries and Food

Allan Stewart
Parliamentary Under Secretary of State
Scottish Office

19th March 1992

David Hunt
Secretary of State for Wales

17th March 1992

Definitions

"*local authority*" and "*officer*": see, by virtue of art.5(2), the Environmental Protection Act 1990, s.149(11), at p.134.

Commentary

This order replaces and extends with effect from April 1, 1992 the Control of Dogs Order 1930 as amended.

Control of Dogs Order 1992

All dogs, except those mentioned in art.2(2), while in a highway or place of public resort are required to carry identification of their owners (art.2(1)).

An offence is created by art.3 for which see, further, the Animal Health Act 1981 s.75 at p.121.

Offending dogs may be seized and treated as strays under the provisions of the 1906 and 1990 Acts referred to (art.4). These provisions may be found at pp.85 and 133.

This order is to be enforced by the local authority officers, and not by the police (art.5(1)).

SI 1995/2767

ROAD TRAFFIC

The Control of Dogs on Roads Orders (Procedure) (England and Wales) Regulations 1995

Made .... *19th October 1995*
Laid before Parliament .... *2nd November 1995*
Coming into force .... *11th December 1995*

The Secretary of State for Transport, as respects England, and the Secretary of State for Wales, as respects Wales, in exercise of the powers conferred by section 27(6) of the Road Traffic Act 1988 and of all other powers enabling them in that behalf, and after consultation with representative organisations in accordance with section 195(2) of that Act, hereby make the following Regulations:—

1. Commencement and citation

These Regulations may be cited as the Control of Dogs on Roads Orders (Procedure) (England and Wales) Regulations 1995 and shall come into force on 11th December 1995.

2. Revocation and transitional provisions

(1) Subject to paragraph (2) below, the Control of Dogs on Roads Orders (Procedure) (England and Wales) Regulations 1962 and the Control of Dogs on Roads Orders (Procedure) (England and Wales) (Amendment) Regulations 1965 are hereby revoked.

(2) Where a notice relating to an order has been published pursuant to regulation 3(b) or 11 of the Control of Dogs on Roads Orders (Procedure) (England and Wales) Regulations 1962, those Regulations shall continue to apply to that order as if they had not been revoked and nothing in these Regulations shall apply to the order.

3. Interpretation

A reference in regulation 2 or regulations 5 to 10 below to an order is a reference to an order or a proposed order, as appropriate and, in the case of a proposed order, any reference to the effect of the order (however expressed) is a reference to its effect if it were to be made.

4. Application of regulations
These Regulations apply to orders made or proposed to be made by a local authority falling within section 27(7)(a) of the Road Traffic Act 1988.

5. Procedure before making an order
Before making an order, a local authority shall—
   (a) without prejudice to section 27(5) of the Road Traffic Act 1988, consult such organisations (if any) representing persons likely to be affected by any provision in the order as it thinks appropriate; and
   (b) publish once at least, in a local newspaper circulating in the area in which any length of road to which the order relates is situated, a notice in the form and containing the particulars specified in Part I of the Schedule to these Regulations.

6. Inspection
(1) During the period mentioned in paragraph (2) below, there shall be made available for inspection at the principal offices of the local authority during normal office hours and at such other places (if any) within its area as it may think fit during such hours as it may determine for each such place, the following documents—
   (a) a copy of the notice published under regulation 5(b);
   (b) a copy of the order; and
   (c) a map which clearly indicates in distinguishing colours or markings all lengths of road to which the order relates.

(2) The period referred to in paragraph (1) above, is the period beginning on the date of publication of the notice under regulation 5(b), and ending at the expiration of the period during which objections to the order may be sent under regulation 7.

7. Objections
(1) Any person desiring to object to an order shall send to the local authority, at the address specified in the notice published under regulation 5(b), a written statement of his objection and the grounds on which it is made on or before the date specified in the notice.

(2) Before making an order the local authority shall consider all objections duly made under this regulation and not withdrawn.

8. Notification of decision to make an order by the local authority

(1) After the local authority has decided to make an order, the decision shall be notified in writing to—
  (a) the chief officer of police who is required to be consulted under section 27(5) of the Road Traffic Act 1988; and
  (b) each person who has duly objected to the order under regulation 7 and has not withdrawn his objection.

(2) Where an objection made under regulation 7 has not been, or not wholly been, acceded to, the local authority shall notify in writing the person making the objection of the reasons for the decision.

9. Procedure after order is made

After an order is made, the local authority shall—

  (a) within 14 days of the making of the order publish in a local newspaper circulating in the area in which any length of road to which the order relates is situated a notice in the form and containing the particulars specified in Part II of the Schedule to these Regulations;
  (b) forthwith keep available for inspection at its principal offices during normal office hours a copy of the order as made and a map showing all lengths of road to which the order relates; and
  (c) forthwith take all such steps as are reasonably practicable to cause to be erected on or near to the lengths of road to which the order relates signs in such positions as the local authority may consider to be appropriate for ensuring that adequate information about the order is given to persons likely to be affected by its provisions.

10. Special provision for certain orders

Regulations 5, 6, 7, 8(1)(b) and (2) shall not apply to—
  (a) an order which revokes and re-enacts another order or a provision of another order, but has no further affect, or

(b) an order which revokes another order or a provision of another order, but has no other effect.

Steven Norris
Parliamentary Under Secretary of State,
Department of Transport

18th October 1995

William Hague
Secretary of State for Wales

19th October 1995

SI 1995/2767

SCHEDULE
FORMS OF NOTICE RELATING TO ORDERS

PART I

FORM OF NOTICE OF PROPOSAL TO MAKE AN ORDER

The (**a**)

The (**b**) propose to make an order under section 27 of the Road Traffic Act 1988 the effect of which will be (**c**)

A copy of the order, a notice of the order and a map showing the length(s) of road that will be affected are available for inspection at (**d**)

during the following hours (**e**)

Any objection to the proposal must be made in writing, must state the grounds upon which the objection is made and must be sent to the undersigned by (**f**)

(Name and address of Proper Officer of Local Authority)

Notes
(**a**) Here insert title of the order;
(**b**) Here insert name of local authority proposing to make the order;
(**c**) Here insert a brief statement of general nature and effect of the order;
(**d**) Here insert addresses where the order, notice of order and map will be available for inspection;
(**e**) Here insert hours during which the order, notice of order and map will be available for inspection; and
(**f**) Here insert date not less than 21 days from the date of first publication of the notice in the local newspaper.

PART II

FORM OF NOTICE OF MAKING OF AN ORDER

The (**a**)

On the (**b**) the (**c**)

made an order under section 27 of the Road Traffic Act 1988 the effect of which is to (**d**)

A copy of the order, notice of the order and a map showing the length(s) of road that will be affected are available for inspection at (**e**)

during the following hours (**f**)

(Name and address of Proper Officer of Local Authority)

Notes
(a) Here insert title of the order;
(b) Here insert date of making of the order;
(c) Here insert name of local authority making the order;
(d) Here insert a brief statement of general nature and effect of the order;
(e) Here insert addresses where the order, notice and map will be available for inspection; and
(f) Here insert hours during which the order, notice of order and map will be available for inspection.

Definitions
"*local authority*": reg.4; Road Traffic Act 1988, s.27(7)(a), at p.124.

Commentary
Section 27 of the Road Traffic Act 1988 (at p.124) enables a local authority by order to designate roads on which it will be an offence to have a dog without a lead. Section 27(6) of that Act allows the Secretary of State to make regulations prescribing the procedure to be followed when an order is made.
　These regulations, so made, provide for:
(1) **Consultation about, and advertisement of, a proposed order (reg.5).**
(2) **Inspection of a proposed order and its associated map (reg.6).**
(3) **The procedure for dealing with objections (reg.7).**
(4) **Notification to objectors and the police of decision to make an order (reg.8).**
(5) **After an order is made, publication in a local paper of its effect, inspection of the order and erection of notices on the roads affected (reg.9).**

SI 1995/2767

(6) The exclusion of certain earlier provisions of the regulations in the case of orders revoking or re-enacting provisions in earlier orders (reg.10).

The Schedule contains forms of notices to be used in connection with regs 5(b) and 9(a).

The earlier regulations made in 1962 and 1965 are revoked, except where a notice thereunder has already been published (reg.2).

SI 1999/3191

ANIMALS, ENGLAND AND WALES

The Sale of Dogs (Identification Tag) Regulations 1999

Made . . . . *29th November 1999*
Laid before Parliament . . . . *7th December 1999*
Coming into force . . . . *30th December 1999*

The Secretary of State, in exercise of the powers conferred on him by the definition of "identifying tag or badge" (and the definition of "regulations") in section 8(5) of the Breeding and Sale of Dogs (Welfare) Act 1999, hereby makes the following Regulations:

1.—(1) These Regulations may be cited as the Sale of Dogs (Identification Tag) Regulations 1999 and shall come into force on 30th December 1999.

. . .

2. In addition to the information required by the definition of "identifying tag or badge" in section 8(5) of the Breeding and Sale of Dogs (Welfare) Act 1999 to be displayed on such a tag or badge, that tag or badge shall also display the following information—
  (a) the date of birth of the dog, and
  (b) an identifying number, if any, allocated to the dog by the licensed breeding establishment at which it was born.

Mike O'Brien
Parliamentary Under-Secretary of State
29th November 1999

Commentary
Section 8(1)(e), (3) of the Breeding and Sale of Dogs (Welfare) Act 1999 (at p.193) makes it an offence if, in specified circumstances, a dog is sold when not wearing a collar with an "identifying tag or badge".

Section 8(5) defines the meaning of that phrase, and enables the Secretary of State for the Home Office to make regulations specifying any further information to be displayed on the tag or badge.

That further information is detailed in reg.2 above.

SI 1999/3192

ANIMALS, ENGLAND AND WALES

The Breeding of Dogs (Licensing Records) Regulations 1999

Made ....29th November 1999
Laid before Parliament ....7th December 1999
Coming into force 30th December 1999

The Secretary of State, in exercise of the powers conferred on him by section 1(4)(i) and (4A) of the Breeding of Dogs Act 1973, hereby makes the following Regulations:

1.—(1) These Regulations may be cited as the Breeding of Dogs (Licensing Records) Regulations 1999 and shall come into force on 30th December 1999.

. . .

2. For the purposes of section 1(4)(i) of the Breeding of Dogs Act 1973, the records referred to in that section shall be in the form set out in the Schedule to these Regulations.

Mike O'Brien
Parliamentary Under-Secretary of State

29th November 1999

Commentary

Section 1(4)(i), (4A) of the Breeding of Dogs Act 1973 (at pp.105–106) authorises the Secretary of State for the Home Office to make regulations prescribing the form in which records are to be kept at dog breeding establishments.

The Schedule to these Regulations supplies the form so prescribed.

Breeding of Dogs (Licensing Records) Regs 1999

SCHEDULE

Regulation 2

FORM OF RECORD TO BE KEPT BY LICENSED DOG BREEDER FOR EACH BREEDING BITCH

Name	Date of birth	Address where kept	Breed	Description*	Date of mating	Details of sire**	Details of litter							Total number in litter
							Male				Female				
							Date of birth	Weight	Description*	Sale details***	Date of birth	Weight	Description*	Sale details***	

* Enter name (in the case of puppies), colour, identifying features (if any) and registration number (if any).
** Enter name, address where kept, breed, colour and registration number (if any).
*** Enter date of sale, and name, address and status (for example, private/pet shop) of purchaser.

SI 2004/2363

ANIMALS, ENGLAND

ANIMAL HEALTH

The Non Commercial Movement of Pet Animals (England) Regulations 2004

Made . . . . *8th September 2004*
Laid before Parliament . . . . *10th September 2004*
Coming into force . . . . *1st October 2004*

The Secretary of State, being a Minister designated for the purposes of section 2(2) of the European Communities Act 1972 in relation to the common agricultural policy of the European Community and in relation to measures in the veterinary and phytosanitary fields for the protection of public health, exercising the powers conferred upon her by that section makes the following Regulations:

PART 1 – INTRODUCTION

1. Title, application and commencement

These Regulations may be cited as the Non Commercial Movement of Pet Animals (England) Regulations 2004; they apply only to England and come into force on 1st October 2004.

2. Interpretation

(1) In these Regulations—

"airport" means the aggregate of the buildings and works comprised in an aerodrome within the meaning of the Civil Aviation Act 1982;

"carrier" means any undertaking carrying goods or passengers for hire by land, sea or air;

"the Community Regulation" means Regulation (EC) No. 998/2003 of the European Parliament and of the Council of 26 May 2003 on the animal health requirements applicable to the non-commercial movement of pet animals and amending Council Directive 92/65/EC as amended by Commission Regulation (EC) No. 592/2004 and as read with Commission Decisions—

(a) 2003/803/EC of 26 November 2003 establishing a model passport for the intra-Community movement of dogs, cats and ferrets,
(b) 2004/203/EC of 18 February 2004 establishing a model health certificate for non-commercial movements from third countries of dogs, cats and ferrets,
(c) 2004/301/EC of 30 March 2004 derogating from Decisions 2003/803/EC and 2004/203/EC as regards the format for certificates and passports for the non-commercial movement of dogs, cats and ferrets and amending Decision 2004/203/EC, and
(d) 2004/539/EC of 1 July 2004 establishing a transitional measure for the implementation of Regulation (EC) No. 998/2003 on the animal health requirements applicable to the non-commercial movement of pet animals;

. . .

"inspector" means a person appointed by the Secretary of State or a local authority to be an inspector for the purposes of these Regulations and a person appointed as an inspector or a veterinary inspector for the purposes of the Animal Health Act 1981 shall be an inspector for the purposes of these Regulations;

"local authority" means—
  (a) in any part of England where there is, within the meaning of the Local Government Changes for England Regulations 1994, a unitary authority for that local government area, that authority;
  (b) where there is not a unitary authority—
    (i) in a metropolitan district, the council of that district;
    (ii) in a non-metropolitan county, the council of that county; or
    (iii) in each London borough, the council of that borough;
  (c) in the City of London, the Common Council;

"microchip" means the electronic identification system (transponder) specified in article 4(1) of the Community Regulation;

"PETS certification" means either the official health certificate relating to rabies required by article 7 of the Pet Travel Scheme (Pilot Arrangements) (England) Order 1999 or the official health certificate required by paragraph 4(a) of Schedule 6 to that Order;

"third country health certificate" means a health certificate complying with Commission Decision 2004/203/EC and the supporting documentation (or a certified copy of that documentation) referred to in article 3 of that Decision.

(2) Expressions defined in the Community Regulation have the same meaning in these Regulations.

3. Approvals
Approvals issued under these Regulations shall be in writing, may be made subject to such conditions as the Secretary of State considers necessary to—
- (a) ensure that the provisions of the Community Regulation and these Regulations are complied with; and
- (b) protect public or animal health

and may be amended, suspended or revoked by notice in writing at any time; in particular approvals granted under regulation 8 may be suspended or revoked if the Secretary of State is reasonably of the opinion that the written procedures and contingency plans produced under Schedule 1 have not been complied with.

4. Exemption from the provisions of the Rabies (Importation of Dogs, Cats and Other Mammals) Order 1974
(1) A person may bring a pet animal into England without complying with the provisions of the Rabies (Importation of Dogs, Cats and Other Mammals) Order 1974 provided the movement complies with the Community Regulation and these Regulations.

(2) Nothing in these Regulations shall apply in relation to an animal brought into England directly from other parts of the British Islands or the Republic of Ireland.

5. Exceptions
These Regulations shall not apply to the movement to England of—
- (a) more than five pet animals if they—
  - (i) are travelling together; and
  - (ii) come from a third country other than one listed in Section 2 of Part B of Annex II to the Community Regulation;
- (b) prairie dogs originating in or travelling from the United States of America; . . .

PART 2 – IDENTIFICATION AND BLOOD-TESTING OF PET ANIMALS

6. Identification of pet dogs, cats and ferrets

For the purposes of article 4 of the Community Regulation, pet dogs, cats and ferrets shall be identified by microchip.

7. Waiting period after satisfactory blood test

The neutralising antibody titration at least equal to 0.5 IU/ml referred to in article 6(1) of the Community Regulation shall be carried out on a blood sample taken at least six months before the pet animal is brought into England.

PART 3 – CARRIERS, CERTIFICATION AND CHECKING ARRANGEMENTS

8. Carriers

(1) Pet dogs, cats and ferrets shall be brought into England under the Community Regulation using a carrier approved to transport them under this regulation.

(2) The Secretary of State may approve a carrier under this regulation if she is satisfied that—
  (a) the carrier complies with the requirements in Schedule 1;
  (b) the written procedures and contingency plans required in that Schedule are adequate; and
  (c) the carrier will comply with the Community Regulation and these Regulations, the written procedures required in Schedule 1 and any conditions of the approval.

(3) The approval shall specify—
  (a) where checks must be carried out;
  (b) the routes to be used by the approved carrier to bring a pet dog, cat or ferret into England; and
  (c) any other conditions the Secretary of State considers appropriate.

(4) The carrier shall provide such information to the Secretary of State as she shall reasonably require.

(5) Every carrier shall comply with the terms and conditions of its approval.

9. Treatment and certification in respect of *echinococcus multilocularis* and ticks

(1) This regulation shall apply to pet dogs, cats and ferrets during the transitional period specified in article 16 of the Community Regulation.

(2) Not less than 24 and not more than 48 hours before embarkation for England the pet dog, cat or ferret shall have been treated by a veterinary surgeon entitled to practise medicine in the country in which the treatment is administered against Echinococcus multilocularis and ticks.

(3) The treatment shall be with a veterinary medicine with a marketing authorisation in the country in which the treatment is administered, shall be at an appropriate dosage, and—
  (a) in the case of treatment against Echinococcus multilocularis shall contain praziquantel as the active ingredient; and
  (b) in the case of treatment against ticks shall not be by means of a collar impregnated with acaricide.

(4) In addition to the certification required by the Community Regulation, the passport or third country health certificate accompanying each pet dog, cat and ferret shall—
  (a) specify the manufacturer of each treatment administered in respect of Echinococcus multilocularis and ticks, the product used for each treatment, and the date and time of such administration; and
  (b) be signed and stamped in respect of those treatments by the veterinary surgeon who administered them.

10. Duties on carriers

(1) A carrier shall check—
  (a) the microchip, and
  (b) either the passport or the third country health certificate
of every pet dog, cat or ferret it brings into England under the Community Regulation.

(2) A carrier shall check the Hendra certificate of every cat it brings into England from Australia.

(3) The checks shall be performed in the place and in the manner specified in the carrier's approval.

(4) The carrier shall satisfy itself that—
  (a) the animal has been implanted with a microchip,
  (b) the number of the microchip corresponds with the number of the

microchip recorded in the passport or the third country health certificate (and such number must appear on both the health certificate and its supporting documentation) and, for a cat travelling from Australia, the Hendra certificate,
(c) the passport or third country health certificate shows that—
 (i) it is current;
 (ii) the animal has been vaccinated against rabies (and revaccinated where required) in accordance with the Community Regulation;
 (iii) a neutralising antibody titration has been carried out on a blood sample from the animal in accordance with the Community Regulation and these Regulations and with a result in accordance with that required by the Community Regulation; and
 (iv) the animal has been treated against Echinococcus multilocularis and ticks in accordance with these Regulations and those treatments have been certified in accordance with regulation 9(4),

. . .

(5) If the passport or third country health certificate of a pet dog or cat shows that it was vaccinated or its blood sample was taken before its microchip was inserted it shall not fail either of the checks in paragraphs (4)(c)(ii) and (4)(c)(iii) for that reason if—
(a) the animal was vaccinated in a country or territory where the competent authority (or a body authorised by that authority) operates a mandatory identification system under which that species is required to be registered and identified by tattoo or microchip, or by tattoo only,
(b) the number of the animal's tattoo corresponds with the number of the tattoo recorded in the passport or third country health certificate (and such number must appear on both the health certificate and its supporting documentation), and
(c) the passport or third country health certificate shows that the animal was vaccinated after it was tattooed and before the blood sample was taken.

(6) If, after carrying out the checks, the carrier is not satisfied that the pet dog, cat or ferret may be brought into England under the Community Regulation and these Regulations—

(a) where the checks were performed outside England (other than during transport directly to England), the carrier shall not bring the animal into England under the Community Regulation;
(b) where the checks were performed in England or during transport directly to England, the carrier shall ensure that the animal is transferred to quarantine facilities in accordance with the Rabies (Importation of Dogs, Cats and Other Mammals) Order 1974 or is otherwise dealt with under the provisions of that Order and compliance with this sub-paragraph shall be a defence to a breach of article 4(1) of that Order.

(7) If, after carrying out the checks, the carrier is satisfied that the pet dog, cat or ferret may be brought into England under the Community Regulations and these Regulations it shall—
(a) issue a certificate to the person in charge of the animal which—
   (i) is signed and dated by a representative of the carrier,
   (ii) states that the animal complies with the provisions of the Community Regulation and these Regulations, and
   (iii) states the date of importation to England; and
(b) if the animal is brought into England in a motor vehicle, give the person in charge a sticker or hanger for display on the vehicle stating that it is carrying a pet animal which has been checked and found to comply with the provisions of the Community Regulation and these Regulations.

11. Duties at the port of arrival

(1) A person bringing a pet dog, cat or ferret into England in a vehicle under the Community Regulation and these Regulations shall display the sticker or hanger given by the carrier in a prominent position in the windscreen until the vehicle leaves the port of arrival or, in the case of the Channel Tunnel, the Folkestone Terminal at Cheriton.

(2) A person bringing a pet dog, cat or ferret into England under the Community Regulation and these Regulations shall produce on demand by an inspector—
(a) in the case of arrival by sea, in the port area,
(b) in the case of transport through the Channel Tunnel, in the Tunnel System as defined in section 1(7) of the Channel Tunnel Act 1987 or the Folkestone Terminal at Cheriton, except that an inspector of a local authority shall only have powers in England,
(c) in the case of air transport, in the airport,

the passport or third country health certificate, any Hendra certificate, and the certificate of entry given by the carrier under regulation 10(7)(a) and shall make the animal available for checking.

PART 4 – ADMINISTRATION AND ENFORCEMENT

12. Designation of competent authority

(1) The Secretary of State shall be the competent authority for the purposes of—
   (a) approving veterinarians in accordance with articles 5(1) and 6(1) of the Community Regulation, and
   (b) granting derogations in relation to animals under three months old in accordance with article 6(2) of the Community Regulation and each such derogation shall be granted by an approval under these Regulations.

(2) Every person granted an approval under this regulation shall comply with its terms and conditions.

13. Powers of inspectors

(1) An inspector shall, on producing if required to do so, some duly authenticated document showing his authority, have a right at all reasonable hours to enter any land or premises (other than premises used exclusively as a dwellinghouse) for the purpose of administering and enforcing these Regulations and the Community Regulation; and in this regulation "premises" includes any vessel, boat, aircraft or vehicle of any other description.

(2) Such an inspector shall have powers to carry out all checks, searches and examinations which may be necessary to ascertain whether the Community Regulation and these Regulations are being complied with and in particular may examine and copy documentary or data processing material.

14. Obstruction

(1) No person shall—
   (a) intentionally obstruct any person acting in the execution of the Community Regulation and these Regulations;
   (b) without reasonable cause, fail to give any person acting in the execution of the Community Regulation and these Regulations any assistance or information which that person may reasonably require for the purposes of his functions under these Regulations; or

(c) furnish to any person acting in the execution of the Community Regulations and these Regulations any information which he knows to be false or misleading.

15. Falsification of documents

(1) No person, other than a duly approved veterinary surgeon or a person acting at his direction, shall alter—
  (a) any part of a passport save for Section I,
  (b) any part of a third country health certificate, or
  (c) any part of a Hendra certificate.
 (2) No person shall knowingly be in possession of—
  (a) a passport, third country health certificate or Hendra certificate which has been unlawfully altered, or
  (b) a document which falsely purports to be a passport, third country health certificate or Hendra certificate.

16. Offences

(1) It shall be an offence for any person to fail to comply with—
  (a) regulation 8(5) (failure by a carrier to comply with the terms and conditions of its approval);
  (b) regulation 10 (duties on carriers);
  (c) regulation 11 (duties at the port of arrival);
  (d) regulation 12(2) (failure by a veterinarian or a person importing animals under three months old to comply with the terms and conditions of their approval);
  (e) regulation 14 (obstruction);
  (f) regulation 15 (falsification of documents).
 (2) Where a body corporate is guilty of an offence under these Regulations, and that offence is proved to have been committed with the consent or connivance of, or to have been attributable to any neglect on the part of—
  (a) any director, manager, secretary or similar officer of the body corporate, or
  (b) any person who was purporting to act in such a capacity,
he as well as the body corporate shall be guilty of an offence and be liable to be proceeded against and punished accordingly.
 (3) For the purposes of paragraph (2), "director" in relation to a body corporate whose affairs are managed by its members, means a member of the body corporate.

17. Penalties

A person guilty of an offence under these Regulations shall be liable on summary conviction to imprisonment for a term not exceeding six months or to a fine not exceeding level 5 on the standard scale or to both.

18. Enforcement

(1) The provisions of these Regulations shall be enforced by the local authority.

(2) The Secretary of State may direct, in relation to cases of a particular description or a particular case, that any duty imposed on a local authority under paragraph (1) shall be discharged by the Secretary of State and not by the local authority.

. . .

Ben Bradshaw
Parliamentary Under Secretary of State
Department for Environment, Food and Rural Affairs
8th September 2004

SCHEDULE 1

Regulation 8(2)

CONDITIONS OF APPROVAL FOR CARRIERS

1. Staff having contact with passengers who may be travelling with pet dogs, cats or ferrets or staff who may be involved in checking pet dogs, cats or ferrets under these Regulations shall be appropriately trained.

2. The carrier shall set out in writing procedures to ensure that a pet dog, cat or ferret presented for travel under the Community Regulation is—

(a) directed to an appropriate checking point;
(b) checked under these Regulations; and
(c) transported in an appropriate part of the vessel, train or aircraft in appropriate conditions.

3. The carrier shall set out in writing procedures on what it will do if a pet dog, cat or ferret presented for travel fails to comply with the Community Regulation or these Regulations, or if a pet dog, cat or ferret is discovered that the carrier reasonably suspects is intended to be transported to England without being presented to the carrier for checking.

4. The carrier shall set out in writing contingency plans for dealing with emergencies, including plans for vessels being diverted to another place of landing.

5. Adequate facilities for checking pet dogs, cats and ferrets under these Regulations shall be provided. They shall be adequately equipped, manned and maintained.

6. The carrier shall make arrangements for veterinary assistance to be provided where necessary.

. . .

Commentary
See Chapter 16 in Part I for commentary on the Regulations.

SI 2006/779

DOGS, ENGLAND

CONTROL OF DOGS

The Controls on Dogs (Non-application to Designated Land) Order 2006

Made .... *10th March 2006*
Laid before Parliament .... *16th March 2006*
Coming into force .... *6th April 2006*

The Secretary of State is, in relation to England, the appropriate person as defined in section 66(a) of the Clean Neighbourhoods and Environment Act 2005, for the purpose of exercising the powers conferred by section 57(3) of that Act, and makes the following Order in exercise of those powers:

1. Title, commencement and application
This Order—
   (a) may be cited as the Controls on Dogs (Non-application to Designated Land) Order 2006;
   (b) comes into force on 6th April 2006;
   (c) applies in England only.

2. Interpretation
In this Order—
"the Act" means the Clean Neighbourhoods and Environment Act 2005;
"land" means any land which is open to the air and to which the public are entitled or permitted to have access (with or without payment), and any land which is covered is to be treated as "open to the air" if it is open on at least one side;
"road" means any length of highway or of any other road to which the public have access, and includes bridges over which a road passes.

3. Land to which Chapter 1 of Part 6 of the Act does not apply

Any land that falls within a description in the first column of the table in the Schedule is designated as land to which Chapter 1 (controls on dogs) of Part 6 of the Act does not apply, for the purposes specified in relation to the particular description in the second column of that table.

Ben Bradshaw
Parliamentary Under Secretary of State
Department for Environment, Food and Rural Affairs

10th March 2006

SCHEDULE
Article 3

LAND TO WHICH CHAPTER 1 OF PART 6 OF THE ACT DOES NOT APPLY

Description of Land	*Purposes for which Chapter 1 of Part 6 of the Act does not apply*
Land that is placed at the disposal of the Forestry Commissioners under section 39(1) of the Forestry Act 1967	For the purpose of making a dog control order under section 55(1) of the Act
Land over which a road passes	For the purpose of making a dog control order under section 55(1) of the Act which provides for an offence relating to the matter described in section 55(3)(c) (the exclusion of dogs from land)

Commentary

This Order designates descriptions of land to which Chapter 1 (Controls on Dogs) of Part 6 (dogs) of the Clean Neighbourhoods and Environment Act 2005 ("the Act") does not apply (art.3), for the purposes specified in relation to each description.

Two descriptions of land are designated in this Order. They are—

Controls on Dogs Order 2006

(a) any land that is placed at the disposal of the Forestry Commissioners under s.39(1) of the Forestry Act 1967, in respect of the making of any dog control order under s.55(1) of the Act; and

(b) any land over which a road passes, in respect of the making of a dog control order under s.55(1) of the Act which provides for an offence relating to the matter described in s.55(3)(c) (the exclusion of dogs from land) (art.3 and the Schedule).

This Order was revoked by the Controls on Dogs (Non-application to Designated Land) Order 2009 (SI 2009/2829) in relation to England only.

SI 2006/798

DOGS, ENGLAND

CONTROL OF DOGS

The Dog Control Orders (Procedures) Regulations 2006

Made ....*10th March 2006*
Laid before Parliament ....*16th March 2006*
Coming into force ....*6th April 2006*

The Secretary of State is, in relation to England, the appropriate person as defined in section 66(a) of the Clean Neighbourhoods and Environment Act 2005, for the purpose of exercising the powers conferred by section 56(4) and (5) of that Act, and makes the following Regulations in exercise of those powers:

1. Title, commencement and application

These Regulations—
  (a) may be cited as the Dog Control Orders (Procedures) Regulations 2006;
  (b) come into force on 6th April 2006;
  (c) apply in England only.

2. Interpretation

In these Regulations—

"access authority" and "access land" have the meaning they bear in Part I of the Countryside and Rights of Way Act 2000;

"the Act" means the Clean Neighbourhoods and Environment Act 2005;

"Authority" means either a primary authority or a secondary authority as defined in section 58 (primary and secondary authorities) of the Act; and

"local access forum" means a local access forum established under section 94 of the Countryside and Rights of Way Act 2000.

3. Procedures before and after making, or amending, a dog control order

(1) Before making a dog control order under section 55 of the Act, an Authority shall—
  (a) consult upon its proposal to make the order by publishing a notice of that proposal in a local newspaper circulating in the area in which the land in respect of which the order would apply is situated;
  (b) consult every other Authority having power under section 55 of the Act to make a dog control order in respect of all or part of the land in respect of which the proposed order would apply; and
  (c) where all or part of the land in respect of which the proposed order would apply is access land, consult—
    (i) the access authority for that access land, and
    (ii) the local access forum for that access land,

  and, in respect of any of that access land that is not situated in a National Park, the Countryside Agency.
(2) The notice referred to in paragraph (1)(a) shall—
(a) identify the land in respect of which the order is to apply, and, if any of the land is access land, state that this is the case;
(b) summarise the order;
(c) where the order refers to a map, state where the map may be inspected at an address within the Authority's area, and that any inspection shall be free of charge at all reasonable hours during the period mentioned in sub-paragraph (d);
(d) state the period within which representations may be made in writing or by e-mail, such period being not less than 28 days after the publication of the notice; and
(e) state the address and e-mail address to which representations may be sent.
(3) After making a dog control order, an Authority shall, not less than seven days before the day on which the order is to come into force—
  (a) where practicable, place signs summarising the order in conspicuous positions on or near the land in respect of which it applies;
  (b) publish, in a local newspaper circulating in the area in which the land in respect of which the order applies is situated, a

notice that the order has been made and stating the place at which it may be inspected and copies of it obtained;
(c) make the information referred to in sub-paragraph (b) available on its website (if any);
(d) send the information referred to in sub-paragraph (b) to every other Authority having power under section 55 of the Act to make a dog control order in respect of all or part of the land in respect of which the order applies;
(e) where the order applies in respect of any access land, send the information referred to in sub-paragraph (b) to—

   (i) the access authority, and
   (ii) the local access forum,

   for that access land, and to the Countryside Agency.

(4) This regulation shall apply to the amendment of a dog control order as if references to its making were to its being amended.

4. Revocation of a dog control order

(1) Before revoking a dog control order it has made, an Authority shall—
(a) consult upon its proposal to revoke the order by publishing a notice of that proposal in a local newspaper circulating in the area in which the land in respect of which the order applies is situated;
(b) consult every other Authority having power under section 55 of the Act to make a dog control order in respect of all or part of the land in respect of which the order applies; and
(c) where all or part of the land in respect of which the order applies is access land, consult—

   (i) the access authority for that access land, and
   (ii) the local access forum for that access land,

   and, in respect of any of that access land that is not situated in a National Park, the Countryside Agency.

(2) The notice referred to in paragraph (1) shall—
(a) identify the land in respect of which the order applies;
(b) summarise the order;
(c) where the order refers to a map, state where the map may be inspected at an address within the Authority's area, and that any inspection shall be free of charge at all reasonable hours during the period mentioned in sub-paragraph (d);

(d) state that representations may be made in writing or by e-mail within the period of 28 days after the publication of the notice; and

(e) state the address and e-mail address to which representations may be sent.

(3) If an Authority decides to revoke a dog control order it shall—

(a) publish a notice of that decision in a local newspaper circulating in the area in which the land in respect of which the order to be revoked is situated, and specifying the date (which shall not be earlier than the date on which the notice is published) on which the revocation is to have effect;

(b) make the information referred to in sub-paragraph (a) available on its website (if any);

(c) send the information referred to in sub-paragraph (a) to every other Authority having power under section 55 of the Act to make a dog control order in respect of all or part of the land in respect of which the order to be revoked applies;

(d) where the order to be revoked applies in respect of any access land, send the information referred to in sub-paragraph (a) to—

(i) the access authority, and

(ii) the local access forum,

for that access land, and the Countryside Agency.

Ben Bradshaw
Parliamentary Under Secretary of State
Department for Environment, Food and Rural Affairs

10th March 2006

Commentary

The Regulations prescribe the procedures to be observed by a primary or secondary authority (as described in s.58 of the Clean Neighbourhoods and Environment Act 2005) in making a dog control order (an "order") under s.55 of that Act, or when amending or revoking such an order. (The offences and penalties capable of being included in, and model forms to be followed when making, a dog control order are prescribed in the Dog Control Orders (Prescribed Offences and Penalties, etc.) Regulations 2006 (SI 2006/1059) – see p.398.)

The Regulations prescribe that before making an order an authority shall consult on its proposal by publishing a notice in a newspaper circulating in the area in which the land to which the order would apply is situated (reg.3(1)(a)) and shall also consult every other Authority that has the power to make an order in respect of all or part of the same land (reg.3(1)(b)). The required contents of the newspaper notice are prescribed in reg.3(2).

Where any of the land to which a proposed order would apply is "access land" as defined in the Countryside and Rights of Way Act 2000, additional consultees are prescribed in respect of that access land (reg.3(1)(c)).

The Regulations require an authority to publicise the making and effect of an order before it comes into force (reg.3(3)). They apply the same consultation and information requirements to the making of any amendment to an order (reg.3(4)) and also prescribe similar consultation and information requirements for the revocation of an order (reg.4).

SI 2006/1059

DOGS, ENGLAND

CONTROL OF DOGS

The Dog Control Orders (Prescribed Offences and Penalties, etc.) Regulations 2006

Made .... 5th April 2006
Coming into force in accordance with regulation 1(b)

The Secretary of State, being the appropriate person in relation to England as defined in section 66(a) of the Clean Neighbourhoods and Environment Act 2005, makes the following Regulations in exercise of the powers conferred by sections 55(4) and (5), 56(1) and (3) and 67(1) of that Act.

In accordance with section 67(3) of that Act, a draft of this instrument has been laid before Parliament and approved by a resolution of each House of Parliament.

1. Title, commencement and application

These Regulations—
(a) may be cited as the Dog Control Orders (Prescribed Offences and Penalties, etc.) Regulations 2006;
(b) come into force on the day after the day on which they are made;
(c) apply in England only.

2. Interpretation

In these Regulations—
"the Act" means the Clean Neighbourhoods and Environment Act 2005;
an "Authority" means either a primary authority or a secondary authority within the meaning of section 58 (primary and secondary authorities) of the Act.

3. Prescribed offences and penalties

(1) For the purposes of section 55(4) of the Act, the offences capable of being provided for in a dog control order are those set out in paragraph 1 of each of Schedules 1 to 5.

(2) The penalty to be provided in relation to any offence in a dog control order is, on summary conviction, a fine not exceeding level 3 on the standard scale.

(3) A dog control order may specify the times at which, or the periods during which, an offence is to apply.

4. Specified wording to be used in, and the form of, a dog control order

An Authority which makes a dog control order shall—
  (a) in providing for any offence, use the wording specified in the Schedule applying to that offence (under the heading "offence"); and
  (b) in all other respects make the order in the form set out in the said Schedule, or in a form substantially to the like effect.

5. Amendment of a dog control order

An Authority which amends a dog control order it has made shall do so in accordance with Schedule 6.

6. Coming into force of a dog control order

The date of coming into force of a dog control order (including an order amending a dog control order) shall be at least 14 days after the date on which the order is made.

Ben Bradshaw
Parliamentary Under Secretary of State
Department for Environment, Food and Rural Affairs

5th April 2006

SCHEDULE 1

Regulations 3 and 4

OFFENCE OF FAILING TO REMOVE DOG FAECES AND FORM OF ORDER

1.—(1) Subject to sub-paragraphs (2) and (3), it is an offence when being in charge of a dog on land to which a dog control order (described

Dog Control Orders (Prescribed Offences etc.) Regs 2006

as a "Fouling of Land by Dogs Order" in the form set out below) applies, not to remove faeces deposited by the dog at any time, or at any time during certain periods prescribed in the order.

(2) No offence is committed where a person has a reasonable excuse for failing to remove the faeces, or the owner, occupier or other person or authority having control of the land has consented (generally or specifically) to his failing to do so.

(3) The offence does not apply to a person who is registered as a blind person in a register compiled under section 29 of the National Assistance Act 1948, or to a person who has a disability which affects his mobility, manual dexterity, physical co-ordination or ability to lift, carry or otherwise move everyday objects, in respect of a dog trained by Dogs for the Disabled (registered charity number 700454), Support Dogs (registered charity number 1088281) or Canine Partners for Independence (registered charity number 803680) and upon which he relies for assistance.

2. In any Fouling of Land by Dogs Order, the offence of failing to remove dog faeces is to be set out in full as stated in article 3 in the form of order given below.

3. In all other respects, a Fouling of Land by Dogs Order providing for that offence is to be in the form given below, or in a form substantially to the like effect.

Form of Order
The Clean Neighbourhoods and Environment Act 2005
The Dog Control Orders (Prescribed Offences and Penalties, etc.) Regulations 2006 (SI 2006/1059)

The Fouling of Land by Dogs ([X][1]) Order [X][2]

The [X][3] hereby makes the following Order:

1. This Order comes into force on [X].[4]
2. This Order applies to the land specified in [the Schedule] [Schedule 1].[5]

---

1 Identify, specifically or generally, the land in respect of which the Order applies.
2 Insert year in which Order is made.
3 Insert name of primary or secondary authority making the Order.
4 Insert date Order comes into force, being at least 14 days after making of the Order.
5 Specify whichever is the case.

Offence

3.—(1) If a dog defecates at any time [during the periods specified in Schedule 2][6] on land to which this Order applies and a person who is in charge of the dog at that time fails to remove the faeces from the land forthwith, that person shall be guilty of an offence unless—

(a) he has a reasonable excuse for failing to do so; or

(b) the owner, occupier or other person or authority having control of the land has consented (generally or specifically) to his failing to do so.

(2) Nothing in this article applies to a person who—

(a) is registered as a blind person in a register compiled under section 29 of the National Assistance Act 1948; or

(b) has a disability which affects his mobility, manual dexterity, physical co-ordination or ability to lift, carry or otherwise move everyday objects, in respect of a dog trained by a prescribed charity and upon which he relies for assistance.

(3) For the purposes of this article—

(a) a person who habitually has a dog in his possession shall be taken to be in charge of the dog at any time unless at that time some other person is in charge of the dog;

(b) placing the faeces in a receptacle on the land which is provided for the purpose, or for the disposal of waste, shall be a sufficient removal from the land;

(c) being unaware of the defecation (whether by reason of not being in the vicinity or otherwise), or not having a device for or other suitable means of removing the faeces shall not be a reasonable excuse for failing to remove the faeces;

(d) each of the following is a "prescribed charity"—

   (i) Dogs for the Disabled (registered charity number 700454);
   (ii) Support Dogs (registered charity number 1088281);
   (iii) Canine Partners for Independence (registered charity number 803680).

---

6 Specify periods if the Order is to apply only during certain periods of the year.

Dog Control Orders (Prescribed Offences etc.) Regs 2006

Penalty
4. A person who is guilty of an offence under article 3 shall be liable on summary conviction to a fine not exceeding level 3 on the standard scale.
[Date]
[Attestation clause]

[SCHEDULE][SCHEDULE 1][7]
[Specification/description of land, or lands, to which the Order applies][8]

[SCHEDULE 2
[Specification of times or periods during which the offence is to apply]][9]

SCHEDULE 2
Regulations 3 and 4

OFFENCE OF NOT KEEPING A DOG ON A LEAD AND FORM OF ORDER

1.—(1) Subject to sub-paragraph (2), it is an offence when being in charge of a dog on land to which a dog control order (described as a "Dogs on Leads Order" in the form set out below) applies, not to keep the dog on a lead or on a lead of a maximum length prescribed in the order, during such times or periods as may be prescribed.
(2) No offence is committed where a person has a reasonable excuse for failing to keep the dog on a lead, or the owner, occupier or other person or authority having control of the land has consented (generally or specifically) to his failing to do so.
2. In any Dogs on Leads Order, the offence of not keeping a dog on a lead is to be set out in full as stated in article 3 in the form of the order given below.
3. In all other respects, a Dogs on Leads Order providing for that offence is to be in the form given below, or in a form substantially to the like effect.

---

7 Specify whichever is the case.
8 Identify, either specifically or by description, the land to which the Order applies.
9 If applicable, include Sch.2 specifying times or periods.

Form of Order
The Clean Neighbourhoods and Environment Act 2005
The Dog Control Orders (Prescribed Offences and Penalties, etc.)
Regulations 2006 (SI 2006/1059)

The Dogs on Leads ([X][10]) Order [X][11]

The [X][12] hereby makes the following Order:

1. This Order comes into force on [X].[13]
2. This Order applies to the land specified in [the Schedule] [Schedule 1].[14]

Offence

3.—(1) A person in charge of a dog shall be guilty of an offence if, [at any time][during the [times][periods] specified in Schedule 2],[15] on any land to which this Order applies he does not keep the dog on a lead [of not more than [X feet/inches] in length],[16] unless—
  (a) he has a reasonable excuse for failing to do so; or
  (b) the owner, occupier or other person or authority having control of the land has consented (generally or specifically) to his failing to do so.

(2) For the purposes of this article a person who habitually has a dog in his possession shall be taken to be in charge of the dog at any time unless at that time some other person is in charge of the dog.

Penalty

4. A person who is guilty of an offence under article 3 shall be liable on summary conviction to a fine not exceeding level 3 on the standard scale.

[Date]
[Attestation clause]

---

10 Identify, specifically or generally, the land in respect of which the Order applies.
11 Insert year in which Order is made.
12 Insert name of primary or secondary authority making the Order.
13 Insert date Order comes into force, being at least 14 days after making of the Order.
14 Specify whichever is the case.
15 Specify whichever of the options in square brackets is to apply.
16 If this is to be specified, insert maximum length of lead.

Dog Control Orders (Prescribed Offences etc.) Regs 2006

[SCHEDULE][SCHEDULE 1][17]
[Specification/description of land, or lands, to which the Order applies][18]

[SCHEDULE 2]
[Specification of times or periods during which the offence is to apply]][19]

SCHEDULE 3

Regulations 3 and 4

OFFENCE OF NOT PUTTING AND KEEPING A DOG ON A LEAD, UNDER DIRECTION AND FORM OF ORDER

1.—(1) Subject to sub-paragraph (2), it is an offence when being in charge of a dog on land to which a dog control order (described as a "Dogs on Leads by Direction Order" in the form set out below) applies, not to put, and thereafter keep, the dog on a lead or on a lead of a maximum length prescribed in the order, during such times or periods as may be prescribed, when directed to do so by an authorised officer of an Authority.

(2) No offence is committed where a person has a reasonable excuse for failing to comply with a direction to put and keep the dog on a lead, or the owner, occupier or other person or authority having control of the land has consented (generally or specifically) to his failing to do so.

2. In any Dogs on Leads by Direction Order, the offence of not putting and keeping a dog on a lead, by direction, is to be set out in full as stated in article 4 in the form of the order given below.

3. In all other respects, a Dogs on Leads by Direction Order providing for that offence is to be in the form given below, or in a form substantially to the like effect.

Form of Order

The Clean Neighbourhoods and Environment Act 2005
The Dog Control Orders (Prescribed Offences and Penalties, etc.)
Regulations 2006 (SI 2006/1059)

---

17 Specify whichever is the case.
18 Identify, either specifically or by description, the land to which the Order applies.
19 If applicable, include Sch.2 specifying times or periods.

The Dogs on Leads by Direction ([X][20]) Order [X][21]

The [X][22] (in this Order called "the Authority") hereby makes the following Order:

1. This Order comes into force on [X].[23]
2. This Order applies to the land specified in [the Schedule] [Schedule 1].[24]
3. In this Order "an authorised officer of the Authority" means an employee of the Authority who is authorised in writing by the Authority for the purpose of giving directions under this Order.

Offence

4.—(1) A person in charge of a dog shall be guilty of an offence if, [at any time][during the [times][periods] specified in Schedule 2],[25] on any land to which this Order applies, he does not comply with a direction given him by an authorised officer of the Authority to put and keep the dog on a lead [of not more than [X feet/inches] in length],[26] unless—

(a) he has a reasonable excuse for failing to do so; or
(b) the owner, occupier or other person or authority having control of the land has consented (generally or specifically) to his failing to do so.

(2) For the purposes of this article—

(a) a person who habitually has a dog in his possession shall be taken to be in charge of the dog at any time unless at that time some other person is in charge of the dog;
(b) an authorised officer of the Authority may only give a direction under this Order to put and keep a dog on a lead if such restraint is reasonably necessary to prevent a nuisance or behaviour by the dog likely to cause annoyance or disturbance to any other person [on any land to which this Order applies] or the worrying or disturbance of any animal or bird.

---

20 Identify, specifically or generally, the land in respect of which the Order applies.
21 Insert year in which Order is made.
22 Insert name of primary or secondary authority making the Order.
23 Insert date Order comes into force, being at least 14 days after making of the Order.
24 Specify whichever is the case.
25 Specify whichever of the options in square brackets is to apply.
26 If this is to be specified, insert maximum length of lead.

Dog Control Orders (Prescribed Offences etc.) Regs 2006

Penalty
5. A person who is guilty of an offence under article 4 shall be liable on summary conviction to a fine not exceeding level 3 on the standard scale.
[Date]
[Attestation clause]

[SCHEDULE][SCHEDULE 1][27]
[Specification/description of land, or lands, to which the Order applies][28]

[SCHEDULE 2]
[Specification of times or periods during which the offence is to apply]][29]

SCHEDULE 4
Regulations 3 and 4

OFFENCE OF PERMITTING A DOG TO ENTER LAND FROM WHICH IT IS EXCLUDED AND FORM OF ORDER
1.—(1) Subject to sub-paragraphs (2) and (3), it is an offence when being in charge of a dog on land to which a dog control order (described as a "Dogs Exclusion Order" in the form set out below) applies, during such times or periods as may be specified in the order, to take the dog onto, or to permit it to enter or to remain on, such land.

(2) No offence is committed where a person has a reasonable excuse for taking the dog onto, or permitting it to enter or remain on, the land, or the owner, occupier or other person or authority having control of the land has consented (generally or specifically) to his doing so.

(3) The offence does not apply to a person who is registered as a blind person in a register compiled under section 29 of the National Assistance Act 1948, to a deaf person in respect of a dog trained by Hearing Dogs for Deaf People (registered charity number 293358), or to a person who has a disability which affects his mobility, manual dexterity, physical co-ordination or ability to lift, carry or otherwise move everyday objects, in respect of a dog trained by Dogs for the Disabled

---
27 Specify whichever is the case.
28 Identify, either specifically or by description, the land to which the Order applies.
29 If applicable, include Sch.2 specifying times or periods.

(registered charity number 700454), Support Dogs (registered charity number 1088281) or Canine Partners for Independence (registered charity number 803680) and upon which he relies for assistance.

2. In any Dogs Exclusion Order, the offence of taking a dog onto, or permitting it to enter or to remain on, land from which it is excluded is to be set out in full as stated in article 3 in the form of the order given below.

3. In all other respects, a Dogs Exclusion Order providing for that offence is to be in the form given below, or in a form substantially to the like effect.

Form of Order
The Clean Neighbourhoods and Environment Act 2005
The Dog Control Orders (Prescribed Offences and Penalties, etc.) Regulations 2006 (SI 2006/1059)

The Dogs Exclusion [X][30] Order [X][31]

The [X][32] hereby makes the following Order:

1. This Order comes into force on [X].[33]
2. This Order applies to the land specified in [the Schedule] [Schedule 1].[34]

Offence

3.—(1) A person in charge of a dog shall be guilty of an offence if, [at any time][during the [times][periods] specified in Schedule 2],[35] he takes the dog onto, or permits the dog to enter or to remain on, any land to which this Order applies unless—

(a) he has a reasonable excuse for doing so; or
(b) the owner, occupier or other person or authority having control of the land has consented (generally or specifically) to his doing so.

(2) Nothing in this article applies to a person who—

(a) is registered as a blind person in a register compiled under section 29 of the National Assistance Act 1948; or

---

30 Identify, specifically or generally, the land in respect of which the Order applies.
31 Insert year in which Order is made.
32 Insert name of primary or secondary authority making the Order.
33 Insert date Order comes into force, being at least 14 days after making of the Order.
34 Specify whichever is the case.
35 Specify whichever of the options in square brackets is to apply.

Dog Control Orders (Prescribed Offences etc.) Regs 2006

(b) is deaf, in respect of a dog trained by Hearing Dogs for Deaf People (registered charity number 293358) and upon which he relies for assistance; or
(c) has a disability which affects his mobility, manual dexterity, physical co-ordination or ability to lift, carry or otherwise move everyday objects, in respect of a dog trained by a prescribed charity and upon which he relies for assistance.
(3) For the purposes of this article—
(a) a person who habitually has a dog in his possession shall be taken to be in charge of the dog at any time unless at that time some other person is in charge of the dog; and
(b) each of the following is a "prescribed charity"—
   (i) Dogs for the Disabled (registered charity number 700454);
   (ii) Support Dogs (registered charity number 1088281);
   (iii) Canine Partners for Independence (registered charity number 803680).

Penalty

4. A person who is guilty of an offence under article 3 shall be liable on summary conviction to a fine not exceeding level 3 on the standard scale.
[Date]
[Attestation clause]

[SCHEDULE][SCHEDULE 1][36]
[Specification/description of land, or lands, to which the Order applies][37]

[SCHEDULE 2]
[Specification of times or periods during which the offence is to apply]][38]

SCHEDULE 5
Regulations 3 and 4

---

[36] Specify whichever is the case.
[37] Identify, either specifically or by description, the land to which the Order applies.
[38] If applicable, include Sch.2 specifying times or periods.

OFFENCE OF TAKING MORE THAN A SPECIFIED NUMBER OF DOGS ONTO LAND AND FORM OF ORDER

1.—(1) Subject to sub-paragraph (2), it is an offence when being in charge of more than one dog on land to which a dog control order (described as a "Dogs (Specified Maximum) Order" in the form set out below) applies, during such times or periods as may be specified in the order, to take more than the maximum number of dogs specified in the order onto that land.

(2) No offence is committed where a person has a reasonable excuse for taking more than the specified maximum number of dogs onto the land, or the owner, occupier or other person or authority having control of the land has consented (generally or specifically) to his doing so.

2. In any Dogs (Specified Maximum) Order, the offence of taking more than a specified number of dogs onto land is to be set out in full as stated in article 4 in the form of order given below.

3. In all other respects, a Dogs (Specified Maximum) Order providing for that offence is to be in the form given below, or in a form substantially to the like effect.

Form of Order
The Clean Neighbourhoods and Environment Act 2005
The Dog Control Orders (Prescribed Offences and Penalties, etc.) Regulations 2006 (SI 2006/1059)

The Dogs (Specified Maximum) [X][39] Order [X][40]

The [X][41] hereby makes the following Order:

1. This Order comes into force on [X].[42]

2. This Order applies to the land specified in [the Schedule] [Schedule 1].[43]

3. On land to which this Order applies, the maximum number of dogs which a person may take onto that land is [X].[44]

---

[39] Identify, specifically or generally, the land in respect of which the Order applies.
[40] Insert year in which Order is made.
[41] Insert name of primary or secondary authority making the Order.
[42] Insert date Order comes into force, being at least 14 days after making of the Order.
[42] Insert date Order comes into force, being at least 14 days after making of the Order.
[43] Specify whichever is the case.
[44] Insert desired maximum number.

Offence

4.—(1) A person in charge of more than one dog shall be guilty of an offence if, [at any time][during the [times][periods] specified in Schedule 2],[45] he takes onto any land in respect of which this Order applies more than the maximum number of dogs specified in article 3 of this Order, unless—
  (a) he has a reasonable excuse for doing so; or
  (b) the owner, occupier or other person or authority having control of the land has consented (generally or specifically) to his doing so.

(2) For the purposes of this article a person who habitually has a dog in his possession shall be taken to be in charge of the dog at any time unless at that time some other person is in charge of the dog.

Penalty

5. A person who is guilty of an offence under article 4 shall be liable on summary conviction to a fine not exceeding level 3 on the standard scale.
[Date]
[Attestation clause]

[SCHEDULE][SCHEDULE 1][46]

[Specification/description of land, or lands, to which the Order applies][47]

[SCHEDULE 2]

[Specification of times or periods during which the offence is to apply]][48]

SCHEDULE 6
Regulation 5

FORM OF ORDER AMENDING A DOG CONTROL ORDER

1. An order amending a dog control order shall be in the form given below, or in a form substantially to the like effect.

2. Where the amendment is to the description of an offence, the amendment shall be made by substituting the entire article which sets

---

[45] Specify whichever of the options in square brackets is to apply.
[46] Specify whichever is the case.
[47] Identify, either specifically or by description, the land to which the Order applies.
[48] If applicable, include Sch.2 specifying times or periods.

out the offence, and the substituted article shall set out the offence as it is required to be stated were it contained in a newly made dog control order.

Form of Order
The Clean Neighbourhoods and Environment Act 2005
The Dog Control Orders (Prescribed Offences and Penalties, etc.) Regulations 2006 (SI 2006/1059)

The [XXXX][49] (Amendment) Order [X][50]

The [X][51] hereby makes the following Order:
1. This Order comes into force on [X].[52]
2. The [XXXX][53] is amended as follows:
[*insert amendments to be made*].[54]

Commentary
These Regulations, which apply in England, came into force on April 6, 2006.

Further to Chapter 1 (control of dogs) of Part 6 (in particular, ss.55–58) of the Clean Neighbourhoods and Environment Act 2005, under which certain authorities are empowered to make dog control orders, these Regulations prescribe for the purposes of s.55 of the Act the offences that may be provided for in any such order (reg.3(1) and Schs 1–5).

The offences are:
(a) failing to remove faeces deposited by a dog on land in respect of which a Fouling of Land by Dogs Order applies (Sch.1, para.1);
(b) failing to keep a dog on a lead on land in respect of which a Dogs on Leads Order applies (Sch.2, para.1);
(c) failing to put, and to keep, a dog on a lead, when directed to do so by an authorised officer, on land in respect of

---

49 [Insert full title (including year) of the Order to be amended.]
50 [Insert year in which amending Order is made.]
51 [Insert name of primary or secondary authority making the Order.]
52 [Insert date Order comes into force, being at least 14 days after making of the Order.]
53 [Insert full title (including year) of the Order to be amended.]
54 [For example: "[Paragraph X of] Article [X] is replaced by the following [paragraph/Article]: . . ."; "after the words [X] insert the following words: "[X]" "; "for the words "[X]", substitute the words "[X]" ", etc.]

Dog Control Orders (Prescribed Offences etc.) Regs 2006

which a Dogs on Leads by Direction Order applies (Sch.3, para.1);
(d) permitting a dog to enter land in respect of which a Dogs Exclusion Order applies (Sch.4, para.1); and
(e) taking more than the maximum number of dogs onto land in respect of which a Dogs (Specified Maximum) Order applies (Sch.5, para.1),

in each case without reasonable excuse or without the consent of the owner, occupier or other person or authority who has control of the land. The offences of failing to remove dog faeces and of permitting a dog to enter land from which dogs are excluded do not apply to a person who is registered as a blind person or to a person who has a disability in respect of which he relies on the assistance of a dog trained by a specified charity; the offence of permitting a dog to enter land from which dogs are excluded also does not apply to a person who is deaf in respect of a dog trained by a specified charity.

The Regulations also prescribe, in fulfilment of the requirement in s.56(1) of the Act, the maximum penalty which may be provided for in a dog control order (reg.3(2)); this shall be, on summary conviction, a fine not exceeding level 3 on the standard scale (currently £1,000).

In respect of the content and form of a dog control order, the Regulations specify the wording that must be used in providing for an offence in such an order (reg.4(a) and para.2 of Schs 1–5), and in all other respects require that a dog control order (including an order amending a dog control order) shall be in the form set out in the appropriate Schedule, or in a form substantially to the like effect as that form (reg.4(b) and para.3 of Schs 1–5; in respect of an amending order, reg.5 and Sch.6, para.1).

SI 2009/2829

DOGS, ENGLAND

CONTROL OF DOGS

The Controls on Dogs (Non-application to Designated Land) Order 2009

Made .... *23rd October 2009*
Laid before Parliament .... *28th October 2009*
Coming into force .... *1st December 2009*

The Secretary of State is, in relation to England, the appropriate person as defined in section 66(a) of the Clean Neighbourhoods and Environment Act 2005, for the purpose of exercising the powers conferred by section 57(3) of that Act, and makes the following Order in exercise of those powers.

Title, commencement and application

1. This Order—
   (a) may be cited as the Controls on Dogs (Non-application to Designated Land) Order 2009;
   (b) comes into force on 1st December 2009; and
   (c) applies in England only.

Interpretation

2. In this Order—
   "the Act" means the Clean Neighbourhoods and Environment Act 2005;
   "land" means any land which is open to the air and to which the public are entitled or permitted to have access (with or without payment), and any land which is covered is to be treated as "open to the air" if it is open on at least one side;
   "road" means any length of highway or of any other road to which the public have access (with or without payment), and includes bridges over which a road passes.

Land to which Chapter 1 of Part 6 of the Act does not apply

3. Any land that falls within a description in the first column of the table in the Schedule is designated as land to which Chapter 1 (controls on dogs) of Part 6 of the Act does not apply, for the purposes specified in relation to the particular description in the second column of that table.

Revocation

4. The Controls on Dogs (Non-application to Designated Land) Order 2006 is revoked.

Jim Fitzpatrick
Minister of State
Department for Environment, Food and Rural Affairs

23rd October 2009

Article 3

THE SCHEDULE

Land to which Chapter 1 of Part 6 of the Act does not apply

First column *Description of Land*	*Second column* *Purposes for which Chapter 1 of Part 6 of the Act does not apply*
Land that is placed at the disposal of the Forestry Commissioners under section 39(1) of the Forestry Act 1967	For the purpose of making a dog control order under section 55(1) of the Act
Land which is or forms part of a road	For the purpose of making a dog control order under section 55(1) of the Act which provides for an offence relating to the matter described in section 55(3)(c) (the exclusion of dogs from land)

Part V

Government Department Circulars

Home Office Circular 67/1991: Dangerous Dogs Act 1991 417

Home Office Circular 80/1992: Further Advice Concerning the
Dangerous Dogs Act 1991 444

Home Office Circular 9/1994: Further Advice Concerning the
Dangerous Dogs Act 1991 448

Home Office Circular 53/1999: Licensing Dog Breeding
Establishments 453

Defra Guidance Circular 2006: Dog Control Orders 463

Defra Guidance Circular 2007: Guidance on Stray Dogs 474

HOME OFFICE CIRCULAR No. 67/1991

4 September 1991

Dangerous Dogs Act 1991

The Dangerous Dogs Act 1991 came into force on 12 August. Associated with it are three statutory instruments, the Dangerous Dogs (Commencement and Appointed Day) Order 1991 (SI 1991/1742), the Dangerous Dogs (Designated Types) Order 1991 (SI 1991/1743), and the Dangerous Dogs Compensation and Exemption Schemes Order 1991 (SI 1991/1744).

2. Attached to this circular at Annex A are notes on sections of the Act. Annex B is a brief summary of the provisions of the Act as it relates to fighting dogs: this has already been sent out with the notification form which the owners of specially controlled dogs are required to collect from local police stations. The Act applies to England, Scotland and Wales. Section 8, which relates to Northern Ireland, is already in force. This circular is issued with the agreement of ACPO. A similar circular will be issued for police forces in Scotland.

3. The Act deals with three distinct aspects of dangerous dogs: section 1 deals with fighting dogs; section 2 contains reserve powers to impose muzzling and leashing conditions on other dogs which are considered to be specially dangerous, but no order has been made under this section; and section 3 deals with dogs which are dangerously out of control either in a public place or in any other place where they are not permitted to be.

SECTION 1: DOGS OF A TYPE BRED FOR FIGHTING
Specially controlled dogs

4. From 12 August 1991, section 1 of the Act applies special controls to
   (i) the pit bull terrier;
   (ii) the Japanese tosa;
and, as the result of SI 1991/1743,
   (iii) the Dogo Argentino; and
   (iv) the Fila Braziliero.

5. There are powers under section 1(1)(c) for other types of fighting dog to be added to this list. In practice, this is more likely to occur in order to support an import ban on new types of fighting dog which are

currently abroad, rather than on additional types of dog already in this country. Cross-breeds of the pit bull terrier with other dogs are not specially controlled by section 1 of the Act.

Offences under section 1

6. Section 1(2) imposes a number of prohibitions on the owners of specially controlled dogs: they cannot breed from them; sell or exchange them; or give them away. The dogs must be muzzled and on a lead in a public place; under 7(1)(a), the muzzle must be sufficient to prevent the dog biting any person; and, as the result of section 7(1)(b), the dogs must be held by a person who is not less than 16 years old. Specially controlled dogs cannot be abandoned or allowed to stray.

7. As the result of section 1(7), these offences attract a fine of level 5 or a term of imprisonment of up to six months or both, (although imprisonment does not apply to those who simply took part in publishing advertisements, or did so unknowingly). The dog must be destroyed and anyone convicted of an offence can also be disqualified from keeping a dog in future.

Prohibition on keeping a specially controlled dog after 30 November 1991

8. Section 1(3) states that after an appointed day, which has been set by SI 1991/1742 to be 30 November 1991, it will be an offence to have a specially controlled dog unless it is being held as the result of seizure or for destruction. An exception to this is given by section 1(5) which allows the Home Secretary to set up an exemption scheme, as has been done under SI 1991/1744.

Compensation scheme

9. The combined effect of the Act and the statutory instruments is that, provided a dog is destroyed by a veterinary surgeon or veterinary practitioner after 12 August and before 30 November 1991, the owner may claim £25 towards the cost of destruction and a further sum in compensation for the dog, which is £25 in the case of a pit bull terrier and £100 in the case of other types of specially controlled dogs.

Exemption scheme

10. The combined effect of the Act and the orders is to set up an exemption scheme whereby, provided certain conditions are met, the owners of specially controlled dogs can continue to keep these dogs after

Home Office Circular No. 67/1991

30 November 1991. These conditions, which are set out in part III of SI 1991/1744, are that the police have been notified; that the dog has been neutered or spayed and permanently identified (see paragraph 18); that there is in force acceptable third party insurance cover; that a fee has been paid; that a certificate of exemption has been issued; and that the requirements applying to the certificate are complied with.

Puppies

11. It is not good veterinary practice to neuter or spay puppies until they are six months old. In the case of dogs which will be less than six months old on 30 November 1991, a notification form must be completed before that date and a certificate of exemption will not be issued until they have reached the age of six months, when they must be neutered or spayed, permanently identified and insured within a month. This means that there may be a small number of young unexempted dogs until the spring of 1992. It is a relatively easy matter for a veterinary surgeon to determine whether a dog is older than about six months from its teeth, so this exception for puppies should not give rise to significant difficulties in enforcement.

Import and export of specially controlled types of dog

12. Under separate orders, the Government has banned the import of all specially controlled types of dog. Section 1(4) of the Act does, however, make provision for the export of these dogs until 30 November 1991 as an alternative to having them destroyed or fulfilling the conditions required for a certificate of exemption.

The Index of Exempted Dogs

13. Under section 1(6) an agency may be appointed to operate the exemption and compensation schemes and this agency is the Index of Exempted Dogs, Chishill Road, Heydon, Royston, Herts SG8 8PN. The fax number is 0763 838318 and the normal public inquiry telephone number is 0763 838329. A reserved number has been provided for inquiries by the police and local authority dog wardens and this is given at paragraph 23 of this circular.

Notification form

14. All owners of pit bull terriers and other specially controlled dogs are required by article 6 of SI 1990/1744 to collect a notification form from their local police station between 12 August and 12 October 1991.

Home Office Circular No. 67/1991

Newspaper advertisements have advised owners of this requirement and all local police stations should have copies of the notification form. If stocks run out, the form may be photocopied. One form, consisting of two parts should be completed for each dog.

15. Part I of the notification form is for police use. It is designed so that local stations can have information readily available about the location of any specially controlled dogs in their immediate locality. This may be of most value during the transition stage up to 30 November 1991.

16. Part I and Part II of the notification form are almost identical and have been printed so that hey can be completed using carbon paper. Owners are not obliged to complete Part I of the form at the police station, but it should be pointed out to them that Part I has to be returned there. The easiest procedure would, therefore, be for owners to complete Part I at the station and send off Part II to the Index of Exempted Dogs soon afterwards. Part II of the notification form starts the process both for compensation and the obtaining of a certificate of exemption. As soon as that part has been received by the Index of Exempted Dogs, the owner will receive information about both the compensation and exemption schemes.

Requirements of certificates of exemption

17. Certificates of exemption remain valid for the life of the dog, provided that the requirements attached to them are observed. These requirements are:
    (i) that the dog is kept in secure conditions at home so that it cannot escape;
    (ii) that the dog is kept in secure conditions when in a public place, i.e. it must be muzzled and held on a lead by someone who is at least 16;
    (iii) if asked to do so by a police or local authority officer (dog warden), the keeper of the dog must show the certificate of exemption, display the dog's tattoo and allow the implanted transponder to be read;
    (iv) that the third party insurance is kept in force; and
    (v) that the Index of Exempted Dogs is informed of any change of address at which the dog is kept for longer than 30 days.

Home Office Circular No. 67/1991

Permanent numbering of specially controlled dogs: tattoos and transponders

18. Each exempted dog will be marked by a tattoo on the inside of the thigh. It is a requirement that the tattoo letters should be at least 10 mm tall, so that they can be easily read. The tattoo will consist of seven characters: the capital letter E, followed by four or five numbers; and a further capital letter A, B, or C. The capital letter E indicates that the dog is exempt and signifies the right way to read the tattoo. The numbers are the dog's reference number on the Index of Exempted Dogs.

19. The final letter indicates which of the three approved permanently-implanted transponders has been put into the dog. The letter A indicates the AVID tag; B indicates an Identichip; and C indicates a Torvan chip. The transponders, which are all shorter than 15 mm, are implanted in the scruff of the neck and are read by passing a device round the neck of the dog. When the reading device comes within about 100–130mm (4–5 inches) of the transponder, a ten character reference, which may be a mixture of letters and numbers, will appear on the digital display of the reader. This uniquely identifies the dog.

Enforcement of section 1: use of tattoos

20. In the normal course of events, the tattoo will be the usual way of ascertaining whether a dog is exempted. As it is a requirement of the certificate of exemption that the keeper of the dog must display the dog's tattoo on request, a police officer or dog warden can ask for this to be done and needs simply note the numbers and make inquires of the Index of Exempted Dogs, as set out in paragraph 23.

Use of transponders

21. In normal circumstances, police officers will not have immediate access to a transponder reader, although they are becoming much more common and there should be no difficulty in getting a transponder read within about 24 or 48 hours. These readers are held variously by local authorities, veterinary surgeons, dog kennels and RSPCA inspectors. The real advantage of the transponder is the quality of the evidence it provides in identifying the dog since, although there are circumstances in which tattoos can become unreadable, transponders remain readable for much longer than the life of the dog. It is our expectation that, whilst tattoos will be used for routine checking of pit bull terriers, transponders (or the absence of them) will be central to

Home Office Circular No. 67/1991

any court proceedings, alongside evidence that these dogs will probably not have been castrated or spayed.

22. The purpose of tattoos and transponders is to simplify the enforcement of section 1(2). For instance, once a dog has been tattooed or had a transponder implanted, the owner or keeper of the dog cannot easily claim that it is not a pit bull terrier and therefore need not be muzzled or on a lead in a public place. Equally, an exempted pit bull terrier which has been picked up as a stray can be easily identified by its tattoo and transponder and put down under the provisions of section 5(4). The transponder evidence alone may well be sufficient to secure a conviction under section 1(2)(e) against the keeper of the dog. By the same token, dogs which are exchanged, sold or given away can readily be traced through the tattoo and transponder.

24-hours-a-day contact with Index of Exempted Dogs

23. In addition to the fax and telephone numbers given in paragraph 13, the Index of Exempted Dogs can be contacted by the police and local authorities on **0763 838989**. This telephone number is ex-directory and is not open to the general public. It provides a 24-hours-a-day, 365-days-a-year inquiry service and details of the dog, the keeper of the dog and the address at which the dog is kept and whether the insurance remains in force should be immediately available. The Index can provide information about an exempted dog on the basis of the tattoo or transponder reference, or any name or address.

24. To ensure that the caller is entitled to receive the information which will be provided, the Index of Exempted Dogs may ask for the name, address and telephone number of the caller and, possibly, his identifying number (eg PC1234). In some instances, the Index may decide to ring back the caller to verify that they are telephoning from the number given.

Notification to the police by the agency

25. The Index of Exempted Dogs will supply information to police forces about any dogs whose owners appear to have infringed the requirements of the Act. This means principally those cases where notification of ownership of a specially controlled dog has been given, but no certificate of exemption or compensation has been obtained; and where, following reminders from the Index of Exempted Dogs, no evidence has been provided that the insurance policy for the dog has been renewed. In both these cases, the police force for the area will be informed by the

Index within a relatively short time so that appropriate action can be taken. **To assist the Index in the distribution of this information it would be helpful if each force could provide one contact name, address and telephone number. The Index should be advised of this point of contact direct, through the fax and telephone numbers given in paragraph 13 or the telephone number given in paragraph 23.**

26. Routine statistical data about the specially controlled dogs in police force areas will be provided by the Index of Exempted Dogs to the Home Office and we will supply it on request.

Identification of types of specially controlled dogs

27. The pit bull terrier is the most common of the four types of controlled dog. It is currently estimated that there are about 10,000 in the UK and a detailed description of the type was sent to Chief Officers on 26 July. The posters sent to all force headquarters on 2 August give a further indication of the typical size and range of colouring of pit bull terriers. However, it is recognised that identification of pit bull terriers is not straightforward and it may be most easily confused with the Staffordshire bull terrier, which is smaller.

28. The evidence that a dog is not a specially controlled type of dog might be a certificate from a veterinary surgeon to that effect; pedigree papers from, for instance, the Kennel Club; or evidence from the breeder from whom the dog was originally obtained and who may be able to provide further information about its pedigree.

29. The difficulty in identifying put bull terriers is recognised by section 5(5) of the Act which reverses the burden of proof so that, instead of the prosecution having to show that the dog is a pit bull terrier, the accused has to show that his dog is not a pit bull terrier. This means that if someone seeks to claim, for instance, that they have a cross-breed of a pit bull terrier which is nevertheless very similar to a normal pit bull terrier, they must be advised that it is up to them to prove that the dog is not actually a pit bull terrier.

30. The identification of the Dogo Argentino, Fila Braziliero and Japanese tosa is a specialist task. It is believed that there are less than half a dozen of these dogs in the country and, now that their import has been banned, there should be no others. Police forces which believe that they may have one of these types of dog in their area should, therefore, contact the Home Office and we will help to obtain specialist advice.

Specially controlled dogs which are not covered by a Certificate of Exemption

31. Difficulties of identification are likely to arise particularly in the case of a dog which is thought to be a pit bull terrier, but which is not exempted and does not therefore have a tattoo or a transponder. It will be an offence under section 1(3) to have such a dog after 30 November 1991 and if the dog were to appear in public without a muzzle or a lead, a further offence would be committed under section 1(2)(d).

32. In such a case, the person in charge of the dog may well seek to claim that his dog is not a pit bull terrier. In dealing with such a claim, officers will be aware of the power of arrest contained in section 25 of the Police and Criminal Evidence Act 1984; that having an unexempted specially controlled dog is an offence; and that there are powers under section 5(1)(a)(i) to seize the dog. This is most likely to be necessary if the officer has reason to believe that the person in charge of the dog might dispose of it illegally. In many circumstances, it may be the best course to take the person's name and address so that further inquiries can be made.

SECTION 3: NEW CONTROLS APPLYING TO ALL DOGS
Dogs dangerously out of control

33. The new offences under section 3 of the Act of a dog being dangerously out of control in a public place (section 3(1)) or in a place where the dog is not permitted to be (section 3(3)) to a large extent supersede the more restricted provisions in the Town Police Clauses Act 1847.

34. The offence in section 3(1) is absolute and an aggravated offence is caused if the dog has injured someone. The phrasing of this section, and others, is such as to exclude circumstances when the dog causes injury, but does not actually injure directly, like when a dog runs out in front of a bicycle and the rider is hurt.

35. The offence in section 3(3) is similar to the offence in section 3(1), except that it is not absolute and the owner of the dog or the person for the time being in charge of it should, in some sense, have allowed it to enter the place where the dog was not permitted to be. This may include negligence.

36. "Dangerously out of control" is defined in section 10(3). A dog is regarded as dangerously out of control on any occasion when there are grounds for reasonable apprehension that it would injure any person,

whether or not it actually does so. The same section provides an exemption for dogs used by the police and the Crown.

37. The penalties for offences under section 3 are given in section 3(4). Where injury has not been caused there is a maximum fine of level 5 and six months' imprisonment; when an aggravated offence has been committed, the fine is unlimited and the sentence of imprisonment is increased to a maximum of two years. The dog may be destroyed and anyone convicted of an offence can also be disqualified from keeping a dog in future.

Public place

38. Section 10(2) defines a public place as meaning any street, road or other place to which the public have, or are permitted to have access. This is a wide definition of a public place which covers some areas, like privately-owned shopping precincts, that have not hitherto been covered in similar legislation. It also covers places which are temporarily open to the public, for instance, a fête or fair.

39. This section specifically includes the common parts of a building containing two or more separate dwellings. This is intended to cover those parts of, for instance, a block of flats where, although there may be a secure front entry door, so that the interior of the flat is not a place to which the public has unrestricted access, nevertheless the common parts are, in all other respects, a public place.

Owners and people in charge of dogs

40. Throughout the Act, reference is made both to the owner of a dog as well as the person for the time being in charge of it and, when an offence has been committed, either or both can be charged, depending on the circumstances. The intention is that people should not be able to escape responsibility for the dog on the basis that they did not own it, or when they were clearly the person for the time being in charge of it.

41. In order to make it more difficult for people to escape responsibility as owners of specially controlled dogs, Part I of the notification form which has to be deposited at police stations, and Part II which has to be sent to the Index of Exempted Dogs, where it will be kept, requires the applicant to name, first, the keeper of the dog; second, the address at which the dog is normally kept if different; and third, the owner of the dog if different from the keeper. In this way it is hoped that, in the event of any court proceedings, it will have already been established who was the owner and who was the keeper of the dog.

Young persons under 16

42. By virtue of section 6 of the Act, where a dog is owned by a person under 16, the head of the household, if any, is included also as the owner. This means that, for instance, parents who give a child a dog remain legally liable as its owner until the child has reached the age of 16.

43. As noted in paragraph 6 above, in the case of specially controlled dogs which have to be kept on a lead in a public place, section 7(1)(b) requires also that the lead must be held by a person who is not less than 16 years old.

Seizure of dogs

44. Section 5 of the Act deals with the seizure of dogs and entry on to premises. Section 5(1)(a)(i) allows the seizure, after 30 November 1991, of any unexempted dog in a public place. An unexempted dog is a specially controlled dog for which no certificate of exemption has been obtained or one for which the requirements of the certificate of exemption have been breached. In the latter case the dog may be seized because such a breach causes the certificate of exemption to lapse automatically. This means that, for instance, a pit bull terrier without a lead or muzzle which is in a public place can be seized as it will be in breach of its certificate of exemption and therefore no longer exempted. After 30 November 1991, specially controlled dogs can continue to be held legally by the police or any agency appointed by them under the provisions of section 1(3)(a) or (b).

45. Section 5(1)(a)(ii) gives a power of seizure before 30 November 1991, when no certificates of exemption may be in force, where a specially controlled dog is in a public place without a lead or muzzle.

46. Section 5(1)(c) enables any dog which is dangerously out of control in a public place to be seized. As stated in paragraph 36 above, the dog does not need to have injured anyone. There need only be grounds for reasonable apprehension that it will injure someone. In the case of a specially controlled dog in a public place without a lead or a muzzle in breach of section 1(2)(d), this will almost invariably be the case and provide additional grounds on which to seize the dog. Section 5(2) enables police officers to apply for a warrant to enter private property to seize a dog or anything else which provides evidence that an offence under the Act is being, or has been, committed.

47. Section 5(4) sets out how seized dogs can be destroyed. Where no prosecution is to be brought, a Justice of the Peace may order the

destruction. It is noted that the power is given to the Justice of the Peace, rather than to a court.

Changes to the Dogs Act 1871

48. Section 3(5) seeks to clarify the application of the Dogs Act 1871. Broadly, section 3 of the 1991 Act is for the control of the owners of dogs or those who are in charge of them. By contrast, the Dogs Act 1871 can be seen as being principally for the control of the dogs themselves and ceases to have effect as soon as the dog has been destroyed.

49. The strength of the Dogs Act 1871 is that, as it is not criminal law, it operates on a lower standard of proof and proceedings can be taken even when a criminal offence has not been committed. It therefore provides a remedy in a wide range of circumstances for the putting down, or imposition of controls on, dangerous dogs. A particular advantage of the 1871 Act is the fact that it applies everywhere, even in and around a private house, which is why it is especially appropriate for action on behalf of people like postmen and women who are regularly at risk from dogs in front gardens.

50. Section 3(5)(b) of the Act enables the court to make an order under the Dogs Act 1871 that a dog is in future muzzled, kept on a lead, tethered or excluded from specified places like, for instance, a school playground or particular recreation field. This is a flexible provision which can be used to deal with a number of nuisance complaints about dogs, including circumstances where dogs in one back garden cause fear or risk of injury to neighbours in another. Section 3(6) enables male dogs to be neutered, in addition to, or instead of, other control measures.

Contact points

51. Chief Officers are reminded that paragraph 25 invites each force to provide the Index of Exempted Dogs with a contact point to which the Index can report.

HUGH MARRIAGE
E Division

Home Office Circular No. 67/1991

DANGEROUS DOGS ACT 1991: NOTES ON SECTIONS

Annex A

Section 1

(1) This section applies to—
  (a) any dog of the type known as the pit bull terrier;
  (b) any dog of the type known as the Japanese Tosa; and
  (c) any dog of type designated for the purposes of this section by an order of the Secretary of State, being a type appearing to him to be bred for fighting or to have the characteristics of a type bred for that purpose.

This subsection sets out the type of dog to which restrictions will apply. "Type" rather than "breed" is used as the dogs specified in (a) and (b) are not recognised breeds in the United Kingdom. (c) enables dogs of different types or descriptions to be added by Order. The Dogo Argentino and Fila Braziliero were added by SI 1991/1743 which came into force on 12 August 1991.

In the United Kingdom, the pit bull terrier is regarded as a crossbreed of a terrier with a larger dog, commonly a mastiff. The Tosa is a dog similar in size to the Great Dane and is bred in Japan for fighting.

(2) No person shall—
  (a) breed, or breed from, a dog to which this section applies;
  (b) sell or exchange such a dog or offer, advertise or expose such a dog for sale or exchange;
  (c) make or offer to make a gift of such a dog or advertise or expose such a dog as a gift;
  (d) allow such a dog of which he is the owner or of which he is for time being in charge to be in a public place without being muzzled and kept on a lead; or
  (e) abandon such a dog of which he is the owner or, being the owner or for the time being in charge of such a dog, allow it to stray.

This subsection lists the restrictions which apply to the dog specified in or under subsection 1(1). (a) prohibits breeding from a specified dog or breeding to obtain one, for instance by crossing a bull terrier with a mastiff to obtain a pit bull terrier. (b) prohibits the sale or advertisement for sale of such a dog. (c) prohibits the giving away of such a dog.

Home Office Circular No. 67/1991

(d) requires that these dogs are muzzled and kept on a lead as defined in section 7 when in a public place, as defined in subsection 10(2). (e) prohibits the abandoning or letting loose of such a dog.

(3) After such day as the Secretary of State may by Order appoint for the purposes of this subsection no person shall have any dog to which this section applies in his possession or custody except—
 (a) in pursuance of the power of seizure conferred by the subsequent provisions of this Act; or
 (b) in accordance with an order for its destruction made under those provisions;
but the Secretary of State shall by Order make a scheme for the payment to the owners of such dogs who arrange for them to be destroyed, before that day of sums specified in or determined under the scheme in respect of those dogs and the cost of their destruction.

This subsection enables the Secretary of State to specify the day after which it becomes an offence to possess a fighting dog (so allowing a period of grace) except (a) if the dog has been seized, for instance by the police or a dog warden; or (b) while it is being held for destruction. The day for the pit bull terrier, Japanese tosa, Dogo Argentino and Fila Braziliero is set by SI 1991/1742 for 30 November 1991. The subsection also requires the Secretary of State to make a scheme for compensation and to reimburse the costs of destruction, where dogs are destroyed before the specified date.

(4) Subsection (2)(b) and (c) above shall not make unlawful anything done with a view to the dog in question being removed from the United Kingdom before the day appointed under subsection (3) above.

This subsection enables fighting dogs to be sold or given away in order to be exported before the date on which these dogs become prohibited under subsection 1(3) (i.e. 30 November 1991).

(5) The Secretary of State may by Order provide that the prohibition in subsection (3) above shall not apply in such cases and subject to compliance with such conditions as are specified in the Order and any such provision may take the form of a scheme of exemption containing such arrangements (including provision for the payment of charges or fees) as he thinks appropriate.

This subsection gives the Secretary of State power to provide for a scheme to exempt certain dogs and therefore allow them to be possessed after the date specified in subsection 1(3) subject to certain conditions being observed. Exempted dogs will, nevertheless, be subject to the restrictions set out in subsection 1(2). Provision is made for a charge to be made for exempting a dog.

(6) A scheme under subsection (3) or (5) above may provide for specified functions under the scheme to be discharged by such person or bodies as the Secretary of State thinks appropriate.

This subsection allows the Secretary of State to appoint an agency to operate the compensation and exemption schemes on his behalf. Heybush Enterprises Ltd., the trading company of Wood Green Animal Shelters, is to administer the scheme.

(7) Any person who contravenes this section is guilty of an offence and liable on summary conviction to imprisonment for a term not exceeding six months or a fine not exceeding level 5 on the standard scale or both except that a person who publishes an advertisement in contravention of subsection (2)(b) or (c)—

- (a) shall not on being convicted be liable to imprisonment if he shows that he published the advertisement to the order of someone else and did not himself devise it; and
- (b) shall not be convicted if, in addition, he shows that he did not know and had no reasonable cause to suspect that it related to a dog to which this section applies.

This subsection creates an offence of contravening the section with penalties of six months' imprisonment or a fine not exceeding level 5 (currently £2,000; £5,000 after the Criminal Justice Bill comes into force) or both. In the case of advertising by a publisher, imprisonment does not apply and the publisher of the advertisement can avoid conviction if he can show that he did not know and had no reasonable cause to suspect that the advertisement related to a fighting dog.

(8) An Order under subsection (1)(c) above adding dogs of any type to those to which this section applies may provide that subsections (3) and (4) above shall apply in relation to those dogs with the substitution for the day appointed under subsection (3) of a later day specified in the Order.

This subsection provides that if a new type of dog is added by Order, the date on which it would become an offence to possess such a dog can also be specified. Without this provision it would become an offence to possess such a dog immediately the Order under subsection (1)(c) was made.

(9) The power to make Orders under this section shall be exercisable by statutory instrument which, in the case of an Order under subsection (1) or (4) or an Order containing a scheme under subsection (3),

Home Office Circular No. 67/1991

shall be subject to annulment in pursuance of a resolution of either House of Parliament.

This subsection provides that all the Orders in section 1 of the Act are to be made by negative resolution statutory instrument.

Section 2

(1) If it appears to the Secretary of State that dogs of any type to which section 1 above does not apply present a serious danger to the public he may by Order impose in relation to dogs of that type restrictions and prohibitions corresponding, with such modifications, if any, as he thinks appropriate, to all or any of those in subsection (2)(d) and (e) of that section.

This subsection gives the Secretary of State reserve powers to impose restrictions relating to muzzling, leashing and abandoning any non-fighting type of dog if it is considered to present a serious danger to the public.

(2) An Order under this section may provide for exceptions from any restriction imposed by the Order in such cases and subject to compliance with such conditions as are specified in the Order.

This subsection enables the Order which applies the muzzling, leashing and abandoning requirements to specified types to provide for exceptions.

(3) An Order under this section may contain such supplementary or transitional provisions as the Secretary of State thinks necessary or expedient and may create offences punishable on summary conviction with imprisonment for a term not exceeding six months or a fine not exceeding level 5 on the standard scale or both.

This subsection enables the Order to incorporate supplementary and transitional provisions (the requirements might be phased in) and to create offences corresponding to those in subsections 1(2)(d) and (e).

(4) In determining whether to make an Order under this section and, if so, what the provision of this Order should be the Secretary of State shall consult with such persons or bodies as appear to him to have relevant knowledge and experience, including a body concerned with animal welfare, a body concerned with veterinary science and practice and a body concerned with breeds of dogs.

This subsection requires the Secretary of State before making an Order to apply restrictions to non-fighting types of dog, to consult at least one body concerned with animal welfare, one veterinary body and one concerned with dog breeds. [In practice the bodies consulted are likely to include the RSPCA, the British Veterinary Association, the Royal College of Veterinary Surgeons and the Kennel Club.]

(5) The power to make an Order under this section shall be exercisable by statutory instrument; and no such Order shall be made unless a draft of it has been laid before and approved by a resolution of each House of Parliament.

This subsection provides that Orders under section 2 are to be made by the affirmative resolution procedure.

Section 3

(1) If a dog is dangerously out of control in a public place—
   (a) the owner; and
   (b) if different, the person for the time being in charge of the dog,
is guilty of an offence, or, if the dog while so out of control injures any person, an aggravated offence, under this subsection.

This subsection creates an offence applying to any dog which is dangerously out of control in a public place. "Dangerously out of control" is defined in section 10(3). "Public place" is also defined in section 10(2). The offence in section 3(1) applies to both the owner and the person who was in charge of the dog at the time. If, as a consequence of the dog being out of control, the dog injures any person, an aggravated offence is committed. The offence is intended to catch the dog which bites a person but would not catch the dog which, for example, knocks a cyclist off his bicycle thereby contributing to an injury.

(2) In proceedings for an offence under subsection (1) above against a person who is the owner of a dog but was not at the material time in charge of it, it shall be a defence for the accused to prove that the dog was at the material time in the charge of a person whom he had reasonable grounds to believe was a fit and proper person to be in charge of it.

This subsection provides for the owner of a dog who was not actually in charge of it at the time when it was dangerously out of control, to have a defence that he had reasonable grounds to believe that the person who was in charge of the dog was a fit and proper person. This might mean that, for instance, the owner could use this defence when the dog was in the charge of an adult, but not when the dog was in the charge of a young child in the absence of an adult.

(3) If the owner or if different the person for the time being in charge of a dog allows it to enter a place which is not a public place but where it is not permitted to be and while it is there—

(a) it injures any person; or

(b) there are grounds for reasonable apprehension that it will do so he is guilty of an offence or if the dog injures any person an aggravated offence under this subsection.

This subsection provides that a criminal offence is committed if an owner allows his dog to enter private property where it is not permitted to be and it then injures someone or there are grounds for reasonable apprehension that it will do so. The result is that the offence will apply on occasions where a dog is let into a school playground or a neighbour's back garden and then injures someone.

(4) A person guilty of an offence under subsection (1) or (3) above other than an aggravated offence is liable on summary conviction to imprisonment for a term not exceeding six months or a fine not exceeding level 5 on the standard scale or both; and a person guilty of an aggravated offence under either of those subsections is liable—

(a) on summary conviction, to imprisonment for a term not exceeding six months or a fine not exceeding level 5 on the standard scale or both;

(b) on conviction on indictment, to imprisonment for a term not exceeding two years or a fine or both.

This subsection provides that the penalties for an offence when the dog is dangerously out of control but has not injured are a term of imprisonment not exceeding six months, or a level 5 fine, or both. For an aggravated offence, i.e. when the dog has injured, the penalties are increased on conviction on indictment, to imprisonment for a term of up to two years or an unlimited fine.

(5) It is hereby declared for the avoidance of doubt that an Order under section 2 of the Dogs Act 1871 (Order on complaint that a dog is dangerous and not kept under proper control)—

(a) may be made whether or not the dog is shown to have injured any person; and

(b) may specify the measures to be taken for keeping the dog under proper control, whether by muzzling, keeping on a lead, excluding from specified places or otherwise.

The Dogs Act 1871 (strengthened by the Dangerous Dogs Act 1989) is non-criminal legislation which enables action to be taken against dogs even in situations where no offence has been committed or can be established. The Act is not confined to a public place, so enables control to be exercised over, for instance, dogs which attack postmen or behave in such a way as to frighten neighbours in their gardens.

Home Office Circular No. 67/1991

(a) enables an Order under section 2 of the Dogs Act 1871 (for a dog to be kept under proper control or to be destroyed) to be made whether or not a dog has previously caused injury. This ensures that there is no "first bite" rule for Orders made under the Dogs Act 1871.

(b) clarifies the powers of the court to make Orders under the Dogs Act 1871. At the moment the court can order only that the dog be kept under proper control but this subsection enables the court to specify how this control might be exercised, for instance by requiring a dog to be muzzled or kept on a lead, or excluded from specific places like school playgrounds.

(6) If it appears to a court on a complaint under section 2 of the said Act of 1871 that the dog to which the complaint relates is a male and would be less dangerous if neutered the court may, under that section, make an Order requiring it to be neutered.

This subsection enables a court which makes an Order under section 2 of the Dogs Act 1871 to require that a male dog is neutered. The subsection only applies to male dogs since spaying a bitch is not a way of rendering it less dangerous.

(7) The reference in section 1(3) of the Dangerous Dogs Act 1989 c.30 (penalties) to failing to comply with an Order under section 2 of the said Act of 1871 to keep a dog under proper control shall include a reference to failing to comply with any other Order made under that section, but no Order shall be made under that section by virtue of subsection (6) above where the matters complained of arose before the coming into force of that subsection.

This subsection provides that the courts cannot make an Order under section 2 of the Dogs Act 1871 to require that a dog is neutered if the matters complained of arose before 12 August 1991 when this section of the Act comes into force.

Section 4

(1) Where a person is convicted of an offence under section 1 or 3(1) or (3) above or of an offence under an Order made under section 2 above the court—

    (a) may order the destruction of any dog in respect of which the offence was committed and shall do so in the case of an offence under section 1 or an aggravated offence under section 3(1) or 3(3) above; and

    (b) may order the offender to be disqualified, for such period as the court thinks fit, for having custody of a dog.

This subsection provides that when an offence is committed with a specially controlled dog or with a dog which is dangerously out of control, the court can order the destruction of the dog and may order the offender to be disqualified from having further custody of a dog, for as long as it likes.

In the case of an aggravated offence under section 3(1) or (3), or where a fighting dog is involved, the court is required under (a) to order that the dog is put down.

(2) Where a court makes an Order under subsection (1)(a) above for the destruction of a dog owned by a person other than the offender, then, unless the Order is one that the court is required to make, the owner may appeal to the Crown Court against the Order.

In some cases a destruction Order will be made on the conviction of a person other than the owner of a dog. This subsection enables the owner of the dog to appeal to the Crown Court against the destruction of his dog.

(3) A dog shall not be destroyed pursuant to an Order under subsection (1)(a) above—
  (a) until the end of the period for giving notice of appeal against this conviction, where the Order was not one which the court was required to make, against the Order; and
  (b) if notice of appeal is given within that period, until the appeal is determined or withdrawn,

unless the offender and, in a case to which subsection (2) above applies, the owner of the dog give notice to the court that made the Order that there is to be no such appeal.

This subsection provides that a dog is not destroyed until any appeal has been heard. An appeal against destruction can be made by the offender or the owner of the dog if that is someone different.

(4) Where a court makes an Order under subsection (1)(a) above it may—
  (a) appoint a person to undertake the destruction of the dog and require any person having custody of it to deliver it up for that purpose; and
  (b) order the offender to pay such sum as the court may determine to be the reasonable expenses of destroying the dog and of keeping it pending its destruction.

This subsection enables a court to require that a dog is handed over for destruction by whoever has custody of the dog (which might not be either the offender or the owner) and gives the court power to reclaim the costs of the destruction of the dog from the offender. Costs for detaining the dog, for instance during the time when an appeal is being heard, can also be reclaimed from the offender.

(5) Any sum ordered to be paid under subsection (4)(b) above shall be treated for the purposes of enforcement as if it were a fine imposed on conviction.

This subsection provides that the court can recover the costs of destruction and/or detention of a dog as if they were a fine.

(6) Any person who is disqualified for having custody of a dog by virtue of an Order under subsection (1)(b) above may, at any time after the end of the period of one year beginning with the date of the Order, apply to the court that made it (or a magistrates' court acting for the same petty sessions area as that court) for a direction terminating the disqualification.

This subsection allows someone who has been disqualified from having custody of a dog to apply after a year to have the disqualification lifted. It mirrors similar provisions in the Dangerous Dogs Act 1989. The subsection is necessary because the court is empowered to disqualify for any period that it considers fit.

(7) On an application under subsection (6) above the court may—
  (a) having regard to the applicant's character, his conduct since the disqualification was imposed and any other circumstances of the case, grant or refuse the application; and
  (b) order the applicant to pay all or any part of the costs of the application;

and where an application in respect of an Order is refused no further application in respect of that Order shall be entertained if made before the end of the period of one year beginning with the date of the refusal.

(a) specifies the basis on which the court may lift the disqualification and (b) gives powers to require the applicant to pay the costs of the application. The subsection further provides that, in the event of an application being unsuccessful, the applicant must wait a year before re-applying.

(8) Any person who—
  (a) has custody of a dog in contravention of an Order under subsection (1)(b) above; or
  (b) fails to comply with a requirement imposed on him under subsection (4)(a) above,

is guilty of an offence and liable on summary conviction to a fine not exceeding level 5 on the standard scale.

This subsection makes it an offence to have a dog whilst disqualified or to fail to hand over a dog for destruction. The penalty is a fine not exceeding level 5. The offence at (a) applies to any dog, not just specially controlled dogs.

(9) In the application of this section in Scotland—
- (a) in subsection (2) for the words "Crown Court against the Order" there shall be substituted the words "High Court of Justiciary against the Order within the period of seven days beginning with the date of the Order":
- (b) for subsection (3)(a) there shall be substituted—
  "(a) until the end of the period of seven days beginning with the date of the Order"; and
- (c) for subsection (5) there shall be substituted—
  (5) section 411 of the Criminal Procedures (Scotland) Act 1975 shall apply in relation to the recovery of sums ordered to be paid under subsection (4)(b) above as it applies to fines ordered to be recovered by civil diligence in pursuance of part II of that Act; and
- (d) in subsection (6) the words "(or a magistrates' court acting for the same petty sessions areas as that court)" shall be omitted.

This subsection is necessary for the operation of the Act in Scotland. The Dogs Act 1871 and the Dangerous Dogs Act 1989 also apply to Scotland.

Section 5

(1) A constable or an officer of a local authority authorised by it to exercise the powers conferred by this subsection may seize—
- (a) any dog which appears to him to be a dog to which section 1 above applies and which is in a public place—
  - (i) after the time when possession or custody of it has become unlawful by virtue of that section; or
  - (ii) before that time, without being muzzled and kept on a lead;
- (b) any dog in a public place which appears to him to be a dog to which an Order under section 2 above applies and in respect of which an offence against the Order has been or is being committed; and
- (c) any dog in a public place (whether or not one to which that section applies) which appears to him to be dangerously out of control.

This subsection gives a constable or local authority dog warden power to seize a dog which appears to be dangerously out of control in a public place; a dog which is the subject of an Order under section 2 which has been abandoned or is not on a lead before 30 November 1991; a fighting dog which has no muzzle and/or is not being kept on a lead; or a fighting dog which does not satisfy all the conditions for exemption set out in the exemption scheme after possession becomes an offence on 30 November 1991.

(2) If a justice of the peace is satisfied by information on oath, or in Scotland a justice of the peace or Sheriff is satisfied by evidence on oath, that there are reasonable grounds for believing—

(a) that an offence under any provision of this Act or of an Order under section 2 above is being or has been committed; and

(b) that evidence of the commission of any such offence is to be found,

on any premises he may issue a warrant authorising a constable to enter those premises (using such force as is reasonably necessary) and to search them and seize any dog or other thing found there which is evidence of the commission of such an offence.

This subsection gives powers to magistrates, following evidence that an offence under the Act has been or is being committed, to issue a warrant authorising the police to enter the premises using force if necessary, to search them and to seize any dog or any other evidence of the offence.

(3) A warrant issued under this section in Scotland shall be authority for opening lockfast places and may authorise persons named in the warrant to accompany a constable who is executing it.

This subsection provides the necessary authority to enter closed premises in Scotland.

(4) Where a dog is seized under subsection (1) or (2) above and it appears to a justice of the peace, or in Scotland a justice of the peace or sheriff, that no person has been or is to be prosecuted for an offence under this Act or an Order under section 2 above in respect of that dog (whether because the owner cannot be found or for any other reason) he may order the destruction of the dog and shall do so if it is one to which section 1 above applies.

This subsection gives powers for a dog which has been seized to be destroyed when no prosecution is being brought under the Act, including when the owner of the dog cannot be traced.

(5) If in any proceedings it is alleged by the prosecution that a dog is one to which section 1 or an Order under section 2 above applies it shall be presumed that it is such a dog unless the contrary is shown

Home Office Circular No. 67/1991

by the accused by such evidence as the court considers sufficient; and the accused shall not be permitted to adduce such evidence unless he has given the prosecution notice of his intention to do so not later than the fourteenth day before that on which the evidence is to be adduced.

This subsection reverses the burden of proof so that, instead of the prosecution having to establish that a dog is of a type that is specially controlled, the owner has to show that it is not of such a type. When the defendant wishes to use this defence, he has to give 14 days notice, in such the same way as notice has to be given when seeking to establish an alibi. This period will enable the prosecution to consider whether it wishes to produce expert evidence of its own about the type of dog.

Section 6

Where a dog is owned by a person who is less than sixteen years old any reference to its owner in section 1(2)(d) or (e) or 3 above shall include a reference to the head of the household, if any, of which that person is a member or, in Scotland, to the person who has his actual care and control.

This section provides that where someone under sixteen owns a dog the head of the household is also included as the owner. It prevents an adult from escaping responsibility for a dog to which section 1 applies or one which is dangerously out of control by claiming that the dog was owned by a minor.

Section 7

(1) In this Act—
   (a) references to a dog being muzzled are to its being securely fitted with a muzzle sufficient to prevent it biting any person; and
   (b) references to its being kept on a lead are to its being securely held on a lead by a person who is not less than sixteen years old.

(2) If the Secretary of State thinks it desirable to do so he may by Order prescribe the kind of muzzle or lead to be used for the purpose of complying in the case of a dog of any type with section 1 or an Order under section 2 above; and if a muzzle or lead of a particular kind is for the time being prescribed in relation to any type of dog the references in subsection (1) above to a muzzle or lead shall, in relation to any dog of that type, be construed as references to a muzzle or lead of that kind.

(3) The power to make an Order under subsection (2) above shall be exercisable by statutory instrument subject to annulment in pursuance of a resolution of either House of Parliament.

Home Office Circular No. 67/1991

This section does three things. First, subsection (1)(a) defines the type of muzzle that dogs to which section 1 or an Order under section 2 applies must wear. Second, subsection (1)(b) provides that section 1 and section 2 dogs must be under the control of a person of 16 or over. Third, subsection (2) contains an order-making power to enable the Home Secretary to prescribe types of lead or muzzle for section 1 or section 2 dogs.

Section 8

An Order in Council under paragraph 1(1)(b) of Schedule 1 to the Northern Ireland Act 1974 (legislation for Northern Ireland in the interim period) which states that it is made only for purposes corresponding to the purpose of the Act:

(a) shall not be subject to paragraph 1(4) and (5) of that Schedule (affirmative resolution of both Houses of Parliament); and
(b) shall be subject to annulment in pursuance of a resolution of either House.

This section enables the Act's provisions to be applied to Northern Ireland by negative resolution Order in Council. The usual procedure for Northern Ireland is affirmative Order.

Section 9

Any expenses incurred by the Secretary of State in consequence of this Act shall be paid out of money provided by Parliament.

This section provides for the costs of any compensation scheme and other costs incurred by the Secretary of State as a result of this Act to be defrayed out of money provided by Parliament.

Section 10

(1) This Act may be cited as the Dangerous Dogs Act 1991.
(2) In this Act—
"advertisement" includes any means of bringing a matter to the attention of the public and "advertise" shall be construed accordingly;
"public place" means any street, road or other place (whether or not enclosed) to which the public have or are permitted to have access whether for payment or otherwise and includes the common parts of a building containing two or more separate dwellings.
(3) For the purposes of this Act a dog shall be regarded as dangerously out of control on any occasion on which there are grounds for reasonable

Home Office Circular No. 67/1991

apprehension that it will injure any person, whether or not it actually does so but references to a dog injuring a person or there being grounds for reasonable apprehension that it will do so do not include references to any case in which the dog is being used for a lawful purpose by a constable or a person in the service of the Crown.

Subsections (2) and (3) set out the definition of specific terms as they apply to this Act. It is to be noted that "public place" extends to privately-owned land because it includes all places to which the public have access, including the communal areas of blocks of flats even when they are secure-entry controlled. This definition of public place is much wider that the "street, unfenced ground adjoining or abutting upon any street, or any place of public resort or recreation ground under the control of the local authority" which applies (in England and Wales) to the offence of having an unmuzzled ferocious dog at large under the Town Police Clauses Act 1847. Subsection (3) provides an exemption in respect of dogs used by policemen or people in the service of the Crown from the dangerously out of control offences in section 3(1) and (3) of the Act.

(4) Except for section 8 this Act shall not come into force until such day as the Secretary of State may appoint by an Order made by statutory instrument and different days may be appointed for different provisions or different purposes.

By virtue of SI 1991/1742, the Act comes into force on 12 August 1991 (section 8 came into force on Royal Assent).

(4)* Except for section 8 this Act does not extend to Northern Ireland.

It should be noted that this Act does not repeal any part of the Dogs Act 1871, the Dangerous Dogs Act 1989, nor the offence of having an unmuzzled ferocious dog at large in section 28 of the Town Police Clauses Act 1847 (and similar provisions, in London, in the Metropolitan Police Act 1839 and the City of London Police Act 1839).

In Scotland, the offence in section 49(1) of the Civic Government (Scotland) Act 1982 of allowing a creature to endanger or injure any person in a public place, or to give that person reasonable cause for alarm also remains in place.

12 August 1991

---

*Note: Repetition of paragraph numbered as "(4)" reproduced from original document.

Home Office Circular No. 67/1991

INFORMATION ABOUT SPECIALLY CONTROLLED DOGS

Annex B

Please read and keep in a safe place

Which dogs are specially controlled by the Dangerous Dogs Act 1991?

The Act controls the four types of dog known as:
(i) the Pit Bull Terrier;
(ii) the Japanese Tosa;
(iii) the Dogo Argentino;
(iv) the Fila Braziliero.

No other types of dog are specially controlled by the Act.

If you have a pit bull terrier, tosa, dogo or fila, you must take action about it at once.

If I have one of these dogs what do I have to do?

From **12 August 1991**, whenever your dog is in a public place, it must be:
(i) muzzled so that it cannot bite anyone; *and*
(ii) on a lead; *and*
(iii) in the charge of someone who is at least 16 years old.

Failure to do any of these things is a criminal offence, for which the maximum penalty is a fine of £2,000 [now £5,000] or six months' imprisonment or both and the dog will be put down.

From **12 August 1991** it will also be a criminal offence to:
(i) breed from your dog;
(ii) sell or exchange the dog or to offer or advertise your dog for sale or exchange;
(iii) give away your dog, or offer to do so, or advertise your dog as a gift;
(iv) abandon your dog; or
(v) allow it to stray.

From **30 November 1991** it will be a criminal offence to keep your dog unless it has a Certificate of Exemption.

The maximum penalty for these offences is a fine of £2,000 [now £5,000] or six months' imprisonment or both and your dog will be put down.

Are there any requirements attached to the Certificate of Exemption?

Yes: when the dog is in a public place, it must always be muzzled and on a lead held by someone who is at least 16.

You must also:
(i) keep the dog in secure conditions so that it cannot escape;
(ii) if asked to do so by a police or local authority officer (dog warden), show the Certificate of Exemption, display the dog's tattoo and allow the implanted chip to be read;
(iii) keep the third party insurance in force;
(iv) inform the Index of Exempted Dogs of any change of address at which the dog is kept for longer than 30 days.

If these requirements are not observed, the Certificate of Exemption will lapse and the dog will have to be put down.

Are there any special arrangements for puppies?

Yes, they do not have to be neutered or spayed until they are six months old. The application form will give more details about this.

What should I do now?

If you have a pit bull terrier, tosa, dogo or fila, fill in this form at once. Leave part 1 at your local police station and send part II to the Index of Exempted Dogs, Chishill Road, Heydon, Royston, Herts SG8 8PN.

If you have an adult dog, you must do this before **12 October**.

In the case of puppies which will be less than six months old on 30 November, you must do this by **30 November**.

DON'T DELAY!

YOU MUST RETURN PART I OF THIS FORM TO THE POLICE BY 12 OCTOBER AT THE LATEST AND SEND PART II TO THE INDEX OF EXEMPTED DOGS SO THAT YOU CAN GET AN APPLICATION FORM AND WILL HAVE TIME TO OBTAIN THE CERTIFICATE OF EXEMPTION BY 30 NOVEMBER 1991. If you do not receive a reply from the Index of Exempted Dogs within 21 days, you should write again or telephone 0763 838329.

The legal basis for these provisions is the Dangerous Dogs (Compensation and Exemption Schemes) Order 1991 (SI 1991/1744), the Dangerous Dogs Act (Commencement and Appointed Day) Order 1991 (SI 1991/1742), the Dangerous Dogs (Designated Types) Order 1991 (SI 1991/1743) and section 1 and 7 of the Dangerous Dogs Act 1991. This notice was prepared in July 1991 by the Home Office, on behalf of HM Government. The legislation applies to England, Scotland and Wales.

HOME OFFICE CIRCULAR No. 80/1992

24 August 1992

Further Advice Concerning the Dangerous Dogs Act 1991

This Circular gives further advice about the implementation and enforcement of the Dangerous Dogs Act 1991. It should be read in conjunction with Home Office Circular No. 67/1991.

Crosses with the pit bull terrier

2. Some police forces have sought clarification about how the legislation affects pit bull crosses.

3. In this country the pit bull terrier is generally regarded as being a cross between a bull breed of dog and larger dogs like the mastiff. It may also, however, be obtained by breeding or cross-breeding pit bull terriers themselves. The terms of section 1 of the Act make it clear that that section applies not only to 'pure' pit bull terriers but to *any* dog of the type known as the pit bull terrier. It is possible that a pit bull terrier may result from the cross of one dog which is a pit bull terrier and one which is not. Whether section 1 of the Act applies to any particular cross will depend on whether the resulting dog is of the type known as the pit bull terrier – that is to say, whether it has the physical and behavioural characteristics of the pit bull terrier. While in the first instance it is for the police, local authority dog wardens and the prosecution authorities to take a view about whether a particular dog comes within the terms of section 1, it is of course ultimately a matter for the courts to decide.

Identification of the pit bull terrier

4. Chief officers were sent a detailed description of the pit bull terrier type on 26 July 1991, and posters giving further indication of typical size and range of colouring of pit bull terriers were sent out on 2 August. In addition, Chief Officers may wish to note that the Staffordshire Bull Terrier Breed Council has provided a list of clubs which are willing to give advice to police officers, local authority dog wardens or the courts if there is any doubt about whether a dog is a Staffordshire Bull Terrier, the type with which the pit bull terrier is

most commonly mistaken. It should be borne in mind however, that the concern of members of the Council is likely to be with whether an animal is a Staffordshire Bull Terrier or a Staffordshire Bull Terrier Cross, and they may not be in a position to confirm or deny if the dog in question is a pit bull type.

5. Attention is drawn to the issue of certificates by the 'Intercontinental Kennel Club' for 'American Staffordshire Terriers'. It is possible that the dogs for which these certificates have been issued may in fact be pit bull terriers. The Intercontinental Kennel Club is not recognised by either the British Kennel Club or the American Kennel Club. Police officers, local authority dog wardens and the courts may wish to bear this in mind should they come across such certificates.

Burden of proof

6. As outlined in the Home Office Circular No. 67/1991, section 5(5) of the Act reverses the burden of proof so that the onus is placed on the accused to show that the dog is not of a type specially controlled by section 1 of the Act. If the defence wish to rebut this presumption, section 5(5) requires that they give fourteen days notice of their intention to do so. It is for the prosecution to decide whether to produce their own expert witnesses to support the presumption. These might include veterinary surgeons with experience in dealing with pit bull terriers or the other types of specially controlled dog, Staffordshire Bull Terrier judges, experienced police dog handlers or representatives of animal welfare organisations.

Mandatory destruction orders

7. Section 4(1)(a) of the Act provides that where an owner is convicted of an offence under section 1 (i.e. where the dog is of a type that is specially controlled by the Act) or an aggravated offence under section 3(1) or (3), the court is *required* to order the destruction of the dog involved in the commission of the offence. The court has no discretion regarding the destruction of the dog in such cases.

The animal welfare and resource implications of kennelling seized dogs

8. Delays in bringing cases to trial, resulting in the need for dogs which have been seized to be kennelled for substantial periods, are undesirable. When dealing with such cases courts will wish to give due consideration

Home Office Circular No. 80/1992

to the well-being of the animal, as well as the resource implications of prolonged kennelling arising from such delays. Courts may therefore wish to consider how these types of cases can best be expedited.

Provisions relating to dangerous dogs of any breed

9. Section 3 of the Dangerous Dogs Act 1991 created offences of having a dog dangerously out of control, including an aggravated offence where the dog injures a person. These offences relate to dogs of any breed. Where a conviction for the aggravated offence is secured, the court must order the destruction of the dog as explained in paragraph 7. There are in force, however, other statutory provisions relating to the control of dogs where the option of having the dog destroyed is either not available or is not mandatory. These include provisions in the Town Police Clauses Act 1847 and the Dogs Act 1871. Where a dog has attacked, Chief Officers and prosecuting authorities will wish to consider under which legislation it would be most appropriate for charges to be brought in the light of the circumstances of each case.

Certificate of exemption

10. Any breach of its conditions invalidates the certificate of exemption and the dog automatically becomes un-exempted. The dog may then be seized and the owner is liable to prosecution under section 1(3). Where the dog was unmuzzled or not kept on a lead action may also be taken under section 1(2)(d) and where the dog strayed or was abandoned, action may also be taken under section 1(2)(e).

Liaison with the Index of Exempted Dogs

11. Chief Officers are reminded that each police force was asked in paragraph 25 of Home Office Circular No. 67/1991 to provide the Index of Exempted Dogs with a contact point. It appears that not all forces have done so yet. It would help the Index considerably if such a contact point could be provided.

Northern Ireland

12. A similar exemption scheme has been set up in Northern Ireland and it has been agreed that certificates issued in Northern Ireland should be recognised in Great Britain and vice versa. If any queries arise about a particular certificate issued in Northern Ireland, enquiries should be made through the Index of Exempted Dogs.

13. It is a requirement of certificates of exemption issued both in Great Britain and Northern Ireland that the Index (or the district

councils in Northern Ireland) should be informed of any change of address lasting more than 30 days. If the change involves a move from Great Britain to Northern Ireland, the authorities maintaining the respective Indexes will pass on relevant information.

14. The major difference between the exemption scheme in Great Britain and that in Northern Ireland is that there is no tattooing requirement in Northern Ireland. Dogs exempted in Northern Ireland need not, therefore, be tattooed and there is no requirement for them to be tattooed if they move to Great Britain. Officers who encounter an un-tattooed dog whose owner states it was exempted in Northern Ireland should ask to see the certificate of exemption and make enquiries with the Index accordingly.

ALAN HARDING
E Division

ANNEX A (amended)

The Staffordshire Bull Terrier Breed Council of Great Britain and Northern Ireland

Website: *http://www.staffords.co.uk*

from which details of the constituent member clubs and societies may be obtained.

HOME OFFICE CIRCULAR No. 9/1994

24 February 1994

Further Advice Concerning the Dangerous Dogs Act 1991

This Circular offers further advice about the implementation and enforcement of the Dangerous Dogs Act 1991. It should be read in conjunction with Home Office Circulars Nos. 67/1991 and 80/1992.

Identification of the pit bull terrier

2. The Government recognises the problems which have been encountered in deciding whether a dog falls into the category of "the type known as the pit bull terrier". The Circular issued in August 1992 (80/1992) offered some advice on this point, particularly in respect of pit bull crosses, and indicated that the ultimate decision for the court to decide is whether the dog in question has the physical and behavioural characteristics of the pit bull terrier. The Circular drew attention to a list of registered Staffordshire Bull Terrier Clubs which could provide contact details of local Staffordshire Bull Terrier Championship Show Judges willing to give advice on whether a particular dog is in fact a Staffordshire Bull Terrier or a Staffordshire Bull Terrier cross. It is understood that some changes have been made to the list of clubs since that Circular was issued. A copy of the updated list may be obtained from either the Chairman of the Staffordshire Bull Terrier Breed Council, Mr Alec Waters, of 34 West Drayton Road, Hillingdon, Middlesex UB8 3LA, telephone 081-561 6951, or the Secretary, Mr David Levy of 6 The Byeway, Rickmansworth, Hertfordshire WD3 1JW, telephone 0923 774608.

3. Since the issue of the last Circular, the Kennel Club (KC) and the British Veterinary Association (BVA) have been considering together what further assistance might be given to those involved in operating the Act in determining whether or not a particular dog appears likely to fall within the Act's controls. They have now produced a joint list of persons who are prepared to give advice to police officers, local authority dog wardens, the courts or members of the general public as to whether or not a dog is a pit bull terrier. A copy of the joint list is available from, either Mr Brian Leonard, The Kennel Club, 1-5 Clarges Street,

Home Office Circular No. 9/1994

Piccadilly, London W1Y 8AB, telephone 071-355 3608, or Miss Victoria Thomas, British Veterinary Association, 7 Mansfield Street, London WIM OAT, telephone 071-636 6541. The Kennel Club and the British Veterinary Association has said that they have no objection to the list of names being made available to defendants, if there should be requests to this effect. It should be noted this list does not purport to include everyone with expertise in this area, and there are likely to be other people known to the police and prosecuting authorities able and willing to provide advice on whether or not a dog is of the type known as the pit bull terrier. It should also be noted that the lists of names produced by the Staffordshire Bull Terrier Breed Council and the KC/BVA should be regarded as complementary to one another. For example, where the issue is whether a dog is a Staffordshire Bull Terrier rather than a pit bull terrier, the Breed Council list may provide the help needed. On the other hand, where the issue is whether or not the dog is a pit bull terrier, but the question of it being a Staffordshire Bull Terrier does not arise, the KC/BVA list may be more appropriate.

4. It is hoped that the KC/BVA list covers a sufficiently wide geographical area to ensure access to a member of the panel in all parts of the country. It is requested that the Kennel Club or the British Veterinary Association should be informed if there are problems in this respect.

5. A number of cases involving the interpretation of the definitions and phrases contained in the Act have now been considered on appeal. In particular, the Divisional Court has addressed the question whether the reference to a "type" in the Act goes wider than simply "breed"; whether the guidelines of the American Dog Breeders Association are relevant to the determination of a dog's identity; and how far behavioural characteristics should influence the decision. These cases may be subject to further appeal: the outcome may well be important in deciding future cases, and further advice will be issued if appropriate.

Access to seized dogs for the purpose of identification

6. Reference has been made in paragraph 5 to the relevance of behavioural characteristics in identifying these dogs, and the final judgements in the cases now subject to appeal may shed more light on the weight to be given to this aspect. Chief Officers and local authorities will wish to bear in mind, however, that where such factors are an issue before the courts, those giving evidence (whether on behalf of the

prosecution or the defence) will need an adequate opportunity to assess this aspect of the dog in question. This may take longer than the observation necessary to consider physical characteristics, and may necessitate allowing the dog greater freedom of movement than it normally enjoys in custody.

Alternative statutory provisions to the Dangerous Dogs Act 1991

7. Circular 80/1992 discussed the anxieties which have been expressed over the use of section 3 of the 1991 Act, which relates to dogs of *any* type or breed which are dangerously out of control. Particular concern has focused on the mandatory destruction order which the court must make where it convicts for an aggravated offence under section 3 – i.e. any offence where injury is caused. Section 3 was included in the 1991 Act to extend the powers of the courts in dealing with dog attacks. It was not intended to replace previously existing legislation – e.g. the Metropolitan Police Act 1839, the Town Police Clauses Act 1847, the Dogs Act 1871 and the Animals Act 1971 – where the option of having a dog destroyed is either not available or is not mandatory. These previous statutes remain in force, and may well be more appropriate where any injury caused is minor, or where there is a degree of provocation to which the dog may have responded. Prosecuting authorities will wish to consider whether proceeding under one of these earlier statutes would be preferable to using the 1991 Act in cases of lesser severity.

8. There may be circumstances involving prosecutions under section 3 of the 1991 Act for non-aggravated offences, where the court, in deciding whether a destruction order is appropriate or not, would welcome the availability of the powers to impose controls over the dog (muzzling, etc.) contained in the 1871 Act. For that option to be available, the prosecution would need to lay a complaint under the 1871 Act, in parallel with proceedings under section 3 of the 1991 Act. The court would then be able to consider immediately after conviction of the owner or person in charge of the dog whether steps (short of destruction) should be taken in respect of the dog.

The animal welfare and resource implications of kennelling seized dogs

9. Paragraph 8 of Home Office Circular 80/1992 drew attention to the undesirability of delays in bringing cases to trial, resulting in the need

for dogs which have been seized to be kennelled for substantial periods. The Home Office is aware of cases which are continuing to take many months before resolution, leading to high costs for kennelling the dogs and possible long term disturbance to the dogs themselves (who may of course be released at the end of the day). It is recognised that the delays may well be due to circumstances beyond the control of the courts, and that the interests of justice may often require other types of case to take priority. However, once again, the Home Office encourages all concerned to do everything possible to speed the progress of these cases.

Dogs being held in custody pending trial

10. Owners whose dogs have been seized by the police or local authority dog wardens and which are being held in custody pending trial often ask to have access to their dogs, or to have information about their dog's condition. This has been a major theme of representations made to the Home Office about the operation of the Act, along with requests for dogs to be released back to their owners, pending trial. It is recognised that these are all matters which raise potentially important security and public safety considerations; it is for Chief Officers and local authorities to form a judgement in each case whether there would be potential problems if the location of kennels were made known to owners, and what the danger might be (either to the public, or of the non-return of dogs) if seized dogs were released back into their owners' custody more frequently than at present. Chief Officers and local authorities will wish to balance these considerations against the undesirability of keeping dogs in prolonged custody, and the anxieties which owners may feel about the well-being of their animals. Where security considerations rule out access by owners, it may be appropriate (where this is requested) to allow access by a veterinary surgeon, and there is no reason why this should not be subject to an undertaking of confidentiality on the latter's part, so far as the location of the dog is concerned.

11. The suggestion has been made to the Home Office that to microchip a detained dog would guarantee its subsequent identification, if released. This is an option which Chief Officers and local authorities might wish to consider (with the owner's consent) where they are minded to release an animal.

Welfare of dogs in custody

12. There are important welfare considerations raised in respect of dogs which have been seized on suspicion of being pit bull terriers, given that they may in due course be released back to their owners if they are found not to be specially controlled for the purposes of section 1 of the Act. Chief Officers and local authorities will obviously pay due regard to the welfare of animals held pending trial, with adequate veterinary inspection as necessary. Owners receiving a dog back after a prolonged period of incarceration may ask for an account of the dog's health while in detention, and an account of any significant developments while it has been out of their custody. A particular problem is raised by the position of puppies born in captivity to bitches which are pregnant when taken into custody on suspicion of being pit bull terriers – and who will subsequently be released if the mother is found not to be a pit bull. Advice which the Home Office has received suggests that if puppies are not properly socialised in the first six weeks of life, they may never be able, and could themselves be a danger subsequently. Those responsible for the custody of pregnant bitches will need to take appropriate veterinary advice on this issue.

Further enquiries

13. Any enquiries about this Circular may be addressed to:
    E Division
    Room 979
    Home Office
    50 Queen Anne's Gate
    London SW1H 9AT
    Tel: 071-273 2316 or 071-273 3804
    Fax: 071-273 2423.

ALAN HARDING

Head of E Division

HOME OFFICE CIRCULAR No. 53/1999

30 November 1999

Licensing Dog Breeding Establishments: Guidance Updated to Take Account of the Breeding and Sale of Dogs (Welfare) Act 1999

1. District/London borough/unitary councils, as enforcing authorities, will already be aware that the Breeding and Sale of Dogs (Welfare) Act 1999 is due to come into force on 30 December 1999. The Act will amend the Breeding of Dogs Act 1973, by introducing additional requirements for the licensing and inspection of establishments at which the business of breeding dogs for sale is conducted. The new Act will also introduce certain requirements in relation to the sale of dogs from licensed breeding establishments.

2. This circular is addressed to local authorities in England and Wales – separate guidance is to be issued to local authorities in Scotland. It supersedes Home Office Circular No.38/1974 (concerning the 1973 Act), that part of Home Office Circular 75/1991 relating to the Breeding of Dogs Act 1991, and Home Office Circular 9/1997 (which reminded local authorities of their powers under both the 1973 and 1991 Acts). It provides in the following Annexes a summary, with explanation where appropriate, of the licensing law concerning dog breeding establishments from 30 December 1999:

- Annex A refers sequentially to each section of the 1973 Act, as it will be amended by the 1999 Act;
- Annex B deals in a similar way with the additional provisions of the 1999 Act;
- Annex C summarises the provisions of the earlier Act of 1991;

. . .

Changes to the law are, for ease of reference, highlighted in these Annexes in ***bold italics***.

3. The Annexes include points of general guidance, but they do not offer authoritative legal interpretations. Local authorities must obtain their own legal advice as necessary. Nor do the Annexes give detailed guidance on the requirements breeders must meet to comply with licence conditions. For that local authorities may find useful updated

Home Office Circular No. 53/1999

guidance and model conditions produced by the British Veterinary Association in consultation with the British Small Animal Veterinary Association, the Chartered Institute of Environmental Health, and the Local Government Association. The guidance may be purchased from T.G. Scott & Son Limited, Unit 6, Bourne Enterprise Centre, Wrotham Road, Borough Green, Kent TN15 8DG (tel: 01732 884023; fax: 01732 884034).

4. Enquiries about this Circular should be made to the Animal Welfare Section at the address above (telephone: 0171 273 3891 or 0171 273 2316; fax: 0171 273 2029).

RICK EVANS
Head of Unit

Annex A: The Breeding of Dogs Act 1973, as amended by the Breeding and Sale of Dogs (Welfare) Act 1999

Under section 1(1) of the Act, no person shall keep a breeding establishment for dogs without a licence from the local authority. The definition in the Act of "keeping a breeding establishment for dogs" is at paragraph 21 below.

2. Section 1(2) provides for the granting of a licence, with such conditions as the local authority deems fit (subject to any court decisions on appeal – see paragraph 10 below), though it must pay particular regard to matters specified later in the Act (see paragraphs 7 and 8 below). Section 1(2) also stipulates that no person is entitled to a licence if he is at the time disqualified from keeping a dog breeding establishment, pet shop or boarding kennels, or if he has been disqualified from keeping dogs or other animals as a result of specified convictions for cruelty.

3. *In deciding whether to grant a licence to a person for the first time, the local authority is required by section 1(2A) to arrange for the inspection of the premises by a veterinary surgeon/practitioner and by an officer of the authority. Inspections are also required on subsequent applications, but can then be by a veterinary surgeon/practitioner or an officer of the authority (or both).* During the passage of the legislation it was suggested in Parliament that local authorities may wish to use for the initial inspection in each case the services of a veterinary surgeon/practitioner other than one normally used by the applicant. This is not

however a requirement in the Act, and may not always be practicable. The main consideration must be whether the veterinary surgeon/ practitioner has the appropriate experience.

4. Local authorities may, after an initial inspection, consider that a licence can be granted, subject to any required changes to premises being made to an agreed timetable during the licence period. They may, however, wish to ensure that the mandatory inspections for second and subsequent applications – "renewals" – are arranged in sufficient time to allow the applicant to comply with any such additional requirements prior to expiry of the existing licence. (For inspections while a licence is in force see paragraph 16 below, and for inspection of unlicensed premises see Annex C on the 1991 Act.)

5. **Under section 1(2B) the local authority shall arrange for a report to be made about the premises, the applicant and other relevant matters, and must consider that report before deciding whether to grant a licence.** The report must be obtained under this section after every inspection to determine a licence application (including "renewals"). It will be of critical importance in each case, as its content could be used to justify granting or refusal of a licence. It must be detailed and comprehensive. It can contain any information a local authority might need in order to be satisfied that licence conditions will be met (see especially paragraphs 7 and 8 below), and that suitably high priority will be given by the applicant to the overall welfare of dogs in his/her charge.

6. Section 1(3) was repealed in 1975.

7. The local authority, in considering an application for a licence, is required under section 1(4) to have particular regard to a number of factors, which should be covered in the inspection report mentioned in paragraph 5 above, and which must under the Act be reflected in the specified conditions attached to any licence granted. These factors do not prejudice the local authority's discretion to withhold a licence on other grounds. The factors include, as specified in section 1(4)(a)–(e), the general suitability of the accommodation for the dogs; the arrangements for ensuring the dogs receive adequate food, drink and bedding material; and the schedule for visiting and exercising the dogs at suitable intervals. Satisfactory precautions also have to be taken at the establishment to prevent and control the spread among the dogs of diseases, and to ensure the dogs are protected in the event of fire or other emergency. The welfare of the dogs must also be addressed in a number of respects when they are being transported to or from the breeding establishment.

Home Office Circular No. 53/1999

8. **Section 1(4)(f),(g) and (h) require that bitches should not be mated if they are less than one year old; should not give birth to more than six litters of puppies each; and should not give birth to more than one litter of puppies in any period of twelve months.** These are new requirements aimed at significantly improving the health and welfare of breeding bitches, and in turn at raising the standards of health of their progeny. Some breeders may contend that there are difficulties with some of these requirements (for example in connection with the length of the cycle for certain breeds of bitches coming into season), but the Act as it now stands provides no scope for flexibility or exceptions. It is however expected that local authorities will be reasonable and show understanding on minor technical infringements, especially those arising from factors beyond a breeder's control (such as when a bitch whelps prematurely, assuming date of mating is correctly recorded).

9. **Section 1(4)(i) requires that the licence holder should keep accurate records in a form, prescribed by regulations. The records must be kept on the premises and made available for inspection by an officer of the local authority, or any veterinary surgeon/practitioner authorised by the local authority to inspect the premises. Section 1(4A) states that the regulations shall be made by the Secretary of State by statutory instrument subject to the negative resolution procedure in Parliament.** The regulations will not cover all the information a local authority might occasionally need for enforcement purposes from a licensed breeder, but they should be an aid to checking compliance with some of the key licence conditions. Local authorities will want the records required by regulation, along with any other relevant records they might require a breeder to keep, to be examined as part of the inspections for second and subsequent applications, as mentioned at paragraph 4, and during any inspections while a licence is in force (see paragraph 16 below). The regulations are at Annex D, and should come into force on 30 December 1999, unless notice is issued to the contrary.

10. Any person aggrieved by a refusal of the local authority to grant a licence, or by any of the conditions attached to the licence may, under section 1(5), appeal to a magistrates' court. The court may give such directions in the matter as it thinks proper.

11. **Under section 1(5A) the local authority shall determine whether to grant a licence within three months from when the application is received.** This, and sections 1(6) and 1(7) described in

the following paragraphs, relate only to applications received **on or after** 30 December 1999.

12. **Sections 1(6) and 1(7) taken together provide for a licence to run for 12 months from its start date, being the date requested by the applicant or the date of issue, whichever is later.** This is a procedural change, as licences have generally until now expired on 31 December each year. Local authorities will wish to put in place administrative arrangements for ensuring that second and subsequent applications, in effect to renew licences, are invited well ahead of the expiry date of the current licences. (See also paragraph 4 above, about the related desirability of arranging inspections in good time in these cases.) In the longer term this could offer local authorities greater flexibility, by avoiding the processing of all applications at the same time of year.

13. Section 1(8) provides that, where a licence-holder dies, the licence shall remain in force for a period of three months following the death. The local authority has discretion to extend this period on application by the deceased person's representatives, if satisfied that an extension is necessary for the purpose of winding up the estate.

14. Section 1(9) makes it an offence to keep a breeding establishment without a licence, or to contravene any condition attached to a licence. For the maximum penalties for this offence, see paragraph 17 below.

15. Section 1(10) provides for an appeal under section 1(5) to be made to a sheriff court in Scotland.

16. Under Section 2(1), a local authority may authorise in writing any of its officers or any veterinary surgeon/practitioner to inspect any premises, including private dwellings, in respect of which a licence has been granted. There is a power of entry for such inspections, which may take place at all reasonable times to ascertain whether offences under the Act are being committed. Animals found on the premises can also be inspected. It is an offence under section 2(2) to obstruct entry or inspection. The whole of section 2, together with the new requirements for inspections when considering applications, should assist local authorities in their enforcement role, in that it enables them in any particular case to check of their own initiative as to whether there is compliance with licence conditions.

17. Subsections (1)–(4) of section 3 deal with penalties and disqualifications for offences committed on or after 30 December 1999. **The maximum penalty for an offence under section 1(9) (unlawfully**

keeping a dog breeding establishment without a licence – paragraph 14 above) is 3 months imprisonment and/or a fine not exceeding level 4 (currently £2500) *on the standard scale.* The maximum penalty for the offence under section 2(2) (obstructing an inspection – preceding paragraph) will be level 4 on the standard scale. If a person is convicted of an offence under the Act, the court may (in addition to or as substitution for the aforementioned penalties) make an order providing for (i) the cancellation of a licence; (ii) disqualification, for such period as the court thinks fit, from keeping an establishment needing to be licensed under the Act; and (iii) disqualification, for such period as the court thinks fit, from having custody of any dog of a description specified in the order. If the court has made such an order, it may suspend its operation pending an appeal. *The courts may not, as previously, make orders under the Act on account of convictions under other animal welfare/licensing legislation (e.g. relating to pet shops or animal boarding establishments).*

18. *Section 3(5) to (11) sets out in more detail the powers available to the courts in respect of orders disqualifying persons from having custody of specified descriptions of dogs. Section 3(5) provides that a court can make a further order in relation to any dog of the specified description that may have been in the offender's custody when the offence was committed or at any time since. Section 3(6) provides that an order, made under section 3(5), can require the offender to deliver the dog to a specified person, and require him/her to pay for the care of the dog until permanent arrangements are made for its care or disposal. Section 3(7) provides that anyone who contravenes an order or fails to comply with a requirement imposed under section 3(6), is guilty of an offence. Section 3(8) provides for representations to be made, when a section 3(5) order is proposed, by the owner of the dog if the owner is a person other than the offender; and for the owner to appeal to a higher court against an order once it has been made. Under section 3(9), a person who is the subject of a disqualification order may, after one year, apply to the court for it to be lifted. If an application is made under section 3(9) then, under section 3(10), the court is required to notify the local authority to allow any representations to be made prior to making a decision, and may order any costs to be met by the applicant. If an application is made under section 3(9) and is subsequently refused by the court,*

section 3(11) provides that no further application may be made before the end of a further year. Local authorities will wish to prepare contingency plans for homing dogs in cases where disqualification is ordered, to include maintenance of a list of inspected and approved sanctuaries/rescue organisations.

19. *Section 3A provides that local authorities may charge fees in respect of both the applications for the licences and the related inspections under the Act. The level of fees may reflect the reasonable administration and enforcement costs incurred by the local authority under both the Act and the 1991 (sic). Fees can be varied to take account of different circumstances.*

20. Section 4 has been repealed.

21. *The definition of keeping a breeding establishment for dogs, for the purposes of the Act, is provided in section 4A. Under section 4A(2) a person keeps a breeding establishment for dogs at any premises if he/she carries on at those premises a business of breeding dogs for sale. Section 4A(3) in effect provides that a person whose bitches give birth to 5 or more litters in any period of 12 months shall be presumed to be carrying on a dog breeding business.* Those breeders whose rate of litter production brings them within section 4A(3) will therefore have to be licensed, without local authorities having to take additional steps to satisfy themselves as to whether or not a business is being carried out (unless no puppies have been sold – see paragraph 23 below about section 4A(5)). Decisions as to whether breeders with bitches producing fewer than 5 litters a year need to be licensed will depend on whether the persons concerned are carrying on a business as per section 4(2). That in turn can only be determined by local authorities on the facts of each case, in consultation as necessary with their legal advisers (and subject to any related decisions by the courts). It may, however, help local authorities to know that it was made clear in Parliament that the legislation was not intended to apply to hobby breeders, and that the expectation is that the "little test" in section 4A(3) will in practice catch most of the dog breeding businesses. There will however be exceptions, and there will no doubt be some breeders producing fewer than 5 litters who will have to be licensed.

22. *Under section 4A(4), bitches count towards the qualifying total if they are kept at any time during the 12 month period by the applicant/licence holder at the premises at which he/she is carrying on the business of breeding dogs for sale; if they are*

kept at those premises by any of his/her relatives (as defined in the Act – see section 4A(6)); if they are kept by him/her elsewhere; or if they are kept by any other person under a breeding arrangement made by him/her (as defined in the Act – see section 4A(6)). These provisions are designed to prevent evasion of licence controls by breeders distributing bitches amongst different people either at the main premises or at separate locations – if the bitches, regardless of location or "ownership", are in effect part of the same breeding business, they must be included in deciding whether a licence is needed. This means that where puppies are born at different premises, these premises must also be inspected at least annually, even if they are situated in other local authority areas (it is assumed local authorities concerned would liaise with each other in such cases).

23. *Section 4A(5) provides that breeders meeting the section 4A(3) "litter test" (see paragraph 21 above) will not be caught by that section if they can prove that none of the puppies born to bitches at their premises (or anywhere under a breeding arrangement) were sold during the 12 months period being considered.* This is expected to apply very rarely, and in effect would be likely to put any breeder affected beyond the scope of the Act.

24. *Section 4A(6) provides definitions of "breeding arrangements" and "relatives" referred to in section 4A(4) (paragraph 21 above), and section 4A(7) indicates that "premises" in section 4A includes a private dwelling.*

25. *Section 4B of the amended Act defines rearing establishments and "premises" in Scotland.*

26. Section 5 ensures the Act does not apply to keeping dogs at any premises on account of the Diseases of Animals Act 1950, and carries forward definitions of "local authority", "veterinary practitioner" and "veterinary surgeon".

Annex B: Additional provisions in the Breeding and Sale of Dogs (Welfare) Act 1999

Section 8 of the 1999 Act seeks, in the interests of animal welfare and consumer protection, to regulate the sale of puppies born at licensed breeding establishments, by ensuring as far as practicable that they can only be sold either by the breeder direct to the puppies' future owners, or at a licensed pet shop (that is a pet shop, the keeper of which is licensed under the Pet Animals Act 1951). Provision is also

Home Office Circular No. 53/1999

made for the puppies to be easily traceable to the licensed establishments where they were born. Details of these important changes are set out in the following paragraphs.

2. *Under section 8(1) of the 1999 Act, a keeper of a licensed breeding establishment will be guilty of an offence if he/she sells a dog anywhere other than at a licensed breeding establishment, a licensed pet shop or a licensed Scottish rearing establishment. He/she will also commit a offence if selling a dog directly to anyone, other than to a keeper of a licensed pet shop or a licensed Scottish rearing establishment, knowing or believing that the dog will be sold on to another person. It is a further offence for a licensed breeder to sell a dog that is less than eight weeks old to anyone other than a keeper of a licensed pet shop or a licensed Scottish rearing establishment. Dogs sold to such businesses by a licensed breeder must also have been bred at his/her establishment(s) and be wearing identification tags.*

3. *As regards keepers of Scottish rearing establishments, section 8(2) provides for a more or less similar set of offences, and also for the offence described in the following paragraph concerning pet shop owners.*

4. *Under section 8(3), the keeper of a licensed pet shop is guilty of an offence if he sells a dog not wearing the identification tag with which it had been supplied to him by a licensed breeder or licensed Scottish rearing establishment.* Note – local authorities will wish to inform keepers of licensed pet shops in their areas of this new requirement, and to advise them for their own protection to ensure that any dogs they receive from licensed breeding/Scottish rearing establishments are wearing identification tags. *It is a defence under section 8(4) for a pet shop owner to show he took all reasonable steps to avoid committing the offence.*

5. *Section 8(5) defines some of the terms used in the rest of section 8, and provides for identification tags/badges to display information indicating the licensed breeding establishments at which dogs are born and other information required by regulations. Relevant regulations are at Annex E* (not reproduced here).

6. *Section 9 details the penalties for offences under section 8. The maximum penalty on summary conviction is 3 months' imprisonment and/or a level 4 fine on the standard scale. A person found guilty under section 8(1) or (2) may also be*

liable to any of the licence cancellation and disqualification penalties laid down in section 3 of the amended 1973 Act (see paragraphs 16 and 17 in Annex A). A person found guilty of contravening a court order by having a dog whilst disqualified, or failing to deliver it to a specified person, and/or not paying for the care of the dog, is liable on summary conviction to a maximum penalty of 3 months' imprisonment and/or a level 4 fine on the standard scale. There are similar provisions to those in the amended 1973 Act for the making of representations, lodging appeals, and seeking removal of disqualifications.

Annex C: Additional Powers Under the Breeding of Dogs Act 1991

The 1991 Act extended powers of inspection for local authorities, for the purposes of the Breeding of Dogs Act 1973, to premises not covered by a licence under that Act.

2. Section 1 of the 1991 Act enables a local authority officer (or authorised veterinary surgeon or practitioner) to obtain a warrant from a justice of the peace (a sheriff in Scotland) to enter premises – excluding a private dwelling house – in which it is believed that a dog breeding business is being unlawfully carried out without a licence. Reasonable force may be used if necessary to effect entry, and all outbuildings, garages and sheds are open to comprehensive inspection. A warrant is valid for one month and power of entry can be gained at all reasonable times. The warrant should be produced if required, and any precautions specified should be adhered to, in order to prevent the spread among animals of diseases.

3. Section 2(1) of the Act makes it an offence to obstruct or delay entry/inspection. The maximum penalty is a level 3 fine (currently £1000) on the standard scale. Under section 2(2) a person convicted of the offence of running an unlicensed dog breeding establishment may be disqualified from keeping a licensed breeding establishment for such period as the court thinks fit, **and also disqualified from having custody of any dog of a specified description. The disqualification provisions of the 1973 Act, as amended by the 1999 Act, apply.**

. . .

DEFRA GUIDANCE CIRCULAR 2006

DOG CONTROL ORDERS

Guidance on Sections 55 to 67 of the Clean Neighbourhoods and Environment Act 2005

Overview

1. This guidance covers the Dog Control Orders (Prescribed Offences and Penalties, etc.) Regulations 2006 and the Dog Control Orders (Procedures) Regulations 2006, which implement sections 55 and 56 of the Clean Neighbourhoods and Environment Act 2005 (prescribing offences and penalties to be contained in, and procedures and forms for making, dog control orders), together with the other sections of the Act relating to dog control orders. Dog Control Orders replace the previous system of byelaws for the control of dogs, and also the Dogs (Fouling of Land) Act 1996, which has been repealed.

2. This guidance is intended for local authorities, parish councils and for other bodies with powers to make dog control orders; these are defined in the Clean Neighbourhoods and Environment Act 2005 as either primary or secondary authorities (see paragraphs 17 and 18 below). It will also be relevant for those interested in seeking to introduce dog control orders, and for dog owners who may be affected by them.

3. The two sets of Dog Control Order Regulations can be found at: www.opsi.gov.uk

General principles

4. The Dog Control Orders (Prescribed Offences and Penalties, etc.) Regulations provide for five offences which may be prescribed in a dog control order:
   (a) failing to remove dog faeces;
   (b) not keeping a dog on a lead;
   (c) not putting, and keeping, a dog on a lead when directed to do so by an authorised officer;
   (d) permitting a dog to enter land from which dogs are excluded;
   (e) taking more than a specified number of dogs onto land.

5. The penalty for committing an offence contained in a Dog Control Order is a maximum fine of level 3 on the standard scale (currently

£1,000). Alternatively, the opportunity to pay a fixed penalty may be offered in place of prosecution.

6. Both primary and secondary authorities may make Dog Control Orders, provided that they are satisfied that an order is justified, and have followed the necessary procedures (see part 2). The offences are described and the forms of the orders are prescribed in the Schedules to the Dog Control Orders (Prescribed Offences and Penalties, etc.) Regulations, and the exact wording of the description of the offence must be used (minor variations of the wording in the other parts of an order are permissible). A Dog Control Order may be brought into force no sooner than 14 days (or longer if preferred) after it has been made; there is no requirement for an order to be confirmed by the Secretary of State. The transitional arrangements for moving from current arrangements to the new system are described in paragraphs 24–27. In brief, existing dog byelaws and designations under the Dogs (Fouling of Land) Act 1996 are not affected by the introduction of the new system.

Land subject to dog control orders

7. Under section 57 of the Clean Neighbourhoods and Environment Act 2005 a Dog Control Order can be made in respect of any land which is open to the air and to which the public are entitled or permitted to have access (with or without payment). As for the provisions on litter, land which is covered is treated as land 'open to the air' if it is open to the air on at least one side. It therefore applies to any covered place with a significant permanent opening on at least one side, such as a bus shelter or garage forecourt that remains open to the air at all times.

8. Section 57 gives the Secretary of State power to designate types of land which, although they fall within the definition above, are not to be subject to all or some Dog Control Orders. The Control of Dogs (Non-application to Designated Land) (England) Order 2006 designates:

- forestry commission land in respect of all Dog Control Orders;
- roads (including highways) in respect of a Dog Control Order excluding dogs from land specified in the order.

9. A 'road' is defined in section 142 of the Road Traffic Regulation Act 1984 as (in England and Wales) 'any length of highway or of any other road to which the public has access, and includes bridges over which a road passes.' This is a wide definition, and includes not only public

rights of way, including footpaths, but also ways to which the public has access by permission of the landowner, rather than by right.

It therefore includes roads and footpaths through private estates provided the public has access to them.

10. All other land that meets the definition in section 57 (other than that exempted under the provisions described in the next paragraph) may be made subject to a Dog Control Order (but see paragraph 31). In particular, the restrictions on the types of land that could be made subject to designation under the Dogs (Fouling of Land) Act 1996 do not apply to Dog Control Orders in respect of dog fouling. There are special consultation and notification requirements for access land under the Countryside and Rights of Way Act 2000; see paragraph 32.

11. Under subsection (5) any person or body with powers under a private act of Parliament to regulate land, by means of byelaws or in any other way, may give notice in writing to the relevant primary and secondary authorities that the land in question is to be excluded from the dog control regime (but see also paragraph 14).

Defences/exemptions

12. There are defences in all Dog Control Orders of:
   (a) having a reasonable excuse for failing to comply with an order; or
   (b) acting with the consent of the owner or occupier of the land, or of any other person or authority which has control of the land.

13. Under (a), no offence is committed if a person in control of a dog has a reasonable excuse for failing to comply with an order. This would include those responsible for dogs such as police dogs which are on land to investigate or prevent crime. In such cases it will be for local authorities to decide whether to pursue cases where this defence is invoked; if they choose to do so it will be for the Courts to decide whether someone had a reasonable excuse for failing to comply with a dog control order. However, the prescribed Fouling of Land by Dogs Order in Schedule 1 to the Dog Control Orders (Prescribed Offences and Penalties, etc.) Regulations states specifically that being unaware of a dog's defecation, or not having a device or other suitable means of removing the faeces is not a reasonable excuse for failing to comply with the order.

14. Under (b) no offence is committed if a person in charge of a dog acts with the consent of the person who owns or is otherwise in control of the land. There is no specific exemption in the Regulations

Defra Guidance Circular 2006

for working dogs, but this provision will cover any dog that is working on land with the consent of the person in control of the land.

15. Dog control orders provide exemptions in particular cases for registered blind people, and for deaf people and for other people with disabilities who make use of trained assistance dogs. Anyone with any type of assistance dog is not subject to a Dog Control Order excluding dogs from specified land in respect of his or her assistance dog, and anyone other than a registered deaf person (whose disability will not prevent him or her from being aware of and removing dog faeces) is similarly exempt from a Dog Control Orders on the fouling of land. These exemptions are not relevant to the other three offences which can be the subject of Dog Control Orders.

16. Both of the exemptions mentioned in the previous paragraph refer to a person whose ability to move 'everyday objects' is affected. Paragraph C18 of the 'Guidance on matters to be taken into account in determining questions relating to the definition of disability', the following items are listed to illustrate what 'everyday objects' might include: books; a kettle of water; bags of shopping; a briefcase; an overnight bag; or, a chair or other piece of light furniture. A copy of the guidance can be downloaded from the Disability Rights Commission's website at: www.drc gb.org/documents/definition_guidance_final.doc

Primary and secondary authorities

17. Primary and secondary authorities are defined in section 58 of the Clean Neighbourhoods and Environment Act. Primary authorities in England are:

    (a) a district council;
    (b) a county council for an area where there is no district council;
    (c) a London borough council;
    (d) the Common Council of the City of London; and
    (e) the Council of the Isles of Scilly.

18. In England parish councils constitute secondary authorities. In addition the Secretary of State has the power to designate other bodies as secondary authorities. This power enables bodies which have byelaw-making powers in respect of dogs, for example some commons conservators under private legislation (but see also paragraph 11), to be designated as secondary authorities, and so be able to make Dog Control Orders rather than byelaws. If such a body is not designated, it will continue to be able to make byelaws for dog control purposes.

However these can be overridden by a Dog Control Order made by a primary or secondary authority (see paragraph 22 below).

19. Section 63 sets out the arrangements for eliminating potential conflicts where the powers of primary and secondary authorities overlap. In sub-section (1) it states that a secondary authority may not make a Dog Control Order in relation to an offence on a specified area of land if a primary authority has already made an order in respect of the same offence on the same land. Similarly, if a primary authority decides to make a dog control order in respect of an offence on a specified area of land, any existing order made by a secondary authority for the same offence on the same land lapses.

20. These arrangements do not prevent a secondary authority from making a Dog Control Order in respect of a different offence on land that is already subject to a primary authority order in relation to another offence. For example, a District Council (primary authority) might make a Fouling of Land by Dogs Order applying throughout its area. This would not prevent a parish council (secondary authority) from making an order to exclude dogs altogether from, say, playing fields within its jurisdiction.

21. In order to avoid potential conflicts, the Dog Control Orders (Procedures) Regulations 2006 require primary and secondary authorities to consult each other before coming forward with proposals for Dog Control Orders.

22. Sub-section 63(2) of the Act provides for the resolution of any conflict between parish councils and other bodies designated as secondary authorities. In these circumstances, the parish council is treated as if it were a primary authority; as a result any Dog Control Order it makes in respect of an offence will have priority over one made by another secondary authority for the same offence.

Other byelaw-making powers

23. Powers to make byelaws affecting dogs can continue to be used but only in relation to offences that cannot be prescribed in a Dog Control Order.

Transitional arrangements

24. Section 64 of the Clean Neighbourhoods and Environment Act 2005 sets out the provisions that apply to existing dog byelaws; similar arrangements apply to land designated under the Dogs (Fouling of Land) Act 1996.

25. Under sub-section (1) from the date the Regulations came into force no new dog byelaws can be made relating to any of the offences set out in the Regulations. The Dogs (Fouling of Land) Act 1996 was repealed with effect from the same date, so no further land can be designated under that Act.

26. Existing byelaws remain in force indefinitely, and can continue to be enforced as normal. However, under subsection (4) if an Authority makes a Dog Control Order in respect of an offence on a specified area of land, any byelaw made by a primary or secondary authority dealing with the same offence on the same land lapses. Other byelaws, dealing with either the same offence on different land, or with different offences on the same land, are not affected. Similarly, under subsection (5) if an action or failure to take action is an offence under a Dog Control Order and contravenes a byelaw made by another body, it will no longer be an offence under the byelaw.

27. Although the Dogs (Fouling of Land) Act 1996 has been repealed, the Order commencing the repeal provision preserves the offence under the 1996 Act in respect of any designation orders made prior to the repeal. Therefore any orders made under the 1996 Act will continue to have effect indefinitely, and enforcement through fixed penalty notices (fixed at £50) and prosecution can continue as normal. This includes Police and Community Support Officers (PCSOs) and persons accredited under the Police Reform Act 2002. However, if any type of Dog Control Order is made that applies to land already subject to the 1996 Act, the 1996 Act ceases to have effect in respect of the land subject to the Dog Control Order. This also applies in respect of Dog Control Orders made by secondary authorities. For example, if a district has designated all its land under the 1996 Act, but makes any type of Dog Control Order in respect of a park, the 1996 Act will cease to apply in respect of the park, but will continue to have effect in the rest of the district.

Making a Dog Control Order

28. The procedure for making a Dog Control Order is set out in regulation 3 of the Dog Control Orders (Procedures) Regulations 2006. It is important that this procedure is adhered to, since a failure to do so will invalidate the order.

29. It is also important for any authority considering a Dog Control Order to be able to show that this is a necessary and proportionate response to problems caused by the activities of dogs and those in charge of them.

30. The authority needs to balance the interests of those in charge of dogs against the interests of those affected by the activities of dogs, bearing in mind the need for people, in particular children, to have access to dog-free areas and areas where dogs are kept under strict control, and the need for those in charge of dogs to have access to areas where they can exercise their dogs without undue restrictions. A failure to give due consideration to these factors could make any subsequent Dog Control Order vulnerable to challenge in the Courts.

31. Authorities should also consider how easy a Dog Control Order would be to enforce, since failure properly to enforce could undermine the effect of an order. This is particularly the case for orders that exclude dogs completely from areas of land. These will be easier to enforce if the land is enclosed. However, such orders should not be ruled out for unenclosed land where a special case for them can be made, for example to provide dog-free sections on beaches.

32. If an authority is considering making a Dog Control Order which would affect open access land (land subject to Part 1 of the Countryside and Rights of Way Act 2000) it must consult the appropriate access authority (the local highway authority or the National Park Authority for land within a National Park); the relevant authority (the National Park Authority for land within a National Park; the Forestry Commission for land that has been dedicated as access land under section 16 of the Countryside and Rights of Way Act 2000 and which consists wholly or predominantly of woodland, or the Countryside Agency in all other cases) if it is not also the access authority; and the local access forum. There are already comprehensive dog control provisions which may be applied to access land, including if necessary the banning of dogs. An authority should therefore pay particular attention to the views of these bodies in deciding whether any proposed order affecting open access land is necessary.

Procedures for making a Dog Control Order

33. The Dog Control Orders (Procedures) Regulations 2006 require that before it can make a Dog Control Order, an authority must consult any other primary or secondary authority within the area in which a Dog Control Order is being made.

34. Authorities must also publish a notice describing the proposed order in a local newspaper circulating in the same area as the land to which the order would apply and invite representations on the proposal. The notice must:

Defra Guidance Circular 2006

(a) identify the land to which the order will apply (and if it is access land state that that is the case);
(b) summarise the order;
(c) if the order will refer to a map, say where the map can be inspected. This must be at an address in the authority's area, be free of charge, and at all reasonable hours during the consultation period;
(d) give the address to which, and the date by which, representations must be sent to the authority. The final date for representation must be at least 28 days after the publication of the notice.

35. At the end of the consultation period the authority must consider any representations that have been made. If it then decides to proceed with the order, it must decide when the order will come into force. This must be at least 14 days from the date on which it was made.

36. Once an order has been made the authority must, at least 7 days before it comes into force, publish a notice in a local newspaper circulating in the same area as the land to which the order applies stating:
(a) that the order has been made; and
(b) where the order may be inspected and copies of it obtained.

37. Where practicable, a copy of the notice must also be published on the authority's website. Also, where the order affects access land the authority should send a copy of the notice to the access authority, the local access forum and the Countryside Agency.

38. If, after considering representations on a proposal to make an order an authority decides significantly to amend its proposal, it must start the procedure again, publishing a new notice describing the amended proposal.

Amendments

39. Amendments to existing Dog Control Orders must be in the form set out in Schedule 6 to the DCOs (Offences and Penalties) Regulations (minor variables are permissible) and must be advertised, and if appropriate, brought into force in the same way as a new order.

Revocation

40. Authorities proposing to revoke an existing Dog Control Order must place a notice in a newspaper (circulating in the area in which the order applies) inviting representations in response to the proposal (see DCOs (Procedures) Regulations, regulation 4). The notice must:

Defra Guidance Circular 2006

(a) identify the land to which the order currently applies;
(b) summarise the order;
(c) state that representations may be made in writing or by e-mail within 28 days of the publication of the notice, and the address and e-mail address to which representations may be sent.

41. Where the order proposed to be revoked covers access land, the access authority, the local access forum and the relevant authority must also be consulted.

42. Authorities must consider any representations made within the period stated in the notice. Should the authority decide to go ahead and revoke the order, another notice must be published to notify the public of the decision and what date the revocation will have effect, which cannot be before the date on which the final notice is published. If the revoked order applied to access land, authorities must also notify the appropriate access authorities after an order has been revoked. Authorities should also make information about the revoked order available on the website (but only where a website is available).

Erecting signage

43. Regulation 3(4)(a) of the Dog Control Orders (Procedures) Regulations provides the legal requirement that, where practicable, signs must be placed summarising the order on land to which a new order applies, thereby informing the public that land is subject to an order. For example, if an order were made excluding dogs from a park, copies of the order should be placed at the entrances to the park when it was first made, and permanent signs should be erected informing the public that dogs are not permitted in the park. Where a Dog Control Order applies to a large area of land, for example, an order in respect of fouling by dogs, it may not be feasible to post copies of the order on the land, but signs warning the public that it is an offence not to clear up dog faeces should be placed at regular intervals.

44. Where orders are made that apply only at certain times of the day or year, any signs provided to summarise the effect of an order should also make clear the periods in which the Dog Control Order will apply.

Setting the maximum number of dogs

45. When setting the maximum number of dogs the most important factor for authorities to consider is the maximum number of dogs which a person can control; expert advice is that this should not

exceed six. Authorities should also take into account the views of dog owning and non-dog owning residents within the area to which the order will apply to establish what they consider to be an appropriate maximum number taking into account all the circumstances in the area. A key factor here will be whether children frequently use the area.

Fixed penalty notices

Note: This section covers the basic principles of fixed penalty notices for Dog Control Orders and outlines changes introduced by the Clean Neighbourhoods and Environment Act 2005. However, detailed information on their use is provided in the separate guidance available on fixed penalties; and litter authorities, parish councils, authorised officers, Police Community Support Officers (PCSOs) and persons accredited into Community Safety Accreditation Schemes are strongly advised to consult this guidance when using the fixed penalty notice provisions.

46. For primary authorities, the general principles that apply to the issue of fixed penalty notices apply equally to notices issued for offences under dog control orders. Secondary authorities, however, have powers in relation to dog control orders that they do not usually have in other areas. In particular, secondary authorities may specify the amount of a fixed penalty for orders they have made as well as providing for discounts for early payment (subject to the constraints provided in the Environmental Offences (Fixed Penalties) (Miscellaneous Provisions) Regulations 2006). In this respect secondary authorities have the same powers as primary authorities and should follow the relevant provisions in the Fixed Penalty Notice Guidance.

47. Fixed penalties for offences under dog control orders may be issued by authorised officers under section 59(1) and (2). Section 59(11) defines who are 'authorised officers':

- Employees of primary and secondary authorities who are authorised for this purpose.
- Any person authorised (including employees of that person) in writing by a primary or secondary authority in pursuance of arrangements made by that person and the relevant authority.

Section 62 extends the same powers to Police Community Support Officers and other persons accredited by Chief Police Officers under the Police Reform Act 2002.

48. In connection with dog control order offences, authorised officers of primary and secondary authorities have the power to require the name and address of a person they wish to issue with a fixed penalty notice. In such cases failure to supply these details or to give a false name and address to an authorised officer is an offence for which a maximum fine of level 3 (currently £1000) on the standard scale may be given upon conviction.

49. In relation to secondary authorities, any person who may be authorised to issue fixed penalties on their behalf, other than Police Community Support Officers, and other persons accredited under the Police Reform Act 2002, must first satisfy certain conditions linked to training. These conditions are specified in the Environmental Offences (Fixed Penalties) (Miscellaneous Provisions) Regulations 2006 (regulation 6).

DEFRA GUIDANCE CIRCULAR 2007

October 2007

Guidance on Stray Dogs

Introduction

1. This guidance covers the expectations of the legal duties that rest with local authorities in England and Wales with respect to stray dogs, including the Environmental Protection Act 1990 (the 1990 Act) and the Environmental Protection (Stray Dogs) Regulations 1992 (the 1992 Regulations), the Control of Dogs Order 1992 (the 1992 Order) and other matters related to the control of dogs.

2. This guidance includes references to animal welfare conditions as set out in section 9 of the Animal Welfare Act 2006 (which imposes a statutory duty of care on all owners and keepers to provide for the welfare needs of their animals – "a duty of care") and the kenneling standards published by the Chartered Institute of Environmental Health, entitled Model Licence Conditions and Guidance for Dog Boarding Establishments.

3. It is intended that this guidance is considered alongside the legislation. It has been prepared for local authorities, including other persons contracted to work on their behalf, and other organisations or people working in partnership with local authorities in connection with the collection, or detainment of stray dogs.

4. Section 68 of the Clean Neighbourhoods and Environment Act 2005 will be commenced on 6 April 2008. It removes from legislation references to the police seizing stray dogs and the duty to accept any brought to them. In order to inform the public about the arrangements for stray dogs the police are expected to advertise in police stations any information given to them by local authorities such as locations where strays may be taken and any phone numbers for officers or information, with particular reference to out of office hours contact and the cover provided.

5. This means that from April 2008 local authorities will be solely responsible for discharging stray dog functions. In short, the minimum requirement of the extended duty is that where practicable local authorities provide a place to which dogs can be taken outside normal office hours (referred to in this guidance as an 'acceptance point'). Local authorities are not expected to provide a round-the-clock call out

service. It is possible that the public will continue to contact the police in relation to stray dogs. Authorities are therefore strongly recommended to supply their local police stations with relevant details such as phone numbers and addresses of acceptance points, especially those that operate outside office hours. It is strongly advised that posters detailing new provisions should be placed at any collection point no longer used to accept stray dogs in the area, and all other places that are relevant to changes in provision.

6. The police retain duties with regard to dealing with dangerous dogs and dogs found to be worrying livestock. Authorities and the police should maintain a working relationship so that such issues can be dealt with effectively.

7. An extra £4 million a year is included in the revenue support grant to fund the local authority costs of the extended duty in England and Wales.

8. This guidance comprises two parts. Part 1 sets out what is required by authorities, and any third parties (e.g. contractors such as private kennels), when discharging their duty. Part 2 covers ancillary issues including partnership working, training, contracts and other sources of general information.

Part 1 – Discharging the duty

Responsible body

9. Sections 149 and 150 of the 1990 Act provide the duty for local authorities to collect and detain stray dogs. The local authorities responsible for discharging the functions of the 1990 Act are defined in section 149(11), in relation to England and Wales, as district councils, London Borough Councils, the Common Council of the City of London and the Council of the Isles of Scilly.

Appointment of an officer

10. Under section 149(1), local authorities must appoint an officer for the purpose of discharging their stray dog functions. Whilst these functions can be delegated to other persons under section 149(2), the appointed officer retains overall responsibility for ensuring that the authority's stray dog functions are discharged correctly.

11. Authorities may find it practical to appoint a senior officer under section 149(1), but to delegate the day to day responsibilities to dog wardens or other persons such as a contractor. If responsibility is

delegated the officer should ensure they have appropriate training and skills. For the purposes of this guidance, the term "officer" means an officer appointed under section 149(1) or a person to whom functions are delegated under section 149(2).

Seizure of stray dogs

12. There is no statutory definition of a stray dog. However, any dog found in a public place, or private place where it should not be, which appears to be without its owner and not under the control of its owner or a person representing them, may be seized and detained as a stray dog by an appropriate person.

13. Where an officer finds in a public place a dog he believes to be stray, he shall (where practicable) seize and detain the dog. However if the dog is on land or premises which is not a public place, the officer must first gain the permission of the owner or occupier of the land or premises. Section 149(11) defines "public place" in England and Wales as any highway and any other place to which the public are entitled or permitted to have access.

14. Authorities must publicise the phone numbers of relevant officers so that the public can report stray dogs. Authorities are advised to publicise such phone numbers as widely as possible including on their website and at local police stations.

15. Authorities are not required to offer a night-time call-out service to seize and detain stray dogs seen or found by the public. However, contact numbers for out of hours cover should be widely publicised to enable 'finders' to take a dog to an acceptance point. As a minimum this should include websites, police and authority offices and acceptance points (past and present).

16. The responsibility for functions can be delegated to third parties. Authorities are expected to provide the most cost effective service possible.

Identifying the owner

17. The Control of Dogs Order 1992 provides that dogs must wear a collar and tag giving the name and address of the owner when in a public place. In most cases, it is expected that this will enable the owner to be identified with relative ease. Failure to comply with this direction is an offence under Animal Health Act 1981 and such dogs may be seized, even if a person is in charge of such a dog. Moreover, the 1992 Order places a duty on local authorities to enforce the

Defra Guidance Circular 2007

requirement for dogs to wear a collar and tag in a public place. The officer is therefore recommended to keep careful notes of such incidents for evidence in legal cases.

18. Due to the prevalence of permanent identification methods, such as micro-chipping and tattooing, local authorities are advised to be adequately equipped to identify micro-chipped or tattooed dogs and that dogs are scanned at the earliest possible opportunity. Scanners/readers employed by authorities should be compatible with as wide a range of formats as possible. In respect of tattooed dogs officers can contact the National Dog Tattoo Register for registered owners' details. It is also advisable that scanners can be accessed by waste management teams and where practicable direction is given on checking dead dogs removed for identification.

Identifying the owners of prohibited type dogs

19. The ownership of four types of dog is prohibited under section 1 of the Dangerous Dogs Act 1991 (as amended 1997). The dogs covered by the ban are of the type known as either: the Pit Bull Terrier, the Japanese Tosa, the Dogo Argentino or the Fila Braziliero. Such breeds can be difficult to identify and therefore it is recommended that all officers have access to the guidance on identifying these types of dog which can be found at www.defra.gov.uk/animalh/welfare/domestic/ddogsleaflet.pdf

20. Ownership of the above types of dog is permitted only where the dog is registered on the Index of Exempted Dogs and it is kept in compliance with the requirements of the Index. Exempted dogs have to be neutered, tattooed, and microchipped, and have to be on a lead and muzzled at all times when in a public place. Owners also have to maintain insurance against their dogs injuring third parties. It is an offence under the 1991 Act to allow an exempted dog to stray.

21. Where officers suspect and/or identify a prohibited type of dog which is on the Index (by either a tattoo and/or microchip) they can, if necessary, contact the Index of Exempted Dogs to help identify the owner of the dog. The Index can be contacted on 07000 783651. In addition officers will need to contact the local police force who will want to consider what further actions are necessary against the owner under the Dangerous Dogs Act.

22. Where officers identify a prohibited type of dog which is not on the Index of Exempted Dogs (i.e. is not microchipped and tattooed) they will need to contact the local police force who will want to consider what action is necessary under the Dangerous Dogs Act.

Return of seized dogs to their owners

23. Where officers can identify the dog owner they must, under section 149(4) of the 1990 Act, serve notice on the owner or person whose address is given on the collar. Such a notice must state:
- that the dog has been seized;
- where it is being kept; and
- that it will be disposed of unless it is claimed within seven clear days after the service of the notice and the full amount liable under subsection 149(5) is paid.

24. Under section 149(5), the authority may charge the owner all expenses incurred during the dog's detention plus a further prescribed amount. The expenses should be calculated as the per day kennel cost plus any costs involved in detaining the dog. Authorities should also include any charges incurred in respect of injured dogs that receive treatment. The additional amount is prescribed in the 1992 Regulations as £25. Any such monies received should be used to discharge ongoing stray dog functions.

25. An authority is within its rights to detain the dog until the owner has paid the full amount.

Accepting strays found by other persons

26. Section 150 provides the duty for any finder of a stray dog to return the dog to its owner (if owner can be identified) or take the dog to the local authority for the area in which the dog was found. The authority must treat such a dog as though it had been seized by an officer under section 149.

27. Authorities must, where practicable, provide at least one acceptance point to which dogs can be taken round the clock. In practice, authorities may have one acceptance point during normal office hours such as council offices and another in use outside office hours such as third party kennels, or to make use of third party kennels at all times. The authority must publicise as widely as possible, including on its website, the place(s) to which strays can be taken, the hours of operation and the phone number of the reception staff at the place where they may take stray dogs.

28. It is possible that finders of stray dogs may continue to take them to police stations, where dogs are no longer accepted. The police are not required to take the stray dog and to enable the finder to take the dog to the correct location, officers must therefore ensure that the details of the authority's dog reception centre(s) and hours of operation, and any

relevant telephone numbers, are given to every police station in the area of the authority.

Finders that request to keep a stray dog

29. Any person who finds and takes a stray dog to the local authority can request to keep the dog under section 150(2) of the 1990 Act. The Regulations specify that if the finder requests to keep the dog he must give his name and address to the officer. The officer must make reasonable attempts to contact the owner to give him reasonable opportunity to collect the dog.

30. The Regulations also require the officer to determine whether the finder is a suitable person to keep the dog. The officer must inform the finder verbally and in writing that he is obliged to keep the dog (if unclaimed by the owner) for at least one month and that failure to comply with that obligation is a criminal offence. The maximum penalty on summary conviction is level 2 on the standard scale.

31. The Act does not purport to deal with the civil law on ownership in this context. The finder has a duty to keep the dog for 28 days after taking possession of it, however they do not become the legal owner of the dog. The officer should make clear to the finder that if a person claiming to be the rightful owner of the dog – and can prove it – requests the return of the dog, then the finder may have to relinquish his custodianship. Disputes over ownership would be subject to the usual civil common law principles governing possession and title. Relinquishment might be required at any time and would not be governed by section 150(3) – the intention of which is simply to prevent a finder abandoning or turning the dog loose to become stray again.

32. An authority is entitled to sell or give a dog to a person or other party if the original owner has not reclaimed the dog. However, the intention is not that the recipient (where not the original owner) is charged the prescribed amounts before a dog is released.

Register of detained dogs

33. Under section 149(8) the officer must keep a register of dogs seized or brought to the authority and those in the possession of 'finders'. Details of newly detained dogs should be added to the register at the earliest possible opportunity. Breed posters and colour charts are a useful guide in identifying dogs. The particulars that must be recorded in the register are prescribed in the Regulations as:

- a brief description of dog, including breed (if known), colour and any distinctive characteristics or markings, tattoos or scars;
- any information contained on collar/tag, or otherwise carried by the dog, this would include micro-chipping;
- date, time and place of the seizure;
- if a notice is served on the owner, details of when/where served.

34. Where the officer disposes of a dog the register must record the date of disposal; method of disposal; the name and address of purchaser and price (if sold), person to whom the dog was gifted or person effecting the destruction. Where the dog is returned to a person claiming to be the owner, the register must record the name and address of that person and the date of return.

35. The register must be made available for inspection by the public free of charge at all reasonable times. Authorities may apply a charge for providing a copy of all or part of the register.

Detention of stray dogs

36. Authorities must make provision to house stray dogs they seize and those brought in by other persons. Authorities will need to ensure that there are appropriate arrangements for receiving and dealing with stray dogs found or reported out of usual officer hours. Also see section on acceptance of dogs found by others. This can be done through third-party kennels.

37. Kennel facilities should comply with the standards specified by the Chartered Institute of Environmental Health. They also need to comply with their general duty of care under the Animal Welfare Act 2006.

38. The authority must detain for seven days any dogs seized or brought to them. The seven day period should commence from either the day of the seizure or the day in which the notice was served under section 149(4); whichever is the later. Under section 149(9) the officer has a duty to properly feed and maintain any stray dog in his custody under section 9 of the Animal Welfare Act that specifies that an animal's basic welfare needs must be provided for by the carer of that animal.

39. Authorities are expected to treat any dogs that are injured or require treatment to keep them alive, unless the costs of doing so are excessive or if the dog's condition is such that it would be more humane to provide euthanasia. In order to minimise costs it is recommended that authorities come to a formal arrangement with local veterinary

surgeons. It is recommended to authorities that they consider making contractual provision for such arrangements; these should include details on emergency treatment they will fund. Authorities should also agree a protocol with third parties such as dog welfare organisations in respect of treatment of dogs they take charge of; to state explicitly the extent of the veterinary treatments the local authority will fund.

40. An officer may have a dog destroyed before the seven day period has elapsed if he is of the view that it must be done to avoid suffering. But officers must consult with a veterinary surgeon prior to making such a decision, and the euthanasia should only be effected by a veterinary surgeon except in cases where the animal is in considerable pain or distress where an officer should take action immediately.

Disposal of stray dogs

41. If a stray has not been collected by its owner after seven days, the officer may under section 149(6) dispose of the dog:
- by selling it or giving it to a person who will in his opinion care properly for the dog;
- by selling it or giving it to an establishment for the reception of stray dogs; or
- by euthanizing it in a manner to cause as little pain and suffering as possible.

42. No dog may be disposed of for the purposes of vivisection.

43. Euthanasia should only be considered after all other avenues have been explored to save the dog by re-homing. It should be noted that banned breeds cannot be re-homed. Euthanasia must only be effected by a veterinary surgeon and in a manner causing as little pain and suffering to the dog as possible.

44. Where a dog is disposed of under section 149(6)(a) or (b) to a person acting in good faith, officers will need to satisfy themselves of the suitability of such persons or establishments. Under section 149(7) the ownership of the dog is vested in the recipient and this provision also protects anyone who has acquired the dog in good faith. It should be noted that this situation is different to that of a finder who elects to keep the dog under section 150(2).

Records keeping

45. Authorities and their agents are required to keep records of stray dogs as set out at sections 149 and 150 of the 1990 Act, and in the 1992 Regulations. The register shall be available, at all reasonable times,

for inspection by the public free of charge. In addition, upon commencement of Section 68 of the Clean Neighbourhoods and Environment Act 2005, Government expects authorities to be able to furnish it with statistics on the total number of dogs accepted out of hours, the total number of days dogs accepted out of hours have been kept in kennels, the number of those dogs returned to their owner and the number that by necessity were put down.

Part 2 – Ancillary issues

Lost, stolen and abandoned dogs

46. Authorities will be aware of the intrinsic link between lost, stolen and stray dogs, but should note the distinction between reporting lost property and reporting a stray. Whilst the local authority is responsible for strays, the police are responsible for recording reported lost property, including dogs, and also dog theft, which is a criminal offence. Local authority officers will record details of any reported stray dog, but they should also advise owners of lost or stolen dogs to file a report with the police. With respect to abandoned dogs, kennels or welfare organisations should be contacted to see if they could rehome the dog.

Dead dogs

47. In the event that officers find a dead dog they should make every attempt to establish the identity of the dog and its owner and, where appropriate, give the owner the opportunity to collect the dog. If practicable dead dogs should be scanned to identify the owner.

Education

48. Education is a key element in reducing the number of stray dogs and dangerous dogs and protecting the welfare of animals. It is therefore important that officers consider the most effective methods for how they can promote and raise the profile of responsible dog ownership within their area. This may include visits to national/local dog welfare or dog owning organisations, kennels and schools in their area. Officers should publish any information on responsible dog ownership on their website.

Neutering

49. Authorities should consider whether there is a need to offer subsidised or free neutering; particularly authorities with high numbers

of stray dogs in their area. Many dog welfare organisations, charities and kennels offer free or subsidised neutering, so authorities are advised to contact any such organisations in their area to establish whether they can come to a local agreement.

Microchipping

50. The onus of ensuring dogs are permanently identified is with the owner themselves, but as a tool for reducing the number of strays authorities should consider the benefits of offering discounted or free micro-chipping, perhaps in conjunction with local dog kennels or welfare organisations.

Training

51. Authorities are strongly advised to ensure that anyone involved in discharging their stray dog duty is adequately trained to do so. Training should be provided by a reputable and accredited trainer.

Partnership working

52. For authorities with minimum budgets developing a partnership approach with local kennels and welfare organisations will be key to addressing problems with stray dogs in the locality, particularly in areas with high numbers of strays. Authorities should seek to develop protocols with any bodies that play a role in dealing with stray dogs. Authorities should explore the benefits of working with other local authorities in the area; authorities in Hampshire have established such a partnership. Contracts should be reviewed regularly to ensure service delivery is of a consistently high standard and that tendering is competitive.

53. Authorities are expected to provide a cost effective service, which can often be delivered through appropriate use of third-party kennels. Tasks can be delegated to other parties, however it should be noted that overall responsibility rests with the officer appointed at section 149 of the 1990 Act.

54. It is at the discretion of the local authority whether council owned kennels or private councils under contract are used to fulfil this duty, however they are expected to comply with the Chartered Institute of Environmental Health's Standards.

Other sources of general information

About animal health and welfare from Defra, including the Animal Welfare Act 2007, prohibited animals and the duty of care:

Defra Guidance Circular 2007

http://www.defra.gov.uk/animalh/index.htm

http://www.defra.gov.uk/animalh/welfare/domestic/ddogsleaflet.pdf

http://www.defra.gov.uk/animalh/welfare/act/affect.htm#2

Chartered Institute of Environmental Health: www.cieh.org

Dogs Trust:

www.dogstrust.org

Kennel Club:

www.the-kennel-club.org.uk

Royal Society for the Prevention of Cruelty to Animals:

www.rspca.org

Index

Note: The following Index covers references to material contained in the first section of this book – Part I: A Summary of the Law.

Advertising rewards
  generally, 3
Agricultural land
  guard dogs, and, 47
  trespass, and, 22
Animal Welfare Act 2006
  animals in distress, 55–56
  baiting, 52–53
  codes of practice, 55
  disqualification from ownership
    generally, 57–58
    termination, 58–59
  docking dogs' tails, 50–51
  enforcement powers, 56
  fighting, 51–53
  improvement notices, 53
  introduction, 49
  mutilation, 49–50
  licensing, 54–55
  miscellaneous provisions, 59
  poisoning, 51–52
  post-conviction powers
    deprivation of ownership, 57
    destruction of animals, 58
    disqualification from ownership, 57–58
    fines, 57
    forfeiture of equipment used in offences, 58
    imprisonment, 57
    licensing-related orders, 58
    pending appeals, 58
    reimbursement of expenses, 59
    seizure of an animal, 58
  prevention of harm
    baiting, 52–53
    docking dogs' tails, 50–51
    fighting, 51–53
    mutilation, 49–50
    poisoning, 51–52
    unnecessary suffering, 49
    wrestling, 52–53
  promotion
    duty of responsible person, 53
    improvement notices, 53
    regulations, 54
    transfer of animals by sale or prize, 54
  prosecutions
    local authorities' power, 56
    penalties, 57–59
    time limits, 57
  registration, 54–55
  suffering, 49
  transfer of animals by sale or prize to persons under 16, 54
  unnecessary suffering, 49
  wrestling, 52–53
Animals in distress
  welfare of dogs, and, 55–56
Baiting
  prevention of harm, and, 52–53
Boarding kennels
  generally, 44–45
Breeding kennels
  generally, 45–46
Byelaws
  nuisance, and, 26–27
Caveat emptor
  sale of dogs, and, 4
Codes of practice
  welfare of dogs, and, 55
Collars
  generally, 35–36
Conditions
  sale of dogs, and, 4–5

485

Index

Damage
  owners' responsibilities, and, 9
Dangerous dogs
  background, 28–29
  current position, 29–33
  generally, 28
Diseases
  generally, 12–13
Distress
  welfare of dogs, and, 55–56
Docking dogs' tails
  prevention of harm, and, 50–51
Dog control orders
  generally, 18–19
Dogs
  See also under individual headings
  boarding, 44–45
  breeding, 45–46
  collars, 35–36
  dangerous dogs, 28–33
  diseases, and, 12–13
  export, 72
  ferocious dogs, 33–34
  game birds, and, 64–66
  guard dogs, 47–48
  hunting, and, 66–68
  import, 69–71
  killing and injuring, 39–43
  nuisance, and, 25–27
  owners' responsibilities, 9–11
  ownership, 3
  performing dogs, 61–63
  roads, and, 14–19
  sale, 4–8
  strays, 36–38
  theft, 3
  trespass, and, 20–24
  welfare, 49–60
Enforcement powers
  welfare of dogs, and, 56
Export
  generally, 72
Ferocious dogs
  generally, 33–34
Fighting
  prevention of harm, and, 51–53

Films
  performing dogs, and, 63
Food safety
  nuisance, and, 27
Fouling pavements and public open spaces
  generally, 16–17
Game
  introduction, 64
  licences, 65
  poaching, 65
  prohibited times for taking game, 64
  protection from dogs, 65–66
Guard dogs
  generally, 47–48
Hunting
  generally, 66–68
Hygiene
  nuisance, and, 27
Illegal sales
  sale of dogs, and, 8
Implied conditions
  sale of dogs, and, 5
Import
  generally, 69–71
Improvement notices
  welfare of dogs, and, 53
Kennels
  boarding, 44–45
  breeding, 45–46
Killing and injuring dogs
  civil law, 39–41
  criminal law, 41–43
Leads
  generally, 15–16
Licensing
  game, and, 65
  welfare of dogs, and, 54–55
Livestock
  killing and injuring dogs, and, 39
  trespass, and, 21–22
Motorways
  generally, 17
Mutilation
  prevention of harm, and, 49–50

Index

Negligence
owners' responsibilities, and, 11
Nuisance
byelaws, 26–27
generally, 25–26
hygiene, 27
Owners' responsibilities
generally, 9–11
Ownership
disqualification
generally, 57–58
termination, 58–59
generally, 3
Pavements
fouling, and, 16–17
Pedigree
sale of dogs, and, 5
Performing dogs
films, 63
generally, 61–63
Pet shops
sale of dogs, and, 5–8
Poaching
generally, 65
Poisoning
prevention of harm, and, 51–52
Prevention of harm
baiting, 52–53
docking dogs' tails, 50–51
fighting, 51–53
mutilation, 49–50
poisoning, 51–52
unnecessary suffering, 49
wrestling, 52–53
Promotion of welfare
duty of responsible person, 53
improvement notices, 53
regulations, 54
transfer of animals by sale or prize, 54
Prosecutions
welfare of dogs, and
local authorities' power, 56
penalties, 57–59
time limits, 57
Public open spaces
fouling, and, 16–17

Puppies
ownership, and, 3
Registration
welfare of dogs, and, 54–55
Reporting accidents
dogs on roads, and, 15
Roads
dog collars, and, 35–36
dog control orders, 18–19
fouling pavements and public open spaces, 16–17
leads, and, 15–16
motorway rules, 17
reporting accidents, 15
stray dogs, and, 36–37
straying dogs, 14
Sale of dogs
caveat emptor, and, 4
conditions, 4–5
generally, 4
illegal sales, 8
implied conditions, 5
pedigree, and, 5
pet shops, by, 5–8
warranties, 4–5
Stray dogs
finding by private person, 37–38
seizure by dog wardens, 38
seizure by police, 36–37
Straying dogs
roads, and, 14
Strict liability
owners' responsibilities, and, 9–11
Suffering
welfare of dogs, and, 49
Tails
prevention of harm, and, 50–51
Theft
generally, 3
Transfer of animals by sale or prize
welfare of dogs, and, 54
Trespass
'agricultural land', 22
generally, 20–24
'livestock', 21–22
'worrying', 22–24

Index

Unnecessary suffering
 prevention of harm, and, 49
Warranties
 sale of dogs, and, 4–5
Welfare
 animals in distress, 55–56
 baiting, 52–53
 codes of practice, 55
 disqualification from ownership
  generally, 57–58
  termination, 58–59
 docking dogs' tails, 50–51
 enforcement powers, 56
 fighting, 51–53
 improvement notices, 53
 introduction, 49
 mutilation, 49–50
 licensing, 54–55
 miscellaneous provisions, 59
 poisoning, 51–52
 post-conviction powers
  deprivation of ownership, 57
  destruction of animals, 58
  disqualification from ownership, 57–58
  fines, 57
  forfeiture of equipment used in offences, 58
  imprisonment, 57
  licensing-related orders, 58
  pending appeals, 58
  reimbursement of expenses, 59
  seizure of animal, 58

 prevention of harm
  baiting, 52–53
  docking dogs' tails, 50–51
  fighting, 51–53
  mutilation, 49–50
  poisoning, 51–52
  unnecessary suffering, 49
  wrestling, 52–53
 promotion
  duty of responsible person, 53
  improvement notices, 53
  regulations, 54
  transfer of animals by sale or prize, 54
 prosecutions
  local authorities' power, 56
  penalties, 57–59
  time limits, 57
 registration, 54–55
 suffering, 49
 transfer of animals by sale or prize to persons under 16, 54
 unnecessary suffering, 49
 wrestling, 52–53
Worrying
 killing and injuring dogs, and, 40
 trespass, and, 22–24
Wrestling
 welfare of dogs, and, 52–53